W9-BOB-237

SECOND EDITION

ASSESSMENT IN SPECIAL EDUCATION

A Practical Approach

ROGER PIERANGELO

Long Island University

GEORGE A. GIULIANI

Hofstra University

PEARSON

Boston ■ New York ■ San Francisco
Mexico City ■ Montreal ■ Toronto ■ London ■ Madrid ■ Munich ■ Paris
Hong Kong ■ Singapore ■ Tokyo ■ Cape Town ■ Sydney

Executive Editor: *Virginia Lanigan*
Editorial Assistant: *Scott Blaszak*
Executive Marketing Manager: *Amy Cronin Jordan*
Editorial Production Service: *Omegatype Typography, Inc.*
Composition Buyer: *Linda Cox*
Manufacturing Buyer: *Andrew Turso*
Electronic Composition: *Omegatype Typography, Inc.*
Cover Administrator: *Joel Gendron*

For related titles and support materials, visit our online catalog at www.ablongman.com.

Between the time website information is gathered and then published, it is not unusual for some sites to have closed. Also, the transcription of URLs can result in typographical errors. The publisher would appreciate notification where these errors occur so that they may be corrected in subsequent editions.

Library of Congress Cataloging-in-Publication Data

Pierangelo, Roger.
    Assessment in special education : a practical approach / Roger Pierangelo, George A. Giuliani.—2nd ed.
        p. cm.
    Includes bibliographical references and index.
    ISBN 0-205-41643-8
        1. Children with disabilities—Education—United States.   2. Disability evaluation—United States.   3. Educational tests and measurements—United States.   4. Special education—United States.   I. Giuliani, George A.   II. Title.

LC4031.P483 2006
371.9'0973—dc22

2004065072

Printed in the United States of America

10 9 8 7 6 5   10 09 08 07

This book is dedicated to my wife, Jackie, and my two children, Jacqueline and Scott, who provide me with the love and purpose for undertaking projects that will hopefully enhance the lives of others. Their lovely presence in my life is a blessing.

I also dedicate this book to my parents, who provided me with the secure and loving foundation from which to grow; my sister Carol, who has always made me smile and laugh; and my brother-in-law George, who has always been a very positive guiding light in my professional journey.
—R. P.

This book is dedicated to my wife, Anita, and our two children, Collin and Brittany, who give me the greatest life imaginable. The long hours and many years it took to finish this book would never have been possible without the support of my loving wife. Her constant encouragement, understanding, and love provided me with the strength I needed to accomplish my goals. I thank her with all my heart.

I also dedicate this book to my parents, who have given me so much support and guidance throughout my life. Their words of encouragement and guidance have made my professional journey a very rewarding and successful experience.
—G. G.

CONTENTS

■ ■ ■ ■ ■

PART II   THE SPECIAL EDUCATION PROCESS   87

CHAPTER EIGHTEEN
Eligibility Procedures for Special Education Services   321

CHAPTER NINETEEN
Development of the IEP   341

CHAPTER TWENTY
Special Topics in Assessment   370

Assessment in Special Education: A Practical Approach represents a new and unique direction in college textbooks. This book is the result of several years of marketing analysis and experience. The format for this text is based on your needs as a student to have a practical, user-friendly, useful, and clearly understood textbook that also can be used as a reference once you enter the workplace. In our market research with undergraduate and graduate students, we found that

- 91% of those interviewed felt that most college texts were very difficult to read
- 87% found them difficult to understand
- 74% felt that most texts contained irrelevant and useless charts and tables
- 93% indicated that they could not see using the book as a practical reference tool after the course was over
- 71% felt that the formats were overwhelming
- 98% felt that most texts contained too much theory and not enough "practical information"
- 90% normally sold back their textbooks at the end of the semester because they had no practical value and would "just sit on a shelf"

We have tried to provide you with a "real-world story" or process for the area of assessment that has a beginning, a middle, and an end. Many texts we have reviewed on assessment have approximately 15 or more chapters that are not connected, but rather offer students separate pieces that never show clearly the overall process in a straight line. In this text, we provide you with the practical tools necessary to understand the process of assessment in schools and to learn how to "put it all together."

FEATURES OF THIS TEXT

Graduates of most assessment courses understand what constitutes validity and reliability, a description of the tests most often used in assessment, legal issues, and basic statistical terminology. Our textbook not only covers these areas, but it also focuses on the practical application of assessment in schools, discussing interpretation of results, diagnosing a suspected disability, writing a professional report, making recommendations from the data, presenting results to parents, and attending the eligibility committee meetings. From our market research, this is where our book is unique.

Other practical features of this text include the following:

- Reflects IDEA 2004
- Combined coverage of formal and informal assessment
- Thorough discussion of all the most up-to-date tests used in school systems

- The most updated information on the assessment of learning disabilities, mental retardation, and emotional disabilities
- Opportunities to take test data and learn their practical application in both writing and recommendations
- Practical approaches to parent–teacher conferences and the sensitivity required in discussing test results with parents
- Determination of classification in the IEP
- The most recent updated requirements on IEP development
- A step-by-step approach from identification of a high-risk child to placement
- Comprehensive coverage of the latest tests and evaluation procedures for all areas of exceptionality
- The full spectrum of special education assessment with an emphasis on the application of information to meet the individual, often unique, requirements of students with special needs
- Assessment from infancy and preschool age, through high school and into adulthood
- An overall practical focus to balance out the strong grounding in theory so necessary for understanding exceptionality
- A firm grasp of all assessment vehicles, both formal and informal, in order to make informed decisions about which technique or tool is best with which students
- Numerous teaching–learning aids
- Samples of actual assessment, evaluation, and procedure forms utilized in school systems

After reading this textbook, you should have a thorough understanding of the assessment process in special education from start to finish. Assessment in special education is a step-by-step approach, and the goal of this text is to give you all the tools necessary to understand what really happens in the assessment process.

ACKNOWLEDGMENTS

In the course of writing this book, we have encountered many professional and outstanding sites. It has been our experience that those resources have contributed and continue to contribute enormous information, support, guidance, and education to parents, students, and professionals in the area of special education. Although we have accessed many worthwhile sites, we would especially like to thank and acknowledge the National Dissemination Center for Children and Youths with Disabilities (NICHCY) and the National Clearing House for Bilingual Education (NCHBE).

Dr. Roger Pierangelo extends thanks to the following: the faculty, administration, and staff in the Department of Graduate Speical Education and Literacy at Long Island University; the students and parents of the Herricks Public Schools he has worked with and known over the past 28 years; the late Bill Smyth, a truly gifted and "extraordinary ordinary" man; Helen Firestone, for her influence on his career and tireless support of him; and Ollie Simmons, for her friendship, loyalty, and great personality.

Dr. George Giuliani extends sincere thanks to all of his colleagues at Hofstra University in the School of Education and Allied Human Services. He is especially grateful to those who have made his transition to Hofstra University such a smooth one, including Dr. James R. Johnson (Dean), Dr. Penelope J. Haile (Associate Dean), Dr. Daniel Sciarra (Chairperson), Dr. Frank Bowe, Dr. Diane Schwartz (Graduate Program Director of Special Education), Dr. Darra Pace, Dr. Vance Austin, Dr. Gloria Wilson (whom he thanks so much for the chance to co-teach assessment courses with at Hofstra), Dr. Laurie Johnson, Dr. Joan Bloomgarden, Dr. Tai Chang, Dr. Jamie Mitus, Dr. Estelle Gelman, Dr. Joseph Lechowicz, Dr. Ron McLean, Adele Piombino, Marjorie Butler, Eve Byrne, Sherrie Basile, and Linda Cappa. Dr. Giuliani would also like to thank the following: his brother and sister, Roger and Claudia; mother-in-law, Ursula Jenkeleit; sister-in-laws, Karen and Cindy; bother-in-laws Robert and Bob; and grandfather, all of whom have provided him with the encouragement and reinforcement in all of his personal and professional endeavors.

We would like to thank Scott Blaszak, our editorial assistant, for always helping us attain any materials or information necessary to complete this textbook, and Virginia Lanigan, our editor, whose outstanding guidance, support, and words of encouragement made writing this book a very worthwhile and enjoyable experience.

We would also like to thank the following reviewers: Nedra Wheeler Atwell, Western Kentucky University; Mary C. Esposito, California State University, Dominguez Hills; Laura Boynton Hauerwas, Providence College; and Patricia R. Renick, Wright State University.

ABOUT THE AUTHORS

Dr. Roger Pierangelo is a full-time associate professor in the Department of Special Education and Literacy at Long Island University and president of the National Association of Special Education Teachers. He has been an administrator of special education programs, served for 18 years as a permanent member of Committees on Special Education, has over 30 years of experience in the public school system as a regular education classroom teacher and school psychologist, and is a consultant to numerous private and public schools, PTA, and SEPTA groups. Dr. Pierangelo has also been an evaluator for the New York State Office of Vocational and Rehabilitative Services and a director of a private clinic. He is a New York State licensed clinical psychologist, certified school psychologist, and Diplomate Fellow in Forensic Psychology.

Dr. Pierangelo earned his B.S. from St. John's University, M.S. from Queens College, Professional Diploma from Queens College, Ph.D. from Yeshiva University, and Diplomate Fellow in Forensic Psychology from the International College of Professional Psychology.

Dr. Pierangelo is a member of the American Psychological Association, New York State Psychological Association, Nassau County Psychological Association, New York State Union of Teachers, and Phi Delta Kappa.

Dr. Pierangelo is the author of *The Educator's Diagnostic Manual of Disabilities and Disorders* (pub. date 2005), *Survival Kit for the Special Education Teacher,* and *The Special Education Teacher's Book of Lists.* He is co-author of *The Special Educator's Complete Guide to 109 Diagnostic Tests* and *The Special Educator's Guide to 301 Diagnostic Tests,* published by Jossey Bass; *Parent's Complete Guide to Special Education* and *The Special Educator's Complete Guide to Transition Services,* published by Prentice Hall; *The Special Education Yellow Pages,* published by Merrill Publishers; *Assessment in Special Education: A Practical Approach, Transition Services in Special Education: A Practical Approach;* and *Learning Disabilities: A Practical Approach to Theory, Diagnosis, Process and Practice* (pub. date 2005), published by Allyn and Bacon; *Why Your Students Do What They Do—and What to Do When They Do It, Grades K–5, Why Your Students Do What They Do—and What to Do When They Do It, Grades 6–12, Creating Confident Children in the Classroom: The Use of Positive Restructuring,* and *What Every Teacher Should Know about Students with Special Needs,* published by Research Press; and *301 Ways to Be a Loving Parent,* by SPI Publishers.

Dr. George A. Giuliani is a full-time assistant professor at Hofstra University's School of Education and Allied Human Services in the Department of Counseling, Research, Special Education, and Rehabilitation. He is the vice president of the *National Association of Special Education Teachers.* Dr. Giuliani earned his B.A. from the College of the Holy Cross, M.S. from St. John's University, J.D. from City University Law School, and Psy.D. from Rutgers University, Graduate School of Applied and Professional Psychology. He is a diplomate fellow in forensic psychology. Dr. Giuliani is also a New York State licensed psychologist, certified school psychologist, and has an extensive private practice focusing on children with special needs. He is a member of the American Psychological Association, New York State Psychological Association, the National Association of School Psychologists, Suffolk County Psychological Association, Psi Chi, and the Council for Exceptional Children.

Dr. Giuliani has been involved in early intervention for children with special needs and is a consultant for school districts and early childhood agencies. Dr. Giuliani has provided numerous workshops for parents and teachers on a variety of psychological and educational topics.

Dr. Giuliani is the co-author of *The Educator's Diagnostic Manual of Disabilities and Disorders* (pub. date 2005), *The Special Educator's Complete Guide to 109 Diagnostic Tests,* and *The Special Educator's Guide to 301 Diagnostic Tests,* published by Jossey Bass; *Assessment in Special Education: A Practical Approach, Transition Services in Special Education: A Practical Approach,* and *Learning Disabilities: A Practical Approach to Theory, Diagnosis, Process and Practice* (pub. date 2005), published by Allyn and Bacon; and *Why Your Students Do What They Do—and What to Do When They Do It, Grades K–5, Why Your Students Do What They Do—and What to Do When They Do It, Grades 6–12, Creating Confident Children in the Classroom: The Use of Positive Restructuring,* and *What Every Teacher Should Know about Students with Special Needs,* published by Research Press.

FOUNDATIONAL CONCEPTS IN ASSESSMENT IN SPECIAL EDUCATION

Welcome to the world of assessment in special education. We hope that you enjoy this book and find it very practical and user friendly. This book is divided into two parts. Part I (Chapters 1 through 6) presents an overview of the most important concepts, laws, statistics, and terms you need to know to understand the assessment process. Part II (Chapters 7 through 20) then takes you step by step through the assessment process as it happens every day in schools.

Chapter 1 presents you with an overview of key terms and definitions used in assessment in special education. You will learn about what constitutes assessment, the professionals involved in the assessment process, and the various children with disabilities you may come in contact with in special education. We then present you with a brief general overview of the different methods of assessment. Finally, you will learn about parental involvement in the assessment process.

Chapter 2 presents an overview of legal issues in assessment. First, you will learn about the most important historical cases in special education. Following these cases, we will discuss current federal legislation and how it influences children, parents, and special educators involved in the assessment process.

Chapter 3 focuses on various methods of assessment used in special education. This chapter presents an overview of both formal (norm-referenced tests) and informal assessment (criterion referenced tests, portfolios, curriculum based assessment, dynamic assessment, and many others). Following a discussion of these methods, you will learn about the decision-making process involved in selecting the appropriate instrument for evaluating students.

Chapter 4 is an overview of the most basic statistical concepts you need to survive the special education process. To fully understand assessment, you must first become familiar with statistics. Statistics are very important in special education, and we will guide you down a very methodical and comfortable road to teach these concepts to you.

Chapter 5 addresses concerns about validity and reliability. You will learn that a test needs to be both valid (assessing what it is supposed to measure) and reliable (consistent) to be useful. This chapter also addresses all the different types of validity and reliability so that you will have a strong working knowledge of when a test is most suitable to use.

Finally, in **Chapter 6,** we present to you basic scoring terminology used every day in assessment. These terms are very important in scoring and analyzing the results of the various measures you will use in the assessment process.

After reading the first six chapters, you will be ready for Part II of this text, which will lead you through a practical, step-by-step process involved in assessing children with special needs.

■ ■ ■ ■ ■

CHAPTER ONE

INTRODUCTION TO ASSESSMENT

KEY TERMS

Analysis	IDEA 2004
Assessment	IEP Development
Autism	Instructional Planning
Collection	Mental Retardation
Consent for Evaluation	Multiple Disabilities
Deaf–Blindness	Orthopedic Impairment
Deafness	Other Health Impairment
Determination	Recommendation
Eligibility and Diagnosis	Specific Learning Disability
Emotional Disturbance	Speech or Language Impairment
Evaluation	Traumatic Brain Injury
Hearing Impairment	Visual Impairment

CHAPTER OBJECTIVES

This chapter presents a general overview of assessment. After reading this chapter, you should be able to do the following:

- Define assessment
- Understand the purpose of assessment
- Know the professionals involved in the assessment process
- List and define the classifications in special education as defined under the Individuals with Disabilities Education Improvement Act of 2004 (IDEA 2004)
- Know the three most common ways students are identified for the assessment process
- Have a general working knowledge of parental consent in the assessment process
- Know the various components of a thorough assessment

OVERVIEW OF ASSESSMENT

> Danielle is in serious danger of failing fourth grade again. She appears to have difficulty following directions, completing assignments on time, progressing in reading and spelling, and interacting with her peers. Her teacher believes that Danielle may have a learning disability and has made a referral to the district's Committee on Special Education.

> Carl has spina bifida and uses a wheelchair. He has recently moved into the community and enrolled in the local high school. His parents are concerned that Carl is not developing the mobility and daily living skills that he needs now and in the future. They request that the new school system evaluate Carl to identify his special needs.

> James has become severely withdrawn in the last year. His grades have been declining steadily, he is starting to skip school, and when the teacher calls on him in class, he responds rudely or not at all. The teacher is worried that James may have an emotional disorder. She makes a referral to the special education department.

Although these children are different from each other in very many ways, they may also share something in common. Each may be a student who has a disability that will require special education services in the school setting. Before decisions may be made about what those special education services will be, each child requires an evaluation conducted by specially trained educational personnel, which may include a school psychologist, a speech–language pathologist, special education and regular education teachers, social workers, and, when appropriate, medical personnel. This is true for any child suspected of having a disability.

Assessment in special education is a process that involves collecting information about a student for the purpose of making decisions. According to Gearheart and Gearheart (1990), assessment is "a process that involves the systematic collection and interpretation of a wide variety of information on which to base instructional/intervention decisions and, when appropriate, classification and placement decisions. Assessment is primarily a problem-solving process" (p. 3). Clearly, gathering information about a student using a variety of techniques and information sources should shed considerable light upon strengths and needs, the nature of a suspected disability and its effect upon educational performance, and realistic and appropriate instructional goals and objectives.

The professional involved in special education in today's schools plays a very critical role in the overall education of students with all types of disabilities. The special educator's position is unique in that he or she can play many different roles in the educational environment. Whatever their role, special educators encounter a variety of situations that require practical decisions and relevant suggestions. No matter which type of professional you become in the field of special education, it is always necessary to fully understand the assessment process and to be able to clearly communicate vital information to professionals, parents, and students.

The importance of assessment should never be underestimated. In special education, you will work with many professionals from different fields. You are part of a team, often referred to as a multidisciplinary team (see Chapter 8), that tries to determine what, if any, disability is present in a student. The team's role is crucial because it helps determine the extent and direction of a child's personal journey through the special education experience. Consequently, the skills you must possess in order to offer a child the most global, accurate, and practical evaluation should be fully understood. The development of these skills should include a good working knowledge of the following components of the assessment process in order to determine the presence of a suspected disability (NICHCY, 1999):

- **Collection:** The process of tracing and gathering information from the many sources of background information on a child such as school records, observation, parent intakes, and teacher reports
- **Analysis:** The processing and understanding of patterns in a child's educational, social, developmental, environmental, medical, and emotional history
- **Evaluation:** The evaluation of a child's academic, intellectual, psychological, emotional, perceptual, language, cognitive, and medical development in order to determine areas of strength and weakness
- **Determination:** The determination of the presence of a suspected disability and the knowledge of the criteria that constitute each category
- **Recommendation:** The recommendations concerning educational placement and program that need to be made to the school, teachers, and parents

PURPOSE OF ASSESSMENT

As will be discussed in great detail throughout this book, following a referral for a suspected disability of a child and with written parental or guardian permission, an individual evaluation is conducted. This means that formal tests, observations, and numerous assessments will be given. The results help to determine if special education is needed and whether factors unrelated to disabilities are affecting a child's school performance. Evaluation results provide information that is useful for determining or modifying a child's program, if necessary. Assessment plays an critical role in the determination of six important decisions (NICHCY, 1999):

- **Evaluation Decisions:** Information collected in the assessment process can provide detailed information of a student's strengths, weaknesses, and overall progress.
- **Diagnostic Decisions:** Information collected in the assessment process can provide detailed information of the specific nature of the student's problems or disability.
- **Eligibility Decisions:** Information collected in the assessment process can provide detailed information of whether a child is eligible for special education services.
- **IEP (IEP Development) Decisions:** Information collected in the assessment process can provide detailed information so that an Individualized Education Program (IEP) may be developed
- **Educational Placement Decisions:** Information collected in the assessment process can provide detailed information so that appropriate decisions may be made about the child's educational placement

■ **Instructional Planning Decisions:** Information collected in the assessment process is critical in planning instruction appropriate to the child's special social, academic, physical, and management needs

INDIVIDUALS INVOLVED IN THE ASSESSMENT PROCESS

Under federal law (the **Individuals with Disabilities Education Improvement Act,** herein cited as IDEA 2004) an evaluation of a child with a suspected disability must be made by a multidisciplinary team or groups of persons including at least one teacher or specialist with knowledge in the area of the suspected disability. These professionals must use a variety of assessment tools and strategies to gather relevant functional and developmental information, including information provided by the parent, that will assist in determining whether a child has a disability as defined under federal law.

The members of the multidisciplinary team often include the following:

■ Regular education teacher
■ School psychologist
■ Special education evaluator
■ Special education teacher
■ Speech and language clinician
■ Medical personnel (when appropriate)
■ Social workers
■ School/guidance counselor
■ Parents
■ School nurse
■ Occupational and physical therapists

The roles that each of these people play in the assessment process is discussed thoroughly in Chapter 8.

CLASSIFICATIONS UNDER IDEA 2004

The Individuals with Disabilities Education Improvement Act, Public Law (P.L.) 108-446, is the federal law that protects students in special education. This law will be discussed at length in Chapter 2, "Legal Issues in Assessment." IDEA 2004 lists separate categories of disabilities under which children may be eligible for special education and related services. Children are eligible to receive special education services and supports if they meet the eligibility requirements for at least one of the disabling conditions listed in P.L. 108-446 and if it is determined that they are in need of special education services (Bigge & Stump, 1999).

According to IDEA 2004, Sec. 602(3)(A), a child with a disability is a child

(1) with mental retardation, hearing impairments (including deafness), speech or language impairments, visual impairments, serious emotional disturbance, orthopedic impairments, autism, traumatic brain injury, other health impairments, or specific learning disability; and

(2) who, by reason thereof, needs special education and related services

The definitions of disabling conditions under IDEA 2004 are listed below:

- **Autism:** A developmental disability significantly affecting verbal and nonverbal communication and social interaction, generally evident before age three, that adversely affects a child's educational performance. Other characteristics often associated with autism are engagement in repetitive activities and stereotyped movements, resistance to environmental change or change in daily routines, and unusual responses to sensory experiences. The term does not apply if a child's educational performance is adversely affected because the child has an emotional disturbance.

- **Deafness:** A hearing impairment that is so severe that the child is impaired in processing linguistic information through hearing, with or without amplification, that adversely affects a child's educational performance.

- **Deaf–Blindness:** Concomitant hearing and visual impairments, the combination of which causes such severe communication and other developmental and educational problems that they cannot be accommodated in special education programs solely for children with deafness or children with blindness.

- **Emotional Disturbance:** A condition exhibiting one or more of the following characteristics over a long period of time and to a marked degree that adversely affects a child's educational performance: (a) An inability to learn that cannot be explained by intellectual, sensory or health factors. (b) An inability to build or maintain satisfactory interpersonal relationships with peers and teachers. (c) Inappropriate types of behaviors or feelings under normal circumstances. (d) A general pervasive mood of unhappiness or depression. (e) A tendency to develop physical symptoms or fears associated with personal or school problems. (ii) The term includes schizophrenia. The term does not apply to children who are socially maladjusted, unless it is determined that they have an emotional disturbance.

- **Hearing Impairment:** An impairment in hearing, whether permanent or fluctuating, that adversely affects a child's performance but that is not included under the definition of deafness in this section.

- **Mental Retardation:** Significantly subaverage general intellectual functioning, existing concurrently with deficits in adaptive behavior and manifested during the developmental period, that adversely affects a child's performance.

- **Multiple Disabilities:** Concomitant impairments (such as mental retardation–blindness, mental retardation–orthopedic impairment, etc.) the combination of which causes such severe educational problems that the problems cannot be accommodated in special education programs solely for one of the impairments. The term does not include deaf–blindness.

- **Orthopedic Impairment:** A severe orthopedic impairment that adversely affects a child's educational performance. The term includes impairments caused by congenital anomoly (e.g., club foot, absence of some member), impairments caused by disease (e.g., poliomyelitis, bone tuberculosis), and impairments from other causes (e.g., cerebral palsy, amputations, and fractures or burns that cause contractures).

- **Other Health Impairment:** Having limited strength, vitality, or alertness due to chronic or acute health problems, such as a heart condition, tuberculosis, rheumatic fever, nephritis, asthma, sickle cell anemia, hemophilia, epilepsy, lead poisoning, leukemia, or diabetes, that adversely affects a child's educational performance.

- **Specific Learning Disability:** A disorder in 1 or more of the basic psychological processes involved in understanding or in using language, spoken or written, which may manifest itself in the imperfect ability to listen, think, speak, read, write, spell, or do mathematical calculations. Such term includes conditions such as perceptual disabilities, brain injury, minimal brain dysfunction, dyslexia, and developmental aphasia. Such term does not include such learning problem that is primarily the result of visual, hearing, or motor disabilities; of mental retardation; of emotional disturbance; or of environmental, cultural, or economic disadvantage. Under IDEA 2004, when determining whether a child has a specific disability, a local education agency shall not be required to take into consideration whether a child has a severe discrepancy between achievement and intellectual ability.

- **Speech or Language Impairment:** A communication disorder such as stuttering, impaired articulation, a language impairment, or a voice impairment that adversely affects a child's educational performance.

- **Traumatic Brain Injury:** An acquired injury to the brain caused by an external physical force, resulting in total or partial functional disability or psychosocial impairment or both, and that adversely affects a child's educational performance. The term applies to open or closed head injuries resulting in impairments in one or more areas, such as cognition; language; memory; attention; reasoning; abstract thinking; judgment; problem solving; sensory, perceptual, and motor abilities; psychosocial behavior; physical functions; information processing; and speech. The term does not apply to brain injuries that are congenital or degenerative or to brain injuries induced by birth trauma.

- **Visual Impairment:** An impairment in vision that, even with correction, adversely affects a child's educational performance. The term includes both partial and sight blindness.

HOW STUDENTS ARE IDENTIFIED FOR ASSESSMENT

There are normally three ways in which a student may be identified for assessment of a suspected disability (Pierangelo & Giuliani, 1999):

1. School personnel may suspect the presence of a learning or behavior problem and ask the student's parents for permission to evaluate the student individually. This may have resulted from a student scoring far below his or her peers on some type of screening measure and thereby alerting the school to the possibility of a problem.

2. The student's classroom teacher may identify that certain symptoms exist within the classroom that seem to indicate the presence of some problem. For example, the student's work is below expectations for his or her grade or age, or the student's behavior is so disruptive that he or she is unable to learn. Further, many attempts at intervention strategies suggested by professional staff members have been met with little or no success.

3. The student's parents may call or write to the school or to the director of special education and request that their child be evaluated. The parents may feel that the child is not progressing as expected or may notice particular problems in how their child learns. When parents note a problem and request an evaluation, the school must follow through on the assessment process. This is the parents' legal right.

PARENTAL CONSENT AND THE ASSESSMENT PROCESS

In order to protect the legal rights of parents and their children, IDEA 2004 mandates that a school must obtain written permission before any school evaluation for a suspected disability is undertaken. Request for consent for evaluation should not be misinterpreted as a decision that a child has a disability. Rather, it is a means of assuring that parents have both full knowledge of school actions and involvement in the decision-making process. It is important that parents fully understand the reasons for an individual evaluation so that they feel comfortable with the decisions that they must make. This process of parents' rights is discussed in great detail in Chapter 8.

COMPONENTS OF A COMPREHENSIVE ASSESSMENT

An evaluation for special education should always be conducted on an individual basis. When completed, it is a comprehensive assessment of the child's abilities.

Under IDEA 2004 (sec. 614(2) (B)), no single measure or assessment is used as the sole criterion for determining an appropriate educational program for a child. Further, the child must be assessed in all areas related to the suspected disability, including, where appropriate, health, vision, hearing, social and emotional status, general intelligence, academic performance, communicative status, and motor abilities.

In light of these mandates, a comprehensive assessment should normally include many of the following:

- An individual *psychological evaluation* including general intelligence, instructional needs, learning strengths and weaknesses, and social–emotional dynamics
- A thorough *social history* based on interviews with parents and student
- A thorough *academic history* with interviews or reports from past teachers
- A *physical examination* including specific assessments that relate to vision, hearing, and health
- A *classroom observation* of the student in the current educational setting
- An appropriate *educational evaluation* specifically pinpointing the areas of deficit or suspected disability including, but not limited to, educational achievement, academic needs, learning strengths and weaknesses, and vocational assessments
- A *functional behavioral assessment* to describe the relationship between a skill or performance problem and variables that contribute to its occurrence. The purpose of a functional behavioral assessment is to gather broad and specific information in order to better understand the specific reasons for the student's problem behavior
- A *bilingual assessment* for students with limited English proficiency
- *Auditory and visual discrimination tests*
- Assessment of *classroom performance*
- *Speech and language evaluations,* when appropriate
- *Physical and/or occupational evaluations,* when indicated
- *Interviewing the student and significant others* in the student's life
- *Examining school records* and past evaluation results
- Using information from *checklists* completed by parents, teachers, or the student
- *Evaluating curriculum requirements and options*
- *Evaluating the student's type and rate of learning* during trial teaching periods
- *Evaluating which skills have been and have not been mastered,* and in what order unmastered skills need to be taught
- *Collecting ratings on teacher attitude toward students with disabilities, peer acceptance, and classroom climate*

This information can be gathered in a variety of ways. These may include, but are not limited to: norm-referenced tests, informal assessment, criterion-referenced tests, standards-referenced tests, ecological assessment, curriculum-based assessment, curriculum-based measurement, dynamic assessment, portfolio assessment, authentic/naturalistic/performance–based assessment, task analysis, outcome-based assessment, and learning styles assessment (Pierangelo & Giuliani, 1999). All of these are discussed in detail in Chapter 3 of this textbook.

CONCLUSION

Assessment is a complex process that needs to be conducted by a multidisciplinary team of trained professionals and involves both formal and informal methods of collecting information about the student. Although the team may choose to administer a series of tests to the student, by law assessment must involve much more than standardized tests. Interviews of all key participants in the student's education and observations of student behaviors in the classroom or in other sites should be included as well. To develop a comprehensive picture of the student and to develop practical intervention strategies to address that student's special needs, the team must ask questions and use assessment techniques that will help them determine the factors that are facilitating—and interfering with—the child's learning. It is also important that assessment be an ongoing process. As you will see as you read through this book, the process begins even before the student is referred for formal evaluation; his or her teacher or parent may have noticed that some aspect of the student's performance or behavior is below expectations and, so, requests an official assessment. After eligibility has been established and the IEP developed for the student, assessment should continue, through teacher-made tests, through ongoing behavioral assessment, or through other methods. This allows teachers and parents to monitor the student's progress toward the goals and objectives stated in his or her IEP. Thus, assessment should not end when the eligibility decision is made or the IEP is developed; it has great value to contribute to the daily, weekly, and monthly instructional decision making that accompanies the provision of special education and related services.

A thorough and comprehensive assessment of a child can greatly enhance his or her educational experience. The assessment process has many steps and needs to be appropriately done. Furthermore, no one individual makes all of the decisions for a child's classification; it is done by a multidisciplinary team. As future special educators, it is your professional responsibility to understand the laws, steps, and various assessment measures and procedures used in the special education process so that when you enter the school systems, you can have a significant and positive impact on all those whom you are involved with in special education.

VOCABULARY

Analysis: The processing and understanding of patterns in a child's educational, social, developmental, environmental, medical, and emotional history.

Assessment: A process that involves collecting information about a student for the purpose of making decisions.

Autism: A developmental disability significantly affecting verbal and nonverbal communication and social interaction, generally evident before age three years.

Collection: The process of tracing and gathering information from the many sources of background information on a child such as school records, observation, parent intakes, and teacher reports.

Consent for Evaluation: A means of assuring that parents have both full knowledge of school actions and involvement in the decision-making process.

Deaf–blindness: Simultaneous hearing and visual impairments.

Deafness: A hearing impairment that is so severe that the child is impaired in processing linguistic information, with or without amplification.

Determination: The determination of the presence of a suspected disability and the knowledge of the criteria that constitute each category.

Eligibility and Diagnosis: One of the primary purposes of assessment to determine whether a child is eligible for special education services and what classification the child will receive.

Emotional Disturbance: A disability whereby a child of typical intelligence has difficulty, over time and to a marked degree, building satisfactory interpersonal relationships; responds inappropriately behaviorally or emotionally under normal circumstances; demonstrates a pervasive mood of unhappiness; or has a tendency to develop physical symptoms or fears.

Evaluation: The evaluation of a child's academic, intellectual, psychological, emotional, perceptual, language, cognitive, and medical development in order to determine areas of strength and weakness.

Hearing Impairment: An impairment in hearing, whether permanent or fluctuating.

IEP Development: One of the primary purposes of assessment whereby a child receives an individualized education program.

Instructional Planning: One of the primary purposes of assessment whereby a plan is developed that is appropriate for a child in special education. The plan should focus on social, academic, physical, and management needs.

Mental Retardation: Significantly subaverage general intellectual functioning existing concurrently with deficits in adaptive behavior.

Multiple Disabilities: The manifestation of two or more disabilities (such as mental retardation and blindness), the combination of which requires special accommodation for maximal learning.

Orthopedic Impairment: Physical disabilities, including congenital impairments, impairments caused by disease, and impairments from other causes.

Other Health Impairment: Having limited strength, vitality or alertness due to chronic or acute health problems (e.g., diabetes, asthma, hypoglycemia, attention deficit disorder).

Recommendation: The recommendations concerning educational placement and program that need to be made to the school, teachers, and parents.

Specific Learning Disability: A disorder in one or more of the basic psychological processes involved in understanding or in using language, spoken or written, which may manifest itself in an imperfect ability to listen, think, speak, read, write, spell, or do mathematical calculations.

Speech or Language Impairment: A communication disorder such as stuttering, impaired articulation, a language impairment, or a voice impairment.

Traumatic Brain Injury: An acquired injury to the brain caused by an external physical force, resulting in total or partial functional disability or psychosocial impairment or both.

Visual Impairment: An impairment in vision (including blindness) that, even with correction, adversely affects a child's educational performance.

CHAPTER TWO

LEGAL ISSUES IN ASSESSMENT

KEY TERMS

Americans with Disabilities Act (ADA)—
P.L. 101-336
Assistive Technology
*Board of Education of Hendrick Hudson School
District v. Rowley*
Brown v. Board of Education of Topeka, Kansas
Daniel R. R. v. State Board of Education
Diana v. State Board of Education
Due Process
Education of All Handicapped Children's
Act (EHA)—P.L. 94-142
The Family Education Rights and Privacy
Act (FERPA)—P.L. 93-380
Fourteenth Amendment
*Georgia State Conference of Branches of
NAACP v. State of Georgia*
Gerstmeyer v. Howard County Public Schools
Guadalupe v. Tempe Elementary School
Hobson v. Hansen
Individualized Education Program (IEP)
Individuals with Disabilities Education Act
(IDEA)—P.L. 101-476
Individuals with Disabilities Education Act
of 1997 (IDEA '97)

Individuals with Disabilities Education
Improvement Act (IDEA 2004)
Informed Consent
Jose P. v. Ambach
Larry P. v. Riles
Least Restrictive Environment
Luke S. and Hans S. v. Nix et al.
Mills v. Board of Education of District
Native Language
P.L. 107-110 No Child Left Behind Act
Nondiscriminatory Assessment
PARC v. Commonwealth of Pennsylvania
PASE v. Joseph P. Hannon
Reauthorization
Section 504 of the Vocational
Rehabilitation Act
Transition Services
Vocational Education Act
of 1984—The Perkins Act
Wyatt v. Stickney
Zero Reject

CHAPTER OBJECTIVES

This chapter focuses on the various legal issues involved in special education and assessment. After reading this chapter, you should be able to understand the following:

- The basic problems with respect to discrimination in special education
- The landmark court cases in special education
- Section 504 of the Vocational Rehabilitation Act
- P.L. 93-380: The Family Education Rights and Privacy Act

- P.L. 94-142: The Education of All Handicapped Children's Act
- The procedural safeguards under P.L. 94-142
- P.L. 98-524: The Vocational Education Act of 1984—the Perkins Act
- P.L. 99-457: Education of the Handicapped Act Amendments of 1986
- P.L. 101-336: The Americans with Disabilities Act
- P.L. 101-476: The Individuals with Disabilities Education Act (IDEA)
- P.L. 105-17: The Individuals with Disabilities Education Act of 1997 (IDEA '97)
- No Child Left Behind Act of 2001
- The role of state and federal government in establishing and implementing laws pertaining to special education

Prior to 1975 in the United States, discrimination against students with disabilities was prevalent in schools. The two types of discrimination most evident were

1. The exclusion of students with disabilities altogether from school.
2. The classification of students with disabilities when, in actuality, no disability was present. This type of discrimination was becoming more apparent with many minority children, many of whom were being classified as mentally retarded when, in truth, there was simply a language barrier.

Has the discrimination stopped? What laws have been enacted to prevent further discrimination from occurring in special education? The focus of this chapter is to discuss the relevant federal laws and court cases that have influenced, and continue to influence, assessment in special education.

LANDMARK COURT CASES IN SPECIAL EDUCATION

The first federal laws designed to assist individuals with disabilities date back to the early days of the nation. In 1798, the Fifth Congress passed the first federal law concerned with the care of persons with disabilities (Braddock, 1987; cited in NICHCY, 1997). This law authorized a Maine Hospital Service to provide medical services to sick and disabled seamen. By 1912, this service became known as Public Health Service. However, prior to World War II, there were relatively few federal laws authorizing special benefits for persons with disabilities. Those that existed were intended to address the needs of war veterans with service-connected disabilities. This meant that, for most of our nation's history, schools were allowed to exclude—and often did exclude—certain children, especially those with disabilities.

In 1948, only 12% of all children with disabilities received some form of special education. By the early 1950s, special education services and programs were available in school districts, but often, undesirable results occurred. For example, students in special classes were considered unable to perform academic tasks. Consequently, they went to special schools or classes that focused on learning manual skills such as weaving and bead stringing. Although programs existed, it was clear that discrimination was still as strong as ever for those with disabilities in schools.

Legislation and court cases to prevent discrimination in education first came to notice in 1954 with the famous case *Brown v. Board of Education of Topeka, Kansas.* In Brown, the Court ruled that it was illegal practice under the Fourteenth Amendment of the U.S. Constitution to arbitrarily discriminate against any group of people. The Court then applied this principle to the schooling of children, holding that a separate education for African American students is not an equal education. In its famous ruling, separate but equal would no longer be accepted (347 U.S. 483).

Brown set the precedent for future discrimination cases in education. People with disabilities were recognized as another group whose rights had been violated because of arbitrary discrimination. For children, the discrimination occurred because they were denied access to schools due to their disabilities. Using Brown as their legal precedent, students with disabilities claimed that their segregation and exclusion from school violated their opportunity for an equal education under the *Fourteenth Amendment of the U.S. Constitution*—the Equal Protection Clause. If Brown could not segregate by race, then schools should not be able to segregate or otherwise discriminate by ability and disability.

In the 1960s, parents began to become advocates for better educational opportunities for their children. Around the same time, many authorities began to agree that segregated special classes were not the most appropriate educational setting for many students with disabilities. By the end of the 1960s, landmark court cases set the stage for enactment of federal laws to protect the rights of children with disabilities and their parents. This section presents an overview of some of the most historical court cases in special education, in their order of occurrence.

Hobson v. Hansen (1967).   In *Hobson v. Hansen,* a U.S. district court declared that the District of Columbia school system's tracking system was invalid. However, special classes were allowed, provided that testing procedures were rigorous and that retesting was frequent (Sattler, 1992).

Diana v. State Board of Education (1970).   In this case, California was mandated by the Court to correct bias in assessment procedures used with Chinese American and Mexican American students. Diana had three very important holdings that would later influence the enactment of federal special education laws:

1. If a student's primary language was not English, the student had to be tested in both English and his or her primary language.
2. Culturally unfair items had to be eliminated from all tests used in the assessment process.
3. If intelligence tests were to be used in the assessment process, they had to be developed to reflect Mexican American culture (*Diana v. State Board of Education,* C-70: 37RFT, N.D. Cal., 1970).

PARC v. Commonwealth of Pennsylvania (1972).   In this case, a U.S. federal court in Pennsylvania ratified a consent agreement assuring that schools may not exclude students who have been classified with mental retardation. Also, the Court mandated that all students must be provided with a free public education. Both of these holdings would play a fundamental role in the enactment of future federal special education laws (***PARC v. Commonwealth of Pennsylvania,*** 343 F. Supp. 279, E.D. PA, 1972).

Wyatt v. Stickney (1972).   In Alabama, a federal court ruled that mentally retarded children in state institutions had a constitutional right to treatment (***Wyatt v. Stickney,*** 344 F. Supp. 387, M.D. Ala 1972).

Guadalupe v. Tempe Elementary School (1972).   In Arizona, a U.S. district court agreed to a stipulated agreement that children could not be placed in educable mentally retarded classes unless they scored lower than two standard deviations below the population mean on an approved IQ test administered in the child's own language. ***Guadalupe v. Tempe Elementary School*** also stipulated that other assessment procedures must be used in addition to intelligence tests, and that parental permission must be obtained for such placements (Sattler, 1992, p. 779).

Mills v. Board of Education of District of Columbia (1972).   This case set forth future guidelines for federal legislation, including the rights of students with disabilities to have access to a free public education, due process protection, and a mandated requirement to receive special education services regardless of the school district's financial capability (***Mills v. Board of Education of District of Columbia,*** 348 Supp. 866, CD. DC 1972; contempt proceedings, EHLR 551:643 CD. DC 1980).

PASE (Parents in Action on Special Education) v. Joseph P. Hannon (1980).   In this case regarding bias in IQ testing, the judge (Judge Grady in Illinois) found that on the IQ tests he examined, only nine of the 488 test questions were racially biased. Consequently, IQ tests were found not to be discriminatory. Furthermore, Judge Grady indicated that clinical judgment also plays a large role in interpreting IQ test results. He stated: "There is no evidence in this record that such misassessments as do occur are the result of racial bias in test items or in any aspect of the assessment process currently in use in the Chicago public school system." Therefore, the decision in PASE resolved some of the controversy about the use of IQ tests for special education classification. As a result, the use of intelligence tests was acceptable in psychoeducational assessment as long as they followed all other procedural safeguards under federal law (***PASE v. Joseph P. Hannon,*** No. 74 C 3586 N.D. Ill. 1980).

Luke S. and Hans S. v. Nix et al. (1982).   In the state of Louisiana, all evaluations had to be completed within a 60-day time period. The plaintiffs in this case argued that thousands of students were not being appropriately evaluated within this time period. The court ruled in favor of the plaintiffs and informed the state of Louisiana that greater prereferral assessment should be done before a referral is made (***Luke S. and Hans S. v. Nix et al.,*** cited in Taylor, 1997, p. 13).

Board of Education of Hendrick Hudson School District v. Rowley (1982).   In Rowley, the parents of Amy Rowley, a deaf student with minimal residual hearing and excellent lip-reading skills, sought the services of a full-time interpreter in her regular classes. Amy had been provided with an FM trainer (a teacher of the deaf) for one hour per day, and speech for three hours per week. Even though Amy was missing about half of what was being discussed in class, she was very well adjusted, was performing better than the average child in the class, and was advancing easily from grade to grade.

Based on these facts, the U.S. Supreme Court determined in ***Board of Education of Hendrick Hudson School District v. Rowley*** that Amy was receiving an "appropriate" education without the sign interpreter. In reaching this opinion, the Court concluded that the obligation to provide an appropriate education does not mean a school must provide the "best" education or one designed to "maximize" a student's potential. However, the program must be based on the student's unique individual needs and be designed to enable the student to benefit from an education. In other words, the student must be making progress (Hager, 1999, p. 5).

Jose P. v. Ambach (1983).   In this case, the plaintiffs filed suit against New York City. Their complaint involved the inappropriate delivery of services. The plaintiffs argued that many students in special education were not receiving services in an appropriate time frame. The court ruled in favor of the plaintiffs and stated that from the time of referral to evaluation a maximum of 30 days can elapse. The court informed the defendants that all evaluations must be "timely evaluations" (***Jose P. v. Ambach,*** cited in Taylor, 1997, p. 13).

Larry P. v. Riles (1984).   In this California case, using IQ tests as the assessment measure for placing African American students in special education as mentally retarded was found to be discriminatory. Schools in California were mandated by the Court to reduce the disproportionate representation of African American students in special education. In ***Larry P. v. Riles,*** the court determined that IQ tests were discriminatory against African Americans in three ways:

1. IQ tests actually measure achievement rather than ability. Because African Americans throughout their educational history have been denied equal educational opportunities through schools segregated by race, they will inevitably have achievement scores lower than the norms and thus be discriminated against in testing.
2. IQ tests rest on the plausible but unproven assumption that intelligence is distributed in the population in accordance with a normal statistical curve (bell shaped), and thus the tests are artificial tools to rank individuals.
3. IQ tests lead to the classification of more African American students than white students in dead-end classes for students with mild to moderate disabilities [(No. C-71-2270 RFP (1979) and No. 80-4027 DC No. CV 71-2270 in the U.S. Court of Appeals for the Ninth Circuit (1984)].

Georgia State Conference of Branches of NAACP v. State of Georgia (1984).   A U.S. court of appeals ruled that African American children schooled in the state of

Georgia were not being discriminated against solely because there was a disproportionate number of them in classes for low achievers. The court explained that there was no evidence of differential treatment of African American and other students. Overrepresentation of African American children in classes for the mentally retarded by itself was not sufficient to prove discrimination (Sattler, 1992).

Daniel R. R. v. State Board of Education (1989).   Daniel R. R. is one of the leading cases opening the door to increased inclusion of children with disabilities in regular education classes. The court noted that Congress created a strong preference in favoring mainstreaming; that is, educating the student in the regular education classroom with supports. Ironically, the court determined that it was not appropriate to include the child in this case in full-time regular education. However, the court's analysis of the least restrictive environment requirement, especially its interpretation of what is meant by providing supplementary aids and services in the regular classroom, has been followed by a number of other courts (Hager, 1999, p. 6).

In determining whether it is appropriate to place a student with disabilities in regular education, the student need not be expected to learn at the same rate as the other students in the class. In other words, part of the required supplementary aids and services must be the modification of the regular education curriculum for the student, when needed. The court in ***Daniel R. R. v. State Board of Education*** noted, however, that the school need not modify the program "beyond recognition." Also, in looking at whether it is "appropriate" for the child to be in regular education—in other words, whether the student can benefit educationally from regular class placement—the school must consider the broader educational benefit of contact with nondisabled students, such as opportunities for modeling appropriate behavior and socialization (Hager, 1999, p. 6).

Gerstmeyer v. Howard County Public Schools (1994).   In the Gerstmeyer case, Howard School District had been told that a child needed an evaluation for the first grade four months before entering the first grade. The evaluation was not done prior to the child's entering the first grade. The parents sent their child to private school and the evaluation was only done six months after the initial referral. The parents sued the district for the costs of private schooling and tutoring caused by the delay. In ***Gerstmeyer v. Howard County Public Schools,*** the Court ruled in favor of the parents and made Howard School District reimburse them for all associated costs (cited in Taylor, 1997, p. 13).

THE HISTORY OF FEDERAL LEGISLATION FOR INDIVIDUALS WITH DISABILITIES

As a result of numerous historical court cases, federal legislation for individuals with disabilities began to develop in the early 1970s. This section discusses relevant federal legislation that has made a significant impact on the health, welfare, safety, and educational rights of these individuals (in the order in which the legislation was enacted).

Section 504 of the Vocational Rehabilitation Act

Section 504 of the Vocational Rehabilitation Act is a civil rights law enacted in 1973. It was created to prevent discrimination against all individuals with disabilities in programs that receive federal funds. For children of school age, Section 504 ensures students of equal opportunity to all school activities.

Section 504 plays a very important role in assessment, especially for students who do not meet the criteria to be classified for special education. Some students not eligible for services in special education may be entitled to receive accommodations under Section 504 to help them in school. For example, a child with attention deficit disorder (ADD) may meet the criteria for special accommodations under 504, because even though attention deficit disorder is not a classification covered under federal law, under Section 504, students with ADD can receive special assistance. Other students who may be helped under Section 504 would be those with asthma, allergies, arthritis, or diabetes, to name just a few.

P.L. 93-380: The Family Education Rights and Privacy Act

The Family Education Rights and Privacy Act (FERPA), often referred to as the *Buckley Amendment,* gives parents of students under the age of 18, and students age 18 and over, the right to examine records kept in the student's personal file. FERPA was passed in 1974 to cover all students, including those in postsecondary education. The major provisions of FERPA follow (NICHCY, 1997):

- Parents and eligible students have the right to inspect and review the student's educational records.
- Schools must have written permission from the parent or eligible student before releasing any information from a student's records.
- Parents and eligible students have the right to have the records explained and interpreted by school officials.
- School officials may not destroy any education records if there is an outstanding request to inspect and review them.
- Parents and eligible students who believe that information in the education records is inaccurate or misleading may request that the records be amended. The parents or eligible students must be advised if the school decides that the records should not be amended, and they have the right to a hearing.

Finally, FERPA mandates that each school district must give parents of students in attendance, or students age 18 or over, an annual notice to inform them of their rights under this law, and the right of parents or eligible students to file a complaint with the U.S. Department of Education.

P.L. 94-142: The Education of All Handicapped Children's Act (EHA)

Because of the victories that were being won for students with disabilities in the early 1970s, parents and student advocates began to lobby Congress for federal laws and money that would ensure that students with disabilities received an education that would meet their needs. In 1975, the stage was clearly set for a national special education law. Years of exclusion, segregation, and denial of basic educational opportunities to students with disabilities and their families set an imperative for a civil rights law guaranteeing these students access to the education system (Smith, 1998, p. 21).

Although it was clear that advancement was being made in providing services to students with disabilities, in 1975 Congress found that:

- Over 1.75 million children with disabilities were being excluded entirely from receiving a public education solely on the basis of their handicap.
- Over 4 million of the estimated 8 million children with handicaps in this country were not receiving the appropriate educational services they needed and were entitled to receive.
- Many other children with handicaps were still being placed in inappropriate educational settings because their handicaps were undetected or because of a violation of their individual rights.
- One million children with disabilities in the United States were excluded entirely from the public school system and would not go through the educational system with their peers.
- Because of the lack of adequate services within the public school system, families were often forced to find services outside the public school system, often at great distance from their residences and at their own expense.
- State and local educational agencies have a responsibility to provide education for all children with disabilities.
- It is in the national interest that the federal government assist state and local efforts to provide programs to meet the educational needs of children with disabilities in order to assure equal protection of the law.

It is evident that Congress recognized the necessity of special education for children with disabilities and was concerned about the widespread discrimination. In response, Congress enacted into federal law the **Education of All Handicapped Children's Act (EHA), P.L. 94-142.** Public Law 94-142 set forth federal procedural safeguards for children with disabilities and their parents. This law outlined the entire foundation upon which current special education practices rest.

The major provisions of P.L. 94-142 are:

- **Before any evaluations, testing, and placement can be done, there must be parental informed consent. Informed consent** is defined as the following:
    - The parent has been fully informed of all information relevant to the activity for which consent is sought, in the family's native language, or other mode of communication.

- The parent understands and agrees in writing to the carrying out of the activity for which consent is sought, and the consent describes that activity and lists the records (if any) that will be released and to whom.
- The parent understands that the gaining of consent is voluntary and may be revoked at any time.

■ **All students in special education must be placed in the least restrictive environment:** Students with disabilities need to be placed in the environment that is best suited for their educational needs or, as it was termed, the **least restrictive environment (LRE).** Under federal law, schools must, to the maximum extent possible, insure that individuals with disabilities, including individuals in public and private institutions or other care facilities, are educated with individuals without disabilities. This is known as mainstreaming, although the federal law did not define this term. Also, special classes and separate schooling are to be used only when the nature or severity of the disability is such that the education in regular classes with the use of supplementary aids and services cannot be satisfactorily achieved. The settings for placement and service delivery are envisioned to fall on a continuum of least restrictive to most restrictive.

■ **All students in special education must have an individualized education program (IEP):** All students in special education are required to have an individualized education program designed to meet their needs. The **IEP** includes both short-term and long-term goals, along with how and where services will be provided (see Chapter 19 for a comprehensive discussion of the components of an IEP).

■ **The evaluation for placement in special education must be nondiscriminatory:** Under federal law, the following requirements must be adhered to for an evaluation to be considered a nondiscriminatory assessment:

1. All instruments used in the evaluation of a student for determination of a disability should be free from bias.
2. When considering eligibility for special education, the evaluation must be done by a multidisciplinary team.
3. All testing materials and procedures used for the purposes of evaluation and placement of children with disabilities must be selected and administered so as not to be racially or culturally discriminatory.
4. All tests and other evaluation materials must be validated for the specific purpose for which they are used.
5. Tests and other evaluation materials must be administered by trained personnel in conformance with the instructions provided by their producer.
6. No single procedure can be used as the sole criterion for determining an appropriate educational program for a child.

■ **The individual is assessed in all areas related to the suspected disability:** This includes, where appropriate, health, vision, hearing, social and emotional status, general intelligence, academic performance, communicative status, and motor abilities.

■ **Tests must be given and reports must be written in the native language:** When doing an assessment, all tests must be given in the child's **native language,** and all reports must be written in the parent's native language.

■ **Parents are entitled to due process:** All students and their parents are afforded **due process.** This means that if a conflict or disagreement ensues concerning a student's eligibility for special education placement or services, no changes can be made until the issue has been settled by an impartial hearing.

■ **Zero reject for all students: Zero reject** means that all students have the right to a public school education and cannot be excluded because of a disability. Students are entitled to a free and appropriate public school education regardless of the extent of the disability. Also, it is the responsibility of each state to find children who may need and be entitled to special education services.

P.L. 98-524: The Vocational Education Act of 1984—The Perkins Act

The Vocational Education Act of 1984, often referred to as the Carl D. Perkins Act or the **Perkins Act,** authorizes federal funds to support vocational education programs. One of the goals for the Perkins Act is to improve the access of either those who have been underserved in the past or those who have greater-than-average educational needs. Under the act, "special populations" include those who have a disability, are disadvantaged, or have limited English proficiency. This law is particularly important, because it requires that vocational education be provided for students with disabilities. The regulations that cover this law are called C.F.R. Title 34; Parts 400–499 (NICHCY, 1997).

The law states that individuals who are members of special populations (including individuals with disabilities) must be provided with equal access to recruitment, enrollment, and placement activities in vocational education. In addition, these individuals must be provided with equal access to the full range of vocational education programs available to others, including occupationally specific courses of study, cooperative education, apprenticeship programs, and, to the extent practical, comprehensive guidance and counseling services. Under the law, vocational educational planning should be coordinated among public agencies, including vocational education, special education, and the state vocational rehabilitation agencies. The provision of vocational education to youth with disabilities should be monitored to ensure that such education is consistent with objectives stated in the student's IEP (NICHCY, 1997).

P.L. 99-457: Education of the Handicapped Act Amendments of 1986

In 1983, Congress amended the Education of All Handicapped Children's Act to expand incentives for preschool special education programs, early intervention, and transition programs. All programs under EHA became the responsibility of the Office of Special Education Programs (OSEP).

In 1986, Public Law 99-457 was passed, amending P.L. 94-142 and requiring the states to provide a free and appropriate public education to children with disabilities age three through age five. The regulations that governed school-age children were then made applicable to the assessment of preschool children. In addition, a new part

(Part H) was added to the law, establishing incentives for serving infants and toddlers with special needs.

In 1990, P.L. 99-457 was retitled the **Individuals with Disabilities Education Act (IDEA)—P.L. 101-476.** The IDEA amendment to P.L. 99-457 requires a timely, comprehensive, multidisciplinary evaluation, including assessment activities related to the child and the child's play. For infants and toddlers (birth to two years of age), a new program (Part H was changed to Part C in the Amendments to IDEA '97) was established to help states develop and implement programs for early intervention services. Every U.S. state currently provides services for infants and toddlers with disabilities under IDEA '97 (P.L. 105-17). A detailed discussion of early intervention law is addressed in Chapter 14.

The Individuals with Disabilities Education Act of 1997 (IDEA '97)

In 1990, the reauthorization of P.L. 94-142 was enacted and became Public Law 101-476. **Reauthorization** is simply the act of amending and renewing a law. Public Law 101-476 is widely known as IDEA—**the Individuals with Disabilities Education Act.** IDEA continued to uphold the provisions set forth in P.L. 94-142. It was amended to P.L. 105-17 on June 4, 1997, and is now often referred to as **IDEA '97.** Some of the changes made were substantial, whereas others fine-tuned processes already in place for schools and parents to follow in planning and providing special education and related services for children with special needs (Venn, 2000).

Under IDEA, most of the mandates under 94-142 remained intact. However, some of IDEA's most important revisions and additions included the following:

- Adding significantly to the provisions for very young children with disabilities and for students preparing to leave secondary school
- Adding two new categories in special education: autism and traumatic brain injury
- Removing the term *handicapped* from the law and substituting the preferred term, *disability*
- Mandating **transition services** no later than 16 years of age
- Requiring further public commenting on defining attention deficit disorder in the law
- Stating that states can be sued in federal courts for violating the laws

Besides the guidelines and procedures set forth from 94-142 and IDEA of 1990, IDEA '97 added many provisions.

- **IDEA '97 strengthened the least restrictive environment mandate:** IDEA '97 fosters increased efforts to educate students with disabilities in the LRE. For example, if a child is to be placed in special education, it must be considered whether and how the child can participate in the general curriculum, and the IEP is to indicate the extent to which the student will not be with nondisabled peers [20 U.S.C.

1414(d)(1)(A)(i)–(iv)]. Prior to IDEA '97, the IEP was to indicate the opposite—the extent to which the student would be educated with nondisabled peers.

- **IDEA '97 strengthened parents' roles further:** Perhaps only making explicit what should already have been obvious, schools must now consider the results of evaluations, the strengths of the child, and the concerns of the parents for enhancing the child's education when developing the IEP [20 U.S.C. 1414(d)(3)(A)]. Under IDEA '97, parents are to be a part of the group that determines their child's eligibility [Section 300.534.535(a)(1)]. IDEA '97 also stated that parents should have the opportunity to examine all records pertaining to their child, not just "relevant" records, as stated in the old law.

- **IDEA '97 added related services to the types of services to be provided for transition services:** Services are to be based on the individual student's needs, taking into account the student's preferences and interests. IDEA '97 enlarged the scope of an appropriate education by requiring that it should not only meet students' unique needs but also "prepare them for employment and independent living" [20 U.S.C. 1400(d)(1)(A)]. See Chapter 20 for a detailed discussion on transition services.

- **IDEA '97 strengthened the obligations of other agencies to provide services to students while they are still in school:** All states must now have interagency agreements to ensure that all public agencies responsible for providing services also considered special education services, fulfill their responsibilities. The agreement must also specify how the various agencies will cooperate to ensure the timely and appropriate delivery of services to students [20 U.S.C. 1412(a)(12)].

- **IDEA '97 emphasized assistive technology:** The need for assistive technology must now be considered for all students when developing the individualized education plan.

- **IDEA '97 expanded the number of members of the IEP team:** This is discussed in detail in Chapter 18. In addition to parents, the team must include at least one special education teacher and at least one teacher from the regular education classroom, if the child participates in regular education.

- **IDEA '97 gave school authorities several options in disciplining a student with a disability:** Schools can suspend a child for up to 10 days or order a change in the child's education setting for up to 10 days, if they discipline students without disabilities in the same way.

- **IDEA '97 changed Part H, serving young children, to Part C:** In doing so, IDEA '97 expanded provisions to "at-risk" children from birth to five years old, in addition to children already being served. This is explained in detail in Chapter 14.

- **Finally, under IDEA '97, children and youth receiving special education had the right to receive the related services necessary to benefit from special education instruction:** Related services include transportation and such developmental, corrective, and other supportive services as are required to assist a child with a disability to benefit from special education, and include speech pathology and audiology; psychological services; physical and occupational therapy; recreation, including therapeutic recreation; early identification and assessment of disabilities in children; counseling services, including rehabilitation counseling; and medical services for diagnostic or evaluation purposes. The term also includes school health services, social work services in schools, and parent counseling and training (C.F.R. Title 34; Education; Part 300.16, 1993).

IDEA '97 and Section 504 of the Vocational Rehabilitation Act of 1973 strengthened each other in important areas. For example, they both:

- Called for school systems to carry out a systematic search for every child with a disability in need of a public education
- Mandated a free and appropriate education (FAPE) regardless of the nature and severity of an individual's disability
- Made it clear that education and related services must be provided at no cost to parents
- Had similar requirements to ensure that testing and evaluation of a child's needs are not based on a single testing instrument
- Emphasized the importance of educating children and youth with disabilities with their nondisabled peers to the maximum extent appropriate (NICHCY, 1997)

The Individuals with Disabilities Education Improvement Act-P.L. 108-446

On November 17, 2004, the unified IDEA bill unveiled by the Conference Committee was passed by Congress. The House passed the bill by a vote of 397–3. The Senate immediately followed suit, passing the bill by voice vote on November 19, 2004. On December 3, 2004, President Bush officially reauthorized IDEA '97 as the Individuals with Disabilities Education Improvement Act (IDEA 2004), Public Law 108-446.

What does this law contain? We will focus on IDEA 2004 and its differences from IDEA '97 in Chapter 20 of this text, *Special Topics in Assessment*. This material is best covered separately, as very few issues in terms of assessment were altered; however, significant revisions were made to various topics in special education that are of importance to special educators.

The Americans with Disabilities Act—P.L. 101-336

In July 1990, President Bush signed into law Public Law 101-336—the Americans with Disabilities Act (ADA). He said, "Let the shameful walls of exclusion finally come tumbling down." Senator Tom Harkin, the chief sponsor of the act, spoke of this law as the "emancipation proclamation" for people with disabilities. This civil rights law is based on Section 504 of the Vocational Rehabilitation Act of 1973, but it further extends the rights of individuals with disabilities. It protects all individuals with disabilities from discrimination and requires most employers to make reasonable accommodations for them.

The ADA plays a very important role in transitional services for students with disabilities. It also figures significantly in making sure that all school buildings are accessible to people with disabilities. For example, if your school is not accessible for wheelchairs, does not have emergency exits for all, or does not have ramps, this would be a violation of the ADA.

IDEA 2004 and ADA differ in certain important areas. These include:

- IDEA 2004 benefits only those who are between certain ages (birth to 21 years). By contrast, ADA benefits all people with disabilities, without regard to their age.
- IDEA 2004 benefits only those people in school. By contrast, ADA benefits people in employment and a wide range of public and private services.
- IDEA 2004 provides money to state and local agencies to help educate students with disabilities, and defines the rights and services afforded by law. By contrast, ADA prohibits discrimination, but does not provide money to help anyone comply with it.

Regardless of their differences, IDEA '97 and ADA work together. IDEA '97 helps state and local education agencies create services to educate students with disabilities, and ADA protects students against discrimination when they are not in school.

P.L. 107-110: No Child Left Behind Act of 2001 (NCLB)

The *No Child Left Behind Act of 2001* (Public Law 107-110: No Child Left Behind-*NCLB*) is a landmark in education reform designed to improve student achievement and change the culture of U.S. schools. President George W. Bush describes this law as the "cornerstone of my administration." Clearly, our children are our future, and, as President Bush has expressed, "Too many of our neediest children are being left behind."

With passage of NCLB, Congress reauthorized the Elementary and Secondary Education Act (ESEA)—the principal federal law affecting education from kindergarten through high school. In amending ESEA, the new law represents a sweeping overhaul of federal efforts to support elementary and secondary education in the United States. It is built on four common-sense pillars: accountability for results, an emphasis on doing what works based on scientific research, expanded parental options, and expanded local control and flexibility.

According to the U.S. Department of Education (2004), NCLB:

- ***Supports learning in the early years, thereby preventing many learning difficulties that may arise later.*** Children who enter school with language skills and pre-reading skills (e.g., understanding that print reads from left to right and top to bottom) are more likely to learn to read well in the early grades and succeed in later years. In fact, research shows that most reading problems faced by adolescents and adults are the result of problems that could have been prevented through good instruction in their early childhood years (Snow, Burns and Griffin, 1998). It is never too early to start building language skills by talking with and reading to children. NCLB targets resources for early childhood education so that all youngsters get the right start.

■ *Provides more information for parents about their child's progress.* Under NCLB, each state must measure every public school student's progress in reading and math in each of grades 3 through 8 and at least once during grades 10 through 12. By school year 2007–2008, assessments (or testing) in science will be underway. These assessments must be aligned with state academic content and achievement standards. They will provide parents with objective data on where their child stands academically.

■ *Alerts parents to important information on the performance of their child's school.* NCLB requires states and school districts to give parents easy-to-read, detailed report cards on schools and districts, telling them which ones are succeeding and why. Included in the report cards are student achievement data broken out by race, ethnicity, gender, English language proficiency, migrant status, disability status, and low-income status; as well as important information about the professional qualifications of teachers. With these provisions, NCLB ensures that parents have important, timely information about the schools their children attend—whether they are performing well or not for all children, regardless of their background.

■ *Gives children and parents a lifeline.* In this new era of education, children will no longer be trapped in the dead end of low-performing schools. Under NCLB, such schools must use their federal funds to make needed improvements. In the event of a school's continued poor performance, parents have options to ensure that their children receive the high-quality education to which they are entitled. That might mean that children can transfer to higher-performing schools in the area or receive supplemental educational services in the community, such as tutoring, after-school programs, or remedial classes.

■ *Improves teaching and learning by providing better information to teachers and principals.* Annual tests to measure children's progress provide teachers with independent information about each child's strengths and weaknesses. With this knowledge, teachers can craft lessons to make sure each student meets or exceeds the standards. In addition, principals can use the data to assess exactly how much progress each teacher's students have made and to better inform decisions about how to run their schools.

■ *Ensures that teacher quality is a high priority.* NCLB defines the qualifications needed by teachers and paraprofessionals who work on any facet of classroom instruction. It requires that states develop plans to achieve the goal that all teachers of core academic subjects be highly qualified by the end of the 2005–06 school year. States must include in their plans annual, measurable objectives that each local school district and school must meet in moving toward the goal; they must report on their progress in the annual report cards.

■ *Gives more resources to schools.* Today, more than $7,000 on average is spent per pupil by local, state, and federal taxpayers. States and local school districts are now receiving more federal funding than ever before for all programs under NCLB. A large portion of these funds is for grants under Title I of ESEA: Improving the Academic Achievement of the Disadvantaged. Title I grants are awarded to states and local education agencies to help states and school districts improve the education of disadvantaged students; turn around low-performing schools; improve teacher quality; and increase choices for parents.

■ *Allows more flexibility.* In exchange for the strong accountability, NCLB gives states and local education agencies more flexibility in the use of their federal education funding. As a result, principals and administrators spend less time filling out forms and dealing with federal red tape. They have more time to devote to students' needs. They have more freedom to implement innovations and allocate resources as policymakers at the state and local levels see fit, thereby giving local people a greater opportunity to affect decisions regarding their schools' programs.

■ *Focuses on what works.* NCLB puts a special emphasis on implementing educational programs and practices that have been clearly demonstrated to be effective through rigorous scientific research. Federal funding is targeted to support such programs. For example, the Reading First program makes federal funds available to help reading teachers in the early grades strengthen old skills and gain new ones in instructional techniques that scientifically based research has shown to be effective.

Finally, according to the U.S. Department of Education (2004), because of No Child Left Behind:

- Parents will know their children's strengths and weaknesses and how well schools are performing; they will have other options and resources for helping their children if their schools are chronically in need of improvement.
- Teachers will have the training and resources they need for teaching effectively, using curricula that are grounded in scientifically based research; annual testing lets them know areas in which students need extra attention.
- Principals will have information they need to strengthen their schools' weaknesses and to put into practice methods and strategies backed by sound, scientific research.
- Superintendents will be able to see which of their schools and principals are doing well and which need help to improve.
- School boards will be able to measure how their districts are doing and measure their districts in relation to others across the state; they will have more and better information on which to base decisions about priorities in their districts.
- Chief state school officers will know how the schools in their states and in other states are doing; they will be better able to pinpoint where guidance and resources are needed.
- Governors will have a yearly report card on how their states' schools are doing; they will be able to highlight accomplishments of the best schools and target help to those schools that are in need of improvement.

- Community leaders and volunteer groups will have information they can use to rally their members in efforts to help children and schools that need the most help.

State Laws Relating to Students with Disabilities

How states implement the requirements of federal laws is covered by the primary and basic source of law for the nation—the United States Constitution. Federal laws passed by Congress must be based on the provisions of the Constitution. State constitutions and laws may go beyond what is provided in the federal law, as long as there is no conflict between them, and as long as state laws do not address areas reserved to the federal government, such as providing for the nation's defense. The major constitutional provisions that are important to children and youth with disabilities are (1) those that provide for the spending of money to protect the general welfare and (2) the Fourteenth Amendment, which provides that no state shall "deprive any person of life, liberty, or property, without the due process of law nor deny equal protection of the laws." It is important to remember that there is no constitutional provision requiring the federal government to provide education for its citizens. The Tenth Amendment to the Constitution states that "powers not delegated to the United States by the Constitution, nor prohibited by the States, are reserved to the States." Therefore, all states have provided for public education, by either state constitution or state law, or both. States are required under the due process and equal protection clauses of the Fourteenth Amendment to provide education on an equal basis and to provide due process before denying equal educational programming (NICHCY, 1997).

Most laws providing for public education are generally state and local rather than federal. Although some educational programs are highly regulated by the federal government, education is, for the most part, a state function. It is important to remember that most federal laws and regulations that provide for educational programming establish minimum standards that states must follow for the delivery of services and programs in order to receive federal funds. Quite often, federal laws give flexibility to the states in implementing the programs or services established with federal funds. Laws and regulations regarding civil rights, on the other hand, are much more firm and concrete.

As future special educators, it is therefore essential that you become familiar with your state laws and regulations. It is important to remember that laws provide a framework for policy, and regulations provide the specific requirements for implementing the policy. Where there are differences, inconsistencies, or ambiguities in interpretation or in implementation, the judicial system is responsible for resolving these disputes. Often, court decisions lead to changes in the law or in regulations. It is important to note that laws are not made in a vacuum. Often, laws are made by one branch of government in response to developments in other arenas. State and federal law are frequently interactive in this process. The development of special education law is an excellent example. It is likely that interaction among the various branches of government (legislative, executive, and judicial) at both the federal and state levels in the development of special education law and laws protecting the civil rights of individuals with disabilities will continue for some time.

CONCLUSION

To prevent discrimination, people must be educated about it. Yet education alone will not solve the problem. We also need legislation that is enforced by federal, state, and local governments. Then, all schools need to comply. It should be evident that the nature of special education has changed dramatically over the past 30 years because of numerous court cases and legal battles. There have been many heroes and heroines in this effort, most certainly the families of children with disabilities. The positive changes in laws and attitudes of the public toward people with disabilities would not have occurred without active and persistent involvement of many dedicated people over the years (NICHCY, 1997). Legislation to protect all people with disabilities is becoming the norm, something we should all be thankful for, especially in education.

VOCABULARY

Americans with Disabilities Act (ADA):   Federal law enacted in 1990 that is antidiscrimination legislation for people with disabilities.

Board of Education of Hendrick Hudson School District v. Rowley: In *Rowley,* the court concluded that the obligation to provide an appropriate education does not mean a school must provide the best education or one designed to maximize a student's potential.

Brown v. Board of Education of Topeka, Kansas: In *Brown,* the U.S. Supreme Court ruled that it was illegal under the Fourteenth Amendment of the U.S. Constitution to arbitrarily discriminate against any group of people.

Daniel R. R. v. State Board of Education: One of the leading cases that opened the door to increased inclusion of children with disabilities in regular education classes.

Diana v. State Board of Education: In this case, California was mandated by the court to correct bias in assessment procedures used with Chinese American and Mexican American students.

Due Process: The right to an impartial hearing if parents do not agree with the decisions made about their child in the assessment process.

Elementary and Secondary Education Act of 1965 (ESEA-P.L. 89-10):   Direct federal support for the education of children with disabilities has its roots in the Elementary and Secondary Education Act of 1965. The purpose of this law was to strengthen and improve educational quality and opportunity in the nation's elementary and secondary schools.

Fourteenth Amendment: The equal protection clause of the U.S. Constitution, which states that all people must have equal protection under the law.

Georgia State Conference of Branches of NAACP v. State of Georgia: Here, a U.S. Court of Appeals ruled that overrepresentation of African American children in classes for the mentally retarded by itself was not sufficient to prove discrimination.

Gerstmeyer v. Howard County Public Schools: Here, the court ruled that when a school district delays an evaluation for six months, parents can sue for costs associated with the delay and be reimbursed for all associated costs.

Guadalupe v. Tempe Elementary School: In Arizona, a U.S. district court agreed to a stipulated agreement that children could not be placed in educable mentally retarded classes unless they scored lower than 2 standard deviations below the population mean on an approved IQ test administered in the child's own language.

Hobson v. Hansen: The first court case that declared that the District of Columbia's school system's tracking system was invalid.

IDEA: The Individuals with Disabilities Education Act is Public Law 105-17, which extends the rights of those set forth in P.L. 94-142.

IDEA 2004:   The federal law that guarantees that a "free appropriate education," including special education and related service programming, is available to all children and youth with disabilities who require it. IDEA 2004 also ensures that the rights of children and youth with disabilities and their parents or guardians are protected (e.g., fairness, appropriateness, and due process in decision making about providing special education and related services to children and youth with disabilities).

Individualized Education Program (IEP):   The document that sets forth the short-term and long-term goals of each child who is classified in special education.

Informed Consent: The rights of parents to know exactly what will happen to their children in the process of assessment.

Jose P. v. Ambach: Here, the court ruled that evaluations in or for special education services must be "timely evaluations."

Larry P. v. Riles: In this California case, using IQ tests as the assessment measure for placing African American students in special education as mentally retarded was found to be discriminatory.

Least Restrictive Environment (LRE):   The idea that all children with disabilities should be educated in an environment that is least restrictive, ensuring to the extent possible that they will receive their education with children without disabilities.

Luke S. and Han S. v. Nix et al.:   A Louisiana court case whereby the court ruled that greater prereferral assessment should be done before a referral is made.

Mills v. Board of Education of District of Columbia: This case set forth future guidelines for federal legislation, including the rights of students to have access to a free public education, due process protection, and a mandated requirement to receive special education services regardless of the school district's financial capability.

Native Language: The language that is the primary language for the child and/or his or her parents.

No Child Left Behind (NCLB):   With passage of No Child Left Behind, Congress reauthorized the Elementary and Secondary Education Act (ESEA). In amending ESEA, the new law represents a sweeping overhaul of federal efforts to support elementary and secondary education in the United States. It is built on four common-sense pillars: accountability for results, an emphasis on doing what works based on scientific research, expanded parental options, and expanded local control and flexibility.

Nondiscriminatory Assessment: Objective and fair testing practices and procedures for all children.

PARC v. Commonwealth of Pennsylvania: In this case, a U.S. Federal Court in Pennsylvania ratified a consent agreement assuring that schools may not exclude students who have been classified with mental retardation.

PASE v. Hannon: Here, the court found that the use of intelligence tests was acceptable in psychoeducational assessment as long as they followed all other procedural safeguards under federal law.

Reauthorization: The act of amending and renewing a law.

Section 504 of the Vocational Rehabilitation Act: A civil rights law created to prevent discrimination against all individuals with disabilities in programs that receive federal funds, as do all public schools.

Transition Services: Services and programs to help students in special education make the transition from high school to college or vocational career.

Wyatt v. Stickney: In Alabama, a federal court ruled that mentally retarded children in state institutions had a constitutional right to treatment.

Zero Reject: All students have the right to a public school education and cannot be excluded because of a disability.

- - - - - -

CHAPTER THREE

METHODS OF ASSESSMENT AND TESTING CONSIDERATIONS

KEY TERMS

Authentic/Naturalistic/Performance–
   Based Assessment
Basal
Ceiling
Criterion-Referenced Tests
Curriculum-Based Assessment (CBA)
Curriculum-Based Measurement (CBM)
Dynamic Assessment
Ecological Assessment
Informal Reading Inventories (IRIs)
Learning Styles Assessment

Limitations of Testing
Norm Group
Norming Group
Norm-Referenced tests (NRT)
Outcome-Based Assessment
Portfolio Assessment
Standardization
Standardized Tests
Standards-Referenced Tests
Task Analysis

CHAPTER OBJECTIVES

The focus of this chapter is to discuss various formal versus informal methods of assessment. After reading this chapter you should understand the following:

- Norm-Referenced Tests
- Intended Purposes of Norm Referenced Tests
- Standardization
- Concerns with Standardized Testing
- Criterion-Referenced Tests
- Standards-Referenced Tests
- Ecological Assessment
- Curriculum-Based Assessment (CBA)
- Curriculum-Based Measurement (CBM)

- Dynamic Assessment
- Portfolio Assessment
- Authentic/Naturalistic/Performance–Based Assessment
- Task Analysis
- Outcome-Based Assessment
- Learning Styles Assessment
- Selecting an Appropriate Instrument
- Selection of Test Content
- Test Interpretation
- Limitations of Testing

ASSESSMENT AND TESTING CONSIDERATIONS

The ways in which children and adolescents can be evaluated for special education vary from individual to individual. The method of assessment utilized needs to determined on a case-by-case basis. However, to obtain the most valid and accurate picture of a student's strengths and weaknesses, a comprehensive measure of assessment involves using both formal and informal methods of assessment.

Formal and informal are not technical psychometric terms; therefore, there are no uniformly accepted definitions. Formal tests assume a single set of expectations for all students and come with prescribed criteria for scoring and interpretation.

Informal tests are used here to indicate techniques that can easily be incorporated into classroom routines and learning activities. Informal assessment techniques can be used at any time without interfering with instructional time. Their results are indicative of the student's performance on the skill or subject of interest. Unlike standardized tests, they are not intended to provide a comparison to a broader group beyond the students in the local project.

This is not to say that informal assessment is casual or lacking in rigor. Informal assessment requires a clear understanding of the levels of ability the students bring with them. Only then may assessment activities be selected that students can attempt reasonably. Informal assessment seeks to identify the strengths and needs of individual students without regard to grade or age norms.

Scores on **norm-referenced tests (NRT)** are not interpreted according to an absolute standard or criterion (e.g., eight out of 10 correct) but rather according to how the student's performance compares with that of a particular group of individuals. In order for this comparison to be meaningful, a valid comparison group—called a norm group—must be defined. A **norm group** is a large number of children who are representative of all the children in that age group. Such a group can be obtained by selecting a group of children that have the characteristics of children across the United States— that is, a certain percentage must be from each gender, from various ethnic backgrounds (e.g., Caucasian, African American, American Indian, Asian, Hispanic), from each geographic area (e.g., Southeast, Midwest), and from each socioeconomic class.

By having all types of children take the test, the test publisher can provide information about how various types of children perform on the test. (This information—what type of students comprised the norm group and how each type performed on the test—is generally given in the manuals that accompany the test.) The school will compare the scores of the child being evaluated to the scores obtained by the norm group. This helps evaluators determine whether the child is performing at a level typical for, below, or above that expected for children of a given ethnicity, socioeconomic status, age, or grade.

Thus, before making assumptions about a child's abilities based upon test results, it is important to know something about the group to which the child is being compared—particularly whether the student is being compared to children who are similar in ethnicity, socioeconomic status, and so on. The more unlike the child the norm group is, the less valuable the results of testing will generally be. This is one of the areas in which standardized testing has fallen under considerable criticism. Often, test administrators do not use the norm group information appropriately, or there may not be children in the norm group who are similar to the child being tested. Furthermore, many tests were originally developed some time ago, and the norm groups reported in the test manual are not similar at all to the children being tested today.

Norm-referenced tests include **basal** and **ceiling** levels. These are used to prevent the examiner from having to administer all of the items with each test. A **basal** is the "starting point." It represents the level of mastery of a task below which the student would correctly answer all items on a test. All of the items prior to the basal are not given to the student. These items are considered already correct. For example, on an IQ test, the examiner may start with question 14 because of the age of the child. That is the basal. Here, the student starts with credit given for the first 13 questions.

Once the basal is determined, the examiner will administer all items until the student reaches a **ceiling.** The ceiling is the point at which the student has made a predetermined number of errors, and therefore, all other items stop being administered because it is assumed that the student will continue to get the answers wrong. The ceiling is the "ending point." It represents the level of mastery of a task above which the student would incorrectly answer all future items on a test. For example, if on a spelling test a child got numbers 15 to 24 wrong, and the ceiling is 10 incorrect in a row, this means that the examiner would stop administering spelling words to the child because the ceiling has been obtained.

Intended Purposes of Norm Referenced Tests

Norm-referenced tests compare a person's score against the scores of a group of people who have already taken the same exam, called the **norming group.** When you see scores in the paper that report a school's scores as a percentage—"the Lincoln school ranked at the 49th percentile"—or when you see your child's score reported that way— "Jamal scored at the 63rd percentile"—the test is usually a norm-referenced test. Norm-referenced tests are designed to "rank order" test takers—that is, to compare students' scores. A commercial norm-referenced test does not compare all the students who take the test in a given year. Instead, test makers select a sample from the target student population (say, ninth graders). The test is "normed" on this sample, which is supposed to fairly represent the entire target population (all ninth graders in the nation). Students' scores are then reported in relation to the scores of this "norming" group. To make comparing easier, test makers create exams in which the results end up looking at least somewhat like a bell-shaped curve (the normal curve, see Chapter 4). Test makers make the test so that most students will score near the middle, and only a few will score low (the left side of the curve) or high (the right side of the curve).

The major reason for using a norm-referenced tests is to classify students. NRTs are designed to highlight achievement differences between and among students to produce a dependable rank order of students across a continuum of achievement from high achievers to low achievers. School systems might want to classify students in this way so that they can be properly placed in remedial or gifted programs. These types of tests are also used to help teachers select students for different ability level reading or mathematics instructional groups.

Tests are normed using a national sample of students. Because norming a test is such an elaborate and expensive process, the norms are typically used by test publishers for seven years. All students who take the test during that seven-year period have their scores compared to the original norm group.

Standardization

All norm-referenced tests include standardized procedures. **Standardization** refers to structuring test materials, administration procedures, scoring methods, and techniques for interpreting results (Venn, 2000). **Standardized tests** have detailed procedures for administration, timing, scoring, and interpretation procedures that must be followed precisely to obtain valid and reliable results. Standardized tests are very much a part of the education scene. Most of us have taken many such tests in our lifetime. A wide variety of standardized tests is available to assess different skill areas. In the field of special education, these include intelligence tests; math, reading, spelling, and writing tests; perceptual tests; and many others. The fact is, standardized tests are a tremendous source of information when assessing a child.

Concerns with Standardized Testing

Criticisms of standardized tests seem to have grown in proportion to the frequency with which, and the purposes for which, they are used (Haney & Madaus, 1989). Pikulski (1990) suggests that the greatest misuse of standardized tests may be their overuse. Many districts now administer such tests at every grade level, define success or failure of programs in terms of test scores, and even link teacher and administrator salaries and job security to student performance on standardized test performance.

Three areas often criticized in regard to standardized tests are content, item format, and item bias. Standardized tests are designed to provide the best match possible to what is perceived to be the "typical" curriculum at a specific grade level. Because a bilingual education program is built on objectives unique to the needs of its students, many of the items on a standardized test may not measure the objectives or content of that program. Thus a standardized test may have low content validity (see Chapter 5) for specific bilingual education programs. In such a situation, the test might not be sensitive to actual student progress. Consequently, the program, as measured by this test, would appear to be ineffective.

Standardized achievement tests generally rely heavily on multiple-choice items. This item format allows for greater content coverage as well as objective and efficient scoring. However, the response required by the format is recognition of the correct answer. This type of response does not necessarily match the type of responses students regularly make in the classroom, for example, the production or synthesis of information. If students are not used to responding within the structure imposed by the item format, their test performance may suffer. On the other hand, students may recognize the correct form when it is presented as a discrete item in a test format, but fail to use that form correctly in communication contexts. In this case, a standardized test may make the student appear more proficient than performance would suggest.

Further, some tests have been criticized for including items that are biased against certain kinds of students (e.g., ethnic minorities, limited English proficiency, rural, inner-city). The basis for this criticism is that the items reflect the language, culture, and/or learning style of the middle-class majority (Neill & Medina, 1989). Although test companies have attempted to write culture-free items, the removal of questions from a meaningful context has proved problematic for minority students.

Thus, there are strong arguments in favor of educators considering the use of alternative forms of assessment to supplement standardized test information. These alternate assessments should be timely, not time-consuming, truly representative of the curriculum, and tangibly meaningful to the teacher and student. Techniques of informal assessment have the potential to meet these criteria as well as programmatic requirements for formative and summative evaluations. Validity and reliability are not exclusive properties of formal, norm-referenced tests. Informal techniques are valid if they measure the skills and knowledge imparted by the project; they are reliable if they measure consistently and accurately.

According to Hart (1994, p. 7, cited in Taylor, 1997) important criticisms of standardized testing include the following:

- It puts too much value on recall and rote learning at the expense of understanding and reflection.
- It promotes the misleading impression that a single right answer exists for almost every problem or question.
- It turns students into passive learners who need only recognize, not construct, answers and solutions.
- It forces teachers to focus more on what can be easily tested than on what is important for students to learn.
- It trivializes content and skill development by reducing whatever is taught to a fill-in-the-bubble format.

NRTs have come under attack recently because they traditionally have purportedly focused on low-level, basic skills. This emphasis is in direct contrast to the recommendations made by the latest research on teaching and learning which calls for educators to stress the acquisition of conceptual understanding as well as the application of skills. The National Council of Teachers of Mathematics (NCTM) has been particularly vocal about this concern. In an NCTM publication (1991), Romberg (1989) cited that "a recent study of the six most commonly used commercial achievement tests found that at grade 8, on average, only 1 percent of the items were problem solving while 77 percent were computation or estimation" (p. 8).

To best prepare their students for the standardized achievement tests, teachers usually devote much time to teaching the information which is found on the standardized tests. This is particularly true if the standardized tests are also used to measure an educator's teaching ability. The result of this pressure placed upon teachers for their students to perform well on these tests has resulted in an emphasis on low-level skills in the classroom (Corbett & Wilson, 1991). With curriculum specialists and educational policy makers alike calling for more attention to higher level skills, these tests may be driving classroom practice in the opposite direction of educational reform.

INFORMAL ASSESSMENT

Criterion-Referenced Tests

Many educators and members of the public fail to grasp the distinctions between criterion-referenced and norm-referenced testing. It is common to hear the two types of testing referred to as if they serve the same purposes, or shared the same characteristics. Much confusion can be eliminated if the basic differences are understood.

While norm-referenced tests ascertain the rank of students, criterion-referenced tests (CRTs) determine ". . . what test takers can do and what they know, not how they compare to others" (Anastasi, 1988, p. 102). CRTs report how well students are doing relative to a predetermined performance level on a specified set of educational goals or outcomes included in the school, district, or state curriculum.

Educators or policy makers may choose to use a CRT when they wish to see how well students have learned the knowledge and skills which they are expected to have mastered. This information may be used as one piece of information to determine how well the student is learning the desired curriculum and how well the school is teaching that curriculum.

CRTs are scored according to a standard, or criterion, that the teacher, school, or test publisher decides represents an acceptable level of mastery. An example of a criterion-referenced test might be a teacher-made spelling test in which there are 20 words to be spelled. The teacher has defined an "acceptable level of mastery" as 16 correct (or 80%). These tests, sometimes called content-referenced tests, are concerned with the mastery of specific, defined skills; the student's performance on the test indicates whether he or she has mastered those skills. Examples of criterion-referenced questions would be

- *Does John correctly read the word "happy"?*
- *Does Jane do eighth-grade math computation problems with 85% accuracy?*
- *Did Joe get 90% of the questions correct on the social studies exam?*

As you can see, in criterion-referenced assessment, the emphasis is on passing one or a series of questions. The test giver is interested in what the student can and cannot do, rather than how his or her performance compares with those of other people (Salvia & Ysseldyke, 1998, p. 35).

Informal reading inventories (IRIs) are an example of a criterion-referenced test. IRIs generally consist of two main sections: word recognition and passage reading. According to Bigge and Stump (1999):

> the interpretation of an IRI is based on criteria or levels of performance, and identifies three reading levels; independent, instructional, and frustration. The independent reading level is the level at which a student reads fluently and for pleasure (word recognition of 96% to 99% correct paired with correct comprehension of 75% to 90%). The instructional reading level is the level at which the student can experience success with assistance (word recognition of 92% to 95% correct paired with correct comprehension of 60% to 75%). The frustration level is the level at which the reading process breaks down for the student (word recognition of 90% to 92% or less paired with correct comprehension of 60% to 75% or less), as demonstrated by depressed comprehension and difficulties with word recognition. (p. 197)

Standards-Referenced Tests

A recent variation of criterion-referenced testing is standards-referenced testing, or standards-based assessment. Many states and districts have adopted content standards (or "curriculum frameworks") that describe what students should know and be able to do in different subjects at various grade levels. They also have performance standards that define how much of the content standards students should know to reach the "basic" or "proficient" or "advanced" level in the subject area. Tests are then based on the standards and the results are reported in terms of these "levels," which, of course, represent human judgment. In some states, performance standards have been steadily increased, so that students continually have to know more to meet the same level.

Educators often disagree about the quality of a given set of standards. Standards are supposed to cover the important knowledge and skills students should learn—they define the "big picture." State standards should be well written and reasonable. Some state standards have been criticized for including too much, for being too vague, for being ridiculously difficult, for undermining higher-quality local curriculum and instruction, and for taking sides in educational and political controversies. If the standards are flawed or limited, tests based on them also will be. In any event, standards enforced by state tests will have—and are meant to have—a strong impact on local curriculum and instruction.

Ecological Assessment

Ecological assessment involves directly observing and assessing a child in the many environments in which he or she routinely operates. The purpose of conducting such an assessment is to probe how the different environments influence the student and his or her school performance. Critical questions to ask in an ecological assessment include:

- *In what environments does the student manifest difficulties?*
- *Are there instances in which he or she appears to function appropriately?*
- *What is expected of the student academically and behaviorally in each type of environment?*
- *What differences exist in the environments in which the student manifests the greatest and the least difficulty?*
- *What implications do these differences have for instructional planning?*

As Wallace, Larsen, and Elksnin (1992) remark: "An evaluation that fails to consider a student's ecology as a potential causative factor in reported academic or behavioral disorders may be ignoring the very elements that require modification before we can realistically expect changes in that student's behavior" (p. 19).

According to Overton (1996), an ecological assessment analyzes a "student's total learning environment" (p. 276). A thorough ecological assessment should include the following:

- Interaction between students, teachers, and others in the classroom and in other school environments
- Presentation of materials and ideas
- Selection and use of materials for instruction
- Physical arrangement and environment of the classroom or target setting
- Students' interactions in other environments

Ecological assessment can also draw on

- The culture and beliefs of the child
- The teacher's teaching style
- The way time is used in the classroom
- Academic, behavioral, and social expectations within the learning environment
- The overall tone of the class (Bigge & Stump, 1999)

The components of an ecological assessment clearly reveal that it involves numerous aspects of the student's life to get a detailed picture of his or her situation.

Curriculum-Based Assessment

Direct assessment of academic skills is one alternative that has recently gained in popularity. Although a number of direct assessment models exist (Shapiro, 1989), they are similar in that they all suggest that assessment needs to be tied directly to instructional curriculum.

Curriculum-based assessment (CBA) is one type of direct evaluation. CBA is defined as a data collection procedure that is a direct measure of a student's progress within a curriculum, with the data serving as a basis for confirmation of adequate and expected progress as well as determination that effective teaching and learning is occurring (King-Sears, 1994, p. 9).

"Tests" of performance in this case come directly from the curriculum. For example, a child may be asked to read from his or her reading book for one minute. Information about the accuracy and the speed of reading can then be obtained and compared with other students in the class, building, or district. CBA is quick and offers specific information about how a student may differ from his or her peers. Because the assessment is tied to curriculum content, it allows the teacher to match instruction to a student's current abilities and pinpoints areas in which curriculum adaptations or modifications are needed. Unlike many other types of educational assessment, such as intelligence tests, CBA provides information that is immediately relevant to instructional programming (Berdine & Meyer, 1987, p. 33).

CBA also offers information about the accuracy and efficiency (speed) of performance. The latter is often overlooked when assessing a child's performance but is an important piece of information when designing intervention strategies. CBA is also useful in evaluating short-term academic progress.

Curriculum-Based Measurement

Curriculum-based measurement (CBM) is an assessment method that involves timing tasks and then charting performance. CBM is most concerned with fluency. This means that we are looking at the rate at which a student is able to perform a given task. After assessing the speed at which the student performs the task, we then chart performance over time so that we can clearly see on a graph the student's progress (or decline) from the initial performance to the goal point. An example of curriculum-based measurement would be to examine the number of words correctly read from a book in five minutes and then continually charting the student's progress over the course of the school year with the goal being set at a predetermined number of 150 words.

Dynamic Assessment

Dynamic assessment refers to several different but similar approaches to evaluating student learning. The goal of this type of assessment "is to explore the nature of learning, with the objective of collecting information to bring about cognitive change and to enhance instruction" (Sewell, 1987, p. 436).

One of the chief characteristics of dynamic assessment is that it includes a dialogue or interaction between the examiner and the student. Depending on the specific dynamic assessment approach used, this interaction may include modeling the task for the student, giving the student prompts or cues as he or she tries to solve a given problem, asking what the student is thinking while working on the problem, sharing on the part of the examiner to establish the task's relevance to experience and concepts beyond the test situation, and giving praise or encouragement (Hoy & Gregg, 1994). The interaction allows the examiner to draw conclusions about the student's thinking processes (i.e., why he or she answers a question in a particular way) and his or her response to a learning situation (i.e., whether, with prompting, feedback, or modeling, the student can produce a correct response, and what specific means of instruction produce and maintain positive change in the student's cognitive functioning).

Dynamic assessment may be framed as a constructivist approach to assessment (Bigge & Stump, 1999). That is, the goal is to determine what students do, can do, and can do with help, and to devote less time and attention to comparing student performance to set standards or to norm-group performance in an attempt to identify deficiencies. In dynamic assessment,

> the assessment is focused on student learning and performance over time, and comparisons are made between a student's current and past performance. Additionally, dynamic assessment is concerned with learning what a student is able to do when provided supports in the form of prompts, cues, or physical supports, some of which naturally exist in the environment. (Bigge & Stump, 1999, p. 182)

Typically, dynamic assessment involves a test–train–retest approach. The examiner begins by testing the student's ability to perform a task or solve a problem without help. Then, a similar task or problem is given to the student, and the examiner models how the task or problem is solved or gives the student cues to assist his or her performance. In Fuerstein's (1979) model of dynamic assessment, the examiner is encouraged to interact constantly with the student, an interaction that is called mediation, which is felt to maximize the probability that the student will solve the problem.

Other approaches to dynamic assessment use what is called graduated prompting (Campione & Brown, 1987), in which "a series of behavioral hints are used to teach the rules needed for task completion" (Hoy & Gregg, 1994, p. 151). These hints do not evolve from the student's responses, as in Fuerstein's model, but rather are scripted and preset, a standardization that allows for comparison across students. The prompts are given only if the student needs help in order to solve the problem. In both these approaches, the "teaching" phase is followed by a retesting of the student with a similar task but with no assistance from the examiner. The results indicate the student's "gains" or responsiveness to instruction—whether he or she learned and could apply the earlier instructions of the examiner and the prior experience of solving the problem.

An approach known as **testing the limits** incorporates the classic training and interactional components of dynamic assessment but can be used with many traditional tests, particularly tests of personality or cognitive ability (Carlson & Wiedl, 1978, 1979, as cited in Jitendra & Kameenui, 1993). Modifications are simply included in the testing situation—while taking a particular standardized test, for example, the student may be encouraged to verbalize before and after solving a problem. Feedback, either simple or elaborated, may be provided by the examiner as well.

Of course, dynamic assessment is not without its limitations or critics. One particular concern is the amount of training needed by the examiner to both conduct the assessment and interpret results. Another is a lack of operational procedures or "instruments" for assessing a student's performance or ability in the different content areas (Jitendra & Kameenui, 1993). Further, conducting a dynamic assessment is undeniably labor intensive.

Even with these limitations, dynamic assessment is a promising addition to current evaluation techniques. Because it incorporates a teaching component into the assessment process, this type of assessment may be particularly useful with students from minority backgrounds who may not have been exposed to the types of problems or tasks found on standardized tests. The interactional aspect of dynamic assessment also can contribute substantially to developing an understanding of the student's thinking process and problem-solving approaches and skills. Certainly, having detailed information about how a student approaches performing a task and how he or she responds to various instructional techniques can be highly relevant to instructional planning.

Portfolio Assessment

Perhaps the most important type of assessment for the classroom teacher is the portfolio assessment. According to Paulson, Paulson, and Meyer (1991), a portfolio is "a purposeful collection of student works that exhibits the student's efforts, progress, and achievement in one or more areas" (p. 60). The collection must include student participation in selecting contents, the criteria for selection, the criteria for judging merit, and evidence of student self-reflection. A portfolio collection contains work samples, permanent products, and test results from a variety of instruments and measures. For example, a portfolio of reading might include a student's test scores on teacher-made tests including curriculum-based assessments, work samples from daily work and homework assignments, error analyses on work and test samples, and the results of an informal reading inventory with miscues noted and analyzed (Overton, 1996, p. 250).

Batzle (1992; cited in Bigge & Stump, 1999) identifies three general types of portfolios:

- **Working portfolio:** Teacher, student, and parents all contribute to the portfolio. Both works in progress and final product pieces are included.
- **Showcase portfolio:** The portfolio houses only the student's best work and generally does not include works in progress. The student manages the portfolio and decides what to place in it.
- **Teacher portfolio or record keeping:** The portfolio houses student test papers and work samples maintained by the teacher. It contains work not selected by the student for inclusion in the showcase portfolio.

When portfolios are used in the classroom, they allow teachers to assess student progress more closely over time, aid teachers and parents in communicating about student's performance, assist in program evaluation efforts, and provide a means through which students can actively participate with their teachers in the assessment process (Hart, 1994).

There is some controversy about what should go into a portfolio, given that it could play a very important role in the educational future of a student. Teachers have been urged to create portfolios and structure them to help them make future decisions for their students.

Yet, the literature on portfolio assessment offers little practical guidance about (1) the types of decisions teachers should be making, (2) the characteristics of the content used for specific decisions, and (3) the criteria to guide decision making about grading, identification of academic weaknesses, instructional improvement, eligibility for entitlement programs, assessing educational outcomes, and educational reform (Salvia & Ysseldyke, 1998, p. 279). Consequently, in order for portfolio assessment to be more useful in special education considerations, more research needs to be done and practical information and suggestions will need to be offered.

Authentic/Naturalistic/Performance–Based Assessment

Another technique that is becoming increasingly popular with classroom teachers to assess classroom performance is authentic assessment. This performance-based assessment technique involves the application of knowledge to real-life activities, real-world settings or a simulation of such a setting using real life, real-world activities (Taylor, 1997). For example, when an individual is being assessed in the area of artistic ability, typically he or she presents artwork and is evaluated according to various criteria; it is not simply the person's knowledge of art, the materials, artists, or the history. Authentic assessment is sometimes referred to as naturalistic-based assessment or performance-based assessment. The terms can be used interchangeably. Each of these assessment methods has common characteristics. These include the following (Herman et al., 1992, p. 6; cited in Bigge & Stump, 1999, p. 183):

- Ask students to perform, create, produce, or do something.
- Tap higher-level thinking and problem-solving skills.
- Use tasks that represent meaningful instructional activities.
- Invoke real-world applications.
- Let people, not machines, do the scoring, using human judgment.
- Require new instructional and assessment roles for teachers.

This category of assessment is up and coming, and as such, an agreement on the appropriate terminology to describe this new type of assessment is still to come.

Task Analysis

Task analysis is very detailed; it involves breaking down a particular task into the basic sequential steps, component parts, or skills necessary to accomplish the task. The degree to which a task is broken down into steps depends upon the student in question; "it is only necessary to break the task down finely enough so that the student can succeed at each step" (Wallace et al., 1992, p. 14).

Taking this approach to assessment offers the teacher several advantages. For one, the process identifies what is necessary for accomplishing a particular task. It also tells the teacher whether the student can do the task, which part or skill causes the student to falter, and the order in which skills must be taught to help the student learn to perform the task. According to Bigge (1990), task analysis is a process that can be used to guide the decisions made regarding

- What to teach next
- Instances in which students encounter problems when they are attempting but are not able to complete a task
- The steps necessary to complete an entire task
- What adaptations can be made to help the student accomplish a task
- Options for those students for whom learning a task is not a possible goal

Task analysis is an approach to assessment that goes far beyond the need to make an eligibility or program placement decision regarding a student. It can become an integral part of classroom planning and instructional decision making.

Outcome-Based Assessment

Outcome-based assessment has been developed, at least in part, to respond to concerns that education, to be meaningful, must be directly related to what educators and parents want the child to have gained in the end. Outcome-based assessment involves considering, teaching, and evaluating the skills that are important in real-life situations. Learning such skills will result in the student becoming an effective adult. Assessment, from this point of view, starts by identifying what outcomes are desired for the student (e.g., being able to use public transportation). In steps similar to what is used with task analysis, the team then determines what competencies are necessary for the outcomes to take place (e.g., the steps or subskills the student needs to have mastered in order to achieve the outcome desired) and identifies which subskills the student has mastered and which he or she still needs to learn. The instruction that is needed can then be pinpointed and undertaken.

Learning Styles Assessment

Learning styles theory suggests that students may learn and problem solve in different ways, and that some ways are more natural for them than others. When they are taught or asked to perform in ways that deviate from their natural style, they are thought to learn or perform less well. A learning style assessment, then, would attempt to determine those elements that impact on a child's learning and "ought to be an integral part of the individualized prescriptive process all special education teachers use for instructing pupils" (Berdine & Meyer, 1987, p. 27).

Some of the common elements that may be included here would be the way in which material is typically presented (visually, auditorily, tactilely) in the classroom, the environmental conditions of the classroom (hot, cold, noisy, light, dark), the child's personality characteristics, the expectations for success that the child and others hold, the response the child receives while engaging in the learning process (e.g., praise or criticism), and the type of thinking the child generally utilizes in solving problems (e.g., trial and error, analyzing). Identifying the factors that positively impact the child's learning may be very valuable in developing effective intervention strategies.

TESTING CONSIDERATIONS

Selecting an Appropriate Instrument

Choosing which test is appropriate for a given student requires investigation. It is extremely important that those responsible for test selection do not use only what is available to or what has "always been used by" the school district or school. The child's test results will certainly influence eligibility decisions, instructional decisions, and placement decisions, all of which have enormous consequences for the child. If the child is assessed with an instrument that is not appropriate for him or her, the data gathered are likely to be inaccurate and misleading, which in turn results in faulty decisions regarding that child's educational program. This is one of the reasons that many educators object vehemently to standardized testing as a means of making decisions about a student's strengths and weaknesses.

Therefore, selecting instruments with care is vital, as is the need to combine any information gathered through testing with information gathered through other approaches. Given the number of standardized tests available today, how do professionals in special education select an appropriate instrument for a given student? Here are some suggestions:

■ Consider the student's skill areas to be assessed, and identify a range of tests that measure those skill areas: A variety of books can help evaluators identify what tests are available. One useful reference book is Pierangelo and Giuliani (2000), *Special Educator's Complete Guide to 109 Diagnostic Tests.* This book describes what each available test claims to measure, the age groups for which it is appropriate, whether it is group or individually administered (all testing of children with suspected disabilities must be individualized), how long it takes to administer the test, and much more.

■ Investigate how suitable each test identified is for the student to be assessed, and select those that are most appropriate: A particularly valuable resource for evaluating tests is *The Fourteenth Mental Measurements Yearbook* (Plake & Impara, 2001), which describes tests in detail and includes expert reviews of many tests. This yearbook is typically available in professional libraries for teachers, university libraries, and in the reference section of many public libraries. Publishers of tests generally also make literature available to help professionals determine whether a test is suitable for a specific student. This literature typically includes sample test questions, information on how the test was developed, a description of what groups of individuals (e.g., ethnic groups, ages, grade levels) were included in the "norm" group, and general guidelines for administration and interpretation.

Some questions professionals consider when reviewing a test follow.

■ According to the publisher or expert reviewers, what, specifically, is the test supposed to measure? Is its focus directly relevant to the skill area(s) to be assessed? Will student results on the test address the educational questions being asked? (In other words, will the test provide the type of educational information that is needed?) If not, the test is not appropriate for that student and should not be used.

■ Is the test valid and reliable? These are two critical issues in assessment (see Chapter 5). Validity refers to the degree to which the test measures what it claims to measure. For example, if a test claims to measure anxiety, a person's scores should be higher under a stressful situation than under a nonstressful situation. Reliability refers to the degree to which a child's results on the test are the same or similar over repeated testing. If a test is not reliable or if its reliability is uncertain—meaning that it does not yield similar results when the student takes the test again—then it should not be used. Test publishers make available specimen sets that will typically report the reliability and validity of the test.

■ Is the content/skill area being assessed by the test appropriate for the student, given his or her age and grade? If not, there is no reason to use the test.

■ If the test is norm-referenced, does the norm group resemble the student? This point was mentioned earlier and is important for interpretation of results.

■ Is the test intended to evaluate students, to diagnose the specific nature of a student's disability or academic difficulty, to inform instructional decisions or to be used for research purposes? Many tests will indicate that a student has a disability or specific problem academically, but results will not be useful for instructional planning purposes. Additional testing may then be needed in order to understand fully what type of instruction is necessary for the student.

■ Is the test administered in a group or individually? By law, group tests are not appropriate when assessing a child for the presence of a disability or to determine his or her eligibility for special education.

■ Does the examiner need specialized training in order to administer the test, record student responses, score the test, or interpret results? In most, if not all, cases, the answer to this question is yes. If the school has no one trained to administer or interpret the specific test, then it should not be used unless the school arranges for the student to be assessed by a qualified evaluator outside of the school system.

■ Will the student's suspected disability impact his or her taking of the test? For example, many tests are timed tests, which means that students are given a certain amount of time to complete items. If a student has weak hand strength or dexterity, his or her performance on a timed test that requires holding a pencil or writing will be negatively affected by the disability. Using a timed test would be appropriate only for determining how speed affects performance. To determine the student's actual knowledge of a certain area, an untimed test would be more appropriate. It may also be possible to make accommodations for the student (e.g., removing time restrictions from a timed test). If an accommodation is made, however, results must be interpreted with caution. Standardized tests are designed to be administered in an unvarying manner; when accommodations are made, standardization is broken, and the norms reported for the test no longer apply.

■ How similar to actual classroom tasks are the tasks the child is asked to complete on the test? For example, measuring spelling ability by asking a child to recognize a misspelled word may be very different from how spelling is usually measured in a class situation (reproducing words from memory). If test tasks differ significantly from classroom tasks, information gathered by the test may do little to predict classroom ability or provide information useful for instruction.

Selection of Test Content

Test content is an important factor when choosing between an NRT test and a CRT test. The content of an NRT test is selected according to how well it ranks students from high achievers to low. The content of a CRT test is determined by how well it matches the learning outcomes deemed most important. Although no test can measure everything of importance, the content selected for the CRT is selected on the basis of its significance in the curriculum, while that of the NRT is chosen by how well it discriminates among students.

Any national, state, or district test communicates to the public the skills that students should have acquired as well as the levels of student performance that are considered satisfactory. Therefore, education officials at any level should carefully consider content of the test which is selected or developed. Because of the importance placed upon high scores, the content of a standardized test can be very influential in the development of a school's curriculum and standards of excellence.

Test Interpretation

As mentioned earlier, a student's performance on an NRT is interpreted in relation to the performance of a large group of similar students who took the test when it was first normed. For example, if a student receives a percentile rank score on the total test of 34, this means that he or she performed as well or better than 34% of the students in the norm group. This type of information can be useful for deciding whether or not a student needs remedial assistance or is a candidate for a gifted program. However, the score gives little information about what the student actually knows or can do. The validity of the score in these decision processes depends on whether or not the content of the NRT matches the knowledge and skills expected of the students in that particular school system.

It is easier to ensure the match to expected skills with a CRT. CRTs give detailed information about how well a student has performed on each of the educational goals or outcomes included on that test. For instance, "... a CRT score might describe which arithmetic operations a student can perform or the level of reading difficulty he or she can comprehend" (U.S. Congress, OTA, 1992, p. 170). As long as the content of the test matches the content that is considered important to learn, the CRT gives the student, the teacher, and the parent more information about how much of the valued content has been learned than an NRT.

Limitations of Testing

Even when all of these considerations have been observed, there are those who question the usefulness of traditional testing in making good educational decisions for children. Many educators see traditional tests as offering little in the way of information useful for understanding the abilities and special needs of an individual child.

Another concern about the overuse of testing in assessment is its lack of usefulness in designing interventions. Historically, it has seemed as if tests have not been interpreted in ways that allow for many specific strategies to be developed. Although scores help to define the areas in which a student may be performing below his or her peers, they may offer little to determine particular instruction or curricular changes that may benefit the child.

Traditional tests often seem to overlap very little with the curriculum being taught. This suggests that scores may not reflect what the child really knows in terms of what is taught in the actual classroom. Other concerns include overfamiliarity with a test that is repeated regularly, inability to apply test findings in any practical way (i.e., generating specific recommendations based on test results), and difficulty in using such measures to monitor short-term achievement gains.

The sometimes circular journey from the referral to the outcome of the assessment process is frustrating. The teacher or parent requests help because the student is having problems, and the assessment results in information that more or less states, "The student is having problems."

It may be, however, that it is not that the tests themselves offer little relevant information but, rather, that the evaluators may fail to interpret them in useful ways. If we ask questions only related to eligibility (e.g., does this child meet the criteria as an individual with mental disabilities?) or about global ability (e.g., what is this child's intellectual potential?), then those are the questions that will be answered. Yet such information is not enough, if the goal is to develop an effective and appropriate educational program for the student.

CONCLUSION

As is evident, various methods of assessment are available to use when evaluating a student for a possible disability. Both formal and informal measures of assessment are necessary in order to get the most complete picture of a student's abilities. Ultimately, it becomes necessary for you to understand all the different measures. Selecting instruments with care is vital, as is the need to combine any information gathered through testing with information gathered through other approaches. Given the number of standardized tests available today, it is your professional responsibility to be sure that you understand the various methods of assessments and the purpose of their use.

VOCABULARY

Authentic Assessment: This is a performance-based assessment technique that involves the application of knowledge to real-life activities, real-world settings, or a simulation of such a setting using real-life, real-world activities.

Basal: The level of mastery of a task below which the student would correctly answer all items on a test.

Ceiling: The point at which the student has made a predetermined number of errors, and therefore, all other items stop being administered because it is assumed that the student will continue to get the answers wrong.

Content-Referenced Tests: Tests that are concerned with the mastery of specific, defined skills; the student's performance on the test indicates whether he or she has mastered those skills.

Criterion: The standard by which criterion reference tests are scored. The criterion represents an acceptable level of mastery.

Criterion-Referenced Tests (CRTs):   Tests that are scored according to a standard, or criterion, that the teacher, school, or test publisher decides represents an acceptable level of mastery.

Curriculum-Based Assessment (CBA):   A type of direct evaluation. "Tests" of performance in this case come directly from the curriculum.

Curriculum-Based Measurement (CBM):   An assessment method that involves timing tasks and then charting performance.

Dynamic Assessment: The goal of this type of assessment "is to explore the nature of learning, with the objective of collecting information to bring about cognitive change and to enhance instruction."

Ecological Assessment: Involves directly observing and assessing the child in the many environments in which he or she routinely operates.

Graduated Prompting: The process in dynamic assessment in which a series of behavioral hints are used to teach the rules needed for task completion.

Informal Reading Inventories: Commercial and teacher-made instruments for diagnosing reading difficulties, assessing a student's progress, and planning interventions for a student.

Informal Tests: Techniques that are not intended to provide a comparison to a broader group beyond the students in the local project.

Learning Style Assessment: An assessment that attempts to determine those elements that impact on a child's learning.

Mediation: In dynamic assessment, the process whereby the examiner is encouraged to interact constantly with the student.

Naturalistic-Based Assessment: A performance-based assessment technique that involves the application of knowledge to real-life activities, real-world settings, or a simulation of such a setting using real-life, real-world activities.

Norm Group: A large number of children who are representative of all the children in that age group.

Norm-Referenced Tests (NRT):   These tests are not interpreted according to an absolute standard or criterion (e.g., eight out of 10 correct) but, rather, according to how the student's performance compares with that of a particular group of individuals.

Outcome-Based Assessment: Involves considering, teaching, and evaluating the skills that are important in real-life situations.

Performance-Based Assessment: See naturalistic-based assessment (terms used interchangeably).

Portfolio Assessment: The process of collecting a student's work to examine efforts, progress, and achievement in one or more areas.

Portfolio: "A purposeful collection of student works that exhibits the student's efforts, progress, and achievement in one or more areas."

Showcase Portfolio: The portfolio houses only the student's best work and generally does not include works in progress. The student manages the portfolio and decides what to place in it.

Standardization: Refers to structuring test materials, administration procedures, scoring methods, and techniques for interpreting results.

Standardized Tests: Tests with detailed procedures for administration, timing, scoring, and interpretation procedures that must be followed precisely to obtain valid and reliable results.

Standards-Reference and Testing: Tests that describe what students should know and be able to do in different subjects at various grade levels.

Task Analysis: Involves breaking down a particular task into the basic sequential steps, component parts, or skills necessary to accomplish the task.

Teacher Portfolio or Record Keeping: The portfolio houses student test papers and work samples maintained by the teacher. It contains work not selected by the student for inclusion in the showcase portfolio.

Testing the Limits: A process whereby modifications are simply included in the testing situation. Its purpose is to assess possible potential without the limits of standardization.

Working Portfolio: Teacher, student, and parents all contribute to the portfolio. Both works in progress and final product pieces are included.

■ ■ ■ ■ ■

CHAPTER FOUR

BASIC STATISTICAL CONCEPTS

KEY TERMS

Bimodal Distribution
Correlation Coefficient
Correlations
Descriptive Statistics
Frequency Distributions
Interval Scales of Measurement
Mean
Measures of Central Tendency
Median
Mode
Nominal Scales of Measurement
Negative Correlation
Negatively Skewed Distributions

Normal Curve
Normal Distribution
Ordinal Scales of Measurement
Positive Correlation
Positively Skewed Distributions
Range
Ratio Scales of Measurement
Multimodal Distribution
Skewed Distributions
Standard Deviation
Variance
Zero Correlation

CHAPTER OBJECTIVES

Statistics! This one 10-letter word tends to instill more fear and anxiety in undergraduate and graduate students than any other word we know. We have learned from our experience as college professors that when we say we are going to cover statistics in our assessment courses, responses from students will be:

■ *Can we take this course pass/fail?*

■ *What is the latest date to drop the course?*

■ *I hate math—I always get confused!*

■ *Do we really have to know this? If so, how come?*

The fact is, whether you are an avid fan of statistics or generally do not enjoy it, you absolutely have to know statistics when you are doing special education assessment. Statistics play a vital role in the understanding of disability awareness. Although there are numerous reasons to know statistics, of primary importance to special educators is that without a proper understanding of it, you cannot interpret test results.

When large sets of data are being presented, it is important that they be organized in a fashion that makes some sense to the reader. In special education, this is done through methods known as **descriptive statistics.** Descriptive statistics summarize and describe data. In this chapter, we discuss basic descriptive statistics used every day in special education. After reading this chapter, you should be able to understand (and in some cases be able to calculate) the following:

- Scales of measurement
- Measures of central tendency (mean, median, and mode)
- Frequency distribution
- Range
- Variance
- Standard deviation
- Normal curve
- Skewed distributions
- Correlations

SCALES OF MEASUREMENT

The way data can be expressed in assessment often depends on the type of score one receives. In descriptive statistics, there are four scales of measurement that can be used to explain data: nominal, ordinal, interval, and ratio.

Nominal

In a **nominal scale of measurement,** nominal data are categorical data. They are created by assigning observations into various independent categories and then counting the frequency of occurrence within each of the categories. This is referred to as nose counting data (Sprinthall, 1994). It is a scale in which scores represent names only but not amount; for example, observing how many males versus females there are in a school.

With nominal data, the concept of quantity cannot be expressed. For example, the numbers on a football jersey are an example of nominal data. A person who wears number 20 is not two times better than the person who wears number 10. Examples of nominal data include telephone numbers, social security numbers, and species of birds.

Ordinal

Ordinal scales of measurement involve the rank order system. It is a scale in which scores indicate only relative amounts or rank order. When we discuss horse races and say first place, second place, and third place, we are using ordinal data. Although ordinal scales tell us rank, they do not tell us the distance between each subject. For example, even though we know which horse finished first, second, and third, we do not know how much farther ahead the first-place horse beat the second-place horse. In schools, class rank is a classic example of ordinal data.

Interval

An **interval scale of measurement** is one in which equal differences in scores represent equal differences in amount of the property measured but with an arbitrary zero point. For example:

- Fahrenheit temperature: A temperature of 40 degrees is not twice as hot as 20 degrees. Also, zero degrees does not mean no temperature; it is an arbitrary zero point.
- IQ scores: A student with an IQ of 100 is not "twice as smart" as someone with an IQ of 50.

Ratio

A **ratio scale of measurement** has all the properties of an interval scale with the additional property of zero indicating a total absence of the quality being measured. A score of zero means zero. For example:

- Distance: The distance 15 feet is three times more than 5 feet.
- Duration: The duration 20 minutes is twice as long as 10 minutes.
- Weight: A 300-pound man is six times heavier than a 50-pound boy.
- On a math test in which a child gets four wrong and another gets eight wrong, the child who missed eight questions got twice as many wrong as the other child.

MEASURES OF CENTRAL TENDENCY

Most students have learned the **measures of central tendency** many times in their academic lives. So, for many of you, this may be a review. There are three ways to describe central tendency in a set of scores. These are mean, median, and mode.

The measures of central tendency can be very important to know because they organize and describe data to see how the data fall together or cluster. Central tendency shows how scores are distributed around a numerical representation of the average score (Overton, 2000).

Mean

The **mean** is the mathematical average of the distribution of scores. Statistically, the mean is represented by the symbol M. The way to calculate the mean score is simply to add up the scores in the distribution and divide by the number of units. For example, suppose the following scores were obtained in a distribution: 8, 10, 8, 14, and 40. Calculate the mean score.

Calculation of the Mean

1. Add up the scores (this is also referred to as summating or summation): 8 + 10 + 8 + 14 + 40 = 80

2. Count the number of units in the distribution. Here, there are five of them (8, 10, 8, 14, and 40 = 5 numbers in total).
3. Take the total score in Step 1 and divide by the number of units calculated in Step 2: 80/5 = 16

The mean is 16 (or you can write it as M = 16).

Important Point: *The mean is greatly affected by extreme scores.* For example, suppose four students take an exam and receive scores of 90%, 95%, 100%, and 7%. The mean of the distribution is 73%. Notice though that three students did extremely well, but the one student who got a 7% took the mean from an A average to a C average.

Median

Another way to measure central tendency is to order the scores relative to where they fall in a distribution. The **median** is the middle score in a distribution. It is the point at which half the scores fall above and half the scores fall below. In the distribution 8, 10, 8, 14, and 40, what is the median?

Calculation of the Median

1. Rank order the data from least to greatest. What you do is simply list the scores from the smallest number to the largest: 8, 8, 10, 14, 40.
2. Now cross off the low score (8), then the high score (40). Repeat this step until there is only one number left. In our example you would next cross off the 8, then the 14. This leaves 10 as the middle number. The median is 10.
3. Now, suppose the distribution of scores had an even number of units. For example: 8, 10, 12, 8, 14, and 40. Calculate the median. In this example, first rank order the data: 8, 8, 10, 12, 14, 40. After crossing out the high and low numbers, you are left with 10 and 12.
4. To find the median, simply take the average of the two numbers left. This would make 11 the median score: (10 + 12 = 22/2 = 11).

Important Point: *The median is less affected by extreme scores than is the mean.* For example, suppose four students take an exam and receive scores of 90%, 95%, 100%, and 7%. Although the mean of the distribution is 73%, the median is 92.5%, a much better indication of how the four students did overall.

Mode

The **mode** is the most frequently occurring score in a distribution. For example: In the distribution 8, 10, 8, 14, and 40, what is the mode? The answer is eight. The number 8 occurs twice, while all other numbers occur only once.

What is the mode in the following distribution: 8, 10, 8, 10, 14, and 40? Here, the scores 8 and 10 occur twice; therefore, we have two modes: 8 and 10. When you have two modes in a distribution, it is referred to as a **bimodal distribution.**

If you have three or more modes in your distribution, it is referred to as a **multi-modal distribution.** For example, what is the mode of this distribution: 8, 10, 8, 10, 14, 14, and 40? Because 8, 10, and 14 are the most frequently occurring numbers (three of them), it is a multimodal distribution.

FREQUENCY DISTRIBUTION

In order to see data more clearly (and often the way to find the mode) in a distribution, it can be extremely helpful to set up a frequency distribution. **A frequency distribution** expresses how often a score occurs in a set of data. For example, suppose you had the following distribution of 11 students' scores on a spelling test:

Student Name	Spelling Test Score (%)
Ted	100
Carmen	85
Ralph	75
Juanna	98
Celeste	98
Mohammed	100
Joaquinne	95
Amy	80
Carol	85
Tony	85
Jesus	100

A frequency distribution sets up a much easier way to look at the data. To set up a frequency distribution simply make three columns: Column 1—Test Score, Column 2—Tally, Column 3—Frequency. Under each column fill in the appropriate information. Table 4.1 shows what the frequency distribution would look like for the above 11 students' spelling test scores.

Important Point: *When setting up a frequency distribution, always rank order the data from the smallest to the largest number or the largest to the smallest.* In Table 4.1, 75 is the smallest and 100 is the largest. Also, notice that when setting up a frequency distribution it

TABLE 4.1   Frequency Distribution for Math Test Scores

TEST SCORE (%)	TALLY	FREQUENCY
75	I	1
80	I	1
85	III	3
95	I	1
98	II	2
100	III	3

is very easy to calculate the mode(s) simply by inspection. (The scores that most frequently occur are 85 and 100—seen by the 3s in the frequency column.)

RANGE

The **range** of a distribution is the difference between the high score and the low score in the distribution (Range = High Score – Low Score). For example, if we have a distribution of 8, 10, 8, 14, and 40, what is the range?

Calculation of the Range

1. Find the high score and the low score in the distribution: 40 and 8.
2. Subtract the low score from the high score: 40 – 8 = 32.
3. The range is 32.

Important Point: The range is very simple to determine, yet there is a serious problem with just giving the range of scores. Think about it: The range tells you nothing about the scores in between the high and low scores. And, if there is *one extreme score, it can greatly affect the range.* Suppose the distribution was 8, 9, 8, 9, 8, and 1,000. The range would be 992 (1,000 – 8 = 992). Yet, only one score is even close to 992, the 1,000.

VARIANCE

When looking at scores within a distribution, it is often very helpful to know how the scores are spread out. In order to get a better idea of the spread of scores within a distribution, it is necessary to calculate the variance. The **variance** is a statistical concept that tells you the spread of scores within a distribution. The variance is an extremely important concept to understand because it is necessary in the calculation of the standard deviation and the analysis of data in the normal curve. (These two areas, discussed later in this chapter, are critical to understand as special educators.)

To explain the importance of variance, let's look at the following two distributions of scores on a 50-question spelling test (each score represents the number of words correctly spelled):

Scores for 5 students in Group A: 28, 29, 30, 31, 32
Scores for 5 students in Group B: 10, 20, 30, 40, 50

Calculate the mean for Groups A and B.

Mean of Group A = 30
Mean of Group B = 30

The mean of both groups is 30. Now, if you knew nothing about these two groups other than their mean scores, you might think they looked similar. However, the spread of scores in Group A (28 to 32) is much smaller than in Group B (10 to 50).

Statistically, we say that the variance of Group B is greater than the variance in group A. According to Sattler (1992), "The general rule is that the greater the spread, the greater the variance. The fact that two different sets of scores have the same mean but different variances means that one has a larger range or spread of scores than the other" (p. 15).

Calculation of the Variance

1. List all test scores in a column (label the column X).
2. Find the mean of the distribution. Set up a column with the mean next to each test score from Step 1. Label this column M.
3. Subtract the mean from each test score (label the column $X - M$).
4. Square each score (multiply it by itself) from Step 3. Label the column $(X - M)^2$.
5. Add all scores from Step 4. This is known as the Sum of Squares (label the column Sum of Squares).
6. Divide the Sum of Squares by the total number of test scores. This score is the variance.

Given the following set of scores, calculate the variance: 5, 3, 7, 8, 2.

1. X
   5
   3
   7
   8
   2

2. $5 + 3 + 7 + 8 + 2 = 25/5 = 5$ The mean is 5: $M = 5$.

3.

X	M	X–M
5	5	0
3	5	−2
7	5	2
8	5	3
2	5	−3

4.

X	M	$X - M$	$(X - M)^2$
5	5	0	0
3	5	−2	4
7	5	2	4
8	5	3	9
2	5	−3	9

5.

X	M	$X - M$	$(X - M)^2$	
5	5	0	0	**Sum of Squares = 26**
3	5	−2	4	**(0 + 4 + 4 + 9 + 9)**
7	5	2	4	
8	5	3	9	
2	5	−3	9	

6. $26/5 = 5.20$ The variance is 5.20.

STANDARD DEVIATION

In almost all cases, we determine the variance in order to calculate the standard deviation. The **standard deviation** is the spread of scores around the mean. It is an extremely important statistical concept to understand when doing assessment in special education. However, before we explain its importance, you need to understand how to calculate it.

Important Point: *The standard deviation is calculated by taking the square root of the variance.* The steps for calculating standard deviation are the exact same steps for calculating the variance except that there is one extra step. After finding the variance, take the square root. This is the standard deviation.

Calculation of Standard Deviation

1. List all test scores in a column.
2. Find the mean of the distribution.
3. Subtract the mean from each test score.
4. Square each score from Step 3 (multiply it by itself).
5. Add all scores from Step 4. This is known as the Sum of Squares.
6. Divide the Sum of Squares by the total number of test scores.
7. Find the square root. This is the standard deviation.

Given the following set of scores, calculate the standard deviation: 5, 3, 7, 8, 2.

To solve this problem, follow the steps as in the previous variance problem given on page 56. The variance was 5.20. Therefore, the standard deviation is the square root of 5.20 = 2.28.

NORMAL CURVE

According to Overton (2000), "a **normal distribution** hypothetically represents the way test scores would fall if a particular test is given to every single student of the same age or grade in the population for whom the test was designed. If educators could administer an instrument in this way and obtain a normal distribution, the scores would fall in the shape of a bell curve (p. 90)."

The **normal curve** (also referred to as the *bell curve*) tells us many important facts about test scores and the population. The beauty of the normal curve is that it never changes. As students, this is great for you because once you memorize it, it will never change on you (and, yes, you do have to memorize it at some point in your academic or professional career). Figure 4.1 shows how the normal curve is always represented.

Now, how does this help you? Well, let's take an example that you will come across numerous times in special education: IQ. The mean IQ score on many IQ tests is 100 and the standard deviation is 15 (the most popular being the Wechsler Scales of Intelligence, see Chapter 10). Now, according to the normal curve, IQ on the Wechsler Scales is distributed as in Figure 4.2.

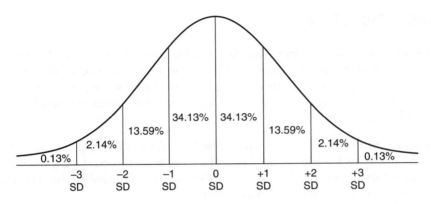

FIGURE 4.1   Diagram of the Normal Curve

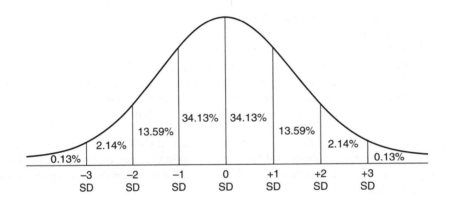

FIGURE 4.2   Diagram of the Normal Curve for the WISC-III with a Mean of 100 and a Standard Deviation of 15

Given this information, there is so much we can say. First, notice that approximately 68% of the entire population has an IQ between 85 and 115 (−1 SD to +1 SD: 34% + 34% = 68%). Also, 13.5% of the population has an IQ between 115 and 130. Furthermore, about 95% of all the scores are found within 2 SD above and below the mean. (Look between the lines on the curve between −2 SD and +2 SD. The percent of scores are 13.5% + 34% + 34% + 13.5%, which totals 95%.)

Do you know what the requirements are for most gifted programs regarding minimum IQ scores (that have a mean of 100 and SD of 15)? By looking at the normal curve you may have figured it out—the minimum is normally an IQ of 130 for entrance. Why? Gifted programs will take only students who are 2 SD or more above the mean. In a sense, they want only those whose IQs are better than 97.5% of the population.

How about mental retardation? On the Wechsler Scales, the classification of mental retardation is determined if a child receives an IQ score of below 70. Why 70? This score was not just randomly chosen. What we are saying is that in order to be mentally retarded, a student is usually 2 or more SD below the mean. In a sense, the child's IQ is only as high as 2.5% (or even lower) of the normal population (or, in other words, 97.5% or more of the population has a higher IQ than this child).

SKEWED DISTRIBUTIONS

As you may have noticed, the normal curve is *symmetrical.* This means that the left side of the bell is exactly the same shape as the right side. However, the normal curve may not always occur when you have only a small number of test scores in your distribution. When the population of a sample is not large, there may be a tendency for the scores to be *skewed.* A **skewed distribution** is one in which the majority of scores fall at either the high end or the low end rather than the middle of a distribution (Venn, 2000).

A distribution can be either positively skewed or negatively skewed (see Figure 4.3). In a **positively skewed distribution,** more of the scores fall below the mean. In a **negatively skewed distribution,** more of the scores fall above the mean.

CORRELATIONS

Correlations tell us the relationship between two variables. There are three types of correlations: positive, negative, and zero (see Figure 4.4).

1. **Positive correlation:** Variables are said to be positively correlated when a high score on one is accompanied by a high score on the other (direct relationship).

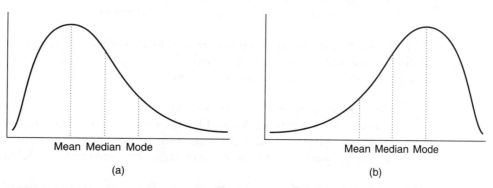

| Mean Median Mode | Mean Median Mode |
| (a) | (b) |

FIGURE 4.3   (a) Positively Skewed Distribution and (b) Negatively Skewed Distribution

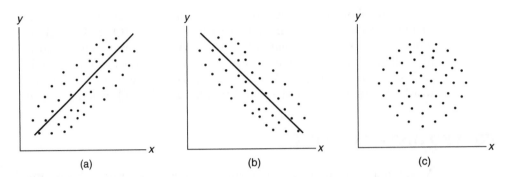

FIGURE 4.4   (a) Positive Correlation, (b) Negative Correlation, and (c) Zero Correlation

Conversely, low scores on one variable are associated with low scores on the other (Runyon & Haber, 1991). Examples include:

- IQ and academic achievement—as IQ increases, academic achievement increases.
- Education and income—as education increases, income tends to increase.

2. **Negative correlation:** Variables are said to be negatively correlated when a high score on one is accompanied by a low score on the other (an inverse relationship). Conversely, low scores on one variable are associated with high scores on the other (Runyon & Haber, 1991). Examples include:

- Teacher stress and job satisfaction—as job stress increases, job satisfaction decreases.
- Student anxiety and student performance—in general, as anxiety increases, student performance decreases.

3. **Zero correlation:** Here, there is *no relationship between the variables.* Examples include:

- Foot size and grades on exams—as foot size increases, nothing changes with respect to grades. They are not related whatsoever.
- Weight and intelligence test scores—as weight increases, nothing changes with respect to IQ. They are not related whatsoever.

When describing the relationship between any two variables, you determine the **correlation coefficient** (see Table 4.2). Statistically, this is represented by the letter r. Now, the general rules for correlations are as follows:

Correlations range from +1.00 to –1.00.
The closer you get to +1.00 or –1.00, the stronger the relationship.
The closer you get to zero, the weaker the relationship
0.00 is the weakest correlation—no relationship between the variables.

For example, a correlation coefficient of –.95 tells you that there is a negative correlation (– sign) and that there is a strong relationship (because .95 is close to 1.0).

Finally, and perhaps the most important point with correlations, is this: *Correlations do not indicate cause and effect.* Just because two things are related to each other does

TABLE 4.2   Interpreting Correlation Coefficients

CORRELATION COEFFICIENT	STATISTICAL INTERPRETATION
.00	*No relationship between the variables.* The two variables **never** occur together
.01–.25	*Weak relationship.* The two variables **rarely** occur together
.26–.50	*Moderate relationship.* The two variables occur together **sometimes**
.51–.75	*Strong relationship.* The two variables occur together **often**
.76–.99	*Very strong relationship.* The two variables occur together **very often**
1.00	*Perfect relationship.* The two variables **always** occur together

not mean that one causes the other to occur. For example, there is a strong positive correlation between depression and anxiety (as depression goes up so does anxiety). But does the depression cause anxiety, or is the anxiety causing the depression? The fact is, you do not know. Therefore, when determining or reading about correlations, never lose sight of the fact that they indicate only relationships, never cause and effect.

CONCLUSION

Descriptive statistics play a very important role in the assessment process. The fact is, without statistics there would be no way to collect truly objective data to be interpreted. Statistics give us the opportunity to compare children to the norms in many different ways. Understanding statistics is a vital part of being an effective special educator. Numerous results will be presented to you on a daily basis. Without the proper understanding or interpretation of data, you will not be able to critically evaluate and properly diagnose a child with a disability. Therefore, being able to look at data and make sense of it are fundamental professional responsibilities of special educators.

VOCABULARY

Bimodal Distribution: When there are two modes in a distribution.

Correlation Coefficient: A numerical value that expresses the degree of relationship between two variables.

Correlations: The relationship between two variables.

Descriptive Statistics: Statistics which describe and summarize data in a meaningful fashion.

Frequency Distribution: Expresses how often a score occurs in a set of data.

Interval Scale of Measurement: An interval scale is one in which equal differences in scores represent equal differences in amount of the property measured but with an arbitrary zero point.

Mean: The arithmetical average of the distribution of scores.

Measures of Central Tendency: The mean, median, and mode of a distribution of scores.

Median: The middle score in a distribution. It is the score that separates the top half of the test takers from the bottom half.

Mode: The score in the distribution that most frequently occurs.

Multimodal Distribution: A distribution with three or more modes.

Negative Correlation: An inverse relationship: Variables are said to be negatively correlated when a high score on one is accompanied by a low score on the other. Conversely, low scores on one variable are associated with high scores on the other.

Negatively Skewed Distribution: A distribution in which more of the scores fall above the mean.

Nominal Scale of Measurement: Nominal data are categorical data. Assigning observations into various independent categories and then counting the frequency of occurrence within each of the categories creates a nominal scale.

Normal Curve (bell curve): In this frequency polygon, most of the scores cluster around the mean. The farther above or below the mean a score appears, the less frequently it occurs.

Normal Distribution: Represents the way test scores would fall if a particular test is given to every single student of the same age or grade in the population for whom the test was designed.

Ordinal Scale of Measurement: Ordinal scales involve the rank order system. It is a scale in which scores indicate only relative amounts or rank order.

Positive Correlation: A direct relationship: Variables are said to be positively correlated when a high score on one is accompanied by a high score on the other. Conversely, low scores on one variable are associated with low scores on the other.

Positively Skewed Distribution: A distribution in which more of the scores fall below the mean.

Range: The difference between the high score and the low score in the distribution (Range = High Score – Low Score).

Ratio Scale of Measurement: A scale having interval properties except that a score of zero indicates a total absence of the quality being measured. A score of zero means zero.

Skewed Distribution: A distribution in which the majority of scores fall at either the high end or the low end rather than the middle of a distribution.

Standard Deviation: The spread of scores around the mean. It is calculated by taking the square root of the variance.

Variance: A statistical concept that tells the spread of scores within a distribution.

Zero Correlation: Here, there is no relationship between the variables.

PRACTICE PROBLEMS

4.1. Given the following set of IQ scores from students, calculate the mean:

Student Name	IQ Score
Billy	100
Juan	110
Carmela	75
Fred	120
Yvonne	95
Amy	80
Carmen	85

4.2. Given the following IQ scores, calculate the median:

Student Name	IQ Score
Ravi	100
Jesus	110
Carmela	75
Fred	120
Yvonne	95
Amy	80
Chenel	85

4.3. Given the following IQ scores, calculate the median:

Student Name	IQ Score
Ralph	100
Marguarita	110
Mike	75
Fred	120
Juanna	95
Amy	80
Carol	85
Ricky	85

4.4. Given the following spelling test scores, calculate the mode:

Student Name	Score
Edwin	100
Marguarita	85
Tom	75
Fredrika	100
Juan	95
Amy	80

Caroline 85
Ravi 85

4.5. Given the following spelling test scores, calculate the mode:

Student Name	Score
Ed	100
Joe	85
Miguel	75
Jean	100
Joan	95
Jose	80
Carol	85
Tony	85
Cory	100

4.6. For the following set of numbers, (a) create a frequency distribution and (b) calculate the mode: 20, 50, 45, 50, 25, 40, 20, 55, 20, 60, 33, 45, 33, 20.

4.7. For the following distribution, calculate the range: 20, 50, 45, 50, 25, 40, 20, 55, 20, 60, 33, 45, 33, 20.

4.8. For the following 10-point Reading Quiz scores, find the measures of central tendency, find the range, and draw a frequency distribution:

Student Name	Score
Caitlyn	10
Erin	8
Tom	7
Kate	6
Lynn	9
Miguel	9
Jen	5
Carol	6
Tony	9
Mohammed	10

4.9. Given the following scores, calculate the variance: 8, 10, 4, 9, 10, 1.

4.10. Given the following scores, calculate the standard deviation: 8, 10, 4, 9, 10, 1.

4.11. For the following correlations, list them in order from strongest correlation to weakest correlation.

a. −.67
b. +.53
c. −.91
d. +.03
e. −.47

ANSWERS TO PRACTICE PROBLEMS

4.1. M = 95. To solve this problem, first summate the IQ scores. This total is 665. Now count the number of IQ scores. There are 7 of them. Now take 665/7, and you get 95 as the mean IQ score.

4.2. 95. Rank order the data from lowest score to highest score: 75, 80, 85, 95, 100, 110, 120. Now, cross off the low and high scores (75 and 120). Do it again (80 and 110). Do it again (85 and 100). You are left with 95 as the median.

4.3. 90. Rank order the data from lowest score to highest score: 75, 80, 85, 85, 95, 100, 110, 120. Now, cross off the low and high scores (75 and 120). Do it again (80 and 110). Do it again (85 and 100). You are now left with 85

and 95. Take the average and you get 90 as the median.

4.4. 85. The test score of 85 occurs three times, the most in the distribution.

4.5. 85 and 100. The test scores of 85 and 100 each occur three times, the most in the distribution.

4.6. (a).

Test Score	Tally	Frequency
20	IIII	4
25	I	1
33	II	2
40	I	1
45	II	2
50	II	2
55	I	1
60	I	1

4.6. (b). The mode is 20.

4.7. The range is 40. The range is calculated by taking the high score (60) and subtracting the low score (20), which equals 40.

4.8.

Reading Quiz Score	Tally	Frequency
5	I	1
6	II	2
7	I	1
8	I	1
9	III	3
10	II	2

The mode is 9. The mean is 7.9. The median is 8.5. The range is 5.

4.9. 11.33.

4.10. 3.37. This is the square root of the variance from Practice Problem 3.9. The square root of 11.33 is 3.37.

4.11. strongest to weakest: c, a, b, e, d.

CHAPTER FIVE

VALIDITY AND RELIABILITY

KEY TERMS

Alternate Forms Reliability
Concurrent Validity
Construct Validity
Constructs
Content Validity
Convergent Validity
Criterion-Related Validity
Discriminant Validity
Interrater Reliability
Obtained Score

Predictive Validity
Reliability
Reliability Coefficient
Reliable Test Scores
Split-Half Reliability
Standard Error of Measurement (SEM)
Target Behavior
Test–Retest Reliability
Validity
Validity Coefficient

CHAPTER OBJECTIVES

This chapter focuses on two very important concepts—*validity* and *reliability*. In order to use any instrument in the assessment process, federal law mandates that the tests be both validated and reliable. What does that mean? How does an evaluator determine which tests are the most valid and reliable? There are many types of validity and reliability that are important to know when doing an assessment in special education. After reading this chapter, you should be able to understand the following:

- The purpose for needing valid and reliable measures
- The most utilized and important types of validity seen in special education assessment
- The most utilized and important types of reliability seen in special education assessment

VALIDITY

Validity denotes the extent to which an instrument is measuring what it is supposed to measure. Validity is the most essential quality needed in a measuring instrument. Obviously, if an instrument is not producing the information that it is supposed to, it is essentially worthless. The greater the validity of a test, the greater our confidence that it measures what it is designed to measure. Questions about validity are of ultimate importance for special educators because they address whether an instrument fulfills the function for which it was created. Accordingly, effort must be put into determining the validity of any measuring instrument that is to be used in a study. This section covers the most important and often utilized types of validity seen in special education assessment.

Criterion-Related Validity

Criterion-related validity is a method for assessing the validity of an instrument by comparing its scores with another criterion (or *criteria*—the plural of *criterion*) known already to be a measure of the same trait or skill. Simply stated, the instrument in question is compared with another instrument that has already been established as being valid. The closer the two tests are to each other, the better the criterion-related validity.

Criterion-related validity is usually expressed as a correlation between the test in question and the criterion measure. This correlation coefficient is referred to as a **validity coefficient.** The closer the correlation coefficient is to +1.00, the stronger the criterion-related validity (see Chapter 4 for a review of correlations). Consequently, when students completing both instruments obtain similar scores, the instrument in question is said to have high criterion-related validity (Overton, 2000).

If you created a new achievement test, the readers would have to know how it compares with an already established and valid achievement test. To establish criterion-related validity for your test, administer your test and then administer an already established test to the same group of students. Whether you give the criterion test soon after or at a much later time will determine the type of criterion-related validity you have chosen.

With respect to criterion-related validity, it is important to understand that a test is only as valid as the criterion measure. If a new test developer reports a high validity coefficient between his new test and a criterion test that is not considered valid, this correlation does not make the new test valid. Therefore, when evaluating criterion-related validity, you must not only look at how strong the validity coefficient is (i.e., how close it is to +1.00), but also examine the criterion measure to which it was compared (McLean et al., 1996).

There are two types of criterion-related validity: (1) concurrent validity and (2) predictive validity. The ultimate difference between concurrent and predictive validity is the time at which scores on the criterion measure are obtained.

Concurrent validity is the extent to which a procedure correlates with the current behavior of subjects. It refers to how precisely a person's present performance (e.g., a test score) estimates that person's performance on the criterion measure administered at approximately the same time.

In order to do a concurrent validity study, both measures must be given in close proximity. Normally, the administration of each of the two measures should not exceed more than two weeks. The procedure consists of administering the first instrument (i.e., the instrument to be validated) and very shortly thereafter, administering the criterion measure. Correlating the data from the two instruments then determines the concurrent validity (Overton, 2000).

Predictive validity is the extent to which a procedure allows accurate predictions about a subject's future behavior. It is a measure of a specific instrument's ability to predict future performance on some other measure or criterion at a later date (Overton, 2000). For example, many colleges believe that the SAT has predictive validity with respect to how well a student will do in college. Similarly, the Graduate Record Exam is often required by admissions committees for graduate school because it is believed to have high predictive validity for future academic performance in graduate school.

Content Validity

Content validity refers to whether the individual items of a test represent what you actually want to assess. When we evaluate content validity, we are asking, "Does the content of our measure fairly and accurately reflect the content desired to be measured?" Thus, when we are measuring academic achievement with a new achievement test, we ask, "Is the score that we obtain truthfully measuring the actual academic achievement of the student?" Overall, content validity describes how well a test's items reflect the area of learning to be assessed (Venn, 2000).

According to the Standards for Educational and Psychological Tests (American Psychological Association, 1985),

> to demonstrate the content validity of a set of test scores, one must show that the behaviors demonstrated in testing constitute a representative sample of behaviors to be exhibited in a desired performance domain. An investigation of content validity requires that the test developer or test user specify his objectives and carefully define the performance domain in light of those objectives. (p. 4)

One of the most commonly known academic screening tests in special education is the Wide Range Achievement Test—(WRAT-3, see Chapter 9). On this test, one of the subtests is Reading. Any valid test of reading will contain various items to assess the proficiency of reading skills. Yet, if you look at what actually is being measured on the reading section of the WRAT-3, it becomes evident that it covers only one area of reading—word recognition. Reading involves so much more than word recognition. For example, you will find as special educators that many children with learning disabilities can adequately read. However, their problem is that they cannot understand what they are reading. This is a reading comprehension issue, something that is not assessed on the WRAT-3. Therefore, one can make the argument that the WRAT-3 lacks content validity on the Reading section of the test because the items contained in the Reading subtest are not representative of the content purported to be measured. It is valid for word recognition, but not reading comprehension, therefore, it does not cover the entire content of reading.

For a test to have good content validity, it must contain the content in a representative fashion (Overton, 2000). For example, a 100-question social studies test on information about the United States that has 50 questions about the East Coast states and 50 questions about the Midwest states has not fairly represented the content of United States knowledge, because there are no questions pertaining to the Southern, Southwestern, or West Coast states. A good representation of content will always include several items for each domain, level, and skill being measured.

The questions college students might raise about an exam are often questions of content validity. A college exam is supposed to measure what students have learned. However, students sometimes feel an exam includes only questions about things they did not understand (Myers & Hansen, 1999).

Finally, when doing an assessment of the content validity of an instrument, you should seek the rationale for item selection as described in the test's technical manual. According to McLean, Bailey, and Wolery (1996),

> An initial test of content validity would be the extent to which the test developer convinces you that a thorough and systematic process has occurred in the selection of test content. Essentially, content validity is assessed through a logical analysis of the item development process of the actual items. (p. 39)

Construct Validity

Construct validity is the extent to which a test measures a theoretical construct or attribute. **Constructs** are abstract concepts, such as intelligence, self-concept, motivation, aggression, and creativity, that can be observed by some type of instrument. They represent relatively abstract concepts that are difficult to define and therefore difficult to measure (Taylor, 1997).

A classic question of construct validity involves intelligence tests, which determine intelligence by measuring subjects in areas such as vocabulary or problem-solving ability. The question of whether intelligence is being measured by these particular variables is an assessment of the test's construct validity.

Because establishing construct validity entails a long and involved process, most tests provide little information about this type of validity. Construct validity is normally determined through extensive research studies using numerous and intensive statistical procedures. According to the Standards for Educational and Psychological Testing (APA, 1985), evidence of construct validity is not found in a single study; rather, judgments of construct validity are based on an accumulation of research results. Consequently, only the most well-established tests in special education present solid evidence of construct validity.

A test's construct validity is often assessed by its convergent and discriminant validity. A test that has good **convergent validity** has high positive correlations with other tests measuring the same construct. In contrast, a test that has good **discriminant validity** has low correlations with tests that measure different constructs. For example, an academic achievement test should correlate highly with established academic achievement tests (convergent validity) and have lower correlations with social and cognitive measures (discriminant validity).

Factors Affecting Validity

Various factors can affect the validity of any test. These include the following:

1. Test-related factors: These consist of, but are not limited to, such things as anxiety, motivation, speed, understanding test instructions, rapport, physical handicaps, language barriers, deficiencies in educational opportunities, and unfamiliarity with testing materials (Sattler, 1992).

2. The criterion to which you compare your instrument may not be well enough established: If your comparison instrument is not valid, then the results you receive are to be questioned as to their validity (Sattler, 1992).

3. Intervening events: These include life experiences such as the death of a parent, divorce, breakup with a boyfriend, and a move to a new school district that occur at the time of testing.

4. Reliability: If the reliability of a test is low, then the validity also will be low. According to McLean, Bailey, and Wolery (1996),

> Validity is both separate and tied to reliability. Although conceptually they ask very different questions, it is a well accepted axiom in test development that test validity can be no higher than the test's reliability, and usually is considerably lower. This makes sense, for how could an unreliable or inconsistent measure have accuracy? However, the fact that a test is reliable does not mean that it has any validity for certain purposes. For example, a screening test may be perfectly reliable but be of no use in planning instructional programs. (p. 42)

RELIABILITY

Reliability refers to the consistency of measurements. If a test lacks reliability, it is not stable, reproducible, predictable, dependable, meaningful, or accurate. In assessment, reliability relates to the confidence in an instrument to give the same score for a student if the test were given more than once. A **reliable test** produces similar scores across various conditions and situations, including different evaluators and testing environments (Venn, 2000).

How do we account for an individual who does not get exactly the same test score every time he or she takes the test? Some possible reasons are the following (America's Learning Exchange, 2000, p. 1):

Test-taker's temporary psychological or physical state: Test performance can be influenced by a person's psychological or physical state at the time of testing. For example, differing levels of anxiety, fatigue, or motivation may affect the applicant's test results.

Environmental factors: Differences in the testing environment, such as room temperature, lighting, noise, or even the test administrator, can influence an individual's test performance.

Test form: Many tests have more than one version or form. Items differ on each form, but each form is supposed to measure the same thing. Different forms of a test are known as parallel forms or alternate forms. These forms are designed to have similar measurement characteristics, but they contain different items. Because the forms are not exactly the same, a test taker might do better on one form than on another.

Multiple raters: In certain tests, scoring is determined by a rater's judgments of the test taker's performance or responses. Differences in training, experience, and frame of reference among raters can produce different test scores for the test taker.

These factors are sources of chance or random measurement error in the assessment process. If there were no random errors of measurement, the individual would get the same test score, the individual's "true" score, each time. The degree to which test scores are unaffected by measurement errors is an indication of the reliability of the test. Reliable assessment tools produce dependable, repeatable, and consistent information about students. In order to interpret test scores meaningfully and make useful assessment decisions, you need reliable instruments.

Reliability Coefficients

The statistic for expressing reliability is the reliability coefficient. The **reliability coefficient** expresses the degree of consistency in the measurement of test scores. The symbol used to denote a reliability coefficient is the letter r with two identical subscripts (r_{xx}). Reliability coefficients can range in value from 0.00 to 1.00. A reliability coefficient of $r_{xx} = 0.00$ indicates absence of reliability, whereas a reliability coefficient of $r_{xx} = 1.00$ demonstrates perfect reliability.

Acceptable reliability coefficients should never be below $r_{xx} = .90$. A coefficient below $r_{xx} = .90$ normally indicates inadequate reliability. A test should not be trusted if its reliability coefficient is low. High reliabilities are especially needed for tests used in individual assessment (Sattler, 1992). A reliability coefficient of $r_{xx} = .95$ on a test means that 95% of a test score is accurate while only 5% consists of unexplained error. However, a test with a reliability coefficient of $r_{xx} = .60$ does not have acceptable reliability because approximately 40% of the test score may be due to error (Venn, 2000).

Test–Retest Reliability

Test–retest reliability suggests that subjects tend to obtain the same score when tested at different times. For example, if an IQ test has strong test–retest reliability, a student who produces a low score now should also produce a low score later. Conversely, a student receiving a high score now should also produce a high score later. In other words, test–retest reliability is evident when there is a high positive correlation between the scores obtained from two testings (Heiman, 1999).

The reliability coefficient expresses the correlation between the scores obtained by the same students on two administrations of test. According to Venn (2000),

> the critical factor with test–retest reliability is the length of time between testing. Too little time between testing and retesting inflates the reliability coefficient, whereas too much time deflates the reliability coefficient. In most cases, a two-week interval allows enough time to adjust from any learning that may take place from the first testing experience. Longer intervals may reduce the reliability estimate due to maturation of the students or the influence of other outside events. (p. 67)

The usual procedure for obtaining a test–retest reliability coefficient is to administer the same test to the same group on two different occasions, usually within a short period of time. Generally, the shorter the retest interval, the higher the reliability coefficient, because within a shorter span of time there are fewer reasons for an individual's score to change (Sattler, 1992).

Split-Half Reliability or Internal Consistency

Split-half reliability (sometimes referred to as *internal consistency*) indicates that subjects' scores on some trials consistently match their scores on other trials. Typically, we make this determination by computing each subject's total odd score and correlating it with the even scores. For example, if the questions on an achievement test have split-half reliability, then subjects producing a low score on the odd questions should also obtain a low score on the even questions (Heiman, 1999).

Split-half reliability is a procedure for determining accuracy that involves correlating two halves of the same test. The steps in the process include giving a test once, splitting the test items in half, and comparing the results of the two halves to each other. The reliability coefficient obtained is an estimate of the correlation between the items on each half of the test (Venn, 2000).

Interrater Reliability

Interrater reliability involves having two raters independently observe and record specified behaviors, such as hitting, crying, yelling, and getting out of the seat, during the same time period. For example, suppose two observers are to determine each time they see a certain child tap his pencil during a math lecture. Tapping the pencil during the math lecture is considered the **target behavior.** A target behavior is a specific behavior the observer is looking to record. After each observer determines the total number of times the target behavior occurs, the scores are compared, and an estimate of the percentage of agreement between the two observations is done (Venn, 2000). The reliability coefficient obtained in this case correlates the observations of two independent observers. According to Overton (2000),

Inter-rater reliability is normally done by administering the test and then having an objective scorer also score the test results. The results of the tests scored by the examiner are then correlated with the results obtained by the objective scorer to determine how much variability exists between the test scores. This information is especially important when tests with a great deal of subjectivity are used in making educational decisions. (p. 129)

The formula for interrater reliability is:

$$\text{Number of agreements/Number of agreements + Disagreements} \times 100 = \text{Percentage of Agreements}$$

For example, suppose you and another observer watch a child to see how many times she looks out the window during a science lesson. Then, the two of you compare when you saw this behavior occurring. The results are listed below, indicating the interrater reliability for your observations.

> You Agree: 47 times
> You Disagree: 3 times

Therefore, $47/50 \times 100 = 94\%$ (.94). Because 90% or higher is our goal, there is adequate interrater reliability.

PRACTICE PROBLEM

5.1. In order to assess interrater reliability, you work with someone to examine how many times a child gets up from his chair over the course of the day. You agree with your partner 55 times but had different recordings on five separate occasions. What is the interrater reliability?

ANSWER TO PRACTICE PROBLEM

5.1. $55/60 \times 100 = 91.67\% = \mathbf{.917}$

Important Point: Accuracy is the unit of measure that compares a child's performance against a standard (e.g., the dictionary). In the English language, *cat* is spelled *c-a-t*. One does not need interrater reliability when an accuracy standard is available.

Alternate Forms Reliability

Alternate forms reliability is also known as *equivalent forms reliability* or *parallel forms reliability*. Here, two different forms of the same instrument are used. Alternate forms reliability is obtained by administering two equivalent tests to the same group of examinees. Determining alternate forms reliability requires a test developer to create two forms of the same test, give both forms to students and compare the scores from the two forms. The reliability coefficient in this case describes the correlation between the scores obtained by the same students on the two forms of the test (Venn, 2000). If the two forms of the test are equivalent, they should have the same means and variances and a high reliability coefficient. If there is no error in measurement, an individual should earn the same score on both forms of the test (Sattler, 1992, p. 26).

In alternate forms reliability, the items are matched for difficulty on each test (Overton, 2000). For example, if three items of long division are on one version of the test, then three long division problems need to be on the alternate form of the test at the same level of difficulty.

Several published achievement and diagnostic tests that are used in special education consist of two equivalent forms (Overton, 2000). The advantage of having alternate forms is that there are two tests of the same difficulty level that can be administered within a short time frame without the influence of practice effects.

To determine alternate forms reliability, it is necessary that the time frame between giving the two forms of the instrument be as short as possible. This eliminates the chance that other factors might affect test performances (Taylor, 1997).

Standard Error of Measurement

When you administer a test you get a score. This score is known as the **obtained score.** In theory, the obtained score consists of two parts: the *true score* and the *error score.* The obtained score is the amount of the trait the child actually possesses (true score) plus the error of measurement (error score). According to Sattler (1992),

> The child's true score is a hypothetical construct; it cannot be observed. The theory assumes that the child possesses stable traits, that errors are random, and that the obtained score results from the addition of true and error scores. (p. 25)

Error exists when doing assessment. The fact is, we are human beings administering tests to human beings. Therefore, it is to be expected that neither the examiner nor the examinee "will be perfect." Errors should always be considered when giving tests. Special educators need to know that all tests contain error, and that a single test score may not accurately reflect the student's true score (Overton, 2000).

> Test manuals report a statistic called the **standard error of measurement (SEM).** It gives the margin of error that you should expect in an individual test score because of imperfect reliability of the test. The SEM represents the degree of confidence that a person's "true" score lies within a particular range of scores. For example, an SEM of "2" indicates that a test taker's "true" score probably lies within 2 points in either direction of the score he or she receives on the test. This means that if an individual receives a 91 on the test, there is a good chance that the person's "true" score lies somewhere between 89 and 93. (America's Learning Exchange, 2000, p. 2)

The SEM is a useful measure of the accuracy of individual test scores. The smaller the SEM, the more accurate the measurements. When evaluating the reliability coefficients of a test, it is important to review the explanations provided in the manual for the following:

> **Types of Reliability Used.** The manual should indicate why a certain type of reliability coefficient was reported. The manual should also discuss sources of random measurement error that are relevant for the test.
>
> **How Reliability Studies Were Conducted.** The manual should indicate the conditions under which the data were obtained, such as the length of time that passed between administrations of a given test in a test–retest reliability study. In general, reliabilities tend to drop as the time between test administrations increases.
>
> **The Characteristics of the Sample Group.** The manual should indicate the important characteristics of the group used in gathering reliability information, such as education level, occupation, and so on. This will allow you to compare the characteristics of the people you want to test with the sample group. If they are sufficiently similar, then the reported reliability estimates will probably hold true for your population as well.

Factors Affecting Reliability

According to Sattler (1992), several factors can affect reliability:

1. **Test length:** The more items on a test and the more homogeneous they are, the greater the reliability.
2. **Test–retest interval:** The smaller the time interval between the administration of two tests, the smaller the chance of change and, hence, the higher the reliability is likely to be.
3. **Variability of scores:** The greater the variance of scores on a test, the higher the reliability estimate is likely to be. Small changes in performance have a greater impact on the reliability of a test when the range or spread of scores is narrow than when it is wide.
4. **Guessing:** The less guessing that occurs on a test, the higher the reliability is likely to be.
5. **Variation within the test situation:** The fewer variations there are in the test situation, the higher the reliability is likely to be. Factors include misleading or misunderstood directions, scoring errors, illness, and daydreaming.

CONCLUSION

In conclusion, an instrument or test should be both valid and reliable. Although both terms define two completely different concepts, they work together. A test needs to measure what it is supposed to measure and it must be consistent with its results.

Therefore, as special educators, when you find out or hear about a new test and wonder if it is technically adequate, examine the various validity and reliability coefficients to determine whether the test will be useful. Remember, making determinations about classifications for children is very serious. Therefore, you always want to be able to defend your decisions by stating that when you did your assessment, you used the most valid and reliable instruments to make your conclusions and recommendations.

VOCABULARY

Alternate Forms Reliability: Reliability obtained by administering two equivalent tests to the same group of examinees.

Concurrent Validity: Refers to how precisely a person's present performance (e.g., a test score) estimates that person's performance on the criterion measure at approximately the same time.

Construct Validity: The extent to which a test measures a theoretical construct or attribute.

Constructs: Theoretical concepts such as self-esteem and intelligence that can be observed by some type of instrument.

Content Validity: Refers to whether the individual items of a test represent what you actually want to assess.

Convergent Validity: A test that has good convergent validity has high positive correlations with other tests measuring the same construct.

Criterion-Related Validity: A method for assessing the validity of an instrument by comparing its scores with another criterion known already to be a measure of the same trait or skill.

Discriminant Validity: A test that has good discriminant validity has low correlations with tests that measure different constructs.

Interrater Reliability: Involves having two raters independently observe and record specified behaviors.

Obtained Score: The score actually calculated in the assessment process.

Predictive Validity: The extent to which a procedure allows accurate predictions about a subject's future behavior. It is a measure of a specific instrument's ability to predict future performance on some other measure or criterion at a later date.

Reliability: Refers to the consistency of measurements.

Reliability Coefficient: Expresses the degree of consistency in the measurement of test scores.

Reliable Test Scores: A test score that produces similar scores across various conditions and situations, including different evaluators and testing environments.

Split-Half Reliability: Indicates that subjects' scores on some trials consistently match their scores on other trials.

Standard Error of Measurement (SEM):   The amount of error that exists when using a specific instrument.

Target Behavior: A specific behavior an observer is looking to record.

Test–Retest Reliability: Suggests that subjects tend to obtain the same score when tested at different times.

Validity: The extent to which a test measures what it is supposed to measure.

Validity Coefficient: Criterion-related validity is usually expressed as a correlation between the test in question and the criterion measure. This correlation coefficient is referred to as a validity coefficient.

CHAPTER SIX

SCORING TERMINOLOGY USED IN ASSESSMENT

KEY TERMS

Age Equivalent   Quartiles
Chronological Age   Raw Score
Data   Scaled Scores
Deciles   Standard Score
Grade Equivalent   Stanine
Percentile Rank (Percentiles) T score
Protocol z score

CHAPTER OBJECTIVES

When you administer tests as special educators, you collect data. **Data** (*datum* is the singular) represent information gathered and collected during the assessment process. However, data need to be interpreted. You do not test a child and then come to the parent meeting with stacks upon stacks of data and test materials. On the contrary, you break the data down into statistical components that describe how the child performed on various parts of the assessment process. This chapter covers the various statistical ways in which data are reported to parents and school personnel when doing assessment. After reading this chapter, you should be able to understand the following:

- Calculation of age
- Raw scores
- Percentiles
- Standard scores
- z scores
- T scores
- Stanines
- Age equivalents
- Grade equivalents

CALCULATION OF AGE

Any time you test a child, perhaps the most important piece of information you must obtain is the child's age at the time of testing (known as **chronological age**). Miscalculating a child's chronological age will result in faulty interpretations and scores. Therefore, it is necessary to take your time and be sure of a child's chronological age when determining how old he or she is at the time of testing.

Now, you may be saying, why not just ask the child his or her age? The answer is threefold:

1. Many children do not know when they were born.
2. Children think they know their date of birth but are incorrect.
3. Ages (when doing an evaluation) are broken down into years, months, and days, something that children would not normally know.

For example, you may calculate that a child has a chronological age of 7-9-13. This means that the child is 7 years, 9 months, and 13 days old. If you determine that a child is 11-5-17, this represents a child who is 11 years, 5 months, and 17 days old.

Now, on every test you give as a special educator, there normally will be a box on the **protocol** (the booklet in which you record the child's response) to calculate the child's chronological age. The box almost always looks like this:

	YEAR	MONTH	DAY
Date of Test	_____	_____	_____
Date of Birth	_____	_____	_____
Chronological Age	_____	_____	_____

To calculate age, the first step is simply to fill in the appropriate lines for Date of Test and Date of Birth. For example, a child who was tested on November 25, 2005, and who was born on July 9, 1991, would have these data in the following box:

	YEAR	MONTH	DAY
Date of Test	2005	11	25
Date of Birth	1991	7	9
Chronological Age	_____	_____	_____

Date of Test of November 25, 2005, is represented by 2005-11-25, whereas Date of Birth of July 9, 1991, is represented by 1991-7-9. Now all you have to do is subtract the Date of Birth from the Date of Test to find the child's Chronological Age.

Important Point: Always start the subtraction process from RIGHT to LEFT (i.e., subtract the Days, then the Months, and lastly, the Years). You must always follow this procedure!

	YEAR	MONTH	DAY
Date of Test	2005	11	25
Date of Birth	1991	7	9
Chronological Age	14	4	16

This child is 14-4-16: 14 years, 4 months, and 16 days old. (On many tests, if the days are over 15, the age is rounded up to 14-5.)

Now, suppose you have a child whose Date of Test DAYS is less than his Date of Birth DAYS. All you need to do is subtract 1 from the Date of Test MONTHS and add 30 to the Date of Test DAYS (you are simply replacing 1 month with 30 days). For example: Suppose you have a child who was tested on August 11, 2005. He was born on May 23, 1995. The box would look like this:

	YEAR	MONTH	DAY
Date of Test	2005	8	11
Date of Birth	1995	5	23
Chronological Age			

You cannot subtract 23 from 11, so simply subtract 1 from the Date of Test MONTHS (8 – 1 = 7) and add 30 to Date of Test DAYS (11 + 30 = 41). Now the box looks like this:

	YEAR	MONTH	DAY
Date of Test	2005	7	41
Date of Birth	1995	5	23
Chronological Age			

Now, simply subtract as you normally would:

	YEAR	MONTH	DAY
Date of Test	2005	7	41
Date of Birth	1995	5	23
Chronological Age	10	2	18

This child is 10-2-18. (For assessment purposes, the child's age probably would be recorded as 10-3.)

Now, suppose the Date of Test MONTHS is less than the Date of Birth MONTHS. Here, subtract 1 from the Date of Test YEARS and add 12 to the Date of Test MONTHS (you are replacing 1 year with 12 months). For example: Suppose you tested a child born on November 4, 2000. He was tested on April 15, 2005. Calculate his age at the time of testing.

	YEAR	MONTH	DAY
Date of Test	2005	4	15
Date of Birth	2000	11	4
Chronological Age			

Subtract the Days as you normally would and you get 11 days. However, you cannot subtract 11 from 4 MONTHS. Therefore, subtract 1 from the Date of Test YEARS (2005 − 1 = 2004) and add 12 to the Date of Test MONTHS (4 + 12 = 16). Subtract as you normally would. Now, the box looks like this:

	YEAR	MONTH	DAY
Date of Test	2004	16	15
Date of Birth	2000	11	4
Chronological Age	4	5	11

This child was 4-5-11 when tested.

If you can do this problem, then you should be able to do any calculation of age. Try this one: A child is tested on March 14, 2005. He was born on December 29, 1998. What was his age at the time of testing? (In both situations, the Date of Test DAYS and MONTHS are less than those of the Date of Birth.)

Answer: This child is 6-2-15. Just for fun, suppose that you were tested today. Calculate how old you are today.

RAW SCORES

When you administer any test, the first step in scoring almost always will be to calculate the number of correct items the student obtained. For example, if a student took a 20-question spelling test in your class, the first thing you would do is determine how many words the student spelled correctly. This score is known as the raw score. The **raw score** normally indicates the number of items correctly answered on a given test. In almost all cases, it is the first score a teacher obtains when interpreting data. A raw score is a test score that has not been weighted, transformed, or statistically manipulated.

In general, raw scores by themselves mean very little. For example, suppose the student in your class got 18 out of 20 correct on the spelling test. The number 18 has no real meaning. What is important is what you do with the 18. For example, most teachers would say the student got 18 out of 20 and turn it into a percentage indicating that the student got 90% (18/20 is 90%) on this test.

PERCENTILE RANKS (PERCENTILES)

A **percentile rank** (often referred to as a **percentile**) is a score indicating the percentage of people or scores that occur at or below a given score. For example, if you have a percentile rank of 75 in a class, this means that you did as well as or better than 75% of the students in the class. A percentile rank of 16 means that you scored as well as or better than only 16% of the population. Percentile ranks range from the lowest (1st percentile) to the highest (99th percentile). A percentile rank of 83 means that a student has scored as well as or better than 83 percent of the students taking a test. Notice, however, it does not mean that the student got a test score of 83%. The percentage correct on a test is not the same as the percentage of people scoring below a given score, the percentile rank. The 50th percentile normally signifies the average ranking or average performance.

There are two other types of percentiles used in assessment: quartiles and deciles. **Quartiles** divide scores into four units: 1–25, 26–50, 51–75, and 76–99. The first quartile (1–25) marks the lower quarter (Bottom 25%) or bottom fourth of all scores, whereas the fourth quartile represents the upper quarter (Top 25%). **Deciles** divide scores into tenths or 10 equal units. For example, the sixth decile is the point at which 60% of the scores fall below, whereas the ninth decile is the point at which 90% of the scores fall below.

In assessment, percentile ranks are very important because they indicate how well a child did when compared to the norms on a test. Knowing that a child had a percentile rank of 97 on a test would tell you that he is exceptional in this testing area; knowing that he got a percentile rank of 7 would tell you that this is an area of weakness.

Important Point: It should be noted that there is a serious drawback to percentiles. According to Venn (2000),

> The major drawback to percentiles involves the unequal length of percentile units, especially at the extremes. This characteristic results in a tendency to overemphasize differences near the middle and under emphasize difference near the ends. In other words, the difference between 50 and 55 may be less than the difference between 90 and 95. This inequality occurs because percentiles, which are calculated from ranked data, designate relative standing, not absolute differences. (p. 97)

STANDARD SCORES

A **standard score** is a score that has been transformed to fit a normal curve, with a mean and standard deviation that remain the same across ages. Normally, standard scores have a mean of 100 and an SD of 15. Perhaps the most well-known version of the standard score with a mean of 100 and an SD of 15 is the Wechsler Intelligence Scales (see Chapter 10 on assessment of intelligence). Using this scoring system, a child with a standard score of 115 would be 1 standard deviation above the mean, whereas a child with a standard score of 85 would be 1 standard deviation below the mean. Also, the percentage of scores between a standard score of 85 and 115 is 68%. (If this is unclear, refer to Chapter 4 for a review of the normal curve.)

Often, when doing assessment, you will have to tell parents and administrators the standard scores the child received on the given test and the appropriate classification that they represent. For some tests with a mean of 100 and a standard deviation of 15, the general classification system may appear as follows:

STANDARD SCORE	CLASSIFICATION
Less than 70	Developmentally Delayed
70–79	Well Below Average or Borderline
80–89	Low Average
90–109	Average
110–119	High Average
120–129	Superior
130 and higher	Very Superior

Important Point: The above classification system is only one form of representing standard scores. Different tests may use different ranges and terminology.

The standard score of 100 with a mean of 15 is the most often utilized representation of standard scores. However, other types of standard scores also represent test performance. The three other types of standard scores that you will come across in doing assessment are z scores, T scores, and stanines.

z SCORES

A **z score** indicates how many standard deviations a score is above or below the mean. A z score is a standard score distribution with a mean of zero and a standard deviation of one. For example, if a student has a z score of +1.0, this means that he scored 1 standard deviation above the mean on the test. If a student has a z score of –1.7, this means that he scored 1.7 standard deviations below the mean. To calculate z scores, the formula is

$$z = \text{Test Score} - \text{Mean Score/Standard Deviation}$$

For example, suppose a student had an IQ of 130 on an IQ test with a mean of 100 and a standard deviation of 15. Use the formula:

130 − 100/15 = +2.0

A student with a 130 IQ would be 2.0 standard deviations above the mean. (You already knew this from the normal curve.)

T SCORES

A *T* **score** is another way to express test performance. *T* scores have a mean of 50 with a standard deviation of 10. Therefore, if you have a *T* score of 40 you are 1 standard deviation below the mean, whereas a *T* score of 60 would be 1 standard deviation above the mean. To calculate *T* scores:

$$T = 50 + 10z$$

For example: A student who scored 1.5 standard deviations above the mean would have a *T* score of 65 because T = 50 + 10(1.5). Here the 1.5 represents 1.5 standard deviations above the mean, which is $z = 1.5$.

STANINES

A **stanine**, an abbreviation for *standard nines*, is a type of standard score that has a mean of 5 and an SD of 2. Stanine scores can range from 1 to 9. A stanine of 7 is 1 SD above the mean (5 + 2). A stanine of 9 is 2 SD above the mean (5 + 2 + 2). Conversely, a stanine of 3 is 1 SD below the mean (5 − 2) and a stanine of 1 is 2 SD below the mean (5 − 2 − 2).

COMPARING *z* SCORES, *T* SCORES, AND STANINES

The table that follows and Figure 6.1 can help you to remember how standard deviations, *z* scores, *T* scores, and stanines compare to each other.

STANDARD DEVIATION	*z* SCORE	*T* SCORE	STANINE
−2.0	−2.0	30	1.0
−1.0	−1.0	40	3.0
0.0 (mean score)	0.0	50	5.0
+1.0	+1.0	60	7.0
+2.0	+2.0	70	9.0

SCALED SCORES

Many tests used for assessment of children have subtests that comprise the entire test. For each subtest, a student receives a raw score. This raw score is often transformed into

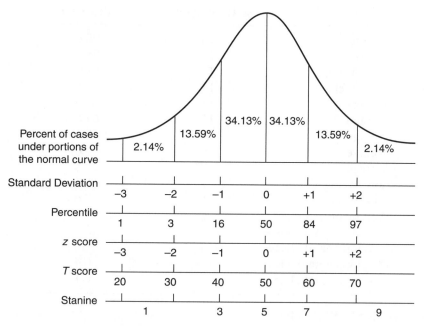

FIGURE 6.1   The Normal Curve

a scaled score. **Scaled scores** are very specific subtest scores. In many cases, scaled scores range from 1 to 19 with a mean of 10. They follow the following classification format:

SCALED SCORE	CLASSIFICATION
1–3	Developmentally Delay
4–5	Well Below Average
6–7	Low Average
8–12	Average
13–14	High Average
15–16	Superior
17–19	Very Superior

For example, if a student gets only a scaled score of 7 on a reading subtest but a 13 on a math subtest, this indicates a much greater strength with respect to math than with reading, compared to the norms of the age group.

**Relationship among Ranges of Scores,
Scaled Scores, and Percentiles**

RANGE	SCALED SCORE	PERCENTILE
Very Superior	19	99.9
Very Superior	18	99.6
Very Superior	17	99.6

(continued)

RANGE	SCALED SCORE	PERCENTILE
Superior	16	98.6
Superior	15	95.6
High Average	14	91.6
High Average	13	84.6
Average	12	75.6
Average	11	63.6
Average	10	50.6
Average	9	37.6
Average	8	25.6
Low Average	7	16.6
Low Average	6	9.6
Well Below Average	5	5.6
Well Below Average	4	2.6
Developmental Delay	3	1.6
Developmental Delay	2	0.4
Developmental Delay	1	0.1

AGE EQUIVALENT SCORES

An **age equivalent** is a very general score that is used to compare the performance of children at the same age with one another. It is the estimated age level that corresponds to a given score. Age equivalent scores are almost always given in years and months. For example, a child who gets an age equivalent score of 11-5 is performing as well as the average 11-year, 5-month-old child.

GRADE EQUIVALENT SCORES

A **grade equivalent** is a very general score that is used to compare the performance of children in the same grade with one another. It is the estimated grade level that corresponds to a given score. Grade equivalent scores are almost always given in years and months in school. For example, a child who gets a grade equivalent score of 3.5 is performing as well as the average student in the 3rd grade, 5th month.

Important Point: Age equivalent scores do not compare the performance of the child at the same age. What they do compare is the child's raw score—the score achieved on the assessment measure—with the average raw score of students in the norm group who took the same test. Likewise, a 6.5 grade equivalent score does not mean that a student is performing as well as the average student in grade 6 midway through the year. It does mean that the student's raw score on the assessment measure was equal to the average raw score of students at the 6.5 level in the norm group.

CONCLUSION

It is evident that there are numerous ways to express test scores in assessment. The fact is, no one way is superior to all others. However, the more information you can give parents and administrators, the more objective and solid the case you make for whether you have determined if a disability is present or in planning a program. Consequently, being able to determine, calculate, and express the various scores from testing in a clear and cogent manner is a very important responsibility as a special educator.

VOCABULARY

Age Equivalent: A very general score that is used to compare the performance of children at the same age with one another.
Chronological Age: The child's actual age.
Deciles: Divide scores into tenths or 10 equal units. For example, the sixth decile is the point at which 60% of the scores fall below, whereas the ninth decile is the point at which 90% of the scores fall below.
Grade Equivalent: A very general score that is used to compare the performance of children in the same grade with one another.
Percentile Rank (Percentile):   A score indicating the percentage of people or scores that occur at or below a given score. If you have a percentile rank of 75, this means that you did as well as or better than 75% of the students in the class.
Protocol: The booklet where responses and scores are recorded.
Quartiles: Divide scores into four units: 1–25, 26–50, 51–75, and 76–99. The first quartile (1–25)

marks the lower quarter (Bottom 25%) or bottom fourth of all scores, whereas the fourth quartile represents the upper quarter (Top 25%).
Raw Score: The raw score indicates the number of items correctly answered on a given test. In almost all cases, it is the first score a teacher obtains when interpreting data.
Standard Score: A score that has been transformed to fit a normal curve, with a mean and standard deviation that remain the same across ages.
Stanine: An abbreviation for *standard nines*, it is a type of standard score that has a mean of 5 and a standard deviation of 2. Stanine scores can range from 1 to 9.
T scores: Another way to express test performance. T scores have a mean of 50 with a standard deviation of 10.
z score: Indicates how many standard deviations a score is above or below the mean. A z score is a standard score distribution with a mean of zero and a standard deviation of one.

PRACTICE PROBLEMS

6.1.   Given the following numerical representation of a child's age, write, in words, his age: 14-3-24.

6.2.   A student is thirteen years, seven months, and twelve days old. How would her age be expressed numerically?

6.3.   A child was tested on June 12, 2004. He was born on January 20, 1994. Calculate his age at the time of testing.

6.4.   A child was born on July 24, 1996. He was tested on May 28, 2005. Calculate his age at the time of testing.

6.5.   A child was tested on February 13, 2005. He was born on August 21, 1991. What was his age at the time of testing?

6.6.   On a test, 1 point represents a correct answer while 0 points represents an incor-

rect answer. On this test, Sally got the following correct and incorrect answers:

0, 1, 0, 1, 1, 0, 1, 1, 1, 0.

What is Sally's raw score?

6.7.   For the following standard scores, assuming a mean of 100 and a SD of 15, give the appropriate classification:

1. 97	**5.** 84
2. 57	**6.** 72
3. 103	**7.** 125
4. 117	**8.** 139

6.8.   A student gets a 75 on a test with a mean of 90 and a standard deviation of 10. How many standard deviations above or below the mean did this student score?

6.9   Calculate the T score of a student who scored 1.5 standard deviations below the mean on a test.

ANSWERS TO PRACTICE PROBLEMS

6.1. 14 years, 3 months, and 21 days old.

6.2. 13-7-12.

6.3. 10-4-22.

6.4. 8-10–4.

6.5. 13-5-22.

6.6. 6.

6.7. **1.** Average, **2.** Developmentally Delayed, **3.** Average, **4.** High Average, **5.** Low Aver-age, **6.** Well Below Average or Borderline, **7.** Superior, **8.** Very Superior.

6.8. $z = 75 - 90/10 = -15/10 = $ **–1.5.** The student scored 1.5 standard deviations below the mean.

6.9. **35.**

$T = 50 + 10 (-1.5)$
$T = 50 - 15$
$T = 35$

■ ■ ■ ■ ■

THE SPECIAL EDUCATION PROCESS

The process of identifying a student with a suspected disability is referred to as the special education process. This process involves a variety of steps that must follow federal, state, and district guidelines. These guidelines have been created to protect the rights of students, parents, and school districts. Working together within these guidelines allows for a thorough and comprehensive assessment of a student and the proper special education services and modifications, if required. When a student is having difficulty in school, the professional staff makes many attempts to resolve the problem. When these interventions do not work, a more extensive look at the student is required.

The remaining chapters in this text outline in detail the step-by-step process that is normally followed in special education. A brief explanation of this assessment continuum follows. Each step is covered in depth in the chapters noted.

Step 1. Prereferral: When concerns are realized by the classroom teacher, he or she attempts simple classroom interventions such as meeting with the child, extra help, simplified assignments, parent conferences, and peer tutoring (discussed in Chapter 7). If unsuccessful, then:

Step 2. Child Study Team and prereferral strategies: Referral to a school-based Child Study Team (sometimes called the Prereferral Team or Pupil Personnel Team) for a prereferral intervention plan is usually made by the classroom teacher (although anyone can make a request for a meeting). More involved prereferral strategies are considered, such as direct classroom intervention strategies that include the following: classroom management, classroom modifications, observation by professional staff, observation and analysis of teaching methods, in-school counseling, assessment of environment, extra help, classroom modifications, change of program, consolidation of program, disciplinary actions, further parent conferences, medical referral, and so forth (discussed in Chapter 7). If strategies prove unsuccessful, then:

Step 3. Screening: The child is screened for a suspected disability by members of the school staff, such as the school psychologist, educational evaluator and speech and language clinician. If screening reveals a possible suspected disability, then a referral for a more comprehensive assessment (discussed in Chapter 7) is made to:

Step 4. Multidisciplinary team (MDT): This team is made up of parents, school staff, and other professionals. When required, they decide which evaluations and professionals will be involved in this specific assessment. The team then provides a thorough and comprehensive assessment for possible special education services. Assessments may include such measures as standardized tests, portfolio assessments, curriculum-based assessment, criterion-referenced assessments, and the like (discussed in Chapters 3, and 8 through 15). If the findings of this team indicate the existence of a disability, then:

Step 5. Putting it all together: Once the MDT team completes the assessment, members of the team determine the strengths and weaknesses of the student; a possible diagnostic category; level of severity of the problem; recommendations to the school, teachers, and parents; and other information that later will be used to determine any appropriate special education recommendations (discussed in Chapter 16).

Step 6. Writing a professional report: Once the members of the team establish their findings, they should write up a professional report (discussed in Chapter 17) clearly outlining their findings. This report will be part of the materials that go to the Eligibility Committee.

Step 7. Preparation for presentation to the Eligibility Committee: The MDT puts together the information packet for the presentation to the Eligibility Committee. This packet contains all the necessary forms, reports, and results of assessment that will be used to determine possible classification and special education services (discussed in Chapter 18).

Step 8. Eligibility Committee meetings: Once the packet is complete, an Eligibility Committee meeting (Committee on Special Education, IEP Committee, Eligibility Committee) is scheduled. This committee determines whether the student meets the criteria for a disability, a special education program, and services (discussed in Chapter 18). If the student is classified, then:

Step 9. IEP development and alternate planning: Final IEP development occurs and placement is instituted (also discussed in Chapter 19). If eligibility is not accepted, alternate planning is formulated and suggested by the eligibility committee to the local school (also discussed in Chapter 19).

Special Topics—State- and District-Wide Assessments and Transition services: Chapter 20 focuses on special topics in special education that are important to the assessment process. The two topics addressed are (1) state- and district-wide assessments and (2) transition services for classified students as they move from high school through adult life.

■ ■ ■ ■ ■

CHAPTER SEVEN

THE CHILD STUDY TEAM AND PREREFERRAL STRATEGIES

KEY TERMS

Change of Program
Classroom Management Techniques
Consolidation of Program
Curriculum-Based Assessment
Disciplinary Action
Hearing Test
Help Classes
In-School Counseling
Medical Exam

Parent Interview
Portfolio Assessment
Prereferral Strategies
Progress Report
Referral to Child Protective Services
Remedial Reading or Math Services
Screening
Team Meeting with Teachers
Vision Test

CHAPTER OBJECTIVES

This chapter focuses on the Child Study Team and the various prereferral procedures that school systems use. After reading this chapter, you should be able to do the following:

■ Understand the purpose of the Child Study Team

■ Understand the purpose of prereferral strategies

■ Identify the prereferral strategies used most often in school systems

THE CHILD STUDY TEAM

When teachers in regular education are having difficulty with a student in their class, they may attempt several strategies to see if the problem can be resolved within the classroom. These strategies may include meeting with the child, extra help, simplified assignments, parent conferences, peer tutoring, and so on. If there is no progress within a realistic amount of time, the teacher may decide to refer the student to a school-based team, often known as the Child Study Team (CST), School Building Level Committee (SBLC), Pupil Personnel Team (PPT), or Prereferral Team (PRT), depending on the state in which the student resides. Depending on the type of referral, this team may be drawn from the following staff members:

- Child's classroom teacher
- Principal
- School psychologist
- Special education teacher
- School nurse
- Social worker
- Speech/language clinician
- Guidance counselor (secondary level)

Many school districts recommend or require that, before a formal assessment of a student for possible placement in special education occurs, his or her teacher meet with this prereferral team to discuss the nature of the problem and what possible modifications to instruction or the classroom might be made. These procedures are known as prereferral strategies. **Prereferral strategies** have arisen out of a number of research studies documenting faulty referral practices. Included among other practices is the overreferral of students who come from backgrounds that are culturally or linguistically different from the majority culture, those who are hard to teach, or those who are felt to have behavioral problems. According to Overton (2000), "the more frequent use of better pre-referral intervention strategies is a step forward in the prevention of unnecessary evaluation and the possibility of misdiagnosis and over identification of special education students" (p. 7).

This process recognizes that many variables affect learning; rather than first assuming that the difficulty lies within the student, the prereferral team and the teacher look specifically at what variables (e.g., classroom, teacher, student, or an interaction of these) might be affecting this particular student. Examining student records and work samples and conducting interviews and observations are part of the team's efforts. These approaches to gathering data are intended to specify the problem more precisely and to document its severity. Modifications to the teacher's approach, to the classroom, or to student activities may then be suggested, attempted, and documented. It is important for teachers to keep track of the specific modifications they attempt with a student who is having trouble learning or behaving, because these can provide valuable information to the school-based team if the student is referred for a comprehensive assessment.

Prior to doing an evaluation for possible classification and placement in special education, it is important to make sure that the school has made every effort to remediate the learning and/or behavioral problems through other means. The assessment process is a very significant and important piece in addressing such concerns but should never be the first step. Before a full battery of tests are administered, many preventative measures are attempted to try to remediate further difficulties. The rest of this chapter is devoted to discussing the prereferral procedures used most often in school systems.

The members of the CST (the prereferral team) usually meet on a regular basis, once or twice a week depending on the caseload. Normally, there is a chairperson on the CST whom the entire faculty and staff can make a referral to during the week for the agenda at the next meeting. For example, if the CST meets on Friday, a teacher can go to the chairperson on Tuesday and say:

> *I have been trying to work with Mary Bell by making some changes in my class. However, she does not seem to be responding, and I am becoming increasingly concerned about her deterioration. I think I need help and would like to discuss her at the next team meeting.*

This type of statement would allow the teacher to come to the team meeting and help develop more formal and comprehensive prereferral strategies that can then be attempted in the classroom. The next statement typifies a different need:

> *We have been working with Luther Santos for a while on prereferral strategies but they do not seem to be working. Therefore, I would like to meet with the CST again to discuss Luther because he is still doing very poorly in my class and nothing we developed is working.*

This type of statement would probably require the team to consider screening Luther for a suspected disability since prereferral strategies have been attempted over a period of time and under a variety of conditions and have made no impact.

The chairperson then puts Mary Bell and Luther Santos on the list of students to discuss at the next CST meeting. He or she informs the members of the CST in writing that both are on the CST agenda. It is each team member's responsibility to bring any important and relevant documentation on Mary Bell and Luther Santos to the next CST meeting.

When the CST meets, team members discuss whatever agenda is put forth for that particular day. On some days, there may be very little to discuss whereas on other days, the CST meeting may run for a few hours based on the number of students that needs to be discussed.

Example Referral Forms to the CST

Many schools utilize a referral form procedure that teachers submit to indicate the possibility of a high-risk student. This is usually the first step in the referral process. The form then goes to the Child Study Team for discussion and future direction. The initial section of these forms is usually the same, containing basic identifying information. The differences are usually in the body of the form. Figures 7.1 and 7.2 are two examples of how this form might be used for referral to the CST.

As shown in Figure 7.1, the classroom teacher has made several attempts to resolve Mary's issues prior to a referral to the CST. When she realized that her attempts were not working, she decided to take her concerns to the CST for a more formal analysis of Mary's situation. At this point, the team, along with the classroom teacher, will develop prereferral strategies for Mary in an attempt to resolve her issues in hopes that a formal referral for a comprehensive assessment is not required.

The referral in Figure 7.2 was made after meetings with the CST established a prereferral intervention strategy plan. This plan had been in operation for several weeks by the time the teacher made the referral.

FIGURE 7.1 Example of Referral Form to Child Study Team

REFERRAL FORM TO THE CHILD STUDY TEAM

Student Name: Mary Bell   **Date of Referral:**   November 21, 2005

Grade Level: 4   **Date of Birth:** 9/21/95

Teacher Name: Mrs. Brown   **Chronological Age:**   10–1

Parents' Names: Julie/Robert   **Phone:**   (516) 555-9876

Please answer the following questions:

What symptoms is the child exhibiting that are of concern at this time?

Mary is having a great deal of problems learning in my class. She rarely hands in work, fails tests, procrastinates, makes excuses, and avoids handing in homework assignments.

What have you tried that has worked?

The only thing that seems to work is contacting her parents, but that is short lived. Any noticeable changes last for only a day or two and Mary is right back to her patterns.

What have you tried that does not seem to work toward alleviating these symptoms?

I have attempted peer tutoring, limiting assignments, change of seat, parent conferences, small group interventions, and shorter but more frequent assignments to see if she could accomplish anything, but nothing has worked.

What are the child's present academic levels of functioning?

From informal testing, I consider Mary to be functioning at a low average level in all academic skills and ability.

Any observable behavioral or physical limitations?

Mary tends to squint a great deal, but does not seem to have any physical limitations.

What is the child's social behavior like?

Mary seems to avoid any social contact with the other children. She spends a great deal of her time alone on the playground and rarely talks to others. She seems to have no friends.

Current performance estimates (below, on, or above grade level)

Reading: __below__   **Math:** __below__   **Spelling:** __below__

Have the parents been contacted? yes __X__ no _____. If not, why not? _____

Further comments?

Parents are very cooperative and concerned. Not sure what to do next.

FIGURE 7.2   Example of Referral Form to Child Study Team

REFERRAL FORM TO THE CHILD STUDY TEAM

Student Name: Luther Santos   **Date of Referral:** February 11, 2005

Grade Level: 3   **Date of Birth:** 2/1/96

Teacher Name: Mrs. Davis   **Chronological Age:** 9–0

Parents' Names: Dalia/Lorenzo   **Phone:** (516) 555-7843

Please answer the following questions:

What symptoms is the child exhibiting that are of concern at this time?

Despite numerous intervention strategies, Luther continues not to follow class or school rules, bothers other children when they are working, gets up out of his seat constantly, throws things at other children, does not finish his class work, and defies authority.

What have you tried that has worked?

Small group instruction in which I can closely monitor Luther by having him close to me. But even that is difficult.

What have you tried that does not seem to work toward alleviating these symptoms?

I have worked with the school psychologist in consultation, tried behavioral plans, behavior modification techniques, parent conferences, small group work, changing his seat, modifying the class environment, and giving him more work in the morning when he seems to have the most attention. He is also receiving in-school counseling and has been observed several times. We have reviewed his work samples and tests and have instituted changes as a result of the weaknesses we have found. We have been trying this intervention plan for several weeks but nothing seems to be working.

What are the child's present academic levels of functioning?

From informal testing I consider Luther to be a very capable boy if he were able to focus. His skills all seem to be at least average, and his ability seems above average based on some of the comments he makes and vocabulary he uses.

Any observable behavioral or physical limitations?

Luther cannot sit still for more than two to three minutes, cannot focus on work for more than a few minutes, and asks questions constantly and at inappropriate times. He does not seem to have any physical limitations and is very good in sports although he has little patience for following rules.

What is the child's social behavior like?

Luther is liked by some children in the class because he is good at sports. However, many of the boys are losing patience because he will walk off during a game when he doesn't feel like playing.

Current performance estimates (below, on, or above grade level)

Reading: _above_   Math: _above_   Spelling: _above_

Have the parents been contacted? yes _X_ no _____. **If not, why not?** _____

Further comments?

Parents do not feel that he is that bad. Father indicated that he was the same way in school and grew out of it.

In the case of Luther, the teacher and the CST have already attempted numerous prereferral strategies in an attempt to improve Luther's class behavior and performance. However, according to the teacher, nothing seems to be working. At this point, the CST might consider screening Luther for a suspected disability. If team members find evidence of a suspected disability, they will make a formal referral for a comprehensive assessment with the parents' permission.

The Child Study Team Meeting

Once a referral is made to the CST, personnel involved on the team will gather as much available information prior to the meeting in order to better understand the child and his or her educational patterns. This information may come from a variety of sources, and the presentation of this information at the meeting is crucial in the determination of the most appropriate direction to proceed. Schools usually have a wealth of information about all of the students, distributed among a number of people and a number of records. Gathering and reviewing this information after a referral, and prior to screening, could reduce the need for more formal testing and provide a very thorough picture of the child's abilities and patterns. School personnel can gather this information from a variety of sources.

Sources of Student Information

School Records.   School records can be a rich source of information about the student and his or her background. For instance, the number of times the student has changed schools may be of interest. Frequent school changes can be disruptive emotionally, as well as academically, and may be a factor in the problems that have resulted in the student's being referred to the CST.

Prior Academic Achievement.   The student's past history of grades is usually of interest to the CST. Is the student's current performance in a particular subject typical of the student or is the problem being observed something new? Are patterns noticeable in the student's grades? For example, many students begin the year with poor grades and then show gradual improvement as they get back into the swing of school. For others, the reverse may be true: During the early part of the year, when prior school material is being reviewed, they may do well, with declines in their grades coming as new material is introduced. Also, transition points such as beginning the fourth grade or middle school may cause some students problems; the nature and purpose of reading, for example, tends to change when students enter the fourth grade, because reading to learn content becomes more central. Similarly, middle school requires students to assume more responsibility for long-term projects (Hoy & Gregg, 1994). These shifts may bring about a noticeable decline in grades.

Prior Test Scores.   Test scores are also important to review. Comparing these scores to a student's current classroom performance can indicate that the student's difficulties are new ones, perhaps resulting from some environmental change that needs to be more fully investigated. Further, the comparison may show that the student has always found a particular skill area to be problematic. "In this situation, the current problems the student is experiencing indicate that the classroom demands have reached a point that the student requires more support to be successful" (Hoy & Gregg, 1994, p. 37).

Group Standardized Achievement Test Results.   A great deal of information can be obtained from group achievement test results. Whereas individual tests should be administered when evaluating a child's suspected disability, group achievement results may reflect certain very important patterns. Most schools administer group achievement tests annually or every few years. If these results are available on a student, you may want to explore the various existing patterns. It is helpful to have several years of results to analyze. Over time this type of pattern can be more reliable for interpretation.

Attendance Records.   Attendance records can provide the CST with a great deal of important information, especially if team members know what they are looking for. Many patterns are symptomatic of more serious concerns, and being able to recognize these patterns early can only facilitate the recognition of a potential high-risk student. When we look at a student's attendance profile over the years, several things may stand out. For instance, a child's pattern of absences might include consistent absences during a specific part of the year, as is the case with some students who have respiratory problems or allergies. In other cases, there may be a noticeable pattern of declining attendance that may be linked to a decline in motivation, an undiagnosed health problem or a change within the family. Specific points to keep in mind when reviewing attendance records include the following:

1. The number of days absent in the student's profile: Ordinarily, more than 10 days a year may need to be investigated for patterns. If a child is out more than 15 to 20 days, this could be indicative of a serious issue if a medical or some other logical reason did not substantiate the absences.

2. The patterns of days absent: Single days may indicate the presence of possible school avoidance, phobia, or dysfunctional or chaotic home environment.

Prior Teacher Reports.   Comments written on report cards or in permanent record folders can provide the CST with a different perspective on the child under a different style of teaching. Successful years and positive comments may be clues to the child's learning style and the conditions under which he or she responds best. Also, write-ups about conferences between previous teachers and parents can provide information important to understanding the child's patterns and history.

Group IQ Test Information.   This information is usually found in the permanent record folder. Many schools administer a group IQ type of test (e.g., Otis Lennon—7) in grades three, six, and nine. It is important to be aware that the term *School Abilities Index* has replaced the term *IQ* or *intelligence quotient* on many group IQ tests.

Prior Teacher Referrals.   The CST should investigate school records for prior referrals from teachers. There could have been a time when a teacher referred but no action was taken due to time of year, parent resistance, delay in procedures, and so on. These referrals may still be on file and may reveal useful information.

Medical History in the School Nurse's Office.   The CST should also investigate school medical records for indications of visual or hearing difficulties, prescribed medication that may have an effect on the child's behavior (e.g., antihistamines), or medical conditions in need of attention or that could be contributing to the child's present difficulties.

Student Work.   Often, an initial part of the assessment process includes examining a student's work, either by selecting work samples that can be analyzed to identify academic skills and deficits or by conducting a portfolio assessment, whereby folders of the student's work are examined (see Chapter 3). When collecting work samples, the teacher selects work from the areas in which the student is experiencing difficulty and systematically examines them. The teacher might identify such elements as how the student was directed to do the activity (e.g., orally, in writing), how long it took the student to complete the activity, the pattern of errors (e.g., reversals when writing), and the pattern of correct answers. Analyzing the student's work in this way can yield valuable insight into the nature of his or her difficulties and suggest possible solutions.

RECOMMENDATIONS BY THE CHILD STUDY TEAM—PREREFERRAL STRATEGIES

After analyzing all of the information presented at the meeting, the CST has to make a decision: What does it recommend at this point? If this is the first time a student is being reviewed by the team, then the CST is very likely to recommend prereferral strategies to the teacher. As previously mentioned, these are techniques and suggestions to attempt to resolve the child's issues without the need for a more comprehensive assessment. What are the benefits of prereferral intervention?

- Alternatives are reviewed and referrals made to other programs. Instructional assistance can be provided if needed.
- Students who do not have a disability, but who need instructional support, will receive it in the regular program.
- Problem solving as a team facilitates professional growth in needed areas; staff development is formative and directly in response to teacher needs. Teachers in the regular program develop a network of peer support.
- Referrals to special education are more valid; that is, students are more likely to truly have a disability.

Prereferral Intervention Strategies

Team Meeting with Teachers.   A team meeting with teachers is a prereferral procedure whereby teachers who have previously worked with or have ideas about this student come together to determine what strategies can be implemented to help this child. In this prereferral procedure, teachers share information about a student to identify patterns of behavior reflective of some particular condition or disability. Sometimes, a group meeting with all of the child's teachers can preclude the need for further involvement. One or several teachers may be using techniques that could benefit others also working with the child. By sharing information or observations, it is possible to identify patterns of behavior reflective of some particular condition or disability. Once this pattern is identified, the student may be handled in a variety of ways without the need for more serious intervention.

Parent Interviews.   A parent interview as a prereferral procedure involves meeting with the parent(s) to discuss what motivates this child along with finding out any family information that may be contributing to the child's behavior in the classroom (e.g., recent separation, death of a loved one). Meeting the parent(s) is always recommended for a child having some difficulty in school. This initial meeting can be informal, with the purpose of clarifying certain issues and gathering pertinent information that may help the child as well as the teacher in the classroom. If testing or serious intervention is required, then a more formal and in-depth parent meeting will take place.

Medical Exam.   The CST should try to rule out any possibility of a medical condition causing or contributing to the existing problems. If the teacher or any other professional who works with the child feels that there is any possibility of such a condition, and the need for a complete medical workup is evident, then a recommendation for a **medical exam** should be made. Available records should be reviewed, and if they are inadequate in light of the presenting problems and symptoms, outside recommendations to the parents such as a neurological examination or opthomological examination should be considered.

Hearing Test.   A **hearing test** should be one of the first prereferral procedures recommended if one has not been administered to the student within the last six months to one year. Be aware of inconsistencies in test patterns from year to year that might indicate a chronic pattern. Some symptoms that might indicate the need for an updated audiological examination are when the child

- Turns head when listening
- Asks you to repeat frequently
- Consistently misinterprets what he or she hears
- Does not respond to auditory stimuli
- Slurs speech, speaks in a monotone voice, or articulates poorly

Vision Test.   As with the hearing exam, this evaluation should be one of the first prereferral procedures recommended. Again, if a **vision test** has not been done within six months to a year, then request this immediately. Possible symptoms that may necessitate such an evaluation are when the child

- Turns head when looking at board or objects
- Squints excessively
- Rubs eyes frequently
- Holds books and materials close to the face or at unusual angles
- Suffers frequent headaches
- Avoids close work of any type

- Covers an eye when reading
- Consistently loses place when reading

Classroom Management Techniques. There are times when the real issue may not be the child but rather in the teaching style of the classroom teacher, that is, having unrealistic expectations, being critical, or being overly demanding. In such instances, help for the teacher can come in the form of classroom management techniques. **Classroom management techniques** are strategies developed to help handle various problems and conflicts within a classroom. An administrator, psychologist, or any realistic and diplomatic team member who feels comfortable with this type of situation may offer these practical suggestions to the teacher. There are many classroom techniques and modifications that should be tried before taking more serious steps. These include the following:

- Display daily class schedule with times so that the student has a structured idea of the day ahead
- Change seating
- Seat the student with good role models
- Use peer tutors when appropriate
- Limit number of directions
- Simplify complex directions
- Give verbal as well as written directions
- Provide extra work time
- Shorten assignments
- Modify curriculum but change content only as a last resort
- Identify and address preferred learning styles
- Provide manipulative materials
- Provide examples of what is expected
- Use color coding of materials to foster organizational skills
- Develop a homework plan with parental support
- Develop a behavior modification plan if necessary
- Uses lots of positive reinforcement
- Use technology as an aid

Help Classes. Certain children may require only a temporary support system to get them through a difficult academic period. Some schools provide extra nonspecial-education services, such as **help classes** that may be held during lunch or before or after school. These classes can clarify academic confusion that could lead to more serious problems if not addressed.

Remedial Reading or Math Services. **Remedial reading or math services** are academic programs within a school designed to help the student with reading or math by going slower in the curriculum or placing him or her with a smaller number of students in the classroom for extra attention. These services can be recommended when reading or math is the specific area of concern. Remedial reading and math classes are not special education services and can be instituted as a means of alleviating a child's academic problems.

In-School Counseling.   **In-school counseling** is normally done by the school psychologist, social worker, or guidance counselor, and is designed to help the child deal with the issues that are currently problematic for him or her. Sometimes, a child may experience a situational or adjustment disorder (a temporary emotional pattern that may occur at any time in a person's life without a prior history of problems) resulting from separation, divorce, health issues, newness to school district, and so on. When this pattern occurs, it may temporarily interfere with the child's ability to concentrate, remember, or attend to tasks. Consequently, a drop in academic performance can occur. If such patterns occur, the school psychologist may want to institute in-school counseling with the parent's involvement and permission. This recommendation should be instituted only to address issues that can be resolved in a relatively short period of time. More serious issues may have to be referred to outside agencies or professionals for longer treatment.

Progress Reports.   A **progress report** is a synopsis of the child's work and behavior in the classroom sent home to the parents in order to keep them updated on the child's strengths and weaknesses over a period of time (e.g., every day, each week, biweekly, or once a month). Sometimes, a child who has fallen behind academically will "hide" from the real issues by avoiding reality. Daily progress reports for a week or two at first and then weekly reports may provide the child with the kinds of immediate gratification and positive feedback necessary to get back on track. They offer the child a greater sense of hope and control in getting back to a more normal academic pattern.

Disciplinary Action.   This recommendation is usually made when the child in question needs a structured boundary set involving inappropriate behavior. If a child demonstrates a pattern of inappropriate behavior, **disciplinary action** is usually used in conjunction with other recommendations because such patterned behavior may be symptomatic of a more serious problem. The appropriate disciplinary actions necessary should be discussed with the school psychologist, and how it should be implemented must be carefully considered before it begins.

Change of Program.   A **change of program** involves examining the child's program and making adjustments to his or her schedule based on the presenting problem. This recommendation usually occurs when a student has been placed in a course that is not suited to his or her ability or needs. If a student is failing in an advanced class, then the student's program should be changed to include more modified classes.

Consolidation of Program.   There are times when reducing a student's course load is necessary. **Consolidation of a program** involves taking the student's program and modifying it so that the workload is decreased. If a child is "drowning in school," then that child's available energy level may be extremely limited. In such cases, you may find that he or she is failing many courses. Temporarily consolidating or condensing the program allows for the possibility of salvaging some courses, because the student's available energy will not have to be spread so thin.

Referral to Child Protective Services.   Child Protective Services is a state agency designed to investigate cases of possible neglect and abuse of children. A **referral to**

Child Protective Services (CPS) is mandated for all educators if there is a suspicion of abuse or neglect. The school official or staff does not have a choice as to referral if such a suspicion is present. Referrals to this service may result from physical, sexual, or emotional abuse and/or educational, environmental, or medical neglect.

Informal Assessment Techniques.   As discussed in Chapter 3, other prereferral intervention strategies may be utilized. See Chapter 3 for more details on the various forms of informal assessment.

Screening.   If the CST feels the prereferral strategies are not working after a realistic period of time, team members may recommend a **screening** for a suspected disability. The source of this suspicion may emanate from the team, a staff member, or the parent. Keep in mind that the team does not have to diagnose a specific disability, but only suspect one in order to begin the referral for a more comprehensive assessment to a multidisciplinary team. This team (see Chapter 8) will administer a comprehensive evaluation conducted by a multitude of professionals to decrease the possibility of subjective and discriminatory assessment.

Informal Screening Tools.   Informal screening tools may include a variety of tests and procedures that can be sensitive enough to allow team members the opportunity to determine the presence of a suspected disability. Other than the very obvious cases involving attempted suicide, neglect, abuse and so on, which must be dealt with immediately, a child with a suspected disability is defined as a child who exhibits one or more of the following symptoms for more than six months:

- Serious inconsistencies in intellectual, emotional, academic, or social performance
- Inconsistency between ability and achievement and/or ability and classroom performance
- Impairment in one or more life functions, that is, socialization, academic performance, or adaptive behavior

In order to accomplish this screening, team members utilize

- Abbreviated intelligence tests
- Selected subtests or screening versions of individual achievement tests
- Informal reading inventories
- Checklists
- Observation scales
- Rating scales
- Prereferral data already discussed

If the screening determines the possibility of a suspected disability, then the CST must make a more formal referral to the district's multidisciplinary team for a comprehensive assessment. This process is discussed in Chapter 8.

CONCLUSION

Although all of these suggestions need not be tried before an evaluation is attempted, parents may be more willing to sign a release for evaluation if they see that other channels have been used and proven unsuccessful. The goal of prereferral procedures is to make sure that all avenues have been explored before the time is invested in doing a comprehensive assessment on a child. If a few modifications can be made to a child's school day that can alleviate the problem at hand, this will benefit all involved.

VOCABULARY

Change of Program: Examining the child's program and making schedule adjustments based on the presenting problem.

Classroom Management Techniques: Strategies created to help handle various problems and conflicts within a classroom.

Consolidation of a Program: Taking the student's program and modifying it so that the workload is decreased.

Curriculum-Based Assessment: An assessment of a student based on performance on the curriculum rather than using scores on standardized, norm-referenced measures.

Disciplinary Action: A prereferral procedure whereby a child is placed in a structured boundary set because of inappropriate behavior.

Hearing Test: A prereferral procedure used to determine whether an auditory problem is causing or contributing to a student's problems.

Help Classes: Classes that provide a student with extra help in a given subject outside of the normal school day.

In-School Counseling: Counseling, normally by the psychologist or social worker, designed to help the child deal with the issues that are currently problematic for him or her.

Medical Exam: A prereferral procedure used to determine whether a medical condition is causing or contributing to a student's problems.

Parent Interview: Meeting with the parent to discuss what motivates this child along with finding out any family information that may be contributing to the child's behavior in the classroom (e.g., recent separation, death of a loved one).

Prereferral Strategies: Many school systems recommend or require that, before an individualized evaluation of a student is conducted for possible placement in special education, the teacher meet with an assistance team to discuss the nature of the problem and what possible modifications to instruction or the classroom might be made. These procedures are known as prereferral strategies.

Progress Report: A synopsis of the child's work and behavior in the classroom sent home to the parents to keep them updated on the child's strengths and weaknesses over a period of time.

Referral to Child Protective Services: A state agency designed to investigate cases of possible neglect and abuse of children.

Remedial Reading or Math Services: Academic programs within a school designed to help students with math or reading by going slower in the curriculum or placing them with a smaller number of students in the classroom for extra attention.

Screening: A prereferral strategy to determine whether a comprehensive assessment for special education is warranted.

Team Meeting with Teachers: A prereferral procedure whereby teachers who have worked with the student or who have ideas about this student come together to determine what helpful strategies can be implemented.

Vision Test: A prereferral procedure used to determine whether a visual problem is causing or contributing to a student's problems.

CHAPTER EIGHT

THE MULTIDISCIPLINARY TEAM AND PARENTAL PARTICIPATION IN THE ASSESSMENT PROCESS

KEY TERMS

Academic History
Association or Organization
Audiologist
Behavioral Consultant
Classroom Teacher
Developmental History
Educational Diagnostician
Family History
Formal Referral
Guidance Counselor
Identifying Data and Family Information

Occupational Therapist
Parent Intake
Perception
Physical Therapist
School Nurse
School Psychologist
School Social Worker
Social History
Special Education Teacher
Speech/Language Clinician

CHAPTER OBJECTIVES

This chapter focuses on the multidisciplinary team (MDT) and parental participation in the assessment process. After reading this chapter, you should be able to understand the following:

- Multidisciplinary team (MDT)
- Purpose of the MDT
- Membership of the MDT
- Formal referral for a suspected disability
- Contents of a referral to the MDT
- Initial referral to the MDT from the school staff
- Initial referral to the MDT from a parent/guardian

- Assessment plans, consent for evaluation
- Assessment options of the MDT
- Parental participation in the assessment process
- How to conduct parent intakes and interviews
- Parent intakes
- Confidentiality

PURPOSE OF THE MULTIDISCIPLINARY TEAM

As a result of the IDEA 2004 regulations, schools are moving toward a more global approach for the identification of students with suspected disabilities through the development of a district-based team. This team may be referred to as the *Multidisciplinary Team (MDT), Multifactor Team (MFT),* or *School-Based Support Team (SBST),* depending on the state in which the student resides. Throughout this text, we refer to this team as the multidisciplinary team. This team usually comes into operation when the local school-based team (Child Study Team) has conducted a screening and suspects a disability. Once that is determined, then the MDT takes over. This team is mandated by IDEA 2004 so that the child and parents are guaranteed that any comprehensive evaluation be conducted by different professionals to decrease the possibility of subjective and discriminatory assessment.

The role of the MDT is to work as a single unit in determining the possible cause, contributing behavioral factors, educational status, prognosis (outcome), and recommendations for a student with a suspected disability. The MDT's major objective is to bring together many disciplines and professional perspectives to help work on a case so that a single person is not required to determine and assimilate all of the factors that affect a particular child. The MDT is responsible for gathering all the necessary information on a child in order to determine the most effective and practical direction for his or her education. In many states, the MDT's findings are then reviewed by another committee (sometimes referred to as the Eligibility Committee, IEP Committee, or Committee on Special Education). Its role is to determine whether the findings of the MDT fall within the guidelines for classification as having an exceptionality and requiring special education services (more on the process of eligibility in Chapter 18). In accomplishing this task, the team members employ several types of assessment and collect data from many sources.

To further comply with IDEA 2004, each local agency must ensure that (IDEA 2004, sec 614 et seq):

a) Assessment materials and other evaluation materials are selected and administered so as not to be discriminatory on a racial or cultural basis.
b) Assessment materials are provided and administered in the language and form most likely to yield accurate information on what the child knows and can do academically, developmentally, and functionally, unless it is not feasible to so provide or administer.

   c) Tests and other assessment materials have been validated for the specific purpose for which they are used.

   d) Tests and other assessment materials are administered by trained personnel in conformance with the instructions provided by the producer of the tests and other assessment materials, except that individually administered tests of intellectual or emotional functioning shall be administered by a credentialed school psychologist.

   e) Tests and other assessment materials are selected and administered to best ensure that when a test administered to a pupil with impaired sensory, manual, or speaking skills produces test results that accurately reflect the pupil's aptitude, achievement level, or any other factors the test purports to measure and not the pupil's impaired sensory, manual, or speaking skills unless those skills are the factors the test purports to measure.

   f) No single procedure is used as the sole criterion for determining an appropriate educational program for an individual with exceptional needs.

   g) The pupil is assessed in all areas related to the suspected disability including, where appropriate, health and development, vision, including low vision, hearing, motor abilities, language function, general ability, academic performance, self-help, orientation and mobility skills, career and vocational abilities and interests, and social and emotional status. A developmental history is obtained, when appropriate. For pupils with residual vision, a low vision assessment shall be provided.

   h) Persons knowledgeable of that disability shall conduct the assessment of a pupil, including the assessment of a pupil with a suspected low incidence disability. For instance, if the screening reveals a suspected learning disability then a learning disabilities specialist becomes part of the team. If the child is suspected of having a hearing impairment then an audiologist becomes a member of the team. Special attention shall be given to the unique educational needs, including, but not limited to, skills and the need for specialized services, materials, and equipment.

MEMBERSHIP OF THE MULTIDISCIPLINARY TEAM

Although specific state regulations may differ on the membership of the MDT, the members are usually drawn from individuals and professionals within the school and community. Depending on the school in which you work, your role may be different than another professional with the same title in a different school (i.e., your roles and responsibilities as an educational evaluator in one school may be different than those of one in another school). Listed here are the general roles and responsibilities of members of a multidisciplinary team:

- **School psychologist:** The role of the school psychologist on the MDT usually involves the administration of individual intelligence tests, projective tests, personality inventories, and the observation of the student in a variety of settings.
- **School nurse:** The role of the school nurse is to review all medical records, screen for vision and hearing, consult with outside physicians, and make referrals to outside physicians, if necessary.

- **Classroom teacher:** The classroom teacher's role is to work with the local school-based Child Study Team to implement prereferral strategies, and plan and implement, along with the special education team, classroom strategies that create an appropriate working environment for the student.
- **School social worker:** The social worker's role on the MDT is to gather and provide information concerning the family system. This may be accomplished through interviews, observations, conferences, and so forth.
- **Special education teacher:** The roles of the special education teacher include consulting with parents and classroom teachers about prereferral recommendations, administering educational and perceptual tests, observing the student in a variety of settings, screening students with suspected disabilities, writing IEPs, including goals and objectives with the team (based on assessed needs), and recommending intervention strategies to teachers and parents.
- **Educational diagnostician:** This professional administers a series of evaluations including norm-referenced and criterion-referenced tests, observes the student in a variety of settings, and makes educational recommendations that get applied to the IEP as goals and objectives.
- **Physical therapist:** The physical therapist is called upon to evaluate a child who may be experiencing problems in gross-motor functioning, living and self-help skills, and vocational skills necessary for the student to be able to function in certain settings. This professional may be used to screen, evaluate, provide direct services, or consult with the teacher, parent, or school.
- **Behavioral consultant:** A behavioral consultant works closely with the team in providing direct services or consultation on issues involving behavioral and classroom management techniques and programs.
- **Speech/language clinician:** This professional is involved in screening for speech and language developmental problems, provides a full evaluation on a suspected language disability, provides direct services, and consults with staff and parents.
- **Audiologist:** This professional is called on to evaluate a student's hearing for possible impairments and, as a result of the findings, may refer the student for medical consultation or treatment. The audiologist may also assist in helping students and parents obtain equipment (i.e., hearing aids) that may affect the child's ability to function in school.
- **Occupational therapist:** The occupational therapist is called on to evaluate a child who may be experiencing problems in fine-motor skills and living and self-help skills. This professional may be used to screen, evaluate, provide direct services, consult with the teacher, parent, or school and assist in obtaining the appropriate assistive technology or equipment for the student.
- **Guidance counselor:** This individual may be involved in providing aptitude test information, providing counseling services, working with the team on consolidating, changing, or developing a student's class schedule, and assisting the Child Study Team in developing prereferral strategies.
- **Parents:** The parent plays an extremely important role on the MDT in providing input for the IEP, working closely with members of the team, and carrying

out, assisting, or initiating academic or management programs within the child's home (parents' roles will be discussed in more detail later in this chapter).

FORMAL REFERRAL FOR A SUSPECTED DISABILITY

Once the CST determines that a suspected disability may exist, a **formal referral** is made to the multidisciplinary team. A formal referral is nothing more than a form starting the special education process. A referral for evaluation and possible special education services is initiated by a written request. However, you should understand that people other than the CST have the right under due process to initiate a formal referral for a child with a suspected disability. Depending on state regulations, these could include

- The child's parent, advocate, person in parental relationship, or legal guardian
- A classroom teacher
- Any professional staff member of the public or private school district
- A judicial officer—a representative of the court
- A student on his or her own behalf if he or she is 18 years of age or older or an *emancipated minor* (a person under the age of 18 who has been given certain adult rights by the court)
- The Chief School Officer of the State or his or her designee responsible for welfare, education, or health of children

The Contents of a Referral to the MDT

This signed formal referral is usually sent to the MDT so that the team can begin the process of formal assessment. At the same time, the referral is sent to the chairperson of the eligibility committee (discussed in Chapter 18) indicating that a child with a suspected disability will be reviewed by the committee in the near future. This referral should be in written form and be dated. This makes it official and gives a start date because time lines are involved. A referral from the CST should include a great deal of information to assist the MDT in its assessment. Further documentation as to why a possible disability exists, descriptions of attempts to remediate the child's behaviors (prereferral strategies), or performance prior to the referral should all be included. All of these are important, especially the attempts that have been made prior to the referral. Remember, the district should try to keep the child in the mainstream, and the documentation it provides at this step in the process should ensure that it has done everything possible before beginning the referral process (prereferral options previously discussed in Chapter 7).

Referrals from the CST for a formal assessment are forwarded to the MDT. If the referral is not from the parents, the district must inform the parents in writing immediately that their child has been referred for assessment of a suspected disability. The referral states that the child may have a disability that adversely affects educational performance. An important point to remember is that a referral to the MDT does not necessarily mean that the child has a disability. It signals that the child is having learning and/or behavioral difficulties, and that there is a concern that the problem may be due to a disability.

Initial Referral to the MDT from the School Staff

As previously stated, once the CST has determined that a disability may exist, the team must alert the chairperson of the MDT that a child with a suspected disability is being referred for review. This, in all actuality, begins the special education process. At this time, the team may fill out a form like the one in Figure 8.1.

Initial Referral to the MDT from a Parent/Guardian

An Initial Referral to the MDT from the School Staff alerts the chairperson of the MDT that the local school has made every attempt to resolve the student's difficulties prior to the formal referral. The form also informs the chairperson that the parent's rights have been followed. In other cases, a student's parent or guardian may initiate a referral to the MDT for suspicion of a disability under special education laws or Section 504 of the Rehabilitation Act. A fully completed referral form and any relevant information is sent to the appropriate special education administrator. Usually, upon the receipt of the parent's referral, the chairperson of the MDT will send to the parent/guardian an assessment plan (discussed next) and the parent's due process rights statement. The building principal is also notified of the referral. If for some reason the possibility of a suspected disability of a child is brought to the school's attention *by the parent*, then the form presented in Figure 8.2 is filled out and forwarded.

Important Point: If a release for testing (assessment plan) is not secured at a separate meeting, the chairperson of the MDT will mail one to the parent along with the letter indicating that a referral has been made. However, no formal evaluations may begin until the district has received signed permission from the parent or guardian.

ASSESSMENT PLANS— CONSENT FOR EVALUATION

Prior to any assessment, the MDT must secure an agreement by the parent to allow the members of the team to evaluate the child. This release is part of the assessment plan and the following characteristics should be included:

- It is in a language easily understood by the general public.
- It is provided in the primary language of the parent or other mode of communication used by the parent, unless to do so is clearly not feasible.
- It explains the types of assessments to be conducted.
- It states that no individualized educational program (IEP) will result from the assessment without the consent of the parent.

FIGURE 8.1   Initial Referral to the MDT from the School Staff

INITIAL REFERRAL TO THE MDT FROM THE SCHOOL STAFF

To: Chairperson of the MDT

From: Bill Wethers   **School:** Harrison   **Date:** 5/15/05

Name/Title: Chairperson of the Child Study Team

The following student is being referred to the MDT for suspicion of a disability:

Student Name: Rosa Carlarzo   **Sex:** F   **Grade:** 5

Ethnicity: Hispanic

Parent/Guardian Name: Livia/Carlos

Address: 12 High Court

City: Birchwood Glen   **State:** NY   **Zip:** 15789

Telephone: (914) 555-9867   **Date of Birth:** 3/2/95

Current Program Placement: Regular mainstream

Teacher (Elem):   Mrs. Buglia

Reasons for Referral: Describe the specific reason and/or needs that indicate the suspicion of a disability. Specify reason why referral is considered appropriate and necessary.

> Rosa is being referred for a formal assessment as the result of a suspected learning disability. The school has attempted a variety of prereferral strategies but has been unable to change Rosa's level of impaired performance. Rosa exhibits severe problems in processing information, retaining information, and expressing her ideas on paper. Although she is a bright girl, and articulates appropriately, her written expression is well below average. Rosa also needs a great deal of attention, encouragement, and monitoring in the classroom. She is not a self-starter and tends to avoid academic tasks.

Describe recent attempts to remediate the pupil's performance prior to referral, including regular education interventions such as remedial reading and math, teaching modifications, behavior modifications, speech improvement, parent conferences, and the like and the results of those interventions.

> The referral is considered necessary at this time because Rosa continues to do poorly in school despite classroom modifications, parent training and conferences, portfolio assessment, observation, remedial reading and math intervention, and changes in teaching strategies and management. The results of these intervention strategies have been unsuccessful and have even added to Rosa's sense of frustration and lack of confidence.

Do you have a signed Parent Assessment Plan?   yes _X_ no ____
(If yes, send copy attached.)

Is there an attendance problem?   yes _X_ no ____

Language spoken at home?   __English__

Did student repeat a grade?   yes ____ no _X_   **If yes, when?** _____

Is an interpreter needed?   yes ____ no _X_   **Deaf:** _____

Is a bilingual assessment needed?   yes ____ no _X_   **If yes, what language?** _____

(continued)

FIGURE 8.1 Continued

Is student eligible to receive ESL (English as a Second Language) services?
yes _____   no __X__

If yes, how many years receiving ESL services? __NA__ If yes, determine how student's educational, cultural, and experiential background were considered to determine if these factors are contributing to the student's learning or behavior problems.

TEST SCORES WITHIN LAST YEAR
(e.g., Standardized Achievement, Regents Competency, etc.)

TEST NAME	AREA MEASURED	PERCENTILE
1. Wechsler Ind. Achievement Test Screening	Basic Reading	22
2. Wechsler Ind. Achievement Test Screening	Reading Comp.	18
3. Wechsler Ind. Achievement Test Screening	Numerical Operations	12
4. Wechsler Ind. Achievement Test Screening	Oral Expression	67
5. Wechsler Ind. Achievement Test Screening	Written Expression	11
6. KBIT-Kauffman Brief Intelligence Test	Intelligence	67

Has school staff informed parent/guardian of referral to MDT?

yes __X__ no _____ By whom? School psychologist

What was the reaction of the parent/guardian to the referral? __Positive__

To Be Completed by School Nurse—Medical Report Summary

Any medication? yes _____ no __X__ If yes, specify: _____

Health Problems? yes _____ no __X__ If yes, specify: _____

Scoliosis screening: Positive _____ Negative __X__

Date of Last Physical: __8/00__ Vision results: __Normal__

Hearing results: __Normal__

Relevant medical information: __None__

Nurse/teacher signature: _____

Principal's signature: _____

To Be Completed by the Appropriate Administrator

Date received: _____ Signature: _____
Chairperson: _____
Date notice and consent sent to parent/guardian: _____
Parent consent for initial evaluation received: _____
Date agreement to withdraw referral received: _____
Projected eligibility meeting date: _____
If eligible, projected date of implementation of services: _____
Projected eligibility board of education meeting date: _____

FIGURE 8.2   Initial Referral to the MDT from a Parent/Guardian

INITIAL REFERRAL TO THE MDT FROM A PARENT/GUARDIAN

To: Chairperson of the MDT

Re: Brian Leader   **Date of Birth:**   7/12/92

I am writing to refer my child Brian, age 13, for consideration of an educational disability under special education laws and/or under Section 504 of the Vocational Rehabilitation Act (mental or physical impairment that substantially limits one of life's functions). I am concerned about my child's educational difficulties in the following areas:

severe and historic reading and writing difficulties.

Parent Name/Signature: _____

Address: 20 Carbondale Rd

Beverly Hills, CA 90210

Telephone No: (314) 555-0507

Date of Referral: 11/9/05

School: Wilson Middle School   **Grade:**   8

Please attach any relevant evaluations or documents or information that support the referral.

Date received by MDT chairperson: _____

- It states that no assessment shall be conducted unless the written consent of the parent is obtained prior to the assessment. The parent shall have at least 15 days (may vary from state to state) from the receipt of the proposed assessment plan to arrive at a decision. Assessment may begin immediately upon receipt of the consent.
- The copy of the notice of parent rights shall include the right to record electronically the proceedings of the eligibility committee meetings.
- The assessment shall be conducted by persons competent to perform the assessment, as determined by the school district, county office, or special education local plan area.
- Any psychological assessment of pupils must be conducted by a qualified school psychologist.
- Any health assessment of pupils shall be conducted only by a credentialed school nurse or physician who is trained and prepared to assess cultural and ethnic factors appropriate to the pupil being assessed.

ASSESSMENT OPTIONS OF THE MULTIDISCIPLINARY TEAM

Only when the parents have been informed of their rights, a release has been obtained, and the assessment plan has been signed, can assessment begin. The MDT has several evaluation options from which to choose. The evaluations most often considered by the MDT to assess a child with a suspected disability include the following:

Academic Achievement Evaluation

An academic achievement evaluation (see Chapter 9) is frequently recommended when a child's academic skill levels (reading, writing, math, and spelling) are unknown or inconsistent. The evaluation will determine strengths and weaknesses in the child's academic performance.

THE PRIMARY OBJECTIVES OF AN ACADEMIC ACHIEVEMENT EVALUATION ARE TO:

- Help determine the child's stronger and weaker academic skill areas. The evaluation may give useful information when making practical recommendations to teachers about academic expectations, areas in need of remediation, and how to best present information to assist the child's ability to learn.
- Help the teacher gear the materials to the learning capacity of the individual child. A child reading two years below grade level may require modified textbooks or greater explanations prior to a lesson.
- Develop a learning profile that can help the classroom teacher understand the best way to present information to the child and therefore increase the child's chances of success.
- Help determine whether the child's academic skills are suitable for a regular class or so severe that a more restrictive educational setting is required (an educational setting or situation best suited to the present needs of the student other than a full-time regular class placement; e.g., resource room, self-contained class, special school, etc.).
- Whatever achievement battery the special educator chooses, it should be one that covers enough skill areas to make an adequate diagnosis of academic strengths and weaknesses.

SOME SYMPTOMS THAT MIGHT SUGGEST THE RECOMMENDATION FOR SUCH AN EVALUATION ARE:

- Consistently low test scores on group achievement tests
- Indications of delayed processing when faced with academic skills
- Labored handwriting after grade three
- Poor word recall
- Poor decoding (word attack) skills
- Discrepancy between achievement and ability
- Consistently low achievement despite remediation

In most cases of a suspected disability, the academic achievement evaluation is always a part of the formal evaluation.

Intellectual and Psychological Evaluation

This recommendation is appropriate when the child's intellectual ability is unknown or when there is a question about his or her inability to learn (see Chapters 9 and 10). It is useful when the CST suspects a potential learning, emotional, or intellectual problem. The psychological evaluation can rule out or rule in emotionality as a primary cause of a child's problem. Ruling this factor out is necessary before a diagnosis of learning disabled (LD) can be made.

OBJECTIVES OF A PSYCHOLOGICAL EVALUATION ARE TO:

- Determine the child's present overall levels of intellectual ability
- Determine the child's present verbal intellectual ability
- Determine the child's nonlanguage intellectual ability
- Explore indications of greater potential
- Find possible patterns involving learning style, that is, verbal comprehension, concentration, and the like
- Ascertain possible influences of tension and anxiety on testing results
- Determine the child's intellectual ability to deal with present grade-level academic demands
- Explore the influence of intellectual ability as a contributing factor to a child's past and present school difficulties, that is, limited intellectual ability found in retardation

SOME SYMPTOMS THAT MIGHT SIGNAL
THE NEED FOR SUCH AN EVALUATION ARE:

- High levels of tension and anxiety exhibited in behavior
- Aggressive behavior
- Lack of motivation or indications of low energy levels
- Patterns of denial
- Oppositional behavior
- Despondency
- Inconsistent academic performance, ranging from very low to very high
- History of inappropriate judgment
- Lack of impulse control
- Extreme and consistent attention-seeking behavior
- Pattern of provocative behavior

As with the academic assessment, the psychological evaluation is a normal part of a referral for a suspected disability.

Perceptual Evaluation

A perceptual evaluation (see Chapter 12) is suggested when the team suspects discrepancies in the child's ability to receive and process information. This assessment may focus on a number of perceptual areas including:

- **Auditory modality:** The delivery of information through sound
- **Visual modality:** The delivery of information through sight
- **Tactile modality:** The delivery of information through touching
- **Kinesthetic modality:** The delivery of information through movement
- **Reception:** The initial receiving of information
- **Perception:** The initial organization of information
- **Association or organization:** Relating new information to other information and giving meaning to the information received
- **Memory:** The storage or retrieval process that facilitates the associational process to give meaning to information or help in relating new concepts to other information that might have already been learned
- **Expression:** The output of information through vocal, motoric, or written responses

THE PRIMARY OBJECTIVES OF THE PERCEPTUAL ASSESSMENT ARE TO:

- Help determine the child's stronger and weaker modality for learning. Some children are visual learners, some are auditory, and some learn well through any form of input. However, if a child is a strong visual learner in a class in which the teacher relies on auditory lectures, then it is possible that his or her ability to process information may be hampered. The evaluation may give useful information for making practical recommendations to teachers about how to best present information to assist the child's ability to learn.
- Help determine a child's stronger and weaker process areas. A child having problems in memory and expression will very quickly fall behind the rest of his or her class. The longer these processing difficulties continue, the greater the chance for secondary emotional problems (emotional problems resulting from continued frustration with the ability to learn) to develop.
- Develop a learning profile that can help the classroom teacher understand the best way to present information to the child, thereby increasing the child's chances of success.
- Help determine whether the child's learning process deficits are suitable for a regular class or so severe that a more restrictive educational setting is required (an educational setting or situation best suited to the present needs of the student other than a full-time regular class placement; e.g., resource room, self-contained class, special school).

Oral Language Evaluation

This recommendation (see Chapter 13) usually occurs when the child is experiencing significant delays in speech or language development, problems in articulation, or problems in receptive or expressive language.

SOME SYMPTOMS THAT MIGHT WARRANT SUCH AN EVALUATION ARE:

- Difficulty pronouncing words through grade three
- Immature or delayed speech patterns
- Difficulty labeling thoughts or objects
- Difficulty putting thoughts into words

Occupational Therapy Evaluation

This evaluation (see Chapter 15) may be considered by the team when the child is exhibiting problems involving fine-motor upper-body functions. Examples of these would include abnormal movement patterns, sensory problems (sensitive to sound, visual changes, etc.), hardship with daily living activities, organizational problems, attention span difficulties, equipment analysis, and interpersonal problems.

Physical Therapy Evaluation

This evaluation (see Chapter 15) may be considered by the team when the child is exhibiting problems with lower body and gross motor areas. Examples of these might be range of motion difficulties; architectural barrier problems; problems in posture, gait, and endurance; and joint abnormalities.

PARENTAL PARTICIPATION IN THE ASSESSMENT PROCESS

Once the CST has made a formal referral for assessment to the MDT for a child with a suspected disability, the parents need to be called in to provide pertinent background information that will assist in the assessment process. The participation of the parents is crucial to this process.

While designing, conducting, interpreting, and paying for the assessment are the school system's responsibilities, parents have an important part to play before, during, and after the evaluation. There is a range of ways in which parents may involve themselves in the assessment of their child. The extent of their involvement, however, is a personal decision and will vary from family to family.

Waterman (1994) lists parental options, responsibilities, and expectations prior to an assessment for a suspected disability:

- Parents may initiate the assessment process by requesting that the school system evaluate their child for the presence of a disability and the need for special education.
- Parents must be notified by the school, and give their consent, before any initial evaluation of the child may be conducted.
- Parents may wish to talk with the professional responsible for conducting the evaluation to find out what the evaluation will involve.
- Parents may find it very useful to become informed about assessment issues in general and any specific issues relevant to their child (e.g., assessment of minority children, use of specific tests or assessment techniques with a specific disability).

- Parents should advocate for a comprehensive evaluation of their child—one that investigates all skill areas apparently affected by the suspected disability and that uses multiple means of collecting information (e.g., observations, interviews, alternative approaches).
- Parents may suggest specific questions to the MDT they would like to see addressed through the assessment.
- Parents should inform the MDT of any accommodations the child will need (e.g., removing time limits from tests, conducting interviews/testing in the child's native language, adapting testing environment to child's specific physical and other needs).
- Parents should inform the MDT if they themselves need an interpreter or other accommodations during any of their discussions with the school.
- Parents may prepare their child for the assessment process, explaining what will happen and, where necessary, reducing the child's anxiety. It may help the child to know that he or she will not be receiving a "grade" on the tests.
- Parents need to share with the MDT their insights into the child's background (developmental, medical, and academic) and past and present school performance.
- Parents may wish to share with the MDT any prior school records, reports, tests, or evaluation information available on their child.
- Parents may need to share information about cultural differences that can illuminate the MDT's understanding of the student.
- Parents need to make every effort to attend interviews the MDT may set up with them and provide information about their child.

How to Conduct Parent Intakes and Interviews

There may be times when a member of the MDT is called on to do a **parent intake,** a gathering of pertinent information from a parent. A thorough parent intake is a crucial part of the assessment process. The parents can offer information on a child that is not seen by teachers or other staff members, and may have profound effects on the outcome of the assessment. This may involve interviewing the parent to obtain a complete **family history.** In some cases, this part of the assessment process may be difficult to obtain because of a number of variables—parents' work restrictions, inability to obtain child care for younger siblings, resistance, or apathy.

In many schools, the psychologist or social worker will normally meet with the parents to collect this information. However, it is important that all members of the MDT understand the process in case anyone is asked to do the interview. When the interview is arranged, there are several things to recognize and consider before a parent meeting.

WHEN CONDUCTING A PARENT INTAKE, YOU SHOULD TRY TO DO THE FOLLOWING:

- Help the parent(s) feel comfortable and at ease by setting up a receptive environment.
- If possible, hold meetings in a pleasant setting, around a table rather than behind a desk. All effort to ease tension should be made, such as offering simple

refreshments or encouraging parents to take brief notes so they feel more in control of your information.

- Never view parents as adversaries even if they are angry or hostile. Any anger or hostility that the parents may exhibit could be a defense because they may not be aware of what the evaluator will be asking or because they may have experienced negative school meetings over the years. Because this may be an opportunity for parents to "vent," evaluators should listen and strive to understand their concerns without being defensive.
- Inform parents every step of the way as to the purpose of meetings and the steps involved in the assessment process. Parents need to be reassured that no recommendation will be made or implemented without their input and permission.
- Inform parents of the types, names, and purposes of the evaluation instruments chosen by the MDT. Parents need to be reassured that the evaluation is looking for a way to help the child.
- Reassure parents about the confidentiality of information gathered about their child. They should know which individuals on the team will be seeing the information and the purpose for their review of the facts. Evaluators should also make every effort to make parents feel free to call with any questions or concerns they may have.

Goals of a Parent Intake

A parent intake should be done with sensitivity and diplomacy. Keep in mind that although some questions may not be of a concern to most parents, they may be perceived as intrusive by others. The questions should be specific enough to help in the diagnosis of the problem, but not so specific as to place the parent in a vulnerable and defensive position. There are four main areas usually covered in a parent intake:

1. **Identifying data and family information:** Confirmation of names, addresses, phone numbers, and dates of birth; siblings' names, ages, and dates of birth; parents' occupations; other adults residing within the home; marital status of parents; and so on.
2. **Developmental history:** Length of delivery; type of delivery; complications if any; approximate ages of critical stages, that is, walking and talking; hospital stays; illnesses other than normal ones; sleeping habits; eating habits; high fevers; last eye exam; last hearing exam; falls or injuries; traumatic experiences; medications; and any prior developmental testing.
3. **Academic history:** Number of schools attended, types of schools attended, adjustment to kindergarten, best school years, worst school year, best subject, worst subject, prior teacher reports, prior teacher comments, and homework behavior.
4. **Social history:** The child's groups or organizations; social behavior in a group situation; hobbies, areas of interest, circle of friends, sports activities.

Shown in Figure 8.3 is an example of a parent intake completed by the school social worker. Here, the intake was done with the mother of the child, Mrs. Bali Shah.

FIGURE 8.3 **Example of a Parent Intake Form**

PARENT INTAKE FORM

Identifying Data

Name of Student: Ravi Muhas   **Date of Intake:** 4-10-05

Address: 12 Conner Street, South Hills, NY 11223

Phone: (631) 555-7863   **Date of Birth:** 3/4/96   **Age:** 9-1

Siblings: Brothers: (names and ages) Mohammed age 15

Sisters: (names and ages) Sari age 4

Mother's name: Bali   **Father's name:** Moshi

Mother's occupation: Medical technician

Father's occupation: Accountant

Referred by: Teacher   **Grade:** 4   **School:** Holland Avenue

Developmental History

Length of pregnancy: Full term   **Type of delivery:** Forceps

Complications: Apgar score 7, jaundice at birth

Long hospital stays: None

Falls or injuries: None

Allergies: Early food allergies, none recently

Medication: none at present

Early milestones (i.e., walking, talking, toilet training):

According to parent, Ravi was late in walking and talking in comparison to brother. He was toilet trained at three years of age. Parent added that he seemed to be slower than usual in learning basic concepts.

Traumatic experiences: None

Previous psychological evaluations or treatment (please explain reasons and dates):

None. However, parent indicated that it was suggested by first-grade teacher but the teacher never followed through.

Previous psychiatric hospitalizations: None

Sleep disturbances: Trouble falling asleep; somnambulism (sleepwalking) at age five but lasted only a few weeks; talks a great deal in his sleep lately

Eating disturbances: Picky eater, likes sweets

Last vision and hearing exams and results: Last eye test in school indicated 20/30 vision. Last hearing test in school was inconclusive. Parent has not followed through on nurse's request for an outside evaluation.

Excessively high fevers: No

Childhood illnesses: Normal ones

(continued)

FIGURE 8.3 Continued

Academic History

Nursery school experience: Ravi had difficulty adjusting to nursery school. The teacher considered him very immature and his skills were well below those of his peers. He struggled through the year.

Kindergarten experience (adjustment, comments, etc.): Ravi's difficulties increased. According to the parent, he had problems with reading and social difficulties. His gross- and fine-motor skills were immature.

First grade through sixth grade (teacher's comments, traumatic experiences, strength areas, comments, etc.): According to past teachers, Ravi struggled through the early elementary school years. He was nice and polite and at times tried hard. But in the later grades (2 and 3), his behavior and academics began to falter. Teachers always considered referral but felt he might grow out of it.

Subjects that presented the most difficulty: Reading, math, spelling

Subjects that were the least difficult: Science

Most recent report card grades (if applicable): Ravi has received mostly NEEDS TO IMPROVE on his report card

Social History

Groups or organizations: Tried Boy Scouts but dropped out. Started Little League but became frustrated.

Social involvement as perceived by parent: Inconsistent. He does not seem to reach out to kids, and lately he spends a great deal of time alone.

Hobbies or interests: Baseball cards, science

CONFIDENTIALITY

Information about the child collected through assessment automatically becomes a part of a child's school records. The school district should establish policies regarding confidentiality of information contained in the school record, such as informing the parent and the child (above age 18) of their right to privacy, of who has access to the information, and their right to challenge those records should they be inaccurate, misleading, or otherwise inappropriate. To communicate this information to the parent, handouts describing the district's policy on confidentiality of school records are usually given out on the day of the parent intake.

Because professionals conducting the evaluation are involved in collecting confidential information about a child's health status and educational development, it is very important that verbal as well as written accounts of the child's performance be held in the strictest confidence. Personnel involved in the evaluation should treat their own impressions and concerns about the children they see in a confidential manner and should refrain from talking about children and their performance with people not directly involved with conducting the evaluation. If parents ask how their child is doing during the evaluation, explain that the screening results are meaningful only after all the testing has been completed and their child's performance in all areas is recorded. You should also inform them at this time that they are entitled to receive a complete typed report from the evaluation personnel. The person in charge of evaluation may choose to designate certain persons responsible for answering specific questions about the evaluation instruments, children's responses, and reports.

CONCLUSION

Once written consent of the parent or legal guardian is given for assessment, the MDT will move to the evaluation phase of the assessment process. The next several chapters address the various evaluation instruments available to the MDT in the formal evaluation of a child with a suspected disability.

The MDT plays a critical role in the assessment of a child with a suspected disability. An effective MDT works as an interdisciplinary team to make many of the most important decisions for a child and his or her possible future in special education. By working as a professional team, the members of the MDT have the opportunity to help numerous children. An efficient MDT gathers much data and takes significant time to analyze each child's potential problems. In the end, its recommendations may be the most important ones for children who are in need of services.

It is very important to remember that referring a child for a suspected disability could have tremendous impact on his or her life. Because this is a formal referral for special education, it has legal implications, and therefore, it is extremely important that the MDT follow all procedures, complete all necessary forms, and make sure that it complies with the specific time limits required by the state in which the child resides.

Parents have many rights during the assessment process. Regardless of race, creed, color, socioeconomic status, and so on, all parents are afforded the same legal rights and protections under federal law. The differences arise in the parents' exercising of their rights. Some parents will be heavily involved in their child's assessment for a suspected disability, whereas others will show little, if any, interest—only signing the release form and never participating nor attending any optional sessions for them. Parents need to be aware of their rights. As a special educator, there are many ways to make parents comfortable when you meet with them. Remember, most parents are scared and confused about the entire process. Normally, all they want is for their child to be evaluated so that success, both in and out of school, becomes a future possibility.

VOCABULARY

Academic History: A section of the parent intake form that asks about number of schools attended, types of schools attended, adjustment to kindergarten, best school years, worse school year, best subject, worse subject, prior teacher reports, prior teacher comments, and homework behavior.

Association or Organization: Relating new information to other information and giving meaning to the information received.

Audiologist: This professional will be called upon to evaluate a student's hearing for possible impairments, and as a result of the findings, may refer the student for medical consultation or treatment. The audiologist may also assist in helping students and parents obtain equipment, i.e., hearing aids that may affect the child's ability to function in school.

Behavioral Consultant: A behavioral consultant works closely with the team in providing direct services or consultation on issues involving behavioral and classroom management techniques and programs.

Classroom Teacher: The member of the MDT who works with the CST to implement prereferral strategies and plans and implements any classroom techniques to help the student.

Developmental History: A section of the parent intake form that asks about length of delivery; type of delivery; complications if any; approximate ages of critical stages, that is, walking, talking; hospital stays; illnesses other than normal ones; sleeping habits; eating habits; high fevers; last eye exam; last hearing exam; falls or injuries; traumatic experiences; medications; and any prior testing.

Educational Diagnostician: Administers a series of evaluations including norm-referenced and criterion referenced tests, observes the student in a variety of settings, and makes educational recommendations that get applied to the IEP as goals and objectives.

Family History: A description of the family life situation.

Formal Referral: Once the CST determines that a suspected disability may exist, a formal referral is made. It is nothing more than a form starting the special education process.

Guidance Counselor: This individual may be involved in providing aptitude test information; provide counseling services; work with the team on consolidating, changing, or developing a student's class schedule; and assist the Child Study Team in developing prereferral strategies.

Identifying Data and Family Information: A section of the parent intake form that asks about confirmation of names, addresses, phone numbers, dates of birth; siblings' names, ages, and dates of birth; parents' occupations; other adults residing within the home; marital status of parents.

Occupational Therapist: The occupational therapist is called upon to evaluate a child who may be experiencing problems in fine motors skills and living and self-help skills. This professional may be used to screen; evaluate; provide direct services; consult with the teacher, parent, or school; and assist in obtaining the appropriate assistive technology or equipment for the student.

Parent Intake: A gathering of pertinent information from a parent.

Parents (on the MDT): The parent plays an extremely important role on the MDT in providing input for the IEP, working closely with other members of the team, and carrying out, assisting, or initiating academic or management programs within the child's home.

Perception: The initial organization of information.

Physical Therapist: The physical therapist is called upon to evaluate a child who may be experiencing problems in gross motor functioning, living and self-help skills, and vocational skills necessary for the student to be able to function in certain settings. This professional may be used to screen, evaluate, provide direct services, or consult with the teacher, parent, or school.

School Nurse: The member of the MDT who reviews all medical records, screens for vision and hearing, and handles other medical concerns.

School Psychologist: The member of the MDT who normally administers intelligence tests, projective tests, personality inventories, and does observations of a student in a variety of settings.

School Social Worker: The member of the MDT who gathers and provides information concerning the family system.

Social History: A section of the parent intake form that asks about groups or organizations, social behavior in a group situation, hobbies, areas of interest, circle of friends, sports activities.

Special Education Teacher: The member of the MDT who consults with parents and teachers about prereferral recommendations, administers educational tests, and observes the student in a variety of settings.

Speech/Language Clinician: This professional will be involved in screening for speech and language developmental problems, be asked to provide a full evaluation on a suspected language disability, provide direct services, and consult with staff and parents.

CHAPTER NINE

ASSESSMENT OF ACADEMIC ACHIEVEMENT

KEY TERMS

Achievement Tests
Affective Comprehension
Arithmetic
Composition
Content Operations Applications
Critical Comprehension
Disregard of Punctuation
Gross Mispronunciation
Handwriting
Hesitation
Incorrect Algorithm
Incorrect Number Fact
Incorrect Operation
Inferential Comprehension
Insertion

Inversion
Lexical Comprehension
Listening Comprehension
Literal Comprehension
Manuscript
Mathematics
Miscue
Omissions
Qualitative Miscues
Quantitative Miscues
Random Error
Spelling
Substitution
Word Attack Skills
Word Recognition Tests

CHAPTER OBJECTIVES

This chapter examines all of the various issues surrounding assessment of academic achievement in special education. It focuses on what to expect on tests of reading, spelling, writing, mathematics, and on comprehensive achievement tests available to special educators today. After reading this chapter, you should be able to do the following:

- Understand the purpose of achievement tests
- Understand why individually administered achievement tests are preferred rather than group achievement tests
- Discuss oral reading and miscues associated with it
- Understand the different types of reading comprehension
- Understand word recognition and word attack skills
- Thoroughly evaluate the various reading assessment measures

- Understand written composition and the tests associated with it
- Differentiate between mathematics and arithmetic
- Identify and thoroughly evaluate the various arithmetic tests
- Identify and thoroughly evaluate tests that measure spelling ability
- Identify and thoroughly evaluate the various comprehensive achievement tests

ACHIEVEMENT TESTS

One of the most important parts of assessment in the special education process is to assess academic achievement. **Achievement tests** are tests designed to assess the academic progress of a student. A student's academic achievement skills are reviewed to determine how well he or she is performing in core skill areas such as reading, writing, mathematics, and spelling. The information obtained from the academic battery of tests is important for both the planning and the evaluation of instruction.

It is important to remember that individual achievement tests (rather than group-administered tests) are preferred for assessment of school performance in special education. When doing an evaluation for identification and/or placement in special education, achievement tests always will be individually administered. Individually administered achievement tests are used because they

- Are designed to assess children at all ages and grade levels
- Can assess the most basic skills of spelling, math, and reading
- Allow the examiner to observe a child's test-taking strategies
- Can focus on a specific area of concern
- Can be given in oral, written, or gestural format
- Allow the examiner to observe the child's behavior in a variety of situations

READING

Reading provides a fundamental way for individuals to exchange information. It is also a means by which much of the information presented in school is learned. As a result, reading is the academic area most often associated with academic failure. Reading is a complex process that requires numerous skills for its mastery. Consequently, identifying the skills that lead to success in reading is extremely important.

Numerous reading tests are available for assessing a student's ability to read. Choosing which test to use depends on what area needs to be assessed. Different reading tests measure different reading subskills: oral reading, reading comprehension, word attack skills, and word recognition.

Oral Reading

A number of tests or parts of tests are designed to assess the accuracy and fluency of a student's ability to read aloud. According to Salvia and Ysseldyke (1998), different oral reading tests record different behaviors as errors or miscues in oral reading. Common errors seen on oral reading tests include, but are not limited to, the following:

- **Omissions:** The student skips individual words or groups of words.
- **Insertion:** The student inserts one or more words into the sentence being orally read.
- **Substitution:** The student replaces one or more words in the passage by one or more meaningful words.
- **Gross mispronunciation of a word:** The student's pronunciation of a word bears little resemblance to the proper pronunciation.
- **Hesitation:** The student hesitates for two or more seconds before pronouncing a word.
- **Inversion:** The student changes the order of words appearing in a sentence.
- **Disregard of punctuation:** The student fails to observe punctuation; for example, may not pause for a comma, stop for a period, or indicate a vocal inflection, a question mark, or an exclamation point.

Analyzing Oral Reading Miscues.   An oral reading error is often referred to as a **miscue.** A miscue is the difference between what a reader states is on a page and what is actually on the page. According to Vacca and colleagues (1986), differences between what the reader says and what is printed on the page are not the result of random errors. Instead, these differences are "cued" by the thought and language of the reader, who is attempting to construct what the author is saying. Analysis of miscues can be of two types:

- **Quantitative miscues:** With this type of miscue analyis, the evaluator counts the number of reading errors made by the student.
- **Qualitative miscues:** With this type of miscue analysis, the focus is on the quality of the error rather than the number of different mistakes. It is not based on the problems related to word identification, but rather on the differences between the miscues and the words on the pages. Consequently, some miscues are more significant than others (Vacca et al., 1986).

According to John (1985), a miscue is *significant* if it affects meaning. Miscues are generally significant when

1. The meaning of the sentence or passages is significantly changed or altered, and the student does not correct the miscue.
2. A nonword is used in place of the word in the passage.
3. Only a partial word is substituted for the word or phrase in the passage.
4. A word is pronounced for the student.

Miscues are generally *not significant* when

5. The meaning of the sentence or passage undergoes no change or only minimal change.
6. They are self-corrected by the student.

7. They are acceptable in the student's dialect.
8. They are later read correctly in the same passage.

Through miscue analysis, teachers can determine the extent to which the reader uses and coordinates graphic, sound, syntactic, and semantic information from the text. According to Goodman and Burke (1972), to analyze miscues you should ask at least four crucial questions:

- **Does the miscue change meaning?** If it does not, then it is semantically acceptable within the context of the sentence or passage.
- **Does the miscue sound like language?** If it does, then it is grammatically acceptable within the context. Miscues are grammatically acceptable if they sound like language and serve as the same parts of speech as the text words.
- **Do the miscue and the text word look and sound alike?** Substitution and mispronunciation miscues should be analyzed to determine how similar they are in approximating the graphic and pronunciation features of the text words.
- **Was an attempt made to self-correct the miscue?** Self-corrections are revealing because they demonstrate that the reader is attending to meaning and is aware that the initial miscuing did not make sense.

Reading Comprehension

Reading comprehension assesses a student's ability to understand what he or she is reading. Many children can read, yet do not understand what they have read. Therefore, when doing a reading assessment, it is always necessary to assess not only decoding but also the ability to understand what is being decoded. Diagnostic reading tests often assess six kinds of reading comprehension skills. According to Salvia and Ysseldyke (1998), these are:

- **Literal Comprehension:** The student reads the paragraph or story and is then asked questions based on it.
- **Inferential Comprehension:** The student reads a paragraph or story and must interpret what has been read.
- **Listening Comprehension:** The student is read a paragraph or story by the examiner and is then asked questions about what the examiner has read.
- **Critical Comprehension:** The student reads a paragraph or story and then analyzes, evaluates, or makes judgments about what he or she has read.
- **Affective Comprehension:** The student reads a paragraph or story, and the examiner evaluates his or her emotional responses to the text.
- **Lexical Comprehension:** The student reads a paragraph or story, and the examiner assesses his or her knowledge of vocabulary words.

When evaluating the reading behavior of a child on reading comprehension subtests, it is important for the evaluator to ask the following questions:

- Does the student *guess* at answers to the questions presented?
- Does the student *show unwillingness to read* or make attempts at reading?
- Does the student *skip* unknown words?

- Does the student *disregard* punctuation?
- Does the student exhibit *inattention* to the story line?
- Does the student *drop the tone of his or her voice* at the end of sentences?
- Does the student *display problems with sounding out* word parts and blends?
- Does the student *exhibit a negative attitude* toward reading?
- Does the student *express difficulty attacking* unknown words?

Word Recognition Skills

The purpose of **word recognition tests** are to explore the student's ability with respect to sight vocabulary. According to Salvia and Ysseldyke (1998),

> A student learns the correct pronunciation of letters and words through a variety of experiences. The more exposure a student has to specific words and the more familiar those words become, the more readily he or she recognizes those words and is able to pronounce them correctly. (p. 464)

Word recognition subtests form a major part of most diagnostic reading tests. Students who recognize many words are said to have good sight vocabularies or good word recognition skills.

Word Attack Skills

When assessing the reading abilities of the student, evaluators will often examine the word attack–word analysis skills of the child. **Word attack skills** are those used to derive meaning and/or pronunciation of a word through context clues, structural analysis, or phonics. In order to assess the word attack skills of the student, the examiner normally reads a word to the student who must then identify the consonant, vowel, consonant cluster, or digraph that has the same sound as the beginning, middle, or ending letters of the word.

> Students must be able to decode words before they can gain meaning from the printed page. Since word-analysis difficulties are among the principal reasons students have trouble reading, a variety of subtests of commonly used diagnostic reading tests specifically assess word-analysis skills. (Salvia and Ysseldyke, 1998, p. 463)

Summary of Reading Assessment

Although most reading tests do cover many of these areas of assessment, each has its own unique style, method of scoring and interpretative value. However, when looking at a student's reading behavior, regardless of the test administered, one must address certain questions:

- Does the student have excessive body movements while reading?
- Does the student prefer to read alone or in a group?
- How does the student react to being tested?
- Does the student avoid reading?

- When the student reads, what types of materials will he or she read?
- Does the student read at home?
- Does the student understand more after reading silently than after listening to someone read the material orally?
- Does the student value reading?
- Is the student's failure mechanical or is he or she deficient in comprehension?

READING ASSESSMENT MEASURES

Many different reading assessment measures are used for determining reading strengths and weaknesses. The various reading tests used in school systems to assess reading abilities follow.

Gates-MacGinitie Silent Reading Tests, 4th Edition (GMRT–4)

Authors: Walter MacGinitie, Ruth MacGinitie, Katherine Maria, and Lois G. Dreyer

Publisher: Riverside Publishing Company

Description of Test: The test comprises a series of multiple-choice pencil-and-paper subtests designed to measure silent reading skills.

Administration Time: About one hour

Age/Grade Levels: Grades 1 through 12

Subtest Information: The test provides a comprehensive assessment of reading skills in two domains:

- *Comprehension*—This subtest domain assesses the ability to read and understand whole sentences and paragraphs.
- *Vocabulary*—This subtest domain assesses reading vocabulary. The difficulty of the task varies with the grade level.

STRENGTHS OF THE GMRT–4

The *GMRT* are efficient, informative, scientifically researched screening tools.

They can help educators understand what beginning readers know—Levels PR and BR determine student achievement in Literacy Concepts, Oral Language Concepts (Phonological Awareness), Letters and Letter/Sound Correspondences, Listening (Story) Comprehension, Initial Consonants and Consonant Clusters, Final Consonants and Consonant Clusters, Vowels, and Basic Story Words.

Educators can pinpoint students' decoding skill challenges—Levels 1 and 2 allow a detailed analysis of students' decoding skills.

Each important stage along the comprehension continuum—from listening skills to mature reading comprehension—can be measured.

The GMRT organizes students into appropriate instructional groups using scale scores, grade equivalents, percentile ranks, stanines, or normal curve equivalents.

Educators can ascertain which students are reading on grade level.

The GMRT help identify students for additional individual diagnosis and special instruction.

Two forms for pre- and posttesting help evaluate the effectiveness of instructional programs.

Educators can report student progress to agencies, parents, and teachers.

Gray Diagnostic Reading Tests–2nd Edition (GDRT2)

Authors: Brian R. Bryant, J. Lee Wiederholt, and Diane P. Bryant

Publisher: PRO-ED

Description of Test: *The Gray Diagnostic Reading Tests–2nd Edition* (GDRT2) has been revised and updated to reflect current research in reading. The GDRT2 assesses students who have difficulty reading continuous print and who require an evaluation of specific abilities and weaknesses. Two parallel forms are provided to allow you to study a student's reading progress over time. Teachers and reading specialists will find this test useful and efficient in gauging reading skills progress.

Administration Time: 45 to 60 minutes

Age Levels: 6-0 to 13-11

Subtest Information: The GDRT2 has four core subtests, each of which measures an important reading skill. The four subtests are: (1) Letter/Word Identification, (2) Phonetic Analysis, (3) Reading Vocabulary, and (4) Meaningful Reading. The three supplemental subtests, Listening Vocabulary, Rapid Naming, and Phonological Awareness, measure skills that many researchers and clinicians think have important roles in the diagnosis or teaching of developmental readers or children with dyslexia.

FIGURE 9.1   Gray Diagnostic Reading Tests

STRENGTHS OF THE GDRT2

The GDRT2, a revision of the Gray Oral Reading Tests–Diagnostic (GORT-D), along with the Gray Oral Reading Tests Fourth Edition (GORT4) and the Gray Silent Reading Tests (GSRT), form the Gray reading test battery.

The GDRT2 was normed in 2001–2002 on a sample of 1,018 students ages 6 through 18.

The normative sample was stratified to correspond to key demographic variables (i.e., race, gender, and geographic region).

The reliabilities of the test are high; all average internal consistency reliabilities for the composites are .94 or above.

Studies showing the absence of culture, gender, race, and disability bias have been added.

Several new validity studies have been conducted, including a comparison of the Wechsler Intelligence Scale for Children–Third Edition (WISC-III) to the GDRT2.

Gray Oral Reading Test–4 (GORT-4)

Authors: J. Lee Wiederholt and Brian R. Byrant

Publisher: PRO-ED & American Guidance Service

Description of Test: The widely used and popular *Gray Oral Reading Tests–3rd Edition* (GORT-3) has been revised and all new normative data provided. The GORT-4 provides an efficient and objective measure of growth in oral reading and an aid in the diagnosis of oral reading difficulties.

Administration Time: The time required to administer each form of the GORT-4 will vary from 15 to 30 minutes. Although the test is best administered in one session, examiners may use two sessions if the reader becomes fatigued or uncooperative.

Age Levels: 6-0 through 18-11.

Subtest Information: The test consists of two parallel forms, each containing 14 developmentally sequenced reading passages with five comprehension questions and can be given to students ages 6–0 through 18–11. The GORT-4 provides examiners with a Fluency Score that is derived by combining the reader's performance in Rate (time in seconds taken to read each passage) and Accuracy (number of deviations from print made in each passage). The number of correct responses made to the comprehension questions provides examiners with an Oral Reading Comprehension Score. All four scores are reported in terms of standard scores, percentile ranks, grade equivalents, and age equivalents. The Fluency Score and the Oral Reading Comprehension Score are combined to obtain an Oral Reading Quotient.

STRENGTHS OF THE GORT-4

The GORT-4 was normed on a sample of more than 1,600 students aged 6 through 18. The normative sample was stratified to correspond to key demographic variables (i.e., race, gender, ethnicity, and geographic region).

The reliabilities of the test are high; all average internal consistency reliabilities are .90 or above.

The test–retest study was conducted with all ages for which the test can be administered and illustrates the stability and reliability of the measure.

The validity is extensive and includes studies that illustrate that the GORT-4 can be used with confidence to measure change in oral reading over time.

Several improvements were made in the GORT-4; a few are discussed here:

- First, we added an easier story to both forms and thus the GORT-4 consists of 14, rather than 13, stories.
- Second, we used a linear equating procedure to adjust scores on the two test forms to allow the examiner to use scores on Forms A and B interchangeably.
- Third, we included bias studies that show the absence of bias based on gender and ethnicity.
- Finally, several new validity studies have been conducted, including an examination of the relationship of the Wechsler Intelligence Scale for Children–3rd Edition (WISC-III) to the GORT-4.
- You can use the GORT-4 in a variety of settings, such as elementary and secondary schools, clinics, and reading centers. The two forms of the test allow you to study an individual's oral reading progress over time.

Gray Silent Reading Tests (GSRT)

Authors: J. Lee Wiederholt and Ginger Blalock

Publisher: PRO-ED

Description of Test: The *Gray Silent Reading Tests* quickly and efficiently measure an individual's silent reading comprehension ability.

Age/Grade Levels: 7-0 through 25-0

Subtest Information: There are no subtests on the GSRT. This test consists of two parallel forms each containing 13 developmentally sequenced reading passages with five multiple-choice questions. It can be given individually or to groups. Each form of the test yields raw scores, grade equivalents, age equivalents, percentiles, and a Silent Reading Quotient.

FIGURE 9.2   Gray Silent Reading Tests

STRENGTHS OF THE GSRT

The GSRT was normed on 1,400 individuals in 31 states. Characteristics of the normative sample have been stratified and approximate those provided in the 1997 Statistical Abstract of the United States with regard to gender, geographic region, ethnicity, race, urban/rural residence, and disability.

The GSRT reliability is sufficiently high to warrant the use of the test in a wide variety of cases. Unlike many other tests of reading, the authors report internal consistency for each one-year interval.

The authors provide evidence for content-description, criterion-prediction, and construct-identification validity for the GSRT.

Durrell Analysis of Reading
Difficulty–3rd Edition (DARD-3)

Authors: Donald O. Durrell and Jane H. Catterson

Publisher: Harcourt Assessment, Inc.

Description of Test: This test has long served a population of experienced teachers whose primary purpose was to discover and describe weaknesses and faulty habits in children's reading. The kit includes an examiner's manual, student record booklets, tachistoscope, and a subtest presentation booklet containing reading passages.

Administration Time: 30 to 90 minutes

Age/Grade Levels: Grades 1 through 6

Subtest Information: The Durrell Analysis consists of 19 subtests designed to assess a student's reading and listening performance. They are included in the following sections:

- *Identifying Sounds in Words*—The examiner reads lists of words at increasing difficulty levels, and the student's score is based on the total number of identifying sounds in words that the student can recall correctly.
- *Listening Comprehension*—The examiner is directed to read one or two paragraphs aloud to determine the student's ability to comprehend information presented orally.
- *Listening Vocabulary*—This test requires the child to listen to a series of words and indicate the category to which it belongs.
- *Oral Reading*—The student reads orally and answers questions that require the recall of explicit information.
- *Phonic Spelling of Words*—The examiner reads lists of words at increasing difficulty levels, and the student's score is based on the total number of words he or she spells phonetically correctly.
- *Prereading Phonics Abilities Inventory*—This optional subtest includes syntax matching, naming letters in spoken words, naming phonemes in spoken words, naming lowercase letters, and writing letters from dictation.
- *Silent Reading*—The student reads silently and answers questions that require the recall of explicit information.
- *Sounds in Isolation*—This test assesses the student's mastery of sound/symbol relationships—including letters, blends, digraphs, phonograms, and affixes.
- *Spelling of Words*—The examiner reads lists of words at increasing difficulty levels, and the student's score is based on the total number of words spelled correctly.
- *Visual Memory of Words*—The examiner reads visually presented lists of words at increasing difficulty levels, and the student's score is based on the total number of words the student can recall correctly when the word list is presented again.
- *Word Analysis*—The examiner reads lists of words at increasing difficulty levels, and the score is based on the total number of words that the child analyzes correctly.

- *Word Recognition*—The examiner reads lists of words at increasing difficulty levels, and the score is based on the total number of words that the child recognizes correctly.

STRENGTHS OF THE DARD-3

The manual for the third edition is improved, providing clearer procedures for testing.

A continuing strength of the test is its set of behavioral checklists, urging close observation of individual reader characteristics.

The checklist can help evaluators analyze reading errors.

The addition of several new subtests makes for a more complete battery for assessment: however, the major focus of the test continues to be on specific skills.

Gates-McKillop-Horowitz Reading Diagnostic Tests

Authors: Arthur I. Gates, Anne S. McKillop, and Elizabeth Horowitz

Publisher: Teachers College Press

Description of Test: This is an 11-part verbal paper-and-pencil test. Not all parts need to be given to all students. Subtests are selected based on the student's reading levels and reading difficulties.

Administration Time: 40 to 60 minutes

Age/Grade Levels: Grades 1 through 6

Subtest Information: The subtests are listed and described below.

- *Auditory Blending*—The student is required to blend sounds to form a whole word.
- *Auditory Discrimination*—The student is required to listen to a pair of words and to determine whether the words are the same or different.
- *Informal Writing*—The student is required to write an original paragraph on a topic of his or her choice.
- *Letter Sounds*—The student is required to give the sound of a printed letter.
- *Naming Capital Letters*—The student is required to name uppercase letters.
- *Naming Lowercase Letters*—The student is required to name lowercase letters.
- *Oral Reading*—The student is required to read seven paragraphs orally. No comprehension is required.
- *Reading Sentences*—The student is required to read four sentences with phonetically regular words.
- *Reading Words*—The student is required to read 15 one-syllable nonsense words.
- *Recognizing and Blending Common Word Parts*—The student is required to read a list of nonsense words made up of common word parts.
- *Spelling*—The student is required to take an oral spelling test.
- *Syllabication*—The student is required to read a list of nonsense words.
- *Vowels*—The student is required to determine which vowel is associated with a nonsense word presented by the examiner.

- *Words/Flash Presentation*—The student is required to identify words presented by a tachistoscope in half-second intervals.
- *Words/Untimed*—The student is required to read the same word list as presented in Words/Flash Presentation. However the student is given the opportunity to use word attack skills in an untimed setting.

STRENGTHS OF THE GATES-MCKILLOP

It tests many critical reading skills.

A careful selection of subtests allows every student some successful reading experiences.

Students can maintain a high level of interest throughout the test because of its varied format and the informal tone of the procedures.

Gilmore Oral Reading Test

Authors: John V. Gilmore and Eunice C. Gilmore (1968)

Publisher: Harcourt Assessment, Inc.

Description of Test: This test measures three aspects of oral reading competency: pronunciation, comprehension, and reading rate. It is used for diagnosing the reading needs of students identified as having reading problems.

Administration Time: 15 to 20 minutes

Age/Grade Levels: Grades 1 through 8

Subtest Information: The test is made up of 10 paragraphs in increasing order of difficulty that form a continuous story about episodes in a family group. There are five comprehension questions on each paragraph and a picture that portrays the characters in the story.

STRENGTHS OF THE GILMORE

The updated Gilmore is among the best standardized tests of accuracy in oral reading of meaningful material.

The test directions are clear and concise.

No special training is required to administer this test satisfactorily.

The test provides informal error analysis.

Nelson-Denny Reading Test

Authors: James I. Brown, Vivian Vick Fishco, and Gerald S. Hanna

Publisher: Riverside Publishing Company

Description of Test: *The Nelson-Denny Reading Test, Forms G and H,* is a reading survey test for high school and college students and adults.

Administration Time: The Nelson-Denny may be administered in 45 minutes, or a single class period.

Age/Grade Levels: High school and college students and adults.

Subtest Information: A two-part test, the Nelson-Denny measures vocabulary development, comprehension, and reading rate. Part I (Vocabulary) is a 15-minute timed test; Part II (Comprehension and Rate) is a 20-minute test.

STRENGTH OF THE NELSON-DENNY

A unique feature of the 1993 edition is the extended-time administration of the test to meet the needs of special populations, such as students with English as a second language or as a foreign language, or returning adults.

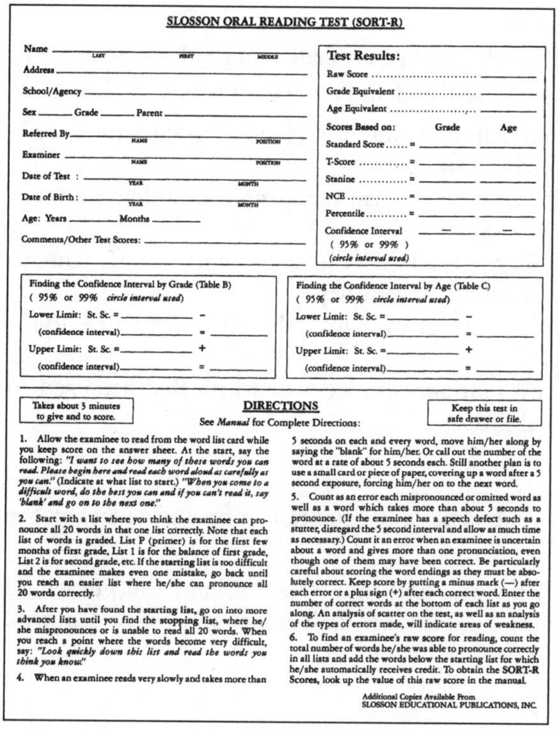

SLOSSON ORAL READING TEST (SORT-R)

Name ______ (LAST) ______ (FIRST) ______ (MIDDLE)
Address ______
School/Agency ______
Sex ______ Grade ______ Parent ______
Referred By ______ (NAME) ______ (POSITION)
Examiner ______ (NAME) ______ (POSITION)
Date of Test : ______ (YEAR) ______ (MONTH)
Date of Birth : ______ (YEAR) ______ (MONTH)
Age: Years ______ Months ______
Comments/Other Test Scores: ______

Test Results:
Raw Score .... ______
Grade Equivalent .... ______
Age Equivalent .... ______

Scores Based on:	Grade	Age
Standard Score...... =		
T-Score .... =		
Stanine .... =		
NCE .... =		
Percentile........ =		
Confidence Interval (95% or 99%) (circle interval used)	—	—

Finding the Confidence Interval by Grade (Table B)
(95% or 99% *circle interval used*)
Lower Limit: St. Sc. = ______ –
(confidence interval) ______ = ______
Upper Limit: St. Sc. = ______ +
(confidence interval) ______ = ______

Finding the Confidence Interval by Age (Table C)
(95% or 99% *circle interval used*)
Lower Limit: St. Sc. = ______ –
(confidence interval) ______ = ______
Upper Limit: St. Sc. = ______ +
(confidence interval) ______ = ______

Takes about 3 minutes to give and to score.

DIRECTIONS

See *Manual* for Complete Directions:

Keep this test in safe drawer or file.

1. Allow the examinee to read from the word list card while you keep score on the answer sheet. At the start, say the following: *"I want to see how many of these words you can read. Please begin here and read each word aloud as carefully as you can."* (Indicate at what list to start.) *"When you come to a difficult word, do the best you can and if you can't read it, say 'blank' and go on to the next one."*

2. Start with a list where you think the examinee can pronounce all 20 words in that one list correctly. Note that each list of words is graded. List P (primer) is for the first few months of first grade, List 1 is for the balance of first grade, List 2 is for second grade, etc. If the starting list is too difficult and the examinee makes even one mistake, go back until you reach an easier list where he/she can pronounce all 20 words correctly.

3. After you have found the starting list, go on into more advanced lists until you find the stopping list, where he/she mispronounces or is unable to read all 20 words. When you reach a point where the words become very difficult, say: *"Look quickly down this list and read the words you think you know."*

4. When an examinee reads very slowly and takes more than 5 seconds on each and every word, move him/her along by saying the "blank" for him/her. Or call out the number of the word at a rate of about 5 seconds each. Still another plan is to use a small card or piece of paper, covering up a word after a 5 second exposure, forcing him/her on to the next word.

5. Count as an error each mispronounced or omitted word as well as a word which takes more than about 5 seconds to pronounce. (If the examinee has a speech defect such as a stutter, disregard the 5 second interval and allow as much time as necessary.) Count it an error when an examinee is uncertain about a word and gives more than one pronunciation, even though one of them may have been correct. Be particularly careful about scoring the word endings as they must be absolutely correct. Keep score by putting a minus mark (—) after each error or a plus sign (+) after each correct word. Enter the number of correct words at the bottom of each list as you go along. An analysis of scatter on the test, as well as an analysis of the types of errors made, will indicate areas of weakness.

6. To find an examinee's raw score for reading, count the total number of words he/she was able to pronounce correctly in all lists and add the words below the starting list for which he/she automatically receives credit. To obtain the SORT-R Scores, look up the value of this raw score in the manual.

Additional Copies Available From
SLOSSON EDUCATIONAL PUBLICATIONS, INC.

FIGURE 9.3 Cover of Slosson Oral Reading Test

Slosson Oral Reading Test–Revised (SORT-R)

Authors: Richard L. Slosson; revised by Charles L. Nicholson (1990)

Publisher: Slosson Educational Publication Inc.

Description of Test: *The Slosson Oral Reading Test–Revised* (SORT-R) contains 200 words arranged in ascending order of difficulty in groups of 20 words. These word groups approximate reading grade levels. For example, Group 1 is at the first-grade level, Group 5 is at the fifth-grade level, and so forth. The last group is listed as grades 9 through 12. This list contains the most difficult words and words frequently encountered at the adult level. Figure 9.3 shows the SORT-R test results box and directions for scoring.

Administration Time: Untimed (3 to 5 minutes)

Age/Grade Levels: Preschool to Adult

Subtest Information: The test has no subtests.

STRENGTHS OF THE SORT-R

The test is easy to administer.
The test is easy to score.
The test is quick.

Spache Diagnostic Reading Scales (DRS)

Author: George D. Spache (1981)

Publisher: CTB Macmillan/McGraw-Hill

Description of Test: *The Diagnostic Reading Scales* consist of a battery of individually administered tests that are used to estimate the instructional, independent, and potential reading levels of a student.

Administration Time: 60 minutes

Age/Grade Levels: Grades 1 through 7 and poor readers in grades 8 through 12

Subtest Information: The subtests are listed and described below:

- *Auditory Comprehension*—The student is required to respond to questions orally about paragraphs read aloud by the examiner.
- *Oral Reading*—The student is required to read paragraphs aloud and answer questions orally.
- *Silent Reading*—The student is required to read a passage silently and to respond orally to questions asked by the examiner.
- *Supplementary Phonics Test*—This subtest measures the student's word attack skills and phonics knowledge.
- *Word Recognition List*—This test contains graded word lists that are used to determine a student's reading ability.

STRENGTHS OF THE DRS

The latest version of the DRS represents a substantial improvement over the previous version.

The revised examiner's manual, the training tape cassette, and the guidelines given for testing students who speak nonstandard dialects are all positive features.

The Woodcock Reading Mastery Tests–Revised (WRMT-R)

Author: Richard W. Woodcock

Publisher: American Guidance Service

Description of Test: *The Woodcock Reading Mastery Tests* (WMRT-R) is composed of six individually administered tests. There are two forms of the test, G and H. Form G includes all six tests, whereas Form H includes only four reading achievement tests.

Administration Time: 40 to 45 minutes

Age/Grade Levels: Grades K through 12

Subtest Information: Form G includes the following six subtests:

- *Letter Identification*—This test measures a student's skill in naming or pronouncing letters of the alphabet. Uppercase and lowercase letters are used.
- *Passage Comprehension*—In this subtest, the student must read silently a passage that has a word missing and then tell the examiner a word that could appropriately fill in the blank space. The passages are drawn from actual newspaper articles and textbooks.
- *Visual Auditory Learning*—The student is required to associate unfamiliar visual stimuli (rebuses) with familiar oral words and to translate sequences of rebuses into sentences.
- *Word Attack*—This test assesses skill in using phonic and structural analysis to read nonsense words.

- *Word Comprehension*—There are three parts to this section: Antonyms, Synonyms, and Analogies. In the Antonyms section, the student must read a word and then provide a word that means the opposite. In the Synonyms section, the student must provide a word with similar meanings to the stimulus words provided. In the Analogies section, the student must read a pair of words, ascertain the relationship between the two words, read a third word, and then supply a word that has the same relationship to the third word as exists between the initial pair of words read.
- *Word Identification*—This tests measures skill in pronouncing words in isolation.

STRENGTHS OF THE WRMT-R

The mandates of the federal Reading First initiative ask teachers to spend more time on diagnostic assessment of their students' skills to form instructional plans. The WRMT-R gives you a test battery with a proven record of accuracy with target grade levels K–3.

The WRMT-R is based on scientific research and tested with years of actual classroom use.

The WRMT-R identifies specific children's strengths and weaknesses in reading skills.

Students' difficulties and their root causes are ascertained, so that you can plan targeted remediation.

Educators can determine the reading strategies so that students with special needs can get needed help learning to read.

The WRMT-R, Normative Update provides an expanded interpretive system and age range to help you assess reading skills of children and adults. Two forms, G and H, make it easy to test and retest, or you can combine the results of both forms for a more comprehensive assessment.

Test of Reading Comprehension–3rd Edition (TORC-3)

Authors: Virginia L. Brown, Donald D. Hammill, and J. Lee Wiederholt (1995)

Publisher: AGS Publishing

Description of Test: The materials in the test kit include an examiner's manual, student booklets, answer sheets, individual and student profile sheets, and separate response forms for several subtests. This current revision of the TORC offers new normative data based on a sample of 1,962 students from 19 states stratified by age, keyed to the 1990 census data, and presented by geographic region, gender, residence, race, ethnicity, and disabling condition. See Figure 9.4 for the TORC-3 Profile/Examiner Record Form.

Administration Time: 30 minutes

Age/Grade Levels: Ages 7 through 18

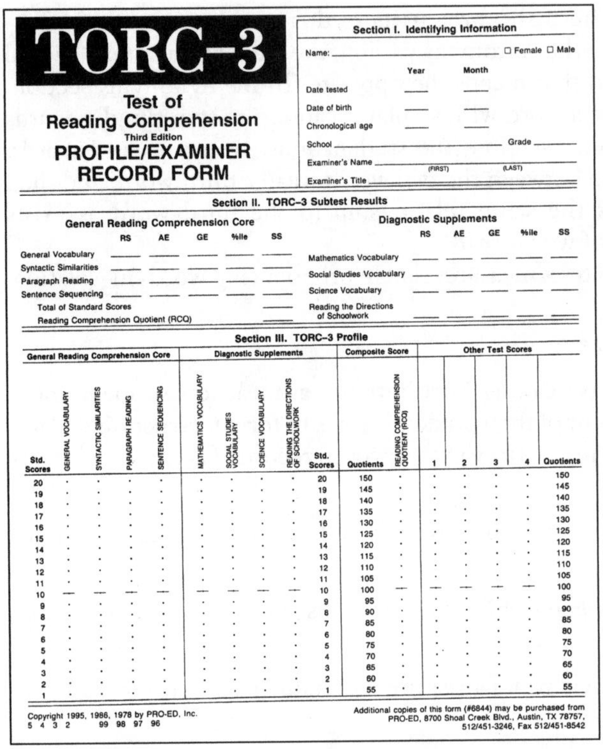
TORC-3

Test of Reading Comprehension

Third Edition

PROFILE/EXAMINER RECORD FORM

Section I. Identifying Information

Name: ☐ Female ☐ Male

	Year	Month
Date tested		
Date of birth		
Chronological age		

School Grade

Examiner's Name (FIRST) (LAST)

Examiner's Title

Section II. TORC–3 Subtest Results

General Reading Comprehension Core	RS	AE	GE	%ile	SS
General Vocabulary					
Syntactic Similarities					
Paragraph Reading					
Sentence Sequencing					
Total of Standard Scores					
Reading Comprehension Quotient (RCQ)					

Diagnostic Supplements	RS	AE	GE	%ile	SS
Mathematics Vocabulary					
Social Studies Vocabulary					
Science Vocabulary					
Reading the Directions of Schoolwork					

Section III. TORC–3 Profile

Std. Scores	General Vocabulary	Syntactic Similarities	Paragraph Reading	Sentence Sequencing	Mathematics Vocabulary	Social Studies Vocabulary	Science Vocabulary	Reading the Directions of Schoolwork	Std. Scores	Quotients	Reading Comprehension Quotient (RCQ)	1	2	3	4	Quotients
20									20	150						150
19									19	145						145
18									18	140						140
17									17	135						135
16									16	130						130
15									15	125						125
14									14	120						120
13									13	115						115
12									12	110						110
11									11	105						105
10									10	100						100
9									9	95						95
8									8	90						90
7									7	85						85
6									6	80						80
5									5	75						75
4									4	70						70
3									3	65						65
2									2	60						60
1									1	55						55

Copyright 1995, 1986, 1978 by PRO-ED, Inc.
5 4 3 2 99 98 97 96

Additional copies of this form (#6844) may be purchased from PRO-ED, 8700 Shoal Creek Blvd., Austin, TX 78757, 512/451-3246, Fax 512/451-8542

FIGURE 9.4 Test of Reading Comprehension–3rd Edition, Profile/Examiner Record Form

Subtest Information: The TORC-3 core subtests include:

- *General Vocabulary*—This subtest measures the reader's understanding of sets of vocabulary items that are all related to the same general concept.
- *Paragraph Reading*—This subtest measures the reader's ability to answer questions related to story-like paragraphs.
- *Reading the Direction of Schoolwork*—This subtest is used for younger or remedial readers. The student must read and follow directions.
- *Sentence Sequencing*—This subtest measures the reader's ability to build relationships among sentences both to each other and to a reader-created whole.
- *Syntactic Similarities*—This subtest measures the reader's understanding of sentence structures that are similar in meaning but syntactically different.

There are also three supplemental tests that measure content area vocabulary in mathematics, social studies, and science and a fourth that measures the student's ability to read directions in schoolwork.

STRENGTHS OF THE TORC-3

Information about the normative sample relative to geographic region, gender, residence, race, ethnicity, and disabling condition is reported.

The normative information has been stratified by age.

Studies showing the absence of gender and racial bias have been added.

Research supporting criterion-related validity has been updated and expanded.

Discussion of content validity has been enhanced, especially that pertaining to the three content-area subtests (i.e., Mathematics, Social Studies, and Science).

The data for test–retest reliability have been reworked to account for age effects.

Stanford Diagnostic Reading Test–Fourth Edition (SDRT-4)

Authors: Bjorn Karlsen and Eric F. Gardner

Publisher: Harcourt Assessment

Description of Test: The *Stanford Diagnostic Reading Test, Fourth Edition* (SDRT-4), provides group-administered diagnostic assessment of the essential components of reading in order to determine students' strengths and needs. SDRT-4 includes detailed coverage of reading skills, including many easy questions, so teachers can better assess students struggling with reading and plan instruction appropriately.

Administration Time: 85 to 105 minutes

Age/Grade Levels: K through 12

Subtest Information: Depending on age level, SDRT-4 subtests include Phonetic Analysis, Vocabulary, Comprehension, and Scanning.

STRENGTHS OF THE SDRT-4

High-quality selections, many written by published children's authors, provide relevant information about students' reading processes and strategies.

- Results can be used to evaluate students for program placement.
- Results can be used to determine reading strengths and weaknesses for instructional planning.
- Results can be used to provide special help for students who lack essential reading skills.
- Results can be used to identify trends in reading achievement at the classroom, school, and district levels.
- Results can be used to provide information about the effectiveness of instructional programs.
- Results can be used to measure changes occurring over a specific instructional period.

WRITTEN EXPRESSION

Writing is a highly complex method of expression involving the integration of eye-hand, linguistic, and conceptual abilities. As a result, it is usually the last skill children master. Whereas reading is usually considered the receptive form of a graphic symbol system, writing is considered the expressive form of that system. The primary concern in the assessment of composition skills is the content of the student's writing, not its form. The term *writing* refers to a variety of interrelated graphic skills, including:

Composition: The ability to generate ideas and to express them in an acceptable grammar, while adhering to certain stylistic conventions

Spelling: The ability to use letters to construct words in accordance with accepted usage

Handwriting: The ability to execute physically the graphic marks necessary to produce legible compositions or messages

Handwriting

Handwriting refers to the actual motor activity that is involved in writing. Most students are taught **manuscript** (printing) initially and then move to cursive writing (script) in later grades. There are those who advocate that only manuscript or only cursive should be taught. In truth, problems may appear among students in either system.

Handwriting skills are usually measured through the use of informal assessment measures—that is, CBA, CBM, portfolio assessments, rating scales, observation measures, or error analysis—rather than norm-referenced measures. Given the fact that most measures are informal, handwriting may or may not be part of a full psychoeducational battery. However, handwriting should always be evaluated, and examples need to be gathered and informally assessed if it appears to warrant concern.

Spelling

Spelling is one of the academic skills often included in the evaluator battery of individual achievement tests used in special education assessment. **Spelling** is the ability to use letters to construct words in accordance with accepted usage. Spelling ability is viewed by some teachers and school administrators equally with other academic skills. Being a poor speller does not necessarily mean that a child has a learning disorder. However, when poor spelling occurs with poor reading and/or arithmetic, then there is reason for concern. It appears that many of the learning skills required for good spelling are the same ones that enable students to become good readers.

Spelling, like all written language skills, is well suited to work sample analysis because a permanent product is produced. Learning to spell is a developmental process, and young children go through a number of stages as they begin to acquire written language skills. Writing begins in the preschool years as young children observe and begin to imitate the act of writing.

Analysis of Spelling Skills

Several questions should be addressed before one begins to analyze the results of the spelling subtest:

Does the child have sufficient mental ability to learn to spell?

This information can be obtained from the school psychologist if an intellectual evaluation was administered. However, if no such test was administered, then a group school abilities index may be present in the child's permanent folder.

Are the child's hearing, speech, and vision adequate?

This information can be obtained through the permanent record folder, information in the nurse's office, or informal screening procedures.

What are the child's general level of spelling ability according to teacher comments, past evaluations, or standardized tests?

Teacher comments and observations about the child's spelling history are very important to show patterns of disability. Also, look at standardized tests to see if patterns exist through the years on such tests.

Other information should be obtained from the classroom teacher as well. The teacher can offer you some foundational information on the child's patterns. You may want to ask the teacher for the following information:

- The child's attitude toward spelling in the classroom
- The extent to which the child relies on a dictionary in the classroom
- The extent of spelling errors in classroom written work
- Any patterns of procrastination or avoidance of written work
- The student's study habits and methods of work in the classroom
- The history of scores on classroom spelling tests
- Any observable handwriting difficulties
- Any evidence of fatigue as a factor in the child's spelling performance

Spelling Errors Primarily Due to Auditory or Visual Channel Deficits

Certain spelling errors may be evident in students with certain auditory channel deficits:

- **Auditory discrimination problems or cultural problems:** The child substitutes *t* for *d* or *sh* for *ch*.
- **Auditory discrimination problems:** The child confuses vowels, for example, spells *bit* as *bet*.
- **Auditory acuity or discrimination problems:** The child does not hear subtle differences in, nor discriminates between, sounds and often leaves vowels out of two syllable words.
- **Auditory–visual association:** The child uses a synonym such as *house* for *home* in spelling.
- **Auditory–visual associative memory:** The child takes wild guesses with little or no relationship between the letters or words used and the spelling words dictated, such as spelling *dog* for *home* or writing *phe* for *home*.

Certain spelling errors may be evident in students with certain visual channel deficits:

- **Visual memory problems:** The child visualizes the beginning or the ending of words but omits the middle of the words, for example, spells *hppy* for *happy*.
- **Visual memory sequence:** The child gives the correct letters but in the wrong sequence, for example, writes the word *the* as *teh* or *hte*.
- **Visual discrimination problems:** The child inverts letters, writing *u* for *n*, *m* for *w*.
- **Visual memory** The child spells words phonetically that are nonphonetic in configuration, for example, *tuff* for *tough*.

TESTS OF WRITTEN LANGUAGE

Many different assessment measures are used for determining written language. Listed next are the various tests of written expression tests.

Test of Early Written Language–2 (TEWL-2)

Author: Wayne P. Hresko

Publisher: PRO-ED & American Guidance Service

Description of Test: The test was developed to assess early writing abilities and covers the five areas of writing transcription, conventions of print, communication, creative expression, and record keeping. The TEWL-2 has a total of 42 items. The starting items vary by age level. An item is graded as 1 if correct and 0 if incorrect. Each item counts equally, although some require more responses or information than others. It is individually administered. See Figure 9.5 for the TEWL-2 Profile/Record Form B.

Administration Time: 10 to 30 minutes

Age/Grade Levels: Ages 3 through 7

Subtest Information: The test consists of two subtests:

The selection of items and the development of the subtests are grounded in the available research literature and other evidence of developing literacy ability. Item types were selected only if recognized experts in the field have related them to developing literacy abilities. The TEWL-2 is a companion to the TOWL-3 for extending the assessment range to younger children.

- *Basic Writing Quotient.* Basic Writing is a subtest (i.e., component) area that results in a standard score quotient. This quotient is a measure of a child's ability in such areas as spelling, capitalization, punctuation, sentence construction, and metacognitive knowledge. The Basic Writing Subtest may be given independent of the Contextual Writing Subtest.
- *Contextual Writing Quotient.* Contextual Writing is a subtest (i.e., component) area that results in a standard score quotient. This quotient is a measure of a child's ability to construct a story when provided with a picture prompt. This subtest measures such areas as story format, cohesion, thematic maturity, ideation, and story structure. Both Form A and Form B consist of 14 items. A detailed, expanded scoring guide is provided to assist in scoring the Contextual Writing Subtest. The Contextual Writing subtest may be given independently of the Basic Writing subtest.

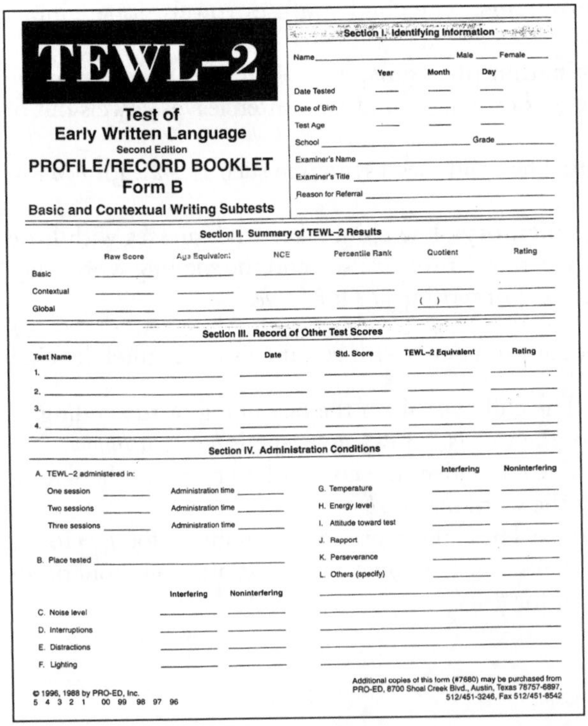
TEWL–2
Test of
Early Written Language
Second Edition
PROFILE/RECORD BOOKLET
Form B
Basic and Contextual Writing Subtests

Section I. Identifying Information

Name ______ Male ___ Female ___

	Year	Month	Day
Date Tested	___	___	___
Date of Birth	___	___	___
Test Age	___	___	___

School ______ Grade ______
Examiner's Name ______
Examiner's Title ______
Reason for Referral ______

Section II. Summary of TEWL–2 Results

	Raw Score	Age Equivalent	NCE	Percentile Rank	Quotient	Rating
Basic						
Contextual						
Global					( )	

Section III. Record of Other Test Scores

Test Name	Date	Std. Score	TEWL–2 Equivalent	Rating
1.				
2.				
3.				
4.				

Section IV. Administration Conditions

A. TEWL–2 administered in:
One session ___ Administration time ___
Two sessions ___ Administration time ___
Three sessions ___ Administration time ___

B. Place tested ______

	Interfering	Noninterfering
C. Noise level		
D. Interruptions		
E. Distractions		
F. Lighting		
G. Temperature		
H. Energy level		
I. Attitude toward test		
J. Rapport		
K. Perseverance		
L. Others (specify)		

© 1996, 1988 by PRO-ED, Inc.
5 4 3 2 1 00 99 98 97 96

Additional copies of this form (#7680) may be purchased from PRO-ED, 8700 Shoal Creek Blvd., Austin, Texas 78757-6897, 512/451-3246, Fax 512/451-8542

FIGURE 9.5 Test of Early Written Language–2nd Edition, Profile/Record Form B

- *Global Writing Quotient.* This composite quotient is formed by combining the standard scores for the Basic Writing Quotient and the Contextual Writing Quotient.

STRENGTHS OF THE TEWL-2

The TEWL is one of several recent efforts to provide assessments for the developmental skills and academic abilities of young children.

The test is useful in assessing and planning educational activities.

The test is useful for evaluating educational programs designed to promote the writing skills of young children.

The test is a good tool to use with other instruments to determine if a child has a mild disability.

Characteristics of the normative group correspond to those for the 1990 census data relative to gender, geographic region, ethnicity, race, and urban/rural residence.

Internal consistency reliability coefficients of all scores meet or exceed .90 for all ages and stability reliability of all scores approximates or exceeds .90.

Extensive content validity data are presented and criterion-related validity is evidenced by correlations with the Woodcock-Johnson, the WIAT, and the Written Language Assessment. Construct-related validity is presented based on correlations with age, cognitive ability, achievement, group discrimination, and the correlation of individual test items with total test scores.

Test of Written Language–3 (TOWL-3)

Authors: Donald D. Hammill and Stephen C. Larsen

Publisher: PRO-ED & American Guidance Service

Description of Test: The TOWL-3 is a completely revised edition of America's most popular test of written composition, the Test of Written Language. It meets the nationally recognized need for a standardized way to document the presence of deficits in this area of literacy. See Figure 9.6 for the TOWL-3 Profile/Story Scoring Form.

Administration Time: Untimed

Age/Grade Levels: Grades 2 through 12

Subtest Information: The TOWL-3 contains eight subtests. The skills measured by each subtest are as follows:

- *Contextual Conventions*—This subtest measures the student's skills in capitalization, punctuation, and spelling.
- *Contextual Language*—This subtest measures the student's vocabulary, syntax, and grammar.
- *Logical Sentences*—This subtest measures the student's ability to recognize and correct through rewriting illogicalities existing in stimulus sentences.
- *Sentence Combining*—This subtest measures the student's ability to incorporate the meaning of several sentences into a comprehensive single sentence containing phrases and clauses.

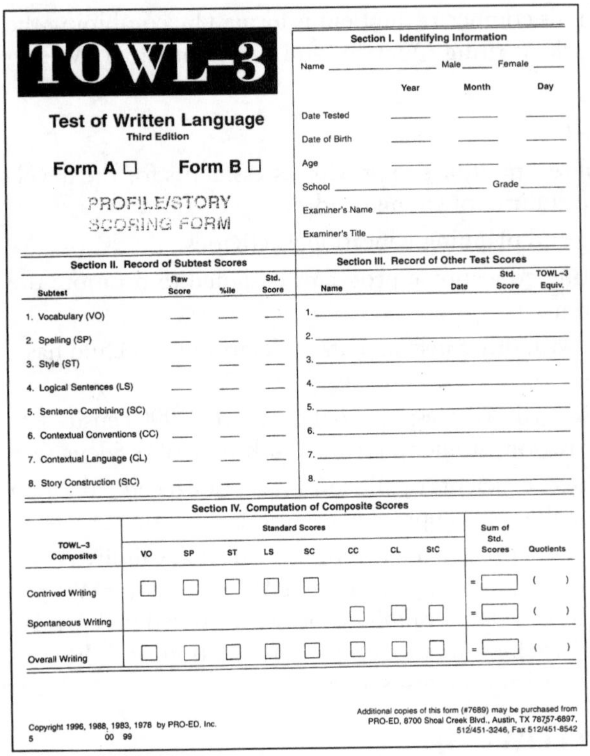

TOWL-3

Test of Written Language
Third Edition

Form A ☐ Form B ☐

PROFILE/STORY SCORING FORM

Section I. Identifying Information

Name ______ Male ____ Female ____

	Year	Month	Day
Date Tested			
Date of Birth			
Age			

School ______ Grade ____

Examiner's Name ______

Examiner's Title ______

Section II. Record of Subtest Scores

Subtest	Raw Score	%ile	Std. Score
1. Vocabulary (VO)			
2. Spelling (SP)			
3. Style (ST)			
4. Logical Sentences (LS)			
5. Sentence Combining (SC)			
6. Contextual Conventions (CC)			
7. Contextual Language (CL)			
8. Story Construction (StC)			

Section III. Record of Other Test Scores

Name	Date	Std. Score	TOWL-3 Equiv.
1.			
2.			
3.			
4.			
5.			
6.			
7.			
8.			

Section IV. Computation of Composite Scores

TOWL-3 Composites	VO	SP	ST	LS	SC	CC	CL	StC	Sum of Std. Scores	Quotients
Contrived Writing	☐	☐	☐	☐	☐				= ☐	( )
Spontaneous Writing						☐	☐	☐	= ☐	( )
Overall Writing	☐	☐	☐	☐	☐	☐	☐	☐	= ☐	( )

Additional copies of this form (#7689) may be purchased from PRO-ED, 8700 Shoal Creek Blvd., Austin, TX 78757-6897, 512/451-3246, Fax 512/451-8542

FIGURE 9.6 Test of Written Language–3rd Edition, Profile/Story Scoring Form

- *Spelling*—This subtest measures the student's ability to spell dictated words.
- *Story Construction*—This subtest measures the student's plot, character development, and general composition
- *Style*—This subtest measures the student's ability to punctuate sentences and capitalize properly.
- *Vocabulary*—This subtest measures the student's knowledge of word meanings and classes through the writing of meaningful sentences.

STRENGTHS OF THE TOWL-3

It is one of the most popular tests used for assessing written language.

Easy items have been added to make the test friendly to poor writers.

All aspects of reliability and validity have been strengthened.

Internal consistency, test–retest with equivalent forms, and interscorer reliability coefficients approximate .80 at most ages, and many are in the .90s.

The validity of the TOWL-3 was investigated extensively. Relevant studies are described in the manual, which has a section that provides suggestions for assessing written language informally and that gives numerous ideas for teachers to use when remediating writing deficits.

The TOWL-3 is by far the most comprehensive, reliable, and valid norm-referenced test of written language available today.

The TOWL-3 has gone further than any other test of written language to detect and eliminate sources of cultural, gender, and racial bias. The TOWL-3 normative sample is representative relative to gender, race, social class, and disability.

Test of Written Expression (TOWE)

Authors: R. McGee, B. Bryant, S. Larsen, and D. Rivera

Publisher: PRO-ED & American Guidance Service

Description of Test: *The Test of Written Expression* (TOWE) provides a comprehensive yet efficient norm-referenced assessment of writing achievement. The TOWE, which can be administered conveniently to individuals or groups of students, uses two assessment methods to evaluate a student's writing skills. The first method involves administering a series of 76 items that tap different skills associated with writing. The second method requires students to read or hear a prepared story starter and use it as a stimulus for writing an essay (i.e., the beginning of the story is provided, and the writer continues the story to its conclusion).

Administration Time: 60 minutes

Age/Grade Levels: 6 through 14 years

Subtest Information: The TOWE provides two separate assessment methods for measuring a comprehensive set of writing skills including:

- Ideation
- Vocabulary
- Grammar
- Capitalization
- Punctuation
- Spelling

STRENGTHS OF THE TOWE

Evidence of validity and reliability (internal consistency, test–retest, interscorer) is provided in the test manual (averaged coefficients are in the .90s). Three types of validity are explored: content validity, criterion-related validity, and construct validity.

Criterion-related validity was determined by correlating the scale's results with writing scores from the Test of Written Language, the Wide Range Achievement Test, and the Diagnostic Achievement Battery, among others.

Construct validity was established by computing the scores of the TOWE with scores from numerous aptitude measures, such as the Wechsler Intelligence Scale for Children and the Detroit Tests of Learning Aptitude, and scores from various scales of achievement, including the Woodcock-Johnson–Revised and the Gray Oral Reading Tests–3rd Edition

Written Expression Scale (WES)

Author: E. Carrow-Woolfolk

Publisher: American Guidance Service

Description of Test: The WES measures the written language of children and young adults. The Written Expression Scale can be administered individually or in small groups. The examiner presents a variety of direct writing prompts—like those tasks found in the classroom—either verbally, with pictures, or in print. Examinees write responses in a booklet. It is one of the three scales on Oral and Written Scales developed by Carrow-Woolkfolk (1995).

Administration Time: Approximately 45 minutes

Age/Grade Levels: Ages 5-0 through 21 years

Subtest Information: Although there are no subtests on the WES it measures three different writing skills: (1) use of conventions; (2) use of linguistic forms; and (3) sentence structure.

STRENGTHS OF THE WES

The Written Expression Scale correlates .84—.88 with global scores on achievement batteries (K-TEA/NU, PIAT-R/NU, and WRMT-R/NU); .57 and .62 with measures of receptive language (OWLS Listening Comprehension Scale and PPVT-R); .66 with the OWLS Oral Expression Scale; and .72 and .67 with measures of verbal intelligence (WISC-III VIQ and K-BIT Vocabulary).

The scale has high validity and reliability.

Writing Process Test (WPT)

Authors: M. R. Warden and T. Hutchinson

Publisher: PRO-ED

Description of Test: The norm-referenced *Writing Process Test* (WPT) is a direct measure of writing that requires the student to plan, write, and revise an original composition. The WPT assesses both written product and writing process. The test can be administered individually or in groups

Administration Time: Varies with age

Age/Grade Levels: Ages 8 through 19 years of age; Grades 2 through 12

Subtest Information: The test rates the writer's effort on two scales, Development and Fluency. The six Development Scales assess Purpose and Focus, Audience, Vocabulary, Style and Tone, Support and Development, and Organization and Coherence. The six Fluency Scales assess Sentence Structure and Variety, Grammar and Usage, Capitalization and Punctuation, and Spelling.

STRENGTHS OF THE WPT

The scales are applicable to virtually all written compositions.

Analytic scoring provides diagnostic information that holistic scoring cannot;

Ten 4-point scales for precise scoring

Uses one score protocol for all grades

Score protocol also works well for grading most teacher-assigned writing

Normed on 5,000+ students in Grades 2 to 12 in class-size groups

Internal consistency reliability averaged .84 (interrater averaged .75).

Mather-Woodcock Group Writing Tests (MWGWT)

Authors: N. Mather and R. Woodcock

Publisher: Riverside Publishing Company

Description of Test: The MWGWT is a revised/modified version of the writing test from the Woodcock-Johnson-Revised Achievement Battery. There are three separate forms of the MWGWT (Basic, Intermediate, and Advanced).

Administration Time: 30 to 60 minutes

Age/Grade Levels: 6 through 18 years of age

Subtest Information: There are four subtests on the MWGWT:

- *Dictation Spelling*—Requires the student to write spelling words orally presented
- *Editing*—Requires the student to detect various grammatical and spelling errors in the text
- *Writing Samples*—Requires the student to express his or her ideas
- *Writing Fluency*—Requires the student to write simple sentences

STRENGTHS OF THE MWGWT

The information obtained by the GWT may be used for early identification of problems/weaknesses, measurement of growth in writing skills, instructional planning, and curriculum evaluation.

The GWT provides an alternative to traditional multiple-choice assessments with open-ended, free-response item types.

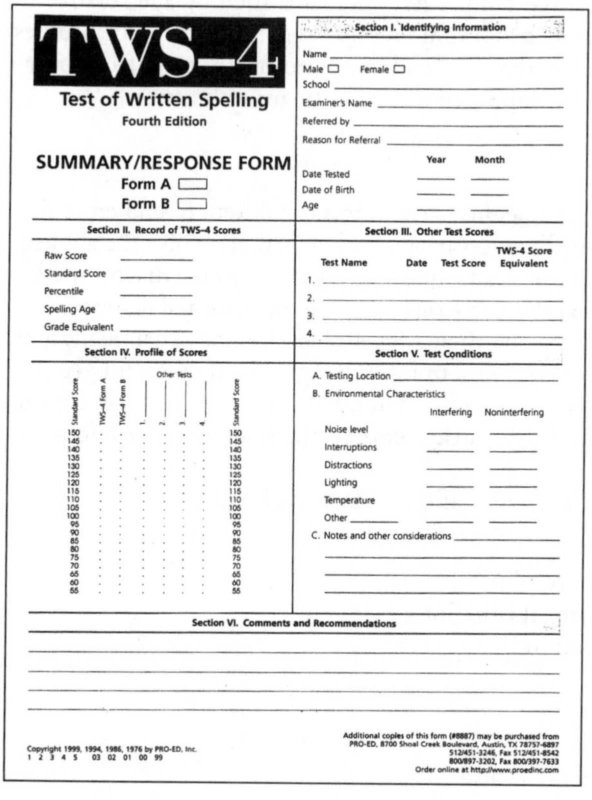
TWS–4
Test of Written Spelling
Fourth Edition
SUMMARY/RESPONSE FORM
Form A
Form B

Section I. Identifying Information
Name
Male Female
School
Examiner's Name
Referred by
Reason for Referral
Year Month
Date Tested
Date of Birth
Age

Section II. Record of TWS–4 Scores
Raw Score
Standard Score
Percentile
Spelling Age
Grade Equivalent

Section III. Other Test Scores

Test Name	Date	Test Score	TWS-4 Score Equivalent
1.			
2.			
3.			
4.			

Section IV. Profile of Scores
Standard Score / TWS–4 Form A / TWS–4 Form B / Other Tests 1. 2. 3. 4. / Standard Score
150 145 140 135 130 125 120 115 110 105 100 95 90 85 80 75 70 65 60 55

Section V. Test Conditions
A. Testing Location
B. Environmental Characteristics

	Interfering	Noninterfering
Noise level		
Interruptions		
Distractions		
Lighting		
Temperature		
Other		

C. Notes and other considerations

Section VI. Comments and Recommendations

Copyright 1999, 1994, 1986, 1976 by PRO-ED, Inc.
1 2 3 4 5 03 02 01 00 99

Additional copies of this form (#8887) may be purchased from PRO-ED, 8700 Shoal Creek Boulevard, Austin, TX 78757-6897 512/451-3246, Fax 512/451-8542 800/897-3202, Fax 800/397-7633 Order online at http://www.proedinc.com

FIGURE 9.7 Test of Written Spelling–4th Edition, Summary/Response Form

Test of Written Spelling–4 (TWS-4)

Authors: Stephen C. Larsen and Donald D. Hammill

Publisher: PRO-ED

Description of Test: The revised TWS-4 (Figure 9.7) is a norm-referenced test of spelling administered using a dictated word format. The TWS-4 now has two alternate or equivalent forms (A and B) which make it more useful in test–teach–test situations. The TWS-4 is appropriate for students in Grades 1 through 12 as well as for those in remedial programs. The TWS was developed after a review of 2,000 spelling rules. The words to be spelled are drawn from 10 basal spelling programs and popular graded word lists. The results of the TWS-4 may be used for four specific purposes: to identify students whose scores are significantly below those of their peers and who might need interventions designed to improve spelling proficiency, to determine areas of relative strength and weakness in spelling, to document overall progress in spelling as a consequence of intervention programs, and to serve as a measure for research efforts designed to investigate spelling.

Administration Time: 15 to 25 minutes

Age/Grade Levels: Ages 6-0 to 18-11

Subtest Information: The test consists of two subtests:

- Predictable words
- Unpredictable words

STRENGTHS OF THE TWS-4

The TWS-4 was standardized on more than 4,000 students. With rare exceptions, internal consistency and test–retest reliability coefficients are greater than .90. Evidence of content, criterion-related, and construct validity also is reported in the test manual. The TWS-4 can be administered in 20 minutes to either groups or individuals and yields the following educationally relevant information: standard scores, percentiles, spelling ages, and grade equivalents.

The characteristics of the normative sample approximate those for the projected 2000 U.S. census. The normative sample has been stratified by age relative to gender, urban or rural residence, geographic region, race, and ethnicity. Studies have been added to show no gender or racial bias, and more study from independent sources has been added supporting reliability and validity.

MATH

Mathematical thinking is a process that begins early in most children. Even before formal education begins, children are exposed to various situations that involve the application of mathematical concepts. As they enter formal schooling, they take the knowledge of what they had previously learned and begin to apply it in a more formal manner.

It is necessary to understand that mathematics and arithmetic are actually two different terms. Although most people use them interchangeably, they each have distinct meanings. **Mathematics** refers to the study of numbers and their relationships to time, space, volume, and geometry. **Arithmetic** refers to the operations or computations performed.

Mathematics involves many different abilities. These include:

- Solving problems
- Recognizing how to interpret results
- Applying mathematics in practical situations
- Using mathematics for prediction
- Estimating
- Using computational skills
- Understanding measurement
- Creating and reading graphs and charts

All schools, whether regular or special education, use some form of mathematical assessment. Schools begin the process of teaching math skills in kindergarten and proceed throughout the child's formal education. Even at the college level, mathematics is often a core requirement in many liberal arts schools. In general, next to reading, mathematics is probably the area most frequently assessed in school systems.

Mathematics can be assessed at the individual or group level. Consequently, it is a skill that is stressed and measured by various tests in schools. Mathematics tests often cover a great many areas. However, according to Salvia and Ysseldyke (1998), three types of classifications are involved in diagnostic math tests. Each classifications measures certain mathematical abilities:

Content: This consists of numeration, fractions, geometry, and algebra.

Operations: This consists of counting, computation, and reasoning.

Applications: This consists of measurement, reading graphs and tables, money and budgeting time, and problem solving.

Furthermore, according to the National Council of Supervisors of Mathematics (1978), basic mathematical skills include

- Arithmetic computation
- Problem solving
- Applying mathematics in everyday situations
- Alertness to the reasonableness of results
- Estimation and approximation
- Geometry
- Measurement
- Reading charts and graphs
- Using mathematics to predict
- Computer literacy

There are fewer diagnostic math tests than diagnostic reading tests. However, math assessment is more clear-cut. Most diagnostic math tests generally sample similar behaviors.

Analysis and Interpretation of Math Skills

According to McLoughlin and Lewis (1990), mathematics is one of the school subjects best suited for error analysis because students respond in writing on most tasks, thereby producing a permanent record of their work. Also, there is usually only one correct answer to mathematics questions and problems, and scoring is unambiguous. Today, the most common use of error analysis in mathematics is assessment of computation skills. Cox (1975) differentiates between systematic computation errors and errors that are random or careless mistakes. With systematic errors, students are consistent in their use of an incorrect number fact, operation, or algorithm (p. 354).

McLoughlin and Lewis (1990) identified four error types in computational analysis:

Incorrect operation: The student selects the incorrect operation. For example, the problem requires subtraction, and the student adds.

Incorrect number fact: The number fact recalled by the student is inaccurate. For example, the student recalls the product of 9×6 as 52.

> **Incorrect algorithm:** The procedures used by the student to solve the problem are inappropriate. The student may skip a step, apply the correct steps in the wrong sequence or use an inaccurate method.
>
> **Random error:** The student's response is incorrect and apparently random. For example, the student writes 100 as the answer to 42×6. (p. 354)

Different types of errors can occur in the mathematics process other than these four mentioned. For example, a student may make a mistake or error in applying the appropriate arithmetical operations. Such an example would be $50 - 12 = 62$. Here, the student used the operation of addition rather than subtraction. The student may understand how to do both operations, but consistently gets these types of questions wrong on the tests he or she takes due to the improper use of the sign involved.

Another problem that the student may encounter is a *slip*. When a slip occurs, it is more likely due to a simple mistake rather than a pattern of problems. For example, if a child correctly subtracts $20 - 5$ in eight problems but for some reason not in the ninth problem, the error is probably due to a simple slip rather than a serious operational or processing problem. One error on one problem is not an error pattern. Error patterns can be assessed by analyzing all correct and incorrect answers. When designing a program plan for a particular child in mathematics, it is critical to establish not only the nature of the problems but also the patterns of problems that occur in the child's responses.

Also, handwriting can play an important role in mathematics. Scoring a math test often involves reading numbers written down on an answer sheet by the student. If a student's handwriting is difficult to interpret or impossible to read, this can create serious problems for the evaluator with respect to obtaining valid scores. When a student's handwriting is not clear on a math test, it is important that the evaluator ask the student to help him or her read the answers. By doing so, the evaluator is analyzing the math skills that need to be assessed rather than spending his or her time trying to decode the student's responses.

ASSESSMENT OF MATHEMATICAL ABILITIES

Many different arithmetic assessment measures are used for determining strengths and weaknesses. The various mathematics tests school systems use to assess students' abilities follow.

Key Math Diagnostic Arithmetic Tests–Revised/ Normative Update (Key Math-R/NU)

> **Authors:** Austin J. Connolly, William Nachtman, and E. Milo Pritchett (2004)
>
> **Publisher:** American Guidance Service
>
> **Description of Test:** The Key Math-R/NU is a point-to and paper-and-pencil test measuring math skills in 14 areas. Two forms of the Key Math-R are available to use: Forms A and B. Each form contains 258 items. The materials include

a test manual, two easel kits for presentation of test items, and individual record forms for recording responses.

Administration Time: Approximately 30 to 45 minutes

Age/Grade Levels: Grades K through 12; Ages 5 to 22 years

Subtest Information: The test is broken down into three major areas consisting of 13 subtests:

- *Basic Concepts*—This part has three subtests that investigate basic mathematical concepts and knowledge: Numeration, Rational Numbers, and Geometry.
- *Operations*—This part consists of basic computation processes: Addition, Subtraction, Multiplication, Division, and Mental Computation.
- *Applications*—This part focuses on the functional applications use of mathematics necessary to daily life: Measurement, Time and Money, Interpretation of Data, Problem Solving, and Estimation.

STRENGTHS OF THE KEYMATH-R/NU

- KeyMath-Revised-Normative Update (KeyMath-R/NU) provides an accurate measurement of students' math skills with up-to-date norms and 516 test items. Because the test does not require reading ability, it is easy to administer to a wide range of students. Educational professionals from classroom aides to school psychologists can administer KeyMath-R effectively.
- With two forms, you can retest, pretest, and posttest confidently. In addition, spring and fall norms let you accurately assess a student's performance at the beginning and the end of the school year to meet Title I evaluation requirements.
- Provides four reports of in-depth information:

  Score Summary Profile provides biographical and test information, and also graphically shows each standard score with its confidence band. An optional Aptitude-Achievement Discrepancy Analysis is also included.

  Domain Performance Summary provides subtest ceiling items, domain scores, average scores, and domain status.

  Narrative Report gives a detailed summary of student performance in each category—total test, general area, and subtest—including teaching strategies for remediation of specific problems.

  Item Objectives and TAP Resources lists item objectives for all missed items and the first item in each ceiling level of each subtest along with references to the KeyMath Teach and Practice (TAP) program for days of already prepared classroom curriculum.

Test of Mathematical Abilities–2 (TOMA-2)

Authors: Virginia L. Brown, Mary E. Cronin, and Elizabeth McEntire

Publisher: PRO-ED & American Guidance Service

Description of Test: The test comprises five paper-and-pencil subtests that assess various areas of mathematical ability. See Figure 9.8 for the TOMA-2 Profile/Record Form.

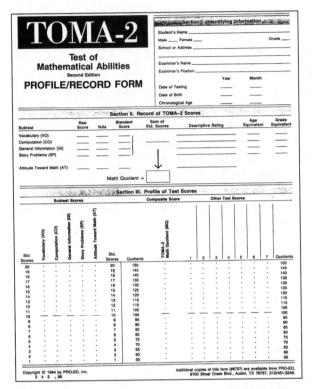

FIGURE 9.8   Test of Mathematical Abilities–2nd Edition, Profile/Record Form

Administration Time: 60–90 minutes

Age/Grade Levels: Ages 8.0 through 18.11

Subtest Information: The test consists of four core subtests and one supplemental subtest:

- *Attitude Toward Math (supplemental subtest)*—Here the child is presented with various statements about math attitudes and must respond with *agree, disagree,* or *don't know.*
- *Computation*—In this subtest, students are presented with computational problems consisting of basic operations and involving manipulation of fractions, decimals, money, percentages, and so on.
- *General Information*—In this subtest, the examiner reads the student questions involving basic general knowledge, and the student must reply orally. This subtest is usually administered individually.
- *Story Problems*—In this subtest, the student reads brief story problems that contain extraneous information and must extract the pertinent information required to solve the problems. Work space is provided for calculation.
- *Vocabulary*—In this subtest, students are presented with mathematical terms, which they are asked to define briefly as they are used in a mathematical sense.

STRENGTHS OF THE TOMA-2

Monitor progress and evaluate the success of your math program with accurate, norm-referenced test results

Analyze students' strengths and needs using five detailed subtests

Broad standardization sample makes this test easy to use for research programs

The TOMA-2 uses a standardization sample comprised of 2,147 students representing 26 states. The characteristics of the sample are similar to those reported in the 1990 Statistical Abstract of the United States for the population as a whole. Normative information is given for students ages 8–0 through 18–11.

The results of the test may be reported in standard scores, percentiles, and grade or age equivalents. The standard scores of the core battery are combined to comprise a total score called the Math Quotient.

Reliability coefficients for the subtests are above .80, and those for the Math Quotient exceed .90. Ample evidence of content, criterion-related, and construct validity are provided in the manual.

Stanford Diagnostic Mathematical Test-4 (SDMT-4)

Authors: Harcourt Brace Educational Measurement

Publisher: Harcourt Brace Educational Measurement

Description of Test: The *Stanford Diagnostic Mathematics Test*, 4th Edition (SDMT-4), measures competence in the basic concepts and skills that are prerequisite to success in mathematics, while emphasizing problem-solving and problem-solving strategies. SDMT-4 identifies specific areas of difficulty for each student so that teachers can plan appropriate intervention.

Designed to be group administered, SDMT-4 provides both multiple-choice and optional free response assessment formats. Students select and apply problem-solving strategies and use their reasoning and communication skills.

Administration Time: Varies with age according to mathematical ability

Age/Grade Levels: Grades 1 through 12

Subtest Information: There are six levels of testing on the SDMT-4 that assess concepts, applications, and computation:

- Red Level: Grades 1.5–2.5
- Orange Level: Grades 2.5–3.5
- Green Level: Grades 3.5–4.5
- Purple Level: Grades 4.5–6.5
- Brown Level: Grades 6.5–8.9
- Blue Level: Grades 9.0–12.9

STRENGTHS OF THE SDMT-4

The free-response component enables teachers to obtain more information regarding students' strengths and needs by observing the problem-solving process used in arriving at the result.

Practice tests are available for grades 1 through 8 to help students become familiar with the types of questions.

Evaluate students for program placement

Determine mathematics strengths and weaknesses for instructional planning

Provide special help for students who lack essential mathematics skills

Identify trends in mathematics achievement

Provide information about the effectiveness of instructional programs

Measure changes occurring over a specific instructional period

Comprehensive Mathematical Abilities Test (CMAT)

Authors: Wayne P. Hresko, Paul L. Schlieve, Shelley R. Herron, Colleen Swain, and Rita J. Sherbenou

Publisher: PRO-ED

Description of Test: Based on actual materials used to teach math in schools and on state and local curriculum guides, the CMAT represents a major advance in the accurate assessment of the mathematics taught in today's schools. All items reflect

FIGURE 9.9   Comprehensive Mathematical Abilities Test

real-world problems using up-to-date, current information and scenarios. Use as few as two subtests or as many as 12, depending on your purpose for testing.

Ages: 7-0 years to 18-11 years

Administration Time: 30 minutes to 2 hours

Subtests: The CMAT has six Core Subtests:

- Addition
- Subtraction
- Multiplication
- Division
- Problem Solving
- Charts, Tables, and Graphs

There are also six Supplemental Subtests:

- Algebra
- Geometry
- Rational Numbers
- Time
- Money
- Measurement

For most testing purposes, you will only want to give the core subtests, which can be administered in about 40 minutes. The Supplemental Subtests are used in those relatively few instances where information about higher-level mathematics ability is needed.

STRENGTHS OF THE CMAT

Both age-based norms (age 7 through 18) and fall and spring grade-based norms (grade 3 through 12) are provided, giving the examiner flexibility in meeting state and local education agency guidelines.

Reliability was determined using standard methods for estimating the internal consistency of the subtests and composites. Reliability estimates are uniformly high, with all composites and most subtest reliability values exceeding or rounding to .90. Coefficients for time sampling and interscorer reliability are also presented.

The CMAT manual provides clear evidence for validity. Strong evidence of content-description validity, criterion-prediction validity, and construct-identification validity is provided, including correlational research with individual and group mathematics tests, intelligence tests, and measures of academic ability.

The CMAT was normed on a national sample of over 1,600 students whose demographic characteristics match those of the United States according to the 2000 census report. The normative group was stratified on the basis of age, gender, race, ethnic group membership, geographic location, community size, and socioeconomic status (as indicated by educational attainment and family income).

FIGURE 9.10   Test of Early Mathematics Ability

The CMAT reflects the National Council of Teachers of Mathematics 2000 Guidelines.

The CMAT helps to identify students who are having difficulty as well as those students who are exceeding expectations.

Test of Early Mathematics Ability–3rd Edition (TEMA3)

Authors: Herbert P. Ginsburg and Arthur J. Baroody

Publisher: PRO-ED

Description of Test: The TEMA3 measures the mathematics performance of children between the ages of 3–0 and 8–11 and is also useful with older children who have learning problems in mathematics. It can be used as a norm-referenced measure or as a diagnostic instrument to determine specific strengths and weaknesses. Thus, the test can be used to measure progress, evaluate programs, screen for readiness, discover the bases for poor school performance in mathematics, identify gifted students, and guide instruction and remediation.

Ages: 3-0 through 8-11

Administration Time: 40 minutes

Subtests: The test measures informal and formal (school-taught) concepts and skills in the following domains: numbering skills, number-comparison facility, numeral literacy, mastery of number facts, calculation skills, and understanding of concepts. It has two parallel forms, each containing 72 items.

STRENGTHS OF THE TEMA3

The all-new standardization sample is composed of 1,219 children. The characteristics of the sample approximate those in the 2000 U.S. Census.

Internal consistency reliabilities are all above .92; immediate and delayed alternative form reliabilities are in the .80s and .90s. In addition, many validity studies are described.

Several important improvements were made in the TEMA3. First, a linear equating procedure is used to adjust scores on the two test forms to allow the examiner to use scores on Form A and B interchangeably. Second, bias studies are now included that show the absence of bias based on gender and ethnicity. Finally, the pictures of animals and money in the Picture Book are now in color to make them more appealing and more realistic in appearance.

COMPREHENSIVE TESTS OF ACADEMIC ACHIEVEMENT

The following tests are comprehensive in their assessment of academic areas. These tests normally offer a thorough approach to the assessment of a child's strengths and weaknesses in reading, writing, math, and spelling.

Brigance Comprehensive Inventory of Basic Skills–Revised

Author: Albert Brigance

Publisher: Curriculum Associates

Description of Test: The test is presented in a plastic ring binder that is designed to be laid open and placed between the examiner and the student. A separate student booklet provided for the student's answers is designed so that the skills range from easy to difficult; thus, the teacher can quickly ascertain the skills level the student has achieved.

Administration Time: Specific time limits are listed on many tests; others are untimed.

Age/Grade Levels: Pre-K through Grade 9.

Subtest Information: There are four subtest areas including 154 pencil-and-paper or oral-response tests:

- *Readiness*—*The skills assessed include color naming; visual discrimination of shapes, letters, and short words; copying designs, drawing shapes from memory; drawing a person; gross-motor coordination; recognition of body parts; following directional and verbal instructions; fine-motor self-help skills; verbal fluency; sound articulation; personal knowledge; memory for sentences; counting; alphabet recitation; number naming and comprehension; letter naming; and writing name, numbers, and letters.*
- *Reading*—This area evaluates word recognition, oral reading, and comprehension, oral reading rate, word analysis (auditorily and while reading), meaning of prefixes, syllabication, and vocabulary.
- *Language Arts*—This area assesses cursive handwriting, grammar and mechanics, spelling, and reference skills.
- *Mathematics*—This area assesses rote counting, writing numerals in sequence, reading number words, ordinal concepts, numeral recognition, writing to dictation, counting in sets, Roman numerals, fractions, decimals, measurement (money, time, calendar, linear/liquid/weight measurement, temperature), and two- and three-dimensional geometric concepts.

STRENGTHS OF THE BRIGANCE

Assesses specific areas of educational need
Facilitates development of performance goals
Provides indicators of progress on specific skills
Facilitates reporting to staff and parents
Is normed in key skill areas for multidisciplinary or classroom-based administration
Can be used for alternate assessment situations

Kaufman Tests of Educational Achievement–2 (KTEA-II)

Authors: Alan S. Kaufman and Nadren L. Kaufman

Publisher: American Guidance Service

Description of Test: The KTEA-II is an individually administered battery that gives a flexible, thorough assessment of the key academic skills in reading, math, written language (new), and oral language (new).

Administration Time: Comprehensive Form: (PreK–K) 25 minutes; (Grades 1–2) 50 minutes; (Grades 3+) 70 minutes; Brief Form: (4 1/2 to 90 years old) 20–30 minutes

Age/Grade Levels: Ages 4 1/2 through 25 (Comprehensive Form), 4 1/2 through 90+ (Brief Form)

Subtest Information: The test contains 14 subtests making up five composite scores

- **Reading Composite**
  Letter & Word Recognition
  Reading Comprehension
  Phonological Awareness
  Nonsense Word Decoding
  Word Recognition Fluency
  Decoding Fluency
  Associated Fluency
  Naming Facility

- **Math Composite**
  Math Concepts & Applications
  Math Computation

- **Written Language Composite**
  Written Expression
  Math Computation

- **Oral Language Composite**
  Listening Comprehension
  Oral Expression

- **Comprehensive Achievement Composite**

STRENGTHS OF THE KTEA-II

The KTEA-II appears to be a well-standardized, reliable measure with some innovative features that could make it the measure of choice for analyzing academic strengths and weaknesses.

The KTEA-II provides valid scores for the basic achievement areas covered in school.

Strong internal consistency has been shown.

Alternate forms to measure progress or response to intervention

Easy to administer, with novel tasks to motivate low-functioning students

Written Expression and Oral Expression subtests use engaging stories or situations

Enhanced reading subtests to measure skills from readiness through advanced levels

Useful comparisons between reading and listening, and writing and speaking

Peabody Individual Achievement Test–Revised (PIAT-R)

Author: Frederick C. Markwardt, Jr.

Description of Test: The PIAT-R is used in special education for identifying academic deficiencies. It is made up of six subtests. The most typical response format on the PIAT-R is multiple choice. The student is shown a test plate with four possible answers and asked to select the correct response.

Administration Time: 50 to 70 minutes

Age/Grade Levels: Grades K–12, ages 5-0 through 22-11; Level 1 (grades K through 1) and Level 2 (grades 2 through 12)

Subtest Information: The test's six subtests include:

- *General information*—This subtest has 100 open-ended questions that are presented orally. They measure the student's factual knowledge related to science, social studies, humanities, fine art, and recreation.
- *Reading Recognition*—There are 100 items. Items 1 through 16 are multiple choice and measure prereading skills. Items 17 through 100 measure decoding skills and require the student to read aloud individually presented words.
- *Reading Comprehension*—This subtest consists of 82 items and measures the student's ability to draw meaning from printed sentences.
- *Spelling*—Items 1 through 15 are multiple-choice tasks that assess reading skills. Items 16 through 100 require the student to select from four possible choices the correct spelling of a word read orally by the examiner.
- *Written Expression*—This subtest has two levels. Level 1 consists of 19 copying and dictation items that are arranged in order of ascending difficulty. In Level 2, the child is presented with one or two picture plates and given 20 minutes to write a story about the picture.
- *Mathematics*—In this subtest, the student is asked the question orally and must select the correct response from four choices. Questions cover topics ranging from numerical recognition to trigonometry.

STRENGTHS OF THE PIAT-R

Simple multiple-choice format helps assess children with severe disabilities

Six subtests ensure a comprehensive assessment

ASSIST report provides scores and a student performance narrative on each subtest and composite

Peabody Individual Achievement Test-Revised-Normative Update (PIAT-R/NU) is an efficient individual measure of academic achievement. Reading, mathematics, and spelling are assessed in a simple, nonthreatening format that requires only a pointing response for most items. This multiple-choice format makes the PIAT-R ideal for assessing low functioning individuals or those having limited expressive abilities.

PIAT-R has "NU" norms. Based on a national sampling of over 3,000 people, it provides accurate score comparisons for reading decoding, reading comprehension, and math applications with the other achievement batteries with which it was conormed: K-TEA/NU, KeyMath-R/NU, and WRMT-R/NU. You gain added flexibility because you can substitute a subtest from a different battery if a subtest is spoiled or if additional diagnostic information is desired.

Wechsler Individual Achievement Test–2 (WIAT-II)

Author: David Wechsler (1999)

Publisher: The Psychological Corporation

Description of Test: The WIAT is made up of eight subtests. The test format includes easels and paper-and-pencil tasks.

Administration Time: 30 to 75 minutes

Age/Grade Levels: Four years and up through 85 years

Subtest Information:

- *Word Reading:* naming letters, phonological skills (working with sounds in words), and reading words aloud from lists. Only the accuracy of the pronunciation (not comprehension) is scored.
- *Pseudoword Decoding:* reading nonsense words aloud from a list (phonetic word attack).
- *Reading Comprehension:* matching words to pictures, reading sentences aloud, and orally answering oral questions about reading passages. Silent reading speed is also assessed.
- *Spelling:* written spelling of dictated letters and sounds and words that are dictated and read in sentences.
- *Written Expression:* writing letters and words as quickly as possible, writing sentences, and writing a paragraph or essay.
- *Numerical Operations:* identifying and writing numbers, counting, and solving paper-and-pencil computation examples with only a few items for each computational skill.
- *Math Reasoning:* counting, identifying shapes, and solving verbally framed "word problems" presented both orally and in writing or with illustrations. Paper and pencil are allowed.
- *Listening Comprehension:* multiple-choice matching of pictures to spoken words or sentences and replying with one word to a picture and a dictated clue.
- *Oral Expression:* repeating sentences, generating lists of specific kinds of words, describing pictured scenes, and describing pictured activities. Content of answers is scored, but quality of spoken language is not for most items.

STRENGTHS OF THE WIAT-II

WIAT-II is a comprehensive yet flexible measurement tool useful for achievement skills assessment, learning disability diagnosis, special education placement, curriculum planning, and clinical appraisal for preschool children through adults. New norms also allow for the evaluation of and academic planning for college students with learning disabilities.

WIAT-II extends the age range down to four years and up through 85 years, including norms for 2-year and 4-year college students.

To better assess both low- and high-functioning individuals, WIAT-II includes more comprehensive items that provide a lower floor and a higher ceiling. Emerging academic skills are also addressed in reading, math, and written and oral language to target instructional needs of young children early and guide them to competency.

With WIAT-II, you can choose the subtests you need to administer, engage examinees with interesting tasks that are instructionally relevant, quickly score the test manually or by computer, and develop plans with detailed skills analysis information.

As with the earlier edition, WIAT-II provides norm-referenced information about all seven areas required by the Individuals with Disabilities Education Improvement Act (IDEA 2004). This comprehensive battery includes a broad sample of curriculum content that exceeds IDEA 2004 requirements with nine subtests.

WIAT-II allows you to go beyond the correctness of a response and begin to examine how the individual solves problems and employs strategies and how this performance matches curricular expectations. Objective scoring guidelines, developed in consultation with leading reading and writing experts, are also provided for the Written Expression subtest to evaluate the writing process as well as the product.

WIAT-II is the only achievement battery empirically linked with the Wechsler Intelligence Scale for Children–Third Edition (WISC-III), the Wechsler Preschool and Primary Scale of Intelligence–Revised (WPPSI-R), and the Wechsler Adult Intelligence Scale–Third Edition (WAIS-III), the most widely used intellectual ability tests. These relationships provide valid discrepancy scores to help you make meaningful comparisons between achievement and ability and develop on-target intervention.

Wide Range Achievement Test–3 (WRAT-3)

Author: Gary S. Wilkinson

Publisher: Jastak Associates/Wide Range Inc.

Description of Test: This new edition of the Wide Range Achievement Test has returned to a single-level format. The test contains a Blue and a Tan form that can be used in a pretest–posttest format, test–retest format, or they can be administered together in a combined test format.

Administration Time: Each form of the WRAT-3 takes approximately 15 to 30 minutes to administer. However, age, ability, and behavioral style of the student will vary the length of the test administration.

Age/Grade Levels: Ages 5 through 75

Subtest Information: The three subtests contained on both the Blue and Tan forms are:

- *Reading*—This is a subtest involving decoding whereby the child is asked to recognize and rename letters and pronounce words in isolation.
- *Spelling*—This is a subtest of written spelling whereby the child is asked to write his or her name, write letters, and write words from dictation.
- *Arithmetic*—This is a subtest of mathematical computation whereby the child is asked to count, read numbers, identify number symbols, solve oral problems, and perform written computation within a defined time limit.

STRENGTHS OF THE WRAT-3

This test makes for a very useful screening instrument because of the short administration time and specific areas measured.

The test is quick and reliable.

The test is reasonably valid in measuring achievement in its subtest areas.

The written spelling subtest is an excellent test and one of the few available.

Woodcock-Johnson Tests of Achievement Test–III (WJ-III)

Author: Richard W. Woodcock and Mary Bonner Johnson

Publisher: Riverside Publishing Company

Description of Test: This test is the first major individual instrument that includes measures of cognitive ability (see Chapter 10 on intelligence tests), academic achievement, and scholastic interest to be standardized on the same norming sample. A complex instrument with many facets and a wide range, it is an individual cognitive and achievement test.

Administration Time: Part I, 60 to 90 minutes; Part II, 30 to 45 minutes; Part III, 15 to 30 minutes

Age/Grade Levels: Ages 3 through 80

Subtest Information: The subtests that make up the Achievement Battery are listed:

BROAD READING

- *Letter-Word Identification*—This subtest measures the subject's word identification skills. The initial items require the individual to identify letters that appear in large type on the subject's side of the Test Book and the remaining items require the individual to pronounce words correctly. The individual is not required to know the meaning of the word. The items become increasingly difficult as the selected words appear less and less frequently in written English.
- *Reading Fluency*—This subtest measures the subject's ability to quickly read simple sentences in the Subject Response Booklet, decide if the statement is

true, and circle Yes or No. The difficulty level of the sentences gradually increases to a moderate level. The individual attempts to complete as many items possible within a 3-minute time limit.

■ *Passage Comprehension*—This subtest involves symbolic learning, or the ability to match a rebus (pictographic representation of a word) with an actual picture of the object. The next items are presented in a multiple-choice format and require the subject to point to the picture represented by a phrase. The remaining items require the subject to read a short passage and identify a missing key word that makes sense in the context of the passage. The items become increasingly difficult by removing pictorial stimuli and by increasing passage length, level of vocabulary, and complexity of syntactic and semantic cues.

BROAD MATH

■ *Calculation*—This subtest is a test of math achievement measuring the ability to perform mathematical computations. The initial items require the individual to write single numbers. The remaining items require the person to perform addition, subtraction, multiplication, division, and combinations of basic operations, as well as some geometric, trigonometric, logarithmic, and calculus operations. The calculations involve negative numbers, percents, decimals, fractions, and whole numbers. Because the calculations presented in a traditional problem format in the Subject Response Booklet, the individual is not required to make any decisions about what operation to use or what data to include.

■ *Math Fluency*—This subtest measures the ability to solve simple addition, subtraction, and multiplication facts quickly. The person is presented a series of sample arithmetic problems in the Subject Response Booklet. This test has a 3-minute time limit.

■ *Applied Problems*—This subtest requires the subject to analyze and solve math problems. To solve the problems, the subject must listen to the problem, recognize the procedure to be followed, and then perform the simple calculations. Because many of the problems include extraneous information, the individual must decide not only the appropriate mathematical operations to use but also which numbers to include in the calculation. Item difficulty increases with complex calculations.

BROAD WRITTEN LANGUAGE

■ *Spelling*—This subtest measures the ability to write orally presented words correctly. The initial items measure prewriting skills such as drawing lines and tracing letters. The next set of items requires the subject to produce upper and lower case letters. The remaining items measure the subject's ability to spell words correctly. The items become increasingly difficult as the words become more difficult.

■ *Writing Fluency*—This subtest measures skills in formulating and writing simple sentences quickly. Each sentence must relate to a given stimulus picture in the Subject Response Booklet and include a given set of three words. This test has a 7-minute time limit.

- *Writing Samples*—This subtest measures skills in writing responses to a variety of demands. The individual must produce written sentences that are evaluated with respect to quality of expression. Item difficulty increases by increasing passage length, level of vocabulary, grammatical complexities, and level of concept abstraction. The individual is not penalized for errors in basic writing skills, such as spelling or punctuation.
- *Handwriting*—This subtest is evaluated on the Handwriting Legibility Scale, a standardized evaluation of the general appearance of the handwriting and an informal evaluation of six handwriting elements such as uniformity of letters, consistency of spacing between letters and words, consistent and uniform slant, a clear distinction between capital and lower case letters, letter formation, and line quality that is even and consistent.

STRENGTHS OF THE WJ-III

The strengths of the test are primarily in the originality of many tasks, in the technical expertise and sophistication involved in the test construction, and in the psychometric properties of the battery.

This test is a multifaceted tool for the assessment of cognitive achievement and scholastic interests.

This test's subtests show validity.

The test is a useful measure for the assessment of school performance across a wide range of academic areas and ages.

Test of Academic Achievement Skills–Revised (TAAS-R)

Author: Morrison F. Gardner

Publisher: Psychological and Educational Publications

Description of Test: The test measures a child's reading, arithmetic, and spelling skills. It is an excellent tool for diagnosing learning disabilities when used in conjunction with other standardized tests.

Administration Time: 15 to 25 minutes

Age/Grade Levels: Ages 5 through 15 years

Subtest Information: The revision of the Test of Academic Achievement Skills has strengthened all of the original subtests and includes a new subtest—Oral Reading Stories and Comprehension. In addition to the new subtest, the revision includes the following subtests:

- Spelling (writing letters and words from dictation)
- Letter Reading and Word Reading (deciphering and pronouncing)
- Listening Comprehension (listening to stories, understanding and remembering in order to answer questions about the stories)

- Oral Reading Stories and Comprehension
- Arithmetic (word problems and computation)

STRENGTHS OF THE TAAS-R

The revision has strengthened all the original subtests and has added another subtest, Oral Reading Stories and Comprehension. Other changes making the revision a more useful instrument in obtaining an estimate of a child's academic achievement skills are the following:

- Extended the upper age levels from 11 years 11 months through 14 years 11 months
- Combined the two age groups (4 years through 5 years 11 months and 6 years through 11 years 11 months to one age group—5 years through 14 years 11 months)
- The revision measures what an academic achievement test should measure; for example, how well a child has mastered various academic subjects. The results obtained from the TAAS-R will provide information about a child's academic progress in kindergarten and readiness for first grade, academic progress in the eighth grade and readiness for ninth grade, and information about other children ages six to fifteen years (grades one through eight) and their readiness for the next grade level or the need for possible remediation.

Hammill Multiability Achievement Test (HAMAT)

Authors: Donald D. Hammill, Wayne P. Hresko, Jerome J. Ammer, Mary E. Cronin, and Sally S. Quinby

Publisher: PRO-ED

Description of the Test: The HAMAT is designed for use by psychologists, educational diagnosticians, counsellors, and other professionals concerned with the assessment of academic achievement.

Ages: 7-0 through 17-11

Administration Time: 30 to 60 Minutes

Subtests: The HAMAT provides four subtests in the areas of:

- Reading (a series of paragraphs based on the cloze procedure)
- Writing (requires students to write sentences from dictation, stressing correctness)
- Mathematics (measures students' mastery of number facts and ability to complete mathematical calculations)
- Facts (requires students to answer questions based on the content of social studies, science, history, and literature)

STRENGTHS OF THE HAMAT

The test was normed on 2,901 students in the United States and provides percentiles, standard scores, and age equivalents.

Reliability of the HAMAT was investigated using estimates of content sampling, time sampling, and scorer differences.

Internal consistency reliability coefficients all exceed or round to .90.

Test–retest coefficients range from .83 to .94 for the subtests, the composite exceed .94.

CONCLUSION

Assessing academic achievement is a vital component of the assessment process. Understanding where a child has strengths and weaknesses in academic areas is necessary if you are going to diagnose a possible disability. There are numerous areas professionals can assess when giving an achievement test. Regardless of the number of areas, reading, writing, math, and spelling are part of every initial assessment battery for possible classification and/or placement in special education. We always need to know how a child compares academically, relative to the norms of the population. Therefore, all special educators should be able to read scores from achievement tests and, at a minimum, have a general understanding of what the assessment measures test and the purpose of the testing. For those who must administer achievement batteries, it is essential that a complete, thorough, valid, and reliable battery be given.

VOCABULARY

Achievement Tests: Tests designed to assess the academic progress of a student. A student's academic achievement skills are reviewed to determine how well he or she is performing in core skill areas such as reading, spelling, mathematics, and writing.

Affective Comprehension: The student reads a paragraph or story, and the examiner evaluates the student's emotional responses to the text.

Applications: In math, this consists of measurement, reading graphs and tables, money and budgeting, time, and problem solving.

Arithmetic: The operations or computations performed in math.

Composition: The ability to generate ideas and to express them in an acceptable grammar, while adhering to certain stylistic conventions.

Content: In math, this consists of numeration, fractions, geometry, and algebra.

Critical Comprehension: The student reads a paragraph or story and then analyzes, evaluates, or makes judgments on what he or she has read.

Disregard of Punctuation: The student fails to observe punctuation; for example, may not pause for a comma, stop for a period, or indicate a vocal inflection, a question mark, or an exclamation point.

Gross Mispronunciation: The student's pronunciation of a word bears little resemblance to the proper pronunciation.

Handwriting: The actual motor activity that is involved in writing.

Hesitation: The student hesitates for two or more seconds before pronouncing a word.

Incorrect Algorithm: The procedures used by the student to solve the problem are inappropriate. The student may skip a step, apply the correct steps in the wrong sequence, or use an inaccurate method.

Incorrect Number Fact: The number fact recalled by the student is inaccurate. For example, the student recalls the product of 9 and 6 as 52.

Incorrect Operation: The student selects the incorrect operation. For example, the problem requires subtraction and the student adds.

Inferential Comprehension: The student reads a paragraph or story and must interpret what has been read.

Insertion: The student inserts one or more words into the sentence being orally read.

Inversion: The student changes the order of words appearing in a sentence.

Lexical Comprehension: The student reads a paragraph or story, and the examiner assesses his or her knowledge of vocabulary words.

Listening Comprehension: The student listens to a paragraph or story read by the examiner and is then asked questions about what was read.

Literal Comprehension: The student reads the paragraph or story and is then asked factual questions based on it.

Manuscript: Printing in writing.

Mathematics: The study of numbers and their relationships to time, space, volume, and geometry.

Miscue: The difference between what a reader states is on a page and what is actually on the page.

Omissions: The student skips individual words or groups of words when reading aloud.

Operations: In math, this consists of counting, computation, and reasoning.

Qualitative Miscues: With this type of miscue analysis, the focus is on the quality of the error rather than the number of different mistakes.

Quantitative Miscues: With this type of miscue analysis, the evaluator counts the number of reading errors made by the student.

Random Error: The student's response is incorrect and apparently random. For example, the student writes 100 as the answer to 42 + 6.

Spelling: The ability to use letters to construct words in accordance with accepted usage.

Substitution: The student replaces one or more words in the passage by one or more meaningful words.

Word Attack Skills: Those used to derive meaning and/or pronunciation of a word through context clues, structural analysis, or phonics.

Word Recognition Tests: Tests that explore the student's ability with respect to sight vocabulary.

CHAPTER TEN

ASSESSMENT OF INTELLIGENCE

KEY TERMS

Adaptive Behavior
Average
Borderline
Developmentally Delayed
Full Scale IQ
High Average
Intellectually Deficient
Intelligence

IQ
Low Average
Mentally Retarded
Performance Subtests
Scaled Scores
Superior
Verbal Subtests
Very Superior

CHAPTER OBJECTIVES

This chapter discusses the importance of intelligence testing in the special education process. After reading this chapter, you should be able to understand the following:

- The complexity of intelligence
- The purpose of intelligence testing
- What IQ scores represent
- Classification of IQ scores
- The Wechsler Scales of Intelligence
- Other measures of intellectual ability

INTELLIGENCE

A very important area to assess in an evaluation for special education is a child's intellectual functioning. Intelligence testing is an area of great controversy because defining intelligence is not an easy task. Many different theorists have conflicting views on the nature of intelligence. Ask yourself what this means: "Sally is intelligent." What do you think you know about Sally? Is she smart? Bright? Exceptional? A great test taker?

Has good common sense? Maybe—maybe not. The fact is, two people may be very intelligent yet have very different capabilities, strengths, and weaknesses. Although the term *intelligence* is not easily defined, the definition we use is as follows: **Intelligence** is a general term referring to the ability to learn and to behave adaptively (Morris, 1999). In essence, intelligence is one's ability to learn new tasks and also be able to adapt to the situations one faces (referred to as **adaptive behavior**—see Chapter 11).

In special education, intelligence testing is usually completed by a psychologist. However, all professionals in special education need to understand intelligence tests and their purpose. Furthermore, it is very important that you learn how to interpret the results of intellectual measures so that you can substantiate a diagnosis, help determine learning styles, assist in making recommendations, and arrive at accurate levels of intellectual expectation.

The Purpose of Intelligence Testing

Intelligence tests are most helpful (and probably most appropriate) when they are used to determine specific skills, abilities, and knowledge that a child either has or does not have. When such information is combined with other evaluation data, it can be directly applied to school programming. Intelligence tests attempt to measure a number of skills, including the following:

- Social judgment
- Level of thinking
- Language skills
- Perceptual organization
- Processing speed
- Spatial abilities
- Common sense
- Long- and short-term memory
- Abstract thinking
- Motor speed
- Word knowledge

Many of these skills are very dependent on the experience, culture, training, and intact verbal abilities of the child being tested. However, responses to items concerning perceptual organization, processing speed, and spatial abilities are less dependent on experience and verbal skill and more on hand–eye coordination and reasoning abilities.

Intelligence tests can yield valuable information about a student's ability to process information. In order to learn, every person must take in, make sense of, store, and retrieve information from memory in an efficient and accurate way. Each of us can process certain kinds of information more easily than others. In school, children need certain skills to function effectively, such as listening attentively so that other movements, sounds, or sights do not distract them. They must be able to understand the words spoken to them. This often requires children to hold multiple pieces of information in memory (e.g., page number, questions to answer) in order to act upon them.

For example, they must be able to find the words they need to express themselves and, ultimately, commit these words to paper. This involves another whole series of processing skills such as holding a writing implement, coordinating visual and motor actions, holding information in memory until it can be transferred to paper, transforming sounds into written symbols, and understanding syntax, punctuation, and capitalization rules. They also must be able to interpret the nonverbal messages of others, such as a frown, a smile, a shake of the head. Moreover, they must do all of these things quickly and accurately and often in a setting with many distractions.

A thorough interpretation of an intelligence test can yield information about how effectively a child processes and retrieves information. Most individually administered intelligence tests can determine, at least to some degree, a child's ability to attend, process information quickly, distinguish relevant from less relevant details, put events in sequence, and retrieve words from memory.

IQ Scores

When children take intelligence tests they normally receive an overall **IQ** score. IQ is an abbreviation for *Intelligence Quotient*. The IQ score often represents a measure of the child's overall potential relative to the norms of his or her age group. On almost all intelligence tests, the mean IQ score is 100 with a standard deviation of 15.0 (a popular exception is the Stanford-Binet–4, which has a standard deviation of 16).

When a child receives an IQ score, a classification often accompanies it. The following is a list of the various IQ scores one can obtain on most intelligence tests, the classifications that directly apply, and the percentages of children who are included (assuming a mean of 100 and an SD of 15):

IQ RANGE	CLASSIFICATION	PERCENT INCLUDED
130 and over	Very Superior	2.2
120–129	Superior	6.7
110–119	High Average	16.1
90–109	Average	50.0
80–89	Low Average	16.1
70–79	Borderline	6.7
	Well-Below Average	
69 and below	Mentally Retarded	2.2
	Developmentally Delayed	
	Intellectually Deficient	

Kamphaus (1993) summarizes a number of research findings related to IQ scores:

■ IQ scores are more stable for school-age children than for preschoolers and more stable among individuals with disabilities than among those without disabilities.
■ IQ scores can change from childhood to adulthood.
■ It is likely that environmental factors, socioeconomic status, values, family structure, and genetic factors all play a role in determining IQ scores.

- Factors such as low birth weight, malnutrition, anoxia (lack of oxygen), and fetal alcohol exposure have a negative impact on intellectual functioning.
- Intelligence and academic achievement appear to be highly related.

Once an IQ score is calculated, the psychologist can make several determinations. The psychologist can then report back to parents, teachers, and all members of the assessment team the following information:

- The child's present overall levels of intellectual functioning
- The child's present verbal intellectual functioning
- The child's nonlanguage intellectual functioning
- Indications of greater intellectual potential
- Possible patterns involving learning style, for example, verbal comprehension and concentration
- Possible influence of tension and anxiety on testing results
- Intellectual capability to deal with present grade-level academic demands
- The influence of intellectual functioning as a contributing factor to a child's past and present school difficulties, for example, limited intellectual level of development found in mental retardation

MEASURES OF INTELLECTUAL ABILITY—THE WECHSLER SCALES

Many intelligence tests are used in special education. Some schools use different tests than others, based on personal preference and the strengths and weaknesses that each test exhibits. This section briefly summarizes some of the intelligence tests most often utilized in school systems.

The Wechsler Scales are one of the most widely used individual evaluation measures of intelligence utilized in today's schools. Although the Wechsler Scales are usually administered by psychologists, there is a great deal of useful information that can be obtained by all special educators from this test. Because special education teachers are likely to come in contact with this test, it is critical that they understand the nature of the scores and the implications of the results. A child's learning style, indications of greater potential, strengths and weaknesses, organizational skills, processing abilities, reasoning abilities, and adjustment to timed tasks are examples of useful information that can be obtained from this test.

The Wechsler Scales used for Preschool Children (*Wechsler Preschool Primary Scales of Intelligence:* WPPSI-III) and the Wechsler Scale used for individuals 17 years of age and older (*Wechsler Adult Intelligence Scale–3rd edition:* WAIS-III) consist of two separate parts—the Verbal and Performance tests. The Verbal Test is a group of **verbal subtests** that assess a student's verbal abilities. The Performance Test consists of a group of **performance subtests** that measure areas of intellectual functioning that do not involve verbal abilities.

On the new Wechsler Scale for Children, *Wechsler Intelligence Scale for Children*–4th edition (WISC-IV), there are four parts called Composite Indexes. These are:

- Verbal Composite Index (VCI)
- Perceptual Reasoning Index (PRI)
- Working Memory Index (WMI)
- Processing Speed Index

All Wechsler Scales of Intelligence produce a Full Scale IQ Score (on the WISC-IV it is referred to as the Full Scale Index-FSIQ), representing the child's overall IQ score.

The Wechsler Scales of Intelligence

Author: David Wechsler

Publisher: Harcourt Educational Assessment

Description of Test: The test is comprised of two areas of assessment: Verbal and Performance. The verbal areas are considered auditory/vocal tasks (auditory input and vocal output), whereas the performance areas are visual/vocal and visual/motor tasks (visual input and vocal or motoric output). The three tests include

- *Wechsler Preschool and Primary Scale of Intelligence–Revised* (WPPSI-III)
- *Wechsler Intelligence Scale for Children–III* (WISC-III)
- *Wechsler Adult Intelligence Scale–III* (WAIS-III)

Administration Time: 60 to 75 minutes

Age/Grade Levels: The three tests are designed for children and adults ages 2–6 to adult. The age ranges for the three Wechsler tests are

- WPPSI-III: ages 2–6 to 7–3 years
- WISC-III: ages 6–0 to 16–11 years
- WAIS-III: ages 17–0 years and older

Subtest Information: The three Wechsler Scales consist of a total of 21 possible subtests. Unless otherwise noted, all subtests are contained in each scale.

WECHSLER SUBTESTS (IN ALPHABETICAL ORDER)

- *Animal House*—Measures ability to associate meaning with symbol, visual-motor dexterity, flexibility, and speed in learning tasks (this subtest is part of the WPPSI-R only).
- *Arithmetic*—Measures mental alertness, concentration, attention, arithmetic reasoning, reaction to time pressure, and practical knowledge of computational facts. This is the only subtest directly related to the school curriculum and is greatly affected by anxiety.
- *Block Design*—Measures ability to perceive, analyze, synthesize, and reproduce abstract forms; visual-motor coordination; spatial relationships; general ability to plan and organize.
- *Cancellation*—Measures processing speed using random and structured animal target forms (forms are common non-animal objects). This subtest is part of the WISC-IV only.

- *Coding*—Measures ability to associate meaning with symbol, visual-motor dexterity (pencil manipulation), flexibility, and speed in learning tasks. This subtest is part of the WPPSI-III and WISC-IV only.
- *Comprehension*—Measures social judgment, commonsense reasoning based on past experience, and practical intelligence.
- *Digit Span*—Measures attention, concentration, immediate auditory memory, auditory attention, and behavior in a learning situation. This subtest correlates poorly with general intelligence.
- *Digit Symbol*—Measures ability to associate meaning with symbol, visual-motor dexterity (pencil manipulation), flexibility, and speed in learning tasks (this subtest is part of the WAIS-III only).
- *Geometric Design*—Measures a child's pencil control and visual-motor coordination, speed and accuracy, and planning capability (this subtest is part of the WPPSI-R only).
- *Information*—Measures general information acquired from experience and education, remote verbal memory, understanding, and associative thinking. The socioeconomic background and reading ability of the student may influence the subtest score.
- *Letter-Number Sequencing*—Measures working memory (adapted from WAIS-III); child is presented a mixed series of numbers and letters and repeats them, numbers first (in numerical order), then letters (in alphabetical order). This subtest is part of the WISC-IV only.
- *Matrix Reasoning*—Measures fluid reasoning a (highly reliable subtest on WAIS-III and WPPSI-III); child is presented with a partially filled grid and asked to select the item that properly completes the matrix.
- *Mazes*—Measures ability to formulate and execute a visual-motor plan, pencil control and visual-motor coordination, speed and accuracy, and planning capability (this subtest is part of the WPPSI-R and WISC-IV only).
- *Object Assembly*—Measures immediate perception of a total configuration, part–whole relationships, and visual-motor-spatial coordination (this subtest is part of the WPPSI-III and WAIS-III only).
- *Picture Arrangement*—Measures visual perception, logical sequencing of events, attention to detail, and ability to see cause–effect relationships (this subtest is part of the WISC-III and WAIS-III only).
- *Picture Completion*—Measures visual alertness to surroundings, remote visual memory, attention to detail, and ability to isolate essential from nonessential detail.
- *Picture Concepts*—Measures fluid reasoning, perceptual organization, and categorization (requires categorical reasoning without a verbal response); from each of two or three rows of objects, child selects objects that go together based on an underlying concept. This subtest is part of the WPPSI-III and WISC-IV only.
- *Picture Naming*—Measures the spoken vocabulary, expressive language ability, and word retrieval from long-term memory (WPPSI-III only).
- *Receptive Vocabulary*—Measures the ability to recognize the meaning of a word (WPPSI-III only).

- *Sentences*—Measures attention, concentration, immediate auditory memory, auditory attention, and behavior in a learning situation (this subtest is part of the WPPSI-R only).
- *Similarities*—Measures abstract and concrete reasoning, logical thought processes, associative thinking, and remote memory.
- *Symbol Search*—Measures visual discrimination (this subtest is part of the WPPSI-III and WISC-IV only).
- *Vocabulary*—Measures a child's understanding of spoken words, learning ability, general range of ideas, verbal information acquired from experience and education, and kind and quality of expressive language. This subtest is relatively unaffected by emotional disturbance, but is highly susceptible to cultural background and level of education. It is also the best single measure of intelligence in the entire battery.
- *Word Reasoning*—Measures reasoning with verbal material; child identifies underlying concept given successive clues. This subtest is part of the WPPSSI-III and WISC-IV only.

Composite Scores for the WISC-IV.   In order to make interpretation more clinical meaningful, the dual IQ and Index structure from WISC-III has been replaced with a single system of four composite scores (consistent with the Four Index Scores in WISC-III) and the Full Scale IQ. This new system helps you better understand a child's needs in relation to contemporary theory and research in cognitive information processing.

Key = * indicates that the subtest is not included in the index total score.

VERBAL COMPREHENSION INDEX (VCI):
Similarities
Vocabulary
Comprehension
*Information
*Word Reasoning

PERCEPTUAL REASONING INDEX (PRI):
Block Design
Picture Concepts
Matrix Reasoning
*Picture Completion

WORKING MEMORY INDEX (WMI):
Digit Span
Letter–Number Sequencing
*Arithmetic

PROCESSING SPEED INDEX (PSI):
Coding
Symbol Search
*Cancellation

PUBLISHER COMMENTS AND STRENGTHS OF THE WECHSLER SCALES

This fourth generation of the most widely used children's intellectual ability assessment meets your testing needs for the twenty-first century. While maintaining the integrity of the Wechsler tradition, the Wechsler Intelligence Scale for Children–4th Edition (WISC-IV) builds on contempary approaches in cognitive psychology and intellectual assessment, giving you a new, powerful and efficient tool to help develop and support your clinical judgements.

Understanding of learning disabilities and attentional disorders has greatly expanded since the publication of the WISC-III. WISC-IV makes important advances from WISC-III in order to provide the most effective clinical tool representing cutting edge research and thinking. This timely revision is the result of over a decade of research and success with the WISC-III. WISC-IV empowers you to use your experience, skills, and judgment to relate test results to referral questions.

Both the look and the feel of the instrument are updated to improve the testing experience for you and the child. The WISC-IV's modern artwork is colorful and engaging and incorporates recent changes in clothing, technology, and demographics. Instructions to both the examiner and the child are improved to make the WISC-IV even more user friendly.

The WISC-IV is designed to expand and strengthen clinical utility to support your decision making, Develop the four Index Scores as the primary interpretive structure, Improve the assessment of fluid reasoning, working memory, and processing speed, Improve subtest reliabilities, floors, and ceilings from WISC-III, and Link to the WIAT-II and to measures of memory (Children's Memory Scale, CMS), adaptive behavior (Adaptive Behavior Assessment System, ABAS), emotional intelligence (Bar-On EQ), and giftedness (Gifted Rating Scale, GRS).

Scaled Scores on the Wechsler Tests.   For each subtest on the Wechsler Tests, a student receives a raw score. This raw score is then transformed into a scaled score (see Chapter 6 for a review). **Scaled scores** are very specific subtest scores on the Wechsler Scales of Intelligence. Scaled scores can range from 1 to 19, with a mean of 10. They follow the following classification format:

SCALED SCORE	CLASSIFICATION
1–3	Developmentally Delayed
4–5	Borderline
6–7	Low Average
8–12	Average
13–14	High Average
15–16	Superior
17–19	Very Superior

For example, if a student gets only a scaled score of 7 on the Vocabulary subtest but a 13 on the Comprehension subtest, this indicates a much greater strength with respect to comprehension than with vocabulary, compared to the norms of his or her age group. Also, when detecting learning disabilities in psychoeducational assessment for a given child, there will often be great variance in the distribution of scaled scores when a learning disability is present.

The protocol reveals many things about the test and its cover contains a great deal of useful information. The first thing we want to look at is the pattern of scaled scores that appears next to the raw scores (the number of correct responses on a given test) on the front of the protocol. The scale scores can range from a low of 1 to a high of 19, with 10 considered the midpoint. However, several scaled scores may constitute a specific range (e.g., scaled scores of 8, 9, 10, and 11 are considered approximately average), as can be seen by the chart that follows.

To get a better idea of the value of a scaled score, simply multiply it by 10, and that will give you a "rough" idea of the correlated IQ value. It is from these scaled scores that our investigation of greater potential begins.

Relationship among IQ Ranges, Scaled Scores, and Percentiles

RANGE	SCALED SCORE	PERCENTILE
Very Superior	19	99.9
Very Superior	18	99.6
Very Superior	17	99
Superior	16	98
Superior	15	95
Above Average	14	91
Above Average	13	84
Average	12	75
Average	11	63
Average	10	50
Average	9	37
Average	8	25
Low Average	7	16
Low Average	6	9
Borderline	5	5
Borderline	4	2
Mentally Retarded	3	1
Mentally Retarded	2	0.4
Mentally Retarded	1	0.1

Note: This chart is used only for a general relationship between IQs, scaled scores, and percentiles, and is not statistically exact. The conversion tables used by the psychologist in deriving the actual IQ from test results are different and are located within the manual.

The scaled scores are calculated to get three separate IQ scores: *Verbal IQ, Performance IQ*, and a **Full Scale IQ** (the student's overall IQ score). When there is a discrepancy between the Verbal and Performance sections on the Wechsler tests, this is one indication of a possible learning disability (see Chapter 16 for a complete discussion of discrepancy scores).

The IQ results from the Wechsler Scales may not always indicate an individual's true intellectual potential. Although the Wechsler Scales are valid tests, the resulting scores can be influenced by many factors—tension, poor self-esteem, language difficulties, culture—and may not be valid, therefore necessitating further analysis. To determine if the resulting scores are valid, four indicators of an individual's true ability are applied to the results of the test. Any one indicator by itself should bring into question the validity of the results and initiate an analysis of the factors that may contribute to such variability.

OTHER MEASURES OF INTELLIGENCE

There are many other measures of intelligence used for assessment in special education. Some of the most popular ones are discussed in this section. They include:

- The Stanford-Binet Intelligence Scales, 5th Edition (SBIS-4)
- Kaufman Assessment Battery for Children (K-ABC)
- Kaufman Brief Intelligence Test (KBIT)
- Slosson Intelligence Test–Revised (SIT-R)
- Comprehensive Test of Nonverbal Intelligence (CTONI)
- Test of Nonverbal Intelligence, 3rd Edition (TONI-3)
- Otis-Lennon School Ability Test, 7th Edition (OLSAT-7)

The Stanford-Binet Intelligence Scale, 5th Edition (SB-5)

Authors: Gaile Roid

Publisher: The Riverside Publishing Company

Description of the Test: The SB5 is an individually administered assessment of intelligence and cognitive abilities.

Ages: 2 to 90+ years

Administration Time: The SB5 includes many untimed tasks with an average testing time of 45 to 60 minutes.

Subtests: The SB5 consists of five Factors covering 10 Domains (subtests):

1. *Fluid Reasoning (FR)*
   Nonverbal Fluid Reasoning*
   Verbal Fluid Reasoning
2. *Knowledge (KN)*
   Nonverbal Knowledge
   Verbal Knowledge*
3. *Quantitative Reasoning (QR)*
   Nonverbal Quantitative Reasoning
   Verbal Quantitative Reasoning
4. *Visual-Spatial Processing (VS)*
   Nonverbal Visual-Spatial Processing
   Verbal Visual-Spatial Processing

5. *Working Memory (WM)*
   Nonverbal Working Memory
   Verbal Working Memory

After completing both Routing Tests, administer all nonverbal subtests, followed by all verbal subtests.

STRENGTHS OF THE SB-5

Wide variety of items requiring nonverbal performance by examinee—ideal for assessing individuals with limited English, deafness, or communication disorders

Comprehensive measurement of five factors—Fluid Reasoning, Knowledge, Quantitative Reasoning, Visual-Spatial Processing, and Working Memory—providing a more complete assessment of individual intelligence

Ability to compare verbal and nonverbal performance—useful in evaluating learning disabilities

Greater diagnostic and clinical relevance of tasks, such as verbal and nonverbal assessment of working memory

Includes Full Scale IQ, Verbal and Nonverbal IQ, and Composite Indices spanning five dimensions with a standard score mean of 100, SD 15

Includes subtest scores with a mean of 10, SD 3

Extensive high-end items, many adapted from previous Stanford-Binet editions and designed to measure the highest level of gifted performance

Improved low-end items for better measurement of young children, low-functioning older children, or adults with Mental Retardation

Enhanced memory tasks provide a comprehensive assessment for adults and the elderly

Conormed with measures of visual-motor perception and test-taking behavior

Scorable by hand or with computer software

Enhanced artwork and manipulatives that are both colorful and child-friendly

Helps identify special needs

In addition to the concurrent validity studies, numerous studies of individuals with special needs or areas of disability have been conducted in order to best reflect the changes in IDEA legislation and to use multiple criteria for identification of children in need of special services. Substantial efforts have been taken to ensure the SB5 will help identify and adequately describe individuals who fall into the following categories:
   Specific learning disability
   Gifted
   Mental Retardation
   ADHD
   Speech and language delays
   Alzheimer's/dementia
   Traumatic brain injury
   Autism

Kaufman Assessment Battery for Children-II (KABC-II) 2nd Edition

Authors: Alan S. Kaufman and Nadeen L. Kaufman

Publisher: American Guidance Service

Description of Test: This individually administered intelligence test was developed in an attempt to minimize the influence of language and acquired facts and skills on the measurement of a child's intellectual ability.

Administration Time: 25 to 55 minutes (core battery, Luria model), 35 to 70 minutes (core battery, CHC model)

Age/Grade Levels: Ages 3 to 18 years

Subtest Information: The intelligence test contains 10 subtests:

- *Face Recognition*—This test requires the child to choose from a group photo the one or two faces that were exposed briefly.
- *Gestalt Closure*—This test requires the child to name an object or scene from a partially constructed inkblot.
- *Hand Movements*—The child is required to perform a series of hand movements presented by the examiner.
- *Magic Windows*—This test requires the child to identify a picture that the examiner exposes slowly through a window—only a small part is shown.
- *Matrix Analogies*—This test requires the child to choose a meaningful picture or abstract design that best completes a visual analogy.
- *Number Recall*—The child is required to repeat a series of digits in the same sequence as presented by the examiner.
- *Photo Series*—This test requires the child to place photographs of an event in the proper order.
- *Spatial Memory*—This test requires the child to recall the placement of a picture on a page that was briefly exposed.
- *Triangles*—This test requires the child to assemble several identical triangles into an abstract pattern.
- *Word Order*—The child is required to touch a series of silhouettes of objects in the same order as presented verbally by the examiner.

PUBLISHER COMMENTS AND STRENGTHS OF THE KABC-II

A dual theoretical foundation—using the Luria neuropsychological model and the Cattell/Horn/Carroll (CHC) approach—helps you obtain the data you need for each individual you test

A new, optional Knowledge/Crystallized Ability scale, so you can use one test with all children

An expanded age range for ages 3 to 18 that allows you to use one test for preschool, elementary, and high school children

Full conorming with the new Kaufman Test of Educational Achievement–2nd Edition (KTEA-II), for in-depth ability/achievement comparisons

The KABC-II now has a broader theoretical base, making it the instrument of choice for all cognitive assessment applications. Extensively redesigned and updated, this test provides detailed, accurate information and unprecedented flexibility. Like the original K-ABC, the second edition more fairly assesses children of different backgrounds and with diverse problems, with small score differences between ethnic groups.

A test of exceptional cultural fairness

KABC-II subtests are designed to minimize verbal instructions and responses. This gives you in-depth data with less "filtering" due to language.

Also, test items contain little cultural content, so children of diverse backgrounds are assessed more fairly. You can be confident you're getting a true picture of a child's abilities—even when language difficulties or cultural differences might affect test scores.

Dual theoretical model gives you options

With the KABC-II, you can choose the Cattell-Horn-Carroll model for children from a mainstream cultural and language background. Or if Crystallized Ability would not be a fair indicator of the child's cognitive ability, you may choose the Luria model, which excludes verbal ability. Administer the same subtests on four or five ability scales. Then, interpret the results based on your chosen model. Either approach gives you a global score that is highly valid and that shows small differences between ethnic groups in comparison with other comprehensive ability batteries. In addition, a nonverbal option allows you to assess a child whose verbal skills are significantly limited.

Kaufman Brief Intelligence Test–2nd Edition (KBIT-2)

Authors: Alan S. Kaufman and Nadeen L. Kaufman (2004)

Publisher: American Guidance Service

Description of Test: This test is an assessment device for developing and evaluating remedial programs for those with mental disabilities. It may also be used for normal children aged birth to 10 years. It is a brief, individually administered screener of verbal and nonverbal ability.

Administration Time: Approximately 20 minutes

Age/Grade Levels: Ages 4 to 90

Subtest Information: KBIT-2 measures two distinct cognitive abilities through two scales—Crystallized and Fluid.

- Crystallized (Verbal) Scale contains two item types: Verbal Knowledge and Riddles
- Fluid (Nonverbal) Scale is a Matrices subtest

STRENGTHS OF THE KBIT-2

Measures verbal and nonverbal intelligence quickly

Is easy to administer and score

Provides valid and reliable results

Attractive test items—offers new, full-color items that are specially designed to appeal to children and reluctant examinees

Conormed with the brief achievement test, KTEA-II Brief Form, for ages 26 to 90

Obtain a quick estimate of intelligence

Screen to identify students who may benefit from enrichment or gifted programs

Identify high-risk children through large-scale screening who require a more comprehensive evaluation

Obtain a quick estimate of the intellectual ability of adults in institutional settings, such as prisons, group homes, rehabilitation clinics, or mental health centers

Slosson Intelligence Test–Revised (SIT-3)

Authors: Richard L. Slosson; Revised by Charles L. Nicholson and Terry L. Hibpschman

Publisher: Slosson Educational Publications & Stoelting Company

Description of Test: The *Slosson Intelligence Test–Revised* (SIT-3) is a quick, reliable, user-friendly instrument for evaluating crystallized verbal intelligence in children and adults (see Figure 10.1). In addition to being one of the few measures assessing the infant, toddler, and preschool years (two and above), it can also be used with Severely/Profoundly Mentally Handicapped populations because its IQ scales range from 36 to 164.

Administration Time: 10 to 20 minutes

Age/Grade Levels: Ages Preschool to Adult

Subtest Information: The SIT-3 test items are derived from the following cognitive domains: Information, Comprehension, Arithmetic, Similarities and Differences, Vocabulary, and Auditory Memory. Cognitive areas of measurements include:

- *Vocabulary:* 33 items
- *General Information:* 29 items
- *Similarities and Differences:* 30 items
- *Comprehension:* 33 items
- *Quantitative:* 34 items
- *Auditory Memory:* 28 items

PUBLISHER COMMENTS ON STRENGTHS

The SIT-3 has been especially constructed so any professional having taken an introductory course in tests and measurements can easily administer this quick screening instrument. A 25-point helpful checklist and sample scoring procedures are included for easy test review.

The SIT-3 is appropriate for the United States and English-speaking countries. Quantitative reasoning questions were designed to be administered to populations who use metric or standard references, using language common to both.

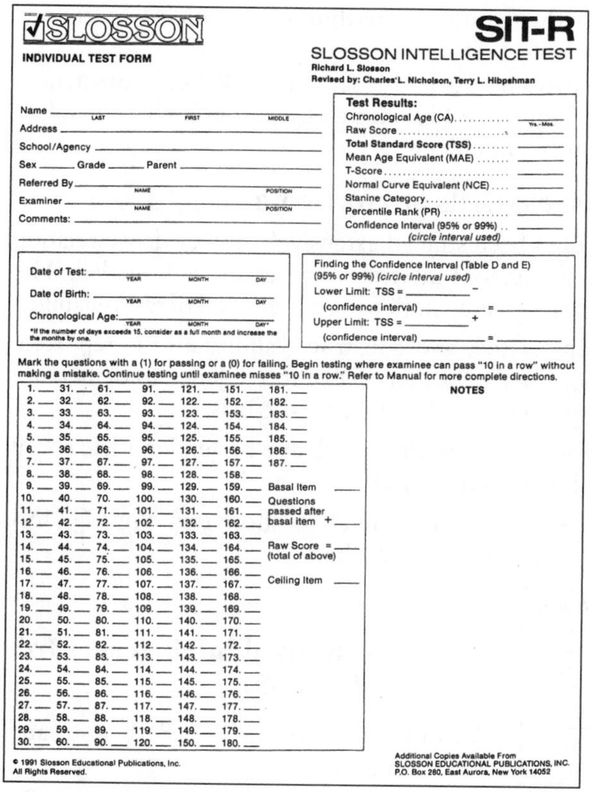

SLOSSON

INDIVIDUAL TEST FORM

SIT-R

SLOSSON INTELLIGENCE TEST

Richard L. Slosson

Revised by: Charles L. Nicholson, Terry L. Hibpshman

Name ________ (LAST, FIRST, MIDDLE)

Address ________

School/Agency ________

Sex ____ Grade ____ Parent ________

Referred By ________ (NAME, POSITION)

Examiner ________ (NAME, POSITION)

Comments: ________

Test Results:

Chronological Age (CA) .... ____ (Yrs.-Mos.)

Raw Score .... ____

Total Standard Score (TSS) .... ____

Mean Age Equivalent (MAE) .... ____

T-Score .... ____

Normal Curve Equivalent (NCE) .... ____

Stanine Category .... ____

Percentile Rank (PR) .... ____

Confidence Interval (95% or 99%) .... ____ *(circle interval used)*

Date of Test: ________ (YEAR, MONTH, DAY)

Date of Birth: ________ (YEAR, MONTH, DAY)

Chronological Age: ________ (YEAR, MONTH, DAY*)

*If the number of days exceeds 15, consider as a full month and increase the the months by one.

Finding the Confidence Interval (Table D and E) (95% or 99%) *(circle interval used)*

Lower Limit: TSS = ________ −

(confidence interval) ________ = ________

Upper Limit: TSS = ________ +

(confidence interval) ________ = ________

Mark the questions with a (1) for passing or a (0) for failing. Begin testing where examinee can pass "10 in a row" without making a mistake. Continue testing until examinee misses "10 in a row." Refer to Manual for more complete directions.

1. ___	31. ___	61. ___	91. ___	121. ___	151. ___	181. ___
2. ___	32. ___	62. ___	92. ___	122. ___	152. ___	182. ___
3. ___	33. ___	63. ___	93. ___	123. ___	153. ___	183. ___
4. ___	34. ___	64. ___	94. ___	124. ___	154. ___	184. ___
5. ___	35. ___	65. ___	95. ___	125. ___	155. ___	185. ___
6. ___	36. ___	66. ___	96. ___	126. ___	156. ___	186. ___
7. ___	37. ___	67. ___	97. ___	127. ___	157. ___	187. ___
8. ___	38. ___	68. ___	98. ___	128. ___	158. ___	
9. ___	39. ___	69. ___	99. ___	129. ___	159. ___	Basal Item ___
10. ___	40. ___	70. ___	100. ___	130. ___	160. ___	Questions passed after basal item + ___
11. ___	41. ___	71. ___	101. ___	131. ___	161. ___	
12. ___	42. ___	72. ___	102. ___	132. ___	162. ___	
13. ___	43. ___	73. ___	103. ___	133. ___	163. ___	
14. ___	44. ___	74. ___	104. ___	134. ___	164. ___	Raw Score = ___ (total of above)
15. ___	45. ___	75. ___	105. ___	135. ___	165. ___	
16. ___	46. ___	76. ___	106. ___	136. ___	166. ___	
17. ___	47. ___	77. ___	107. ___	137. ___	167. ___	Ceiling Item ___
18. ___	48. ___	78. ___	108. ___	138. ___	168. ___	
19. ___	49. ___	79. ___	109. ___	139. ___	169. ___	
20. ___	50. ___	80. ___	110. ___	140. ___	170. ___	
21. ___	51. ___	81. ___	111. ___	141. ___	171. ___	
22. ___	52. ___	82. ___	112. ___	142. ___	172. ___	
23. ___	53. ___	83. ___	113. ___	143. ___	173. ___	
24. ___	54. ___	84. ___	114. ___	144. ___	174. ___	
25. ___	55. ___	85. ___	115. ___	145. ___	175. ___	
26. ___	56. ___	86. ___	116. ___	146. ___	176. ___	
27. ___	57. ___	87. ___	117. ___	147. ___	177. ___	
28. ___	58. ___	88. ___	118. ___	148. ___	178. ___	
29. ___	59. ___	89. ___	119. ___	149. ___	179. ___	
30. ___	60. ___	90. ___	120. ___	150. ___	180. ___	

NOTES

Additional Copies Available From
SLOSSON EDUCATIONAL PUBLICATIONS, INC.
P.O. Box 280, East Aurora, New York 14052

FIGURE 10.1 Slosson Intelligence Test–Revised, Individual Test Form

The comprehensive test manual addresses appropriate usage and interpretation, and test items use contemporary vocabulary and are free of significant group biases.

Standardized on 2,000 individuals, approximating the contemporary U.S. census, SIT-3 uses a deviational IQ and provides standard scores and percentiles for scores as well.

Excellent reliability (.90 or higher) across all age groups.

The SIT-3 provides an excellent complement to other educational assessments that look at learning ability, readiness, or achievement.

The SIT-3 includes the manual, norm tables, and a package of score sheets and Braille supplies. Computer scoring is available separately.

Comprehensive Test of Nonverbal Intelligence (CTONI)

Authors: Donald D. Hammill, Nils A. Pearson, and Lee Wiederholt

Publisher: PRO-ED

Description of Test: The CTONI is a seemingly unbiased test that measures six different types of nonverbal reasoning ability. No oral responses, reading, writing, or object manipulation are involved.

Administration Time: 60 minutes

Age/Grade Levels: Ages 6 to 18

Subtest Information: The subtests of the CTONI require students to look at a group of pictures or designs and to solve problems involving analogies, categorizations, and sequences. Individuals indicate their answer by pointing to alternative choices. There are six subtests arranged according to three abilities. The three ability areas are:

- *Analogical Reasoning*—The two subtests on Analogical Reasoning are Pictorial Analogies and Geometric Analogies. This section identifies the ability to recognize a fourth object that bears the same relation to the third as the second does to the first.
- *Categorical Classification*—The two subtests in this section are Pictorial Categories and Geometric Categories. Categorical Classification assesses

the ability to understand the common attributes by which objects are grouped.

■ *Sequential Reasoning*—The two subtests in this section are Pictorial Sequences and Geometric Sequences. Sequential Reasoning assesses the ability to understand the successive relationship of objects.

PUBLISHER COMMENTS ON STRENGTHS OF THE CTONI

The reliability of the CTONI has been studied extensively, and evidence relating to content sampling, time sampling, and interscorer reliability is provided. The reliability coefficients are all .80 or greater, indicating a high level of test reliability.

Evidence of content, criterion-related, and construct validity also is reported. The CTONI has gone further than any other test of intelligence to detect and eliminate sources of cultural, gender, racial, and linguistic bias.

The CTONI normative sample is representative relative to gender, race, social class, language spoken in the home, and disability.

Convincing evidence is presented in the manual to show that the CTONI items contain little or no bias for the groups studied.

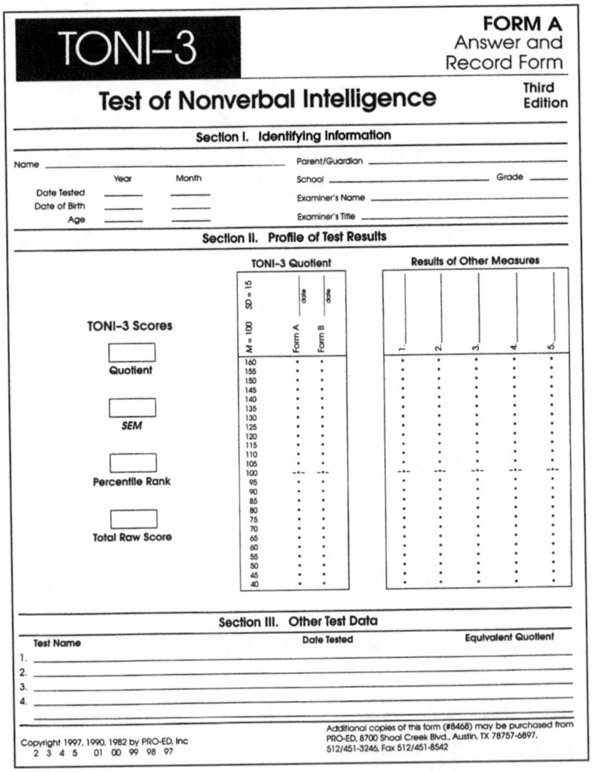

FIGURE 10.2   Test of Nonverbal Intelligence–Third Edition, Answer and Record Form

Test of Nonverbal Intelligence–3rd Edition (TONI-3)

Authors: L. Brown, R. J. Serbenou, and S. K. Johnsen

Publisher: PRO-ED

Description of Test: The TONI-3 is designed to measure the nonverbal intelligence of students who are bilingual, speak a language other than English, or are socially/economically disadvantaged, deaf, language disordered, motor impaired, or neurologically impaired (see Figure 10.2). The test requires no reading, writing, speaking, or listening on the part of the test subject. It is completely nonverbal and largely motor-free, requiring only a point, nod, or symbolic gesture to indicate response choices.

Administration Time: 15 to 20 minutes

Age/Grade Level: Ages 5 to 85

Subtest Information: There are no subtests on the TONI-3. Each form of the TONI-3 contains 50 items arranged in easy to difficult order.

PUBLISHER COMMENTS ON STRENGTHS OF THE TONI-3

This unique language-free format makes the TONI-3 ideal for evaluating subjects who have previously been difficult to test with any degree of confidence or precision. It is particularly well suited for individuals who are known or believed to have disorders of communication or thinking such as aphasia, dyslexia, language disabilities, learning disabilities, speech problems, specific academic deficits, and similar conditions that may be the result of mental retardation, deafness, developmental disabilities, autism, cerebral palsy, stroke, disease, head injury, or other neurological impairment. The format also accommodates the needs of subjects who do not read or write English well, due to disability or lack of exposure to the English language and U.S. culture.

THE TONI-3:

- Meets the highest psychometric standards for norms, reliability, and validity
- Is language free, requiring no reading, writing, or listening
- Is culturally reduced, utilizing novel abstract/figural content
- Is motor reduced, with only a meaningful gesture required in response
- Is quick to score, requiring less than 15 minutes to administer and score
- Is appropriate for use with children, adolescents, and older adults ages 6 through 89 years
- Has two equivalent forms suitable for test–retest and pre- and posttesting situations
- Provides detailed directions for administering, scoring, and interpreting the test in the manual
- Has a 20-year body of reliability and validity research cited and summarized in the test manual

Otis-Lennon School Ability Test–8th Edition (OLSAT-8)

Authors: Arthur S. Otis and Roger T. Lennon

Publisher: Harcourt Assessment, Inc.

Description of Test: OLSAT-8 measures the cognitive abilities that relate to a student's ability to learn in school. By assessing a student's abstract thinking and reasoning abilities, OLSAT-8 supplies educators with information they can use to enhance the insight that traditional achievement tests provide.

Administration Time: A–C (Grades K through 2), 75 minutes over two sessions; Levels D–G (Grades 3 through 12), 60 minutes

Age/Grade Levels: Grades K through 12

Subtest Information: The test is broken down into five clusters:

- *Verbal Comprehension*—This cluster includes following directions, antonyms, sentence completion, and sentence arrangement.
- *Verbal Reasoning*—This cluster includes logical selection, verbal analogies, verbal classification, and inference.

- *Pictorial Reasoning*—This cluster includes picture classification, picture analogies, and picture series.
- *Figural Reasoning*—This cluster includes figural classification, figural analogies, and figural series.
- *Quantitative Reasoning* (given in Levels E—G)—This cluster includes number series, numeric inference, and number matrix.

PUBLISHER COMMENTS STRENGTHS

When administered with the *Stanford Achievement Test Series, Tenth Edition* (Stanford 10), OLSAT-8 scores may also be used to relate a student's actual achievement with his or her school ability.

OLSAT 8 assesses students' thinking skills and provides an understanding of a student's relative strengths and weaknesses in performing a variety of reasoning tasks. This information allows educators to design educational programs that will enhance students' strengths while supporting their learning needs.

CONCLUSION

Intelligence tests are very important in the determination of various disabilities. As you will see later in this book, a determination of whether a child has a learning disability, emotional disturbance, or mental retardation cannot be done without an IQ score. When all is said and done, IQ scores give the special educator a solid indicator of a child's overall potential. Furthermore, when properly evaluated, intelligence tests can uniquely describe in detail numerous strengths and weaknesses of a child as no other tests can do. Utilizing this data appropriately is critical for future placement, recommendations, expectations, and appropriate services for a child.

V O C A B U L A R Y

Adaptive Behavior: The effectiveness or degree with which individuals meet the standards of personal independence and social responsibility expected for age and cultural groups.

Average: A classification that refers to an IQ score of 90 to 109, with a mean of 100 and standard deviation of 15.

Borderline: A classification that refers to an IQ score of 70 to 79, with a mean of 100 and standard deviation of 15.

Developmentally Delayed: A classification that refers to an IQ score of 69 or below, with a mean of 100 and standard deviation of 15.

Full Scale IQ: On the Wechsler Scales, the student's overall IQ score.

High Average: A classification that refers to an IQ score of 110 to 119, with a mean of 100 and standard deviation of 15.

Intellectually Deficient: A classification that refers to an IQ score of 69 and below, with a mean of 100 and standard deviation of 15.

Intelligence: A general term referring to the ability to learn and to behave adaptively.

IQ: An abbreviation for Intelligence Quotient. It is the score one receives on the IQ test.

Low Average: A classification that refers to an IQ score of 80 to 89, with a mean of 100 and standard deviation of 15.

Mentally Retarded: A classification on the Wechsler Tests that refers to an IQ score of 69 and below, with a mean of 100 and standard deviation of 15.

Performance Subtests: Sections on IQ tests that measure a child's nonverbal abilities.

Scaled Score: Scores on the Wechsler scales ranging from 1 to 19, (with a mean of 10 and a standard deviation of 3) that are calculated to provide three separate IQ scores: Verbal IQ, Performance IQ, and a Full Scale IQ.

Superior: A classification that refers to an IQ score of 120 to 129, with a mean of 100 and standard deviation of 15.

Verbal Subtests: Sections on IQ tests that measure a child's verbal abilities.

Very Superior: A classification that refers to an IQ score of 130 and over, with a mean of 100 and standard deviation of 15.

......

CHAPTER ELEVEN

ASSESSMENT OF BEHAVIOR

KEY TERMS

Anecdotal Recording
Apperception Tests
Duration Recording
Event Recording
Functional Behavioral Assessment (FBA)
Interview
Latency Recording

Projective Drawing Tests
Rating Scales
Sentence Completion Tests
Structured Interview
Target Behaviors
Unstructured Interview

CHAPTER OBJECTIVES

When a referral is made for a child who is suspected to have a disability, a behavioral and emotional assessment is a normal part of the evaluation. Behavioral and emotional measures are usually administered and reported on by the school psychologist. The behavior of a given child can have a serious impact on his or her learning processes. For example, a child with problems staying on task or focusing may have the intelligence to do math or social studies but consistently gets low grades because he or she cannot sit still in order to complete the assignments given by the teacher.

Behaviors that are not appropriate in school can occur for many different reasons. Some include:

Attention deficit problems
Emotional disturbance
Environmental factors at home

Problems with teachers of certain classes
Depression
Anxiety

When behaviors are believed to be a contributing factor to a child's problems in school, a variety of methods can be used for assessment. Because there are so many different possibilities for a child to act inappropriately in school, it is critical to do a thorough behavioral assessment. By doing this, reasons for future placement in special education programs and the nature of the appropriate services will be more easily accomplished.

This chapter focuses on the assessment of behavior. After reading this chapter, you should be able to understand the following:

- The purpose of a behavioral assessment
- Observational techniques

- Recording behaviors
- Interviews
- A student's behavior during testing
- Psychological tests
- Projective drawing tests
- Apperception tests
- Sentence completion tests
- Adaptive behavior
- Functional behavioral assessment
- Behavioral intervention plans

ASSESSING PROBLEM BEHAVIOR

Observation

Observation as part of the assessment process is often done when parents, teachers, or any other individuals working with a child feel there are possible concerns involving emotional, social, or behavioral issues. The purpose of observation is to gain an awareness of what factors, if any, are influencing the behavior that the child is exhibiting. In order to do a complete and thorough observation, it is critical to include the following situations:

- **Observation of a specific situation:** Here, an observation of the child is done during a specified time, such as during lunchtime, recess, or show and tell.
- **Observation in various settings:** Here, an observation of the child is done across different settings, such as in the classroom, on the playground, and during band.
- **Observation at different times during the day:** Here, an observation of the child is done in the morning, in the afternoon, and by parents in the evening.

There are many different ways to record a child's behavior for assessment purposes. Regardless, the first goal of observation is to determine the target behaviors. **Target behaviors** are those that the observer seeks to record when doing the observation. For example, an observer could be looking for how many times a child taps his or her pencil during a 30-minute period. Here, the target behavior would be tapping the pencil. Once the target behavior is established, recording of behaviors can begin. In assessment, various types of recording are often used when doing an observation. Four of the most common are:

- **Anecdotal recording:** Here, the observer records behaviors and interactions within a given time frame (e.g., recording a child's behavior from 9:00 A.M. until 9:30 A.M.).

- **Event recording:** Here, the observer is looking specifically for one or more target behaviors and records the frequency with which they occur. Event recording is also referred to as *frequency counting* because the observer is simply "counting" the number of times a behavior occurs (e.g., recording the number of times a child gets out of his chair in a given period of time).
- **Latency recording:** Here, the observer determines the amount of time between a given stimulus for the child and the response (e.g., the time it takes a student to get out her pencil after the teacher says, "Take out your pencil").
- **Duration recording:** Here, the observer notes the amount of time a target behavior occurs (e.g., watching a child for one hour who is supposed to be reading—the child reads only 12 minutes of that time).

When doing the above observations, information about the child becomes much more comprehensive. Collectively, observations should provide the following:

- The nature of the most frequently seen behaviors
- Information that can be related to the types of services the child may need
- Information to help with intervention plans and instructional goals for the child
- An understanding of where the child is currently functioning in certain areas.

Later, this can be compared to the child's behavior after intervention begins. Therefore, progress can be measured from the first observation (baseline) to after a plan or program has been implemented for the child to determine if it is actually working and signs of progress are being noticed.

Interviews

Besides observations, interviews become a very important part of the behavioral assessment. An **interview** is a method of gathering information that is conducted face to face between two people (the interviewer and the interviewee) whereby recorded responses to questions are obtained. Interviews can be very effective because they are personal, emotional, and flexible. Interviews can be of two types:

- **Structured interview:** An interview in which the individual is asked a specific set of predetermined questions in a controlled manner.
- **Unstructured interview:** An interview in which the questions are not predetermined, thereby allowing for substantial discussion and interaction between the interviewer and interviewee.

Parents, teachers, and the child should be interviewed in order to gain insight into the nature and history of the child's difficulties. It is important to interview the child because the evaluator needs to know whether the child has any awareness that there is a concern about his or her behaviors and the degree to which he or she may be willing to change.

UNDERSTANDING A STUDENT'S
BEHAVIOR DURING ASSESSMENT

There are many behaviors that should be watched when doing an assessment for a child with a suspected disability. It is important that evaluators consider carefully any peculiarities exhibited by a student during evaluation. Almost any peculiarity can be seen as either a symptom or a problem. For example, a student who hesitates for long periods before answering may be doing so as a symptom of a difficulty processing information or as a symptom of low self-esteem. However, this hesitation itself becomes a problem during evaluation because it slows the student down considerably and therefore limits strong performance. Evaluations must consider what peculiarities reveal as well as the impact they have. Accordingly, the following behaviors should be recorded in the final report: adjustment to the situation, reaction time, nature of responses, verbalizations, organizational approach used during testing, adaptability, and attitude.

Adjustment to the Situation

Children's adjustment to a new situation (e.g., initial meeting with evaluator, IQ testing, fine-motor testing, etc.) can vary greatly. The significance of any adjustment period is not necessarily the student's initial reactions but the duration of the period of maladjustment. Some children may be initially nervous and uptight but relax as time goes on with the reassurance of the examiner. However, children who maintain a high level of discomfort throughout the sessions may be harboring more serious problems.

Elements of the testing environment itself should be considered as possible distracters for the student being tested. Noise, poor lighting, the presence of antagonistic peers, even an intimidating examiner can adversely impact a student during testing. It is the evaluator's responsibility to limit such variables and to consider the special needs of each student. Examiners should be aware of any overt signs of tension (observable behaviors indicative of underlying tension) exhibited by a child that may affect the outcome of the test results: constant leg motion, little or no eye contact with the examiner, consistent finger or pencil tapping. Any oppositional behaviors (behaviors that test the limits and guidelines of the examiner) should also be noted: singing or making noises while being tested, keeping a jacket on or covering most of his or her face with a hat, and so forth. If this type of tension is extreme, the examiner may want to note in the report the effects of such factors on performance and alert the reader to the possibility that the results may be minimal indicators of ability.

Reaction Time

The speed with which a child answers questions can indicate several things. The child who impulsively answers incorrectly without thinking may be one with high levels of anxiety that interfere with the ability to concentrate before responding. On the other hand, the child who blocks or delays may be afraid of reaction or criticism and may be using these techniques to ward off what he or she perceives will be an ego-deflating situation.

Nature of Responses

The types of responses a child gives during an evaluation may indicate certain difficulties. For example, a child who constantly asks to have questions repeated may have hearing difficulties. (Hearing and vision acuity should be determined prior to a testing situation.) Or, the child who asks to have questions repeated may be having problems processing information and may need more time to understand what is being asked. If a child is overtly negative or self-defeating in responding—for example, "I'm so stupid," "I'll never get any right"—the child is probably exhibiting a very low level of self-esteem or hiding a learning problem.

Verbalizations

A student's verbal interaction with the examiner during an evaluation can be very telling. Some children with high levels of anxiety may try to vent their tension through constant verbalizations. Of course, the tension can interfere with their ability to think clearly and to focus on task, and the verbalizing can also disrupt hearing and thought processes. Examiners should also be aware that verbal hesitations may indicate other problems: immature speech patterns, expressive language problems, poor self-esteem, or lack of understanding of the question due to limited intellectual capacity.

Organizational Approach Used during Testing

A child who sizes up a situation and systematically approaches a task using trial and error may have excellent internal organization, the ability to concentrate, and low levels of tension and anxiety. However, some children with emotional problems may also perform well on short-term tasks because they see it as a challenge and can organize themselves to perform well over a relatively short period of time. Their particular problems in organization and consistency may come when they are asked to perform this way over an extended period of time. On the other hand, some children become less organized under the stress of a time constraint. A child's organizational and performance styles when dealing with a task under time restrictions are factors considered in the investigation of his or her overall learning style.

Children with chaotic internal organization may appear to know what they are doing, but the overall outcome of the task indicates a great deal of energy input with very low production. They essentially "spin their wheels," and the energy output is a cover for not knowing what to do. Children with Attention Deficit Hyperactive Disorder also may exhibit a confused sense of organization. However, there are other factors besides attention span that go into the diagnosis of this disorder, which is discussed later in this chapter.

Adaptability

The ability of a student to adapt or shift from one task to another without difficulty is a very important factor in determining learning style and may be one predictor for the successful completion of a task. A student's ability to shift without expending a great deal of energy results in more available resources for the next task. A student who is rigid and does not adapt well uses much available energy to switch tasks, thereby reducing the chances of success on a new task.

The ability to sustain interest may also be a direct result of available energy. A child who loses interest quickly may be immature, overwhelmed, or preoccupied. Some of these reactions may be normal for the early ages. However, as the child gets older, such reactions may be symptomatic of other factors, e.g., learning problems, emotional issues, or limited intellectual capacity.

Attitude

The attitude that a child demonstrates toward a testing situation may be reflective of his or her attitude within the classroom. A child who is oppositional or uncoopera-tive may be one who needs to feel in control of the situation. The more controlling a child is, the more out of control he or she feels. Control on the part of a child is aimed at securing predictability to be able to deal with a situation even though his or her energy levels may be lowered by conflict and tension. Children under tension do not adapt well and are easily thrown by new situations or people. By controlling a sit-uation or a person, they know what to expect. On the other hand, a child who tries hard to succeed may do so for several reasons, such as parental approval or personal satisfaction. He or she may enjoy success and find the tasks normally challenging. Generally, this type of child is not thrown by a mistake and can easily move to the next task without difficulty.

All behavior is essentially a message, and the way a child reacts to being tested can be a clue to learning style or problem areas. The evaluator who can attend to a child's behavior by being aware of significant signs may come to a better understanding of the child's needs and may learn even more about the child than the test results will indicate.

ASSESSING EMOTIONAL AND SOCIAL DEVELOPMENT

Assessment of emotional and social development is not an easy task. Throughout the course of a given day, children are involved in many situations with different people. It is not like assessing math or reading, whereby we can normally compare numbers of a given child to national norms and make conclusions based on the quantifiable data. A child may act completely different with one person than another. Assessment of a child's behaviors involves knowledge about the following:

- The degree to which the child believes that personal behaviors make a difference in his or her life
- The child's tolerance for frustration
- General activity level
- The child's self-view

- How the child responds emotionally
- How much conflict the child is experiencing

Psychological Tests

There are numerous psychological tests used in the assessment of behavior in children. Psychological tests are almost always administered exclusively by the school psychologist. One of the most common types of psychological tests is called a projective test. *Projective tests* try to elicit feelings from the student about how he or she feels about life through projection of emotions onto the test stimuli. The three most common types of projective tests used in school systems for assessment are projective drawing tests, apperception tests, and sentence completion tests.

A **projective drawing test** requires an individual to respond to indistinct stimuli. The individual's interpretation of the stimuli is meant to reveal personality traits. The tests are used to get the child to "project" his feelings about himself onto paper. The examiner looks for certain patterns in the drawings and the way in which the child handles what is being asked of him or her (e.g., a child who draws himself away from everyone else may have low self-esteem; or a child who takes the pencil and writes very hard on the paper may be exhibiting anger).

Goodenough-Harris Drawing Test (GHDT)

Authors: Florence L. Goodenough and Dale B. Harris

Publisher: Harcourt Assessment, Inc.

Description of Test: Developed in 1926 and revised in the late 1940s, the GHDT's purpose is to assess mental maturity nonverbally. The test is a formal system of administering and scoring human figure drawings to screen children for intellectual maturity as well as emotional problems. Practitioners can detect children who are at risk of having an emotional disturbance by comparing the scores obtained on their figure drawings with the scores from a normative sample.

Administration Time: 15 to 20 minutes

Age/Grade Levels: Ages 3 to 15-11, but the preferred ages are 3 to 10 years

Subtest Information: The Goodenough-Harris Drawing Test is composed of two scales: Man and Woman. Performance may be scored by a short, holistic method with Quality Scale Cards or by a more detailed method. Each drawing may also be scored for the presence of up to 73 characteristics.

STRENGTHS OF THE GHDT

The test's reliability is relatively high.

The test manual provides a clear description of the scoring system. The record form is clear and efficient.

The test is psychometrically sound as well as easily and objectively quantified.

It is a popular test to administer because it is so easy to do.

Draw-A-Person: Screening Procedure for Emotional Disturbance (DAP:SPED)

Authors: Jack A. Naglieri, Timothy J. McNeish, and Achilles N. Bardos (1991)

Publisher: Harcourt Assessment Inc.

Description of Test: The purpose of the DAP:SPED is to identify emotional or behavioral disorders. The test comprises a formal system of administering and scoring human figure drawings to screen children for emotional problems. Practitioners can detect children who are at risk of having an emotional disturbance by comparing the scores obtained on their figure drawings with the scores from the normative sample.

Administration Time: 15 minutes

Age/Grade Levels: Ages 6 to 17 years

Subtest Information: There are no subtests. The DAP:SPED scoring system is composed of two types of criteria, or items. With the first type, eight dimensions of each drawing are scored; a separate template for each age group is provided. With the second type of criteria, each drawing is rated according to 47 specific items. Cutoff scores are divided into three categories: additional assessment is not indicated; additional assessment is indicated; and additional assessment is strongly indicated.

STRENGTHS OF THE DAP:SPED

The test reliability is relatively high.

The test manual provides a clear description of the scoring system. The record form is clear and efficient.

The test is psychometrically sound as well as easily and objectively quantified.

Apperception Tests

Apperception tests require a child to view various picture cards and "tell a story" about what is shown. The child would normally tell a story of what happened before, during, and after the scene shown. Apperception tests try to elicit central themes from the child. For example, a child may consistently tell stories of loneliness, sadness, or perhaps anger. The examiner normally writes down every word the child says in narrative form and then tries to decipher general patterns of self-thoughts that the child may be projecting.

Children's Apperception Test (CAT)

Authors: Leopold Bellack and Sonya Sorel Bellak (1974)

Publisher: C.P.S. Incorporated

Description of Test: This projective technique presents situations of special concern to children. It consists of 10 animal pictures in a social context that involve the child in conflict, identities, roles, family structures, and interpersonal interaction. This test uses a storytelling technique for personality evaluation. It employs pictures of animal figures in a variety of situations because it is assumed that children will be more comfortable expressing their feelings with pictures of animals than of humans.

Administration Time: Untimed

Age/Grade Levels: Ages 5 to 10 years

Subtest Information: There are no subtests.

STRENGTHS OF THE CAT

This test is a good indicator of the presence of psychological needs.

This test is easy to administer.

This is a very popular test within school systems as part of a psychological battery.

Thematic Apperception Test (TAT)

Author: Henry A. Murray

Publisher of the Test: Pearson Assessments

Description of Test: Created in 1943, the TAT is still a widely-used projective test that helps assess an individual's perception of interpersonal relationships. The 31 picture cards included in the TAT are used to stimulate stories or descriptions about relationships or social situations and can help identify dominant drives, emotions, sentiments, conflicts, and complexes.

Administration Time: Variable (31 picture cards/2 series of 10 cards for boys, girls, men, and women)

Age/Grade Levels: Age 10 years and older

Subtest Information: No subtests: Individuals react (orally or in writing) to a series of picture cards

STRENGTHS OF THE TAT

The test is a good indicator of the presence of psychological needs.

The test is easy to administer.

The test is very popular within school systems as part of a psychological battery because of the easy administration and the quality of information that can be obtained.

Sentence Completion Tests

Sentence completion tests provide the beginning of a sentence that the student needs to finish. The "fill ins" are believed to give indications of the emotions and feelings that the student is experiencing. Sentence completion tests can be extremely useful because one response can elicit many questions to ask the child in future interviews. For example, if a child responds to "I could do better if _____," with a response of "I tried harder," you can later ask the child many questions about why his effort is poor or not up to a certain level.

Examples from a Sentence Completion Test

1. I wish _____
2. When I grow up _____
3. My mother _____
4. My best subject is _____
5. I wish my teacher would _____
7. On the school bus _____
8. I could do better if _____

Rating Scales

Rating scales are often given not only to the student but also to the parents and teachers. A rating scale gives a statement about a behavior of a child whereupon the individual (*the rater*) has to rate the frequency, intensity, and/or duration. By rating various situations, the examiner gets an idea of the child's strengths and weaknesses. Raters are normally asked to evaluate whether a given behavior is present or absent. The tremendous value of a rating scale is that it allows the examiner to get a differing viewpoint from other people who interact with the child. A teacher may have a different perception of a child's behavior than a parent does. By getting various viewpoints, a more comprehensive evaluation of the child's daily functioning can be established.

Conners' Rating Scales–Revised (CRS-R)

Author: C. Keith Conners

Publisher: Pearson Assessments

Description of Test: An instrument that uses observer ratings and self-report ratings to help assess attention deficit/hyperactivity disorder (ADHD) and evaluate problem behavior in children and adolescents. Various CRS-R versions offer flexible administration options while also providing the ability to collect varying perspectives on a child's behavior from parents, teachers, caregivers, and the child or adolescent.

Administration Time: Long Version, 15 to 20 minutes; Short Version, 5 to 10 minutes

Age/Grade Levels: Parents and teachers of children and adolescents ages 3 to 17 years; and adolescent self-report, ages 12 to 17 years.

Subtest Information: There are three versions—parent, teacher, and adolescent self-report—all of which also have a short and long form available. In addition, there are three screening tools that offer the option of administering a 12-item ADHD Index or the 18-item DSM-IV Symptom Checklist, or both. These instruments also offer versions for parents, teachers, and adolescents.

These forms measure a variety of behavioral characteristics grouped into several scales:

Oppositional	Social Problems
Cognitive Problems/Inattention	Psychosomatic
Hyperactivity	Conners' Global Index
Anxious-Shy	DSM-IV Symptom Subscales
Perfectionism	ADHD Index

STRENGTHS OF THE CRS-R

Measures hyperactivity in children and adolescents through routine screening

Provides a perspective of the child's behavior from those who interact with the child daily

Establishes a base point prior to beginning therapy and monitors treatment effectiveness and changes over time

Provides valuable structured and normed information to further support conclusions, diagnoses, and treatment decisions when the parent, teacher, and self-report scales are combined

Teacher, parent, and self-report scales are in long and short formats

Applicable to managed care situations through the quantification and measurement of a variety of behavior problems

Attention Deficit Disorders Evaluation Scale–Third Edition (ADDES-3)

Author: Stephen B. McCarney, Ed.D.

Publisher: Hawthorne Educational Services

Description of the Test: The Attention Deficit Disorders Evaluation Scale–Third Edition (ADDES-3) enables educators, school and private psychologists, pediatricians, and other medical personnel to evaluate and diagnose ADHD in children and youth from input provided by primary observers of the student's behavior. The scale is available in two versions: *School Version*, a reporting form for educators, and *Home Version*, a reporting form for parents.

Ages: 4.0 through 18 years of age

Administration Time: The Home Version can be completed by a parent or guardian in approximately 12 minutes and includes 46 items representing behaviors exhibited in and around the home environment. The School Version can be completed in approximately 15 minutes and includes 60 items easily observed and documented by educational personnel.

Subtest Information: The ADDES-3 was developed from research in behavior disorders, learning disabilities, and ADHD; current literature in psychology, neurology, and education; and current practices in identification and diagnosis.

The subscales, *Inattentive and Hyperactive–Impulsive*, are based on the current subtypes of ADHD.

The results provided by the scale are commensurate with criteria used by educational, psychiatric, and pediatric professionals to identify ADHD in children and youth.

STRENGTHS OF THE ADDES-3

The ADDES-3 is based on the APA definition of Attention-Deficit/Hyperactivity Disorder (DSM-IV) and the criteria most widely accepted by educators and mental health professionals. The ADDES-3 School Version was standardized on a total of 3,903 students, including students identified as having ADHD.

The standardization sample included students from 26 states and represented all geographic regions of the United States.

The ADDES-3 was factor analyzed to create the factor clusters (subscales).

The Pre-Referral Attention Deficit Checklist provides a means of calling attention to specific behaviors for the purpose of early intervention before formal assessment of the student.

The Parent's Guide to Attention Deficit Disorders provides parents with specific, practical strategies to use in helping their child be more successful in the home environment.

Internal consistency, test–retest, and inter-rater reliability; item and factor analysis; and content, diagnostic, criterion-related, and construct validity are documented and reported for the scale.

Attention Deficit Disorders Evaluation Scale: Secondary-Age Student (ADDES-S)

Author: Stephen B. McCarney

Publisher: Hawthorne Educational Services

Description of Test: There are two versions of this test: (1) Home Version, completed by parents, has 46 items that assess certain behaviors in the home, and (2) School Version has 60 items that teachers must rate. The ADDES-S is based on the APA definition of Attention-Deficit/Hyperactivity Disorder (DSM-IV) and the criteria most widely accepted by educators and mental health providers.

Administration Time: The **School Version** can be completed in approximately 15 minutes and includes 60 items easily observed and documented by educational personnel.

Age/Grade Levels: Ages 11 to 18

FIGURE 11.1   Attention Deficit Disorders Evaluation Scale

Subtest Information: The subscales, *Inattentive* and *Hyperactive–Impulsive*, are based on the most currently recognized subtypes of ADHD.

STRENGTHS OF THE ADDES-S

The ADDES-S School Version was standardized on a total of 1,280 students, including students with ADHD.

The standardization sample included students from 19 states and represented all geographic regions of the United States.

The ADDES-S was factor analyzed to create the factor clusters (subscales).

The ADDES-S provides separate norms for male and female students 11.5 through 18 years of age.

The Pre-Referral Attention Deficit Checklist provides a means of calling attention to the behavior for the purpose of early intervention before formal assessment of the student.

ASSESSMENT OF ADAPTIVE BEHAVIOR

The assessment of adaptive behavior is a very important part of the overall assessment process. **Adaptive behavior** refers to the effectiveness or degree with which individuals meet the standards of personal independence and social responsibility expected for age and cultural groups. When doing an evaluation of adaptive behavior, the examiner should focus on a number of areas. These areas include:

Communication Skills	*Self-Care*
Community Use	*Home Living*
Self-Direction	*Social Skills*
Health and Safety	*Leisure*
Functional Academics	*Work Skills*

Understanding adaptive behavior is very important when working with or assessing the mentally retarded population. Adaptive behavior is a required area of assessment when a classification of mental retardation is being considered for a student. IDEA 2004 specifies "deficits in adaptive behavior" as one of the two characteristics necessary for a student to be classified as mentally retarded (the other being "significantly subaverage general intellectual functioning").

There are many different ways in which an evaluator can measure adaptive behavior. Because these measures are often used to assess persons with lower levels of intellectual functioning, the student being evaluated may not have to directly take part in the evaluation. The way many of these diagnostic assessment instruments work is that the examiner records information collected from a third person who is familiar with the student (e.g., parent, teacher, direct service provider). Perhaps the greatest problem with doing an assessment on adaptive behavior is the fact that many of the scales and tests do not have high validity and reliability. Also, there are serious concerns about the cultural bias of the tests. Consequently, great care must be taken when selecting the most appropriate measure for an individual student. With respect to minority students, it should also be noted that it is imperative to develop an understanding of what types of behavior are considered adaptive (and thus appropriate) in the minority culture before making diagnostic judgments about the particular functioning of a student.

AAMR Adaptive Behavior Scale, Residential and Community–2 (ABS-RC:2)

Authors: Kazuo Nihira, Henry Leland, and Nadine Lambert

Publisher: PRO-ED

Description of Test: The test is intended for persons with disabilities in residential and community settings. It measures various domain areas and is available as a kit or as software for administration and scoring.

Administration Time: 15 to 30 minutes

Age/Grade Levels: Ages 18 to 80 years

Subtest Information: The test has no subtests.

STRENGTHS OF THE ABS-RC:2

It is one of the few tests available to measure adaptive behaviors and factors in persons with disabilities.

Many different factors are considered; this is helpful for evaluation.

There is evidence of strong reliability.

AAMR Adaptive Behavior Scale–School (ABS-S:2)

Authors: Nadine Lambert, Kazuo Nihira, and Henry Leland

Publisher: PRO-ED

Description of Test: There are 16 subscores that are measured from this test. The test includes an examiner's manual, examiner booklets, computer scoring systems, and profile summary forms.

Administration Time: 15 to 30 minutes

Age/Grade Levels: Ages 3 to 18.11 years

Subtest Information: The scale is divided into two parts Part I focuses on personal independence and is designed to evaluate coping skills considered to be important to independence and responsibility in daily living. The skills within Part I are grouped into nine behavior domains:

Independent Functioning   *Numbers and Time*
Physical Development   *Prevocational/Vocational Activity*
Economic Activity   *Self-Direction*
Language Development   *Responsibility*
Socialization

Part II of the scale contains content related to social adaptation. The behaviors in Part II are assigned to seven domains:

Social Behavior   *Social Engagement*
Conformity Disturbing   *Interpersonal Behavior*

Trustworthiness   *Stereotyped and Hyperactive Behavior*
Self-Abusive Behavior

STRENGTHS OF THE ABS-S:2

The scale has an excellent standardization sample and is appropriate for use with a wide variety of individuals.

The scale's psychometric qualities are good.

It has been and remains one of the best available scales for assessment of adaptive behavior.

The Adaptive Behavior Evaluation Scale–Revised (ABES-R)

Author: Stephen B. McCarney

Publisher: Hawthorne Educational Services

Description of Test: The ABES-R consists of 105 items assessing adaptive behaviors that are not measured by academic skill testing, but are necessary for success in an educational setting.

Administration Time: 20 to 25 minutes

Age/Grade Levels: Norms are for students from Grades K through 12

Subtest Information: The test is comprised of 10 adaptive skill areas:

Communication Skills   *Self-Direction*
Self-Care   *Health and Safety*
Home Living   *Functional Academics*
Social Skills   *Leisure*
Community Use   *Work Skills*

STRENGTHS OF THE ABS-S:2

This test is a good measure of adaptive behavior for the identification of students with intellectual disabilities.

The test comes with an Adaptive Behavior Intervention Manual, which may be useful in developing a student's IEP.

Vineland Adaptive Behavior Scale (VABS)

Authors: Sara S. Sparrow, David A. Balla, and Domenie V. Cicchetti

Publisher: American Guidance Service

Description of Test: The VABS assesses the social competence of handicapped and nonhandicapped individuals. It requires that a respondent familiar with the behavior of the individual participate in question-answer behavior orientation questions posed by a trained examiner. The three versions of this test are: (1) the Interview Edition—Survey Form, (2) the Interview Edition—Expanded Form, and (3) the Classroom Edition.

Administration Time: 20 to 60 minutes

Age/Grade Levels: Birth to 18 months and low-functioning adults, ages 3 through 12-11 years

Subtest Information: All of the versions measure the following domains:

- *Communication*—This contains the subdomains of receptive, expressive, and written communication.
- *Daily Living Skills*—This contains the subdomains of personal, domestic, and community daily living skills.
- *Socialization*—This contains the subdomains of interpersonal relationships, play and leisure time, and coping skills.
- *Motor Skills*—This contains the subdomains of gross- and fine-motor skills.

STRENGTHS OF THE VABS

The test is a useful tool for the assessment of adaptive behavior.

The test has adequate validity and reliability.

It is one of the most popular instruments to assess adaptive behavior.

Developmental Assessment for the Severely Handicapped–Second Edition (DASH-2)

Author: Mary Kay Dykes and Jane Erin

Publisher: PRO-ED

Description of Test: The assessment system is a developmentally sequenced, fine-grained, behaviorally defined criterion-referenced measure of current and developing skills in different domains. The instrument may be useful in identifying and measuring very discrete changes in behavior in very low-functioning individuals in order to pinpoint skills and facilitate training.

Administration Time: 120 to 180 minutes

Age/Grade Levels: Individuals functioning within the developmental range of birth to 8 years

Subtest Information: The DASH-2 consists of five pinpoint scales which assess performance in the following areas:

- Dressing
- Feeding
- Toileting
- Home Routines
- Travel and Safety

STRENGTHS OF THE DASH-2

Provides multiple examples of behavior at young ages.

Provides a scoring method to measure the condition under which behavior occurs.

DASH-2 begins with an individual's areas of strength and builds from there. Therefore, it can function as an initial assessment instrument, a tool for curriculum planning, and a means of monitoring progress. This information can be applied to program planning, communicating with families and other team members, and developing intervention strategies.

FUNCTIONAL BEHAVIORAL ASSESSMENT AND BEHAVIORAL INTERVENTION PLANS

Problem behavior is one of the most complex yet frequent aspects confronted by all educators. Problem behaviors range from minor to severe, and not only affect the child's ability to learn, but also may affect the instructional time of those students involved with the student with severe problem behavior patterns.

Various models of behavioral intervention plans have been documented in the literature (Batsche, 1997; Curwin & Mendler, 1994; Wood, 1994). Prior to functional behavior assessments, most school-based models did not provide the degree of flexibility when students exhibited severe behavior patterns in classroom settings. Functional behavior assessment provides a viable problem-solving model in such instances while providing effective program recommendations for students who present such a wide and serious pattern of inappropriate behavior (Bambara and Knoster, 1995; Dunlap et al., 1991).

IDEA 2004 focuses on prevention and proactively addressing behavioral concerns of students with disabilities that may affect their ability to learn. The use of functional behavioral assessments provides an important and meaningful opportunity to improve the IEP and services for students with disabilities, to promote access to general education curriculum, and to ensure safe and well-disciplined schools.

Further, functional behavioral assessments should be viewed as an integral part of assessment and reevaluation procedures and not as an isolated practice reserved for a student who has engaged in behavior that may have violated a school district's code of conduct. Functional behavioral assessments should be integrated, as appropriate, throughout the process of developing, reviewing, and revising a student's IEP (see Chapter 19) when students demonstrate behaviors that impede learning.

FBA Defined

Functional behavioral assessment (FBA) is the process of determining why a student engages in challenging behavior and how the student's behavior relates to the environment. Functional assessments describe the relationship between a skill or performance problem and variables that contribute to its occurrence. The purpose of a functional behavioral assessment is to gather broad and specific information in order to better understand the specific reasons for the student's problem behavior. Functional behavioral assessments can provide the district's Eligibility Committee (see Chapter 18) with information to develop a hypothesis as to:

- Why the student engages in the behavior
- When the student is most likely to demonstrate the behavior
- Situations in which the behavior is least likely to occur

This type of assessment often involves reviewing:

- Curriculum
- Instructional and motivational variables in relation to the student's behavior
- Classroom arrangements
- Individuals present in the classroom
- Current health issues
- Instructional subject and work demands

The focus of IDEA 2004 in terms of functional behavioral assessments includes the following:

- Functional behavioral assessments should be implemented as an integrated set of practices throughout the IEP decision-making process.
- Functional behavioral assessments identify and measure specific problem behaviors (as opposed to diagnosing). The function of a behavior can be determined only by describing and analyzing the student's interactions within his or her environment.
- It is not appropriate to conduct all functional behavioral assessments using the same set of resources and procedures. The nature of the assessment provided must match the level of need demonstrated by the student.
- Functional behavioral assessments provide data for the design of behavioral strategies and supports (i.e., intervention programs).

Requirements of the Individuals with Disabilities Education Improvement Act

References to consideration of student behavior that may impede learning can be found in several sections of IDEA 2004, including the sections on evaluation, considerations in the development of the IEP, and the role of the general education teacher in the development of the IEP and discipline.

From the Section on Evaluation

In conducting the evaluation, the local educational agency shall use technically sound instruments that may assess the relative contribution of cognitive and behavioral factors, in addition to physical or developmental factors (IDEA 2004, Section 614[b][2][C])

Each local educational agency shall ensure that the child is assessed in all areas of suspected disability; and assessment tools and strategies that provide relevant information that directly assist persons in determining the educational needs of the child are provided. (IDEA 2004, Section 614[b][3][C]–[D])

From the Section on the IEP Team (Eligibility Committee)

The regular education teacher of the child as a member of the IEP team shall, to the extent appropriate, participate in the development of the IEP of the child, including the determination of appropriate positive behavioral interventions and supports, and other strategies, and the determination of supplementary aids and services, program modifications, and support for school personnel. . . . (IDEA 2004, Section 614[d][3][C])

From the Section on the IEP Contents and Considerations

In developing each child's IEP, the IEP team shall, in the case of a child whose behavior impedes the child's learning or that of others, consider the use of positive behavioral interventions, supports and other strategies to address that behavior. (IDEA 2004, Section 614[d][3][B][i])

Writing Functional Behavioral Assessments and Intervention Plans

A variety of techniques are available to conduct a functional behavioral assessment including, but not limited to, the following:

- Indirect assessment (e.g., structured interviews, review of existing evaluation information)
- Direct assessment (e.g., standardized assessments or checklists or observing and recording situational factors surrounding the behavior)
- Data analysis (e.g., a comparison and analysis of data to determine whether patterns are associated with the behavior)

A functional behavioral assessment should minimally include the following components:

- Identification of the problem area
- Definition of the behavior in concrete terms
- Identification of the contextual factors that contribute to the behavior (including affective and cognitive factors)
- Formulation of the hypothesis regarding the general conditions under which a behavior usually occurs and probable consequences that serve to maintain it

When writing the FBA you may need to consider the various requirements for each stage in the plan. These may include the following:

Stage I: Identify and define the target behavior. These behaviors should be observable, descriptive, and defined in such a way that everyone is in agreement with what the behavior(s) actually means (operational definition). In order to collect this information, one can:

- Determine the student's perception of the problem behavior, through an interview.
- Interview the student's parents.
- Interview all the child's past and present teachers for their analysis and history concerning the targeted behavior(s).
- Use direct observation.
- Use behavioral checklists or rating scales and ask parents and teachers to fill them out.

- Speak with the principal or dean of students to determine if there is a history of this target behavior in the records.

Stage II: Gather broad information about the student's skills, abilities, interests, preferences, general health, and well-being. This can be accomplished by:
- Speaking with the school nurse
- Asking the parents for recent medical records
- Having the child fill out an interest inventory checklist
- Speaking with the physical education teacher to determine physical strengths and weaknesses and any areas of exception
- Asking the parents for a list of activities, clubs, organizations, lessons and so on that the child may have been involved with over the years
- Identifying the student's strengths

Stage III: The IEP team gathers contextual information that pinpoints the circumstances or situations that are regularly associated with the occurrence of problem behavior and the function of the student's problem behavior. Six basic questions may be asked during this stage:
1. When is the student most likely to engage in the problem behavior?
2. What specific events or factors appear to be contributing to the student's problem behavior?
3. What function(s) does the problem behavior serve the student?
4. What might the student be communicating through the problem behavior?
5. When is the student most successful, and therefore less likely to engage in the problem behavior?
6. What other factors might be contributing to the student's problem behavior?

Stage IV: Define the function or reason the behavior continues. This is usually the result of getting something, avoidance, or control.

Stage V: Develop a hypothesis about the target behavior in which statements are formed that describe the relationship of the behavior to the event and circumstances. Further, in this stage, the person writing the FBA attempts to identify specific variables to be manipulated and observed.

Stage VI: Develop an intervention plan based on the results from Stage V. In this intervention plan, the student is taught acceptable alternatives by the teacher shaping the student's behavior and manipulating variables within the classroom and school.

Role of the Eligibility Committee in the FBA

IDEA 2004 requires that, in the case of a child whose behavior impedes the learning of the child or others, the district's Eligibility Committee (see Chapter 18), as appropriate, must consider strategies, including positive behavioral interventions and supports, to address that behavior. The results of a student's individual evaluation information, including the functional behavioral assessment, are reviewed at an eligibility meeting. IDEA 2004 requires that one of the members of the Eligibility Committee be an individual who can interpret the instructional implications of evaluation results. Therefore, for students with behaviors that impede learning, it is recommended that an individual knowledgeable about behavioral assessments and intervention planning participate in these meetings. This individual could be the school psychologist or the special or regular education teacher. In addition, the regular education teacher of the child, as a member of the Eligibility Committee, participates in the development of the IEP of the student, including the determination of appropriate positive behavioral interventions and strategies.

It may be the responsibility of the Eligibility Committee to ensure that functional behavioral assessments, where appropriate, are conducted and reviewed to:

- Identify supplementary aids and services, modifications, and related services appropriate to address the identified behaviors, to promote a student's involvement and progress in the general curriculum
- Determine a student's eligibility for special education services
- Develop the IEP, which includes behavioral goals and objectives and positive behavioral supports and strategies

Behavioral Intervention Plans

Functional behavioral assessments provide specific information to the Eligibility Committee concerning the design and implementation of effective strategies to address a student's behaviors. The identification of positive behavioral supports should be based on the functional behavioral assessment and should address:

- Short-term prevention
- Teaching of alternative skills
- Responses to problem behaviors
- Long-term prevention

CONCLUSION

Assessment of behavior is essential for a comprehensive evaluation of a child for special education. Understanding the psychological makeup of a child can help tremendously with recommendations for future educational programs. Psychological tests play a very important role in the understanding of a student's behavior. Using many different psychological tests helps to identify general themes and patterns in the child's emotional well-being. When properly conducted, an assessment of a child's social and emotional development greatly enhances the assessment process because it enables us to try and understand the child's emotional state at the time of testing.

VOCABULARY

Anecdotal Recording: Here, the observer records all behaviors and interactions within a given time frame (e.g., recording a child's behavior from 9:00 A.M. until 9:30 A.M.).

Apperception Tests: Tests that require the child to view various picture cards and "tell a story" about what is shown. Apperception tests try to elicit central themes from the child.

Duration Recording: Here, the observer notes the amount of time a target behavior occurs (e.g., watching a child for one hour who is supposed to be reading—the child reads only 12 minutes of that time).

Event Recording: Here, the observer is looking specifically for one or more target behaviors and records the frequency with which they occur. Event recording is also referred to as frequency counting because the observer is simply counting the number of times a behavior occurs (e.g., recording the number of times a child gets out of his chair in a given period of time).

Functional Behavioral Assessment (FBA):   The process of determining why a student engages in challenging behavior and how the student's behavior relates to the environment.

Interview: A research method conducted face to face between two people (the interviewer and the interviewee) whereby recorded responses to questions are obtained.

Latency Recording: Here, the observer determines the amount of time between a given stimulus for the child and the response (e.g., the time it takes a student to get out her pencil after the teacher says, "Take out your pencil").

Projective Drawing Tests: Tests that simply ask the child to draw a picture. The tests are used to get the child to "project" his feelings about himself onto paper.

Rating Scales: Scales that are often given not only to the student but also to the parents and teachers. A rating scale gives a statement about a behavior of a child whereupon the individual has to rate the frequency, intensity, and/or duration.

Sentence Completion Tests: Tests that provide the student with a beginning of a sentence that the student needs to finish. The "fill ins" are supposed to give indications of the emotions and feelings that the student is experiencing.

Structured Interview: An interview in which the individuals are asked a specific set of predetermined questions in a controlled manner.

Target Behaviors: Specific behaviors an observer seeks to record when doing the observation.

Unstructured Interview: An interview in which the questions are not predetermined, thereby allowing for substantial discussion and interaction between the interviewer and interviewee.

CHAPTER TWELVE

━━━━━

ASSESSMENT OF
PERCEPTUAL ABILITIES

KEY TERMS

Association or Organization
Auditory Association
Auditory Discrimination
Auditory Long-Term Memory
Auditory Modality
Auditory Motoric Expression
Auditory Sequential Memory
Auditory Short-Term Memory
Auditory Vocal Expression
Kinesthetic Modality
Memory
Multisensory Approaches
Perception

Tactile Modality
Visual Association
Visual Coordination
Visual Discrimination
Visual Figure–Ground Discrimination
Visual Form Perception
Visual Long-Term Memory
Visual Modality
Visual Motoric Expression
Visual Sequential Memory
Visual Short-Term Memory
Visual Spatial Relationships
Visual Vocal Expression

CHAPTER OBJECTIVES

This chapter discusses the importance of assessment of perceptual abilities in the special education process. After reading this chapter, you should understand the following:

■ The purpose of perceptual evaluations
■ Visual perception
■ Assessment of visual perception
■ Auditory perception
■ Assessment of auditory perception
■ Comprehensive measures of perceptual abilities

THE LEARNING PROCESS

The perceptual evaluation is theoretically based upon the concept of the learning process. When we evaluate a child's perceptual abilities, we are looking to see if there is a deficit in some area of the learning process that may be slowing down the processing of information, thereby interfering in the child's ability to receive, organize, memorize, or express information. Severe deficits in the learning process can have adverse effects on a child's ability to function in the classroom.

In order to understand how learning takes place, we must first understand the process by which information is received and the manner in which it is processed and expressed. In very simple terms, the learning process can be described in the following way:

- Step 1: Input of Information
- Step 2: Organization of Information
- Step 3: Expression of Information

Information is received in some manner and is filtered through a series of internal psychological processes. As information progresses along this "assembly line," it is given meaning, organized in some fashion, and then expressed through a variety of responses. In order to understand how learning takes place, we must first understand the specific parts that make up the learning process. There are six modalities or channels (avenues through which information is received):

- **Auditory modality:** The delivery of information through sound
- **Visual modality:** The delivery of information through sight
- **Tactile modality:** The delivery of information through touching
- **Kinesthetic modality:** The delivery of information through movement
- **Gustatory modality:** The delivery of information through taste
- **Olfactory modality:** The delivery of information through smell

Skills are usually taught using all six modalities in the primary grades—nursery school through Grade 1. By Grade 2, most teachers teach through approximately four of the modalities with a greater emphasis on visual and auditory input. By the upper elementary grades, this can shift to skill development through the use of only two modalities, visual and auditory. Generally, this remains the source of informational input in most classrooms until possibly college, at which level information in many cases is presented through only one modality, auditory (lectures).

Children should be taught using **multisensory approaches** (the input of information through a variety of receptive mechanisms, i.e., seeing, hearing, touching, etc.) whenever possible because increased sensory input enhances retention of information.

Information is delivered to the senses through one or several of the previously mentioned modalities. Once received, the information goes through a series of processes that attempts to give meaning to the material received. Several processes comprise the learning process:

- **Reception:** The initial receiving of information.
- **Perception:** The initial organization of information.

- **Association or organization:** Relating new information to other information and giving meaning to the information received.
- **Memory:** The storage or retrieval process that facilitates the associational process to give meaning to information or help in relating new concepts to other information that might have already been learned. This process involves short-term, long-term, and sequential memory.
- **Expression:** The output of information through vocal, motoric, or written responses.

THE PURPOSE OF PERCEPTUAL EVALUATIONS

Now that you have some understanding of how the learning process functions, we can explore the objectives of the perceptual evaluation. These include:

- **To help determine the child's stronger and weaker modality for learning:** Some children are visual learners, some are auditory, and some learn best through any form of input. However, if a child is a strong visual learner in a class in which the teacher relies on auditory lectures, then it is possible that the child's ability to process information may be hampered. The evaluation may give us this information, which is very useful when making practical recommendations to teachers about how best to present information to assist the child's ability to learn.
- **To help determine a child's stronger and weaker process areas:** A child having problems in memory and expression will quickly fall behind the rest of the class. The longer these processing difficulties continue, the greater the chance for secondary emotional problems to develop (emotional problems resulting from continued frustration with the ability to learn).
- **To develop a learning profile:** This can help the classroom teacher understand the best way to present information to the child, and therefore, increase his or her chances of success.
- **To help determine if the child's learning process deficits are suitable for a regular class:** Along with other information and test results, the child may require a more restrictive educational setting (an educational setting or situation best suited to the present needs of the student other than a full-time regular class placement; e.g., resource room, self-contained class, special school, etc.).

VISUAL PERCEPTION

Visual perception is considered to be one of the more important specific ability areas in early assessment because of the assumed relationship between visual perception deficits and reading performance. The following assessment area skills are most often associated with visual perception:

- **Visual coordination:** The ability to follow and track objects with coordinated eye movements
- **Visual discrimination:** The ability to differentiate visually the forms and symbols in one's environment

- **Visual association:** The ability to organize and associate visually presented material in a meaningful way
- **Visual long-term memory:** The ability to retain and recall general and specific long-term visual information
- **Visual short-term memory:** The ability to retain and recall general and specific short-term visual information
- **Visual sequential memory:** The ability to recall in correct sequence and detail prior visual information
- **Visual vocal expression:** The ability to reproduce vocally prior visually presented material or experiences
- **Visual motoric expression** (visual motor integration): The ability to reproduce motorically prior visually presented material or experiences
- **Visual figure–ground discrimination:** The ability to differentiate relevant stimuli (the figure) from irrelevant stimuli (the background)
- **Visual spatial relationships:** The ability to perceive the relative positions of objects in space
- **Visual form perception** (visual constancy): The ability to discern the size, shape, and position of visual stimuli

Diagnostic Symptoms for Visual Perceptual Disabilities

There are many symptoms that may indicate problems in a certain perceptual area. Some of these are observable, whereas others are discovered through intakes and testing. What follows is a list of symptoms that may reflect perceptual disabilities in a variety of visual areas.

General Visual Perceptual Problems

The student

- Exhibits poor motor coordination
- Is awkward motorically—frequent tripping, stumbling, bumping into things, having trouble skipping and jumping
- Demonstrates restlessness, short attention span, perseveration
- Exhibits poor handwriting, artwork, drawing
- Exhibits reversals of b, d, p, q, u, n when writing (beyond a chronological age of seven or eight)
- Inverts numbers (17 for 71), reverses as well
- Gives correct answers when teacher reads test, but cannot put answers down on paper
- Exhibits poor performance on group achievement tests
- Appears brighter than test scores indicate
- Has poor perception of time and space

Visual-Receptive Process Disability

The student

- Does not enjoy books, pictures
- Fails to understand what is read

- Is unable to give a simple explanation of contents of a picture
- Is unable to categorize pictures

Visual-Association Disability

The student

- Is unable to tell a story from pictures; can only label objects in the pictures
- Is unable to understand what he or she reads
- Fails to handle primary workbook tasks
- Needs auditory cues and clues

Manual–Expressive Disability

The student

- Has poor handwriting and drawing
- Communicates infrequently with gestures
- Is poor at "acting out" ideas, feelings
- Is clumsy, uncoordinated
- Plays games poorly; can't imitate other children in games

Visual–Memory Disability

The student

- Exhibits frequent misspellings, even after undue practice
- Misspells own name frequently
- Cannot write alphabet, numbers, computation facts
- Identifies words one day and fails to the next

Assessment of Visual Perception

There are many assessment measures used in school systems to assess visual–motor integration and perceptual abilities. This section examines the most commonly used visual–motor perceptual measures and identifies the strengths and weaknesses of each.

Beery-VMI (Developmental Test of Visual Motor Integration)–5th Edition (VMI-5)

Author: Keith E. Beery

Publisher: PRO-ED

Description of Test: Beery VMI, now in its fifth edition, offers a convenient and economical way to screen for visual–motor deficits that can lead to learning, neuropsychological, and behavior problems. The VMI-5 helps assess the extent to which individuals can integrate their visual and motor abilities. The Short Format and Full Format tests present drawings of geometric forms arranged in order of increasing difficulty that the individual is asked to copy.

Administration Time: 10 to 15 minutes

Age/Grade Levels: Ages 3 to 18; Grades preschool through 12

Subtest Information: There are no subtests

STRENGTHS OF THE VMI-5

The Beery VMI is among the few psychological assessments that provide standard scores as low as 2 years, 0 months.

The Examiner's Manual provides approximately 600 age-specific norms from birth through age 6. These consist of basic gross motor, fine motor, visual, and visual-fine motor developmental "stepping stones" that have been identified by research criteria. Many examiners find the age norm information to be useful in helping parents better understand their child's current level of development. The manual also presents teaching suggestions.

As a culture-free, nonverbal assessment, the VMI-5 is useful with individuals of diverse environmental, educational, and linguistic backgrounds.

The VMI-5 provides time-efficient screening tools, with the Short and Full Format tests taking only 10 to 15 minutes to complete and the supplemental tests taking only about 5 minutes each.

The Short and Full Format tests can be administered individually or to groups. (Individual administration is recommended for the supplemental tests.)

Test of Gross Motor Development– 2nd Edition (TGMD-2)

Author: Dale Ulrich

Publisher: PRO-ED

Description of Test: The TGMD–2 assesses common motor skills. The primary uses of this test are to

- Identify children who are significantly behind their peers in gross-motor skill development
- Assist in the planning of an instructional program in gross-motor skill development
- Evaluate the gross-motor program

The test is a multiple-item task performance test consisting of two subtests. The examiner records observations in a student record book. The TGMD-2 allows examiners to administer one test in a relatively brief time and gather data for making important educational decisions.

Administration Time: 15 minutes

Age/Grade Levels: Ages 3 to 10 years

Subtest Information: The test is divided into two subtests:

- *Locomotion*—This subtest measures the run, gallop, hop, leap, horizontal jump, and slide skills that move a child's center of gravity from one point to another.

■ *Object Control*—This subtest measures the ability to strike a stationary ball, stationary dribble, catch, kick, underhand roll, and overhand throw skills that include projecting and receiving objects.

STRENGTHS OF THE TGMD-2

The TGMD-2 includes several updates to the first edition:

All new normative information was keyed to the projected 2000 census.

Normative information is now stratified by age relative to geography, gender, race, and residence.

Age norms have been divided into half-year increments for both subtests for ages 3-0 through 7-11.

New reliability and validity studies, including exploratory and confirmatory factor analyses that empirically support the skills chosen for each subtest.

Evidence related to content sampling and test–retest time sampling reliability is provided. Reliability coefficients for the Locomotor subtest average .85, the Object Control subtest average .88, and the Gross Motor composite average .91. Standard Error of Measurement (SEM) is 1 at every age interval for both subtests and 4 or 5 for the composite score at each age interval. Coefficient alphas for selected subgroups are all above .90 for the subtest and the composite. Time sampling reliability coefficients range from .84 to .96. Content–description, criterion–prediction, and construct–identification validity that further support the use of the TGMD-2 in identifying children who are significantly behind their peers in gross motor development are also provided.

Using the TGMD-2, you will obtain standard scores, percentile scores, and age equivalents. The test also provides you with a Gross Motor Quotient if both subtests are completed.

Bender Visual–Motor Gestalt Test (Bender-Gestalt II)

Publisher: Pearson Assessments and The American Orthopsychiatric Association

Description of Test: Originally published in 1938 by Lauretta Bender M. D., the Bender Visual–Motor Gestalt Test is one of the most widely used psychological tests since that time. The Bender Visual–Motor Gestalt Test, Second Edition (Bender-Gestalt II) updates this classic assessment and continues its tradition as a brief test of visual–motor integration that may provide interpretive information about an individual's development and psychological functioning.

Administration Time: 5 to 10 minutes (14 stimulus cards), 5 minutes (visual, motor tests)

Age/Grade Levels: Ages 3 years and older

Subtest Information: There are no subtests; patient reproduces Gestalt figures presented on stimulus cards

STRENGTHS OF THE BVMGT

The test is quick to administer.

The test is easy to administer.

The test is one of the oldest and most popular tests used to assess visual–motor abilities.

The test provides developmental data on a child's perceptual maturity.

Group administration is a time-saver.

The test is effective as a screening instrument when combined with other tests.

New recall procedures to assess visual–motor memory provide a more comprehensive assessment of visual–motor skills.

Supplemental tests of simple motor and perceptual ability help identify specific visual–motor deficits.

Comprehensive testing observations including physical demeanor, drawing technique, and test-taking behavior and attitude.

Developmental Test of Visual Perception–2 (DTVP-2)

Authors: Donald Hammill, N. Pearson, and J. Voress

Publisher: PRO-ED

Description of Test: The test is designed to measure specific visual perceptual abilities and to screen for visual perceptual difficulties at early ages. The DTVP-2 is a revision of the Developmental Test of Visual Perception (Frostig et al., 1966). The DTVP-2 is a comprehensive diagnostic instrument for assessing the visual-processing skills of children from ages 4 to 10 years. See Figures 12.1 and 12.2 for the DTVP Cover Sheet and example of Subtest 1.

Administration Time: Varies based on individual ability levels

Age/Grade Levels: Ages 4 to 10 years

Subtest Information: The tasks are arranged in increasing order of difficulty in eight areas:

- *Eye motor coordination*—This task requires the child to draw lines between increasingly narrow boundaries. These may include straight, curved, or angled lines.
- *Figure ground*—This task requires the child to distinguish and then outline embedded figures between intersecting shapes.
- *Form constancy*—This task requires the child to discriminate common geometric shapes presented in different shapes, sizes, positions, and textures from other similar shapes.
- *Position in space*—This test requires the child to distinguish between figures in an identical position and those in a reversed rotated position.
- *Spatial relations*—This task requires the child to copy simple forms and patterns by joining dots.

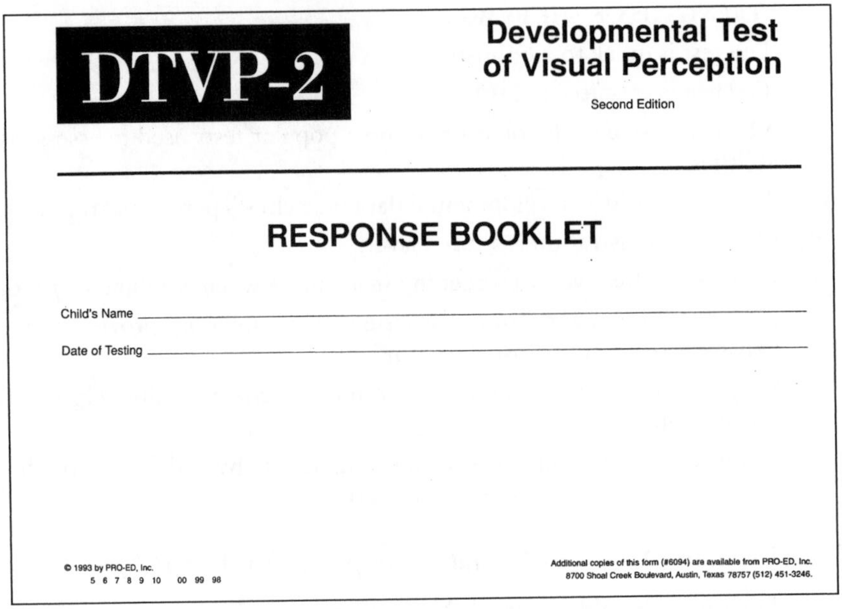

DTVP-2

Developmental Test of Visual Perception

Second Edition

RESPONSE BOOKLET

Child's Name ____________________

Date of Testing ____________________

© 1993 by PRO-ED, Inc.
5 6 7 8 9 10 00 99 98

Additional copies of this form (#6094) are available from PRO-ED, Inc.
8700 Shoal Creek Boulevard, Austin, Texas 78757 (512) 451-3246.

FIGURE 12.1 Developmental Test of Visual Perception, Second Edition, Cover Sheet

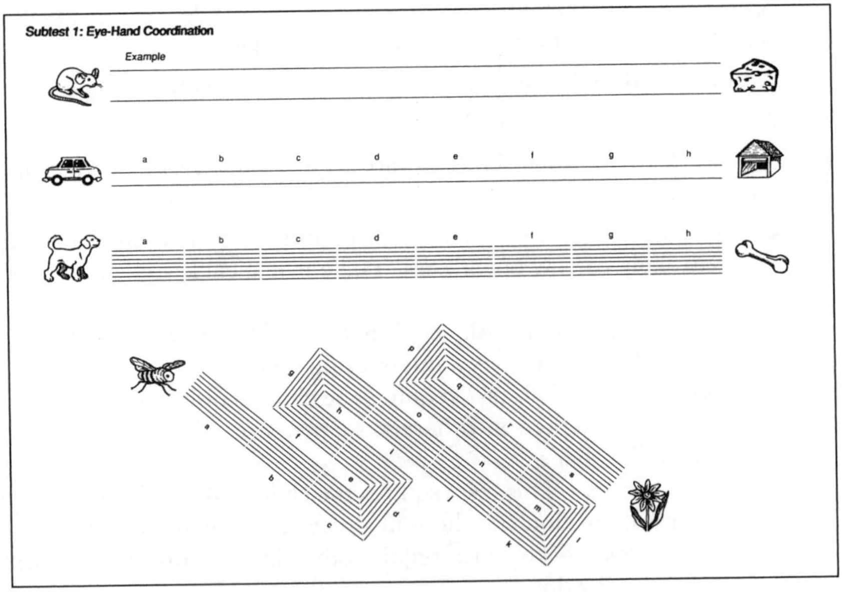

FIGURE 12.2 Example DTVP-2, Subtest 1

- *Copying*—The child is asked to copy increasingly complex figures from model drawings.
- *Visual closure*—The child is required to view a geometric figure and then select the matching figure from a series of figures that all have missing parts
- *Visual–motor speed*—On this test, the child is required to draw special marks in selected geometric designs on a page filled with various designs.

STRENGTHS OF THE DTVP-2

Of all the tests of visual perception and visual–motor integration, the DTVP-2 is unique in that its scores are reliable at the .8 or .9 levels for all age groups; its scores are validated by many studies; its norms are based on a large representative sample keyed to the 1990 census data; it yields scores for both pure visual perception (no motor response) and visual–motor integration ability; and it has been proven to be unbiased relative to race, gender, and handedness.

The DTVP-2 was standardized on 1,972 children from 12 states. Characteristics of the normative sample approximate those provided in the 1990 Statistical Abstract of the United States with regard to gender, geographical region, ethnicity, race, and urban/rural residence.

Internal consistency reliabilities (i.e., alphas) and stability reliabilities (i.e., test–retest) for all scores exceed .8 at all ages.

Criterion-related validity is evidenced by correlating DTVP-2 scores with those from the Developmental Test of Visual-Motor Integration (VMI) and Motor-Free Visual Perception Test.

Construct validity is supported by correlations with mental ability tests, achievement tests, and age. Studies also show that the subtests are intercorrelated and that groups known to have visual perceptual difficulties do poorly on the DTVP-2. Results of factor structure and gender/race/handedness bias studies also reinforce the validity of the DTVP-2.

Motor-Free Perceptual Test–3rd Edition (MVPT-3)

Authors: Ronald Colarusso and Donald D. Hammill

Publisher: PRO-ED

Description of Test: Designed to assess visual perception without reliance on an individual's motor skills, the MVPT-3 is particularly useful with those who may have learning, cognitive, motor, or physical disabilities.

Administration Time: 20 minutes

Age/Grade Levels: Ages 4-0 to 85-0 years

Subtest Information: The MVPT-3 measures skills without copying tasks. It contains many new, more difficult items at the upper end for older children and adults. Tasks include matching, figure–ground, closure, visual memory, and form discrimination. Stimuli are line drawings. Answers are presented in multiple-choice format. Responses may be given verbally or by pointing.

STRENGTHS OF THE MVPT-R

The MVPT-3 can be used for screening as well as diagnostic and research purposes by teachers, psychologists, educational specialists, rehabilitation therapists, and others who need a quick, highly reliable, and valid measure of overall visual–perceptual processing ability in children and adults.

AUDITORY PERCEPTION

Auditory perception has long been a concern for special educators because of its relationship to speech and language development. The areas that compromise auditory perception are:

- **Auditory discrimination:** The ability to differentiate auditorally the sounds in one's environment
- **Auditory association:** The ability to organize and associate auditorily presented material in a meaningful way
- **Auditory long-term memory:** The ability to retain and recall general and specific long-term auditory information
- **Auditory short-term memory:** The ability to retain and recall general and specific short-term auditory information
- **Auditory sequential memory:** The ability to recall in correct sequence and detail prior auditory information
- **Auditory vocal expression:** The ability to reproduce vocally prior auditorily presented material or experiences
- **Auditory motoric expression:** The ability to reproduce motorically prior auditorally presented material or experiences

Diagnostic Symptoms for Auditory Perceptual Disabilities

As previously indicated, a major objective of a perceptual evaluation is to identify those areas that may have a direct impact on a child's ability to process information adequately and that may interfere in his or her academic achievement. What follows is a list of symptoms that may reflect perceptual disabilities in a variety of auditory areas.

General Auditory Perceptual Indicators

The student

- Appears less intelligent than IQ tests indicate
- Does many more things than one would expect: puts puzzles together, fixes broken objects, and so on
- Appears to have a speech problem

- May emphasize wrong syllables in words
- May sequence sounds oddly
- May use "small words" incorrectly
- Appears not to listen or comprehend
- Watches teacher's or adult's faces intently, trying to grasp words

Auditory Receptive Process Disability

The student

- Fails to comprehend what he or she hears
- Exhibits poor receptive vocabulary
- Fails to identify sounds correctly
- Fails to carry out directions

Auditory Association Disability

The student

- Fails to enjoy being read to by someone else
- Has difficulty comprehending questions
- Raises hand to answer question but gives foolish response
- Is slow to respond; takes a long time to answer
- Has difficulty with abstract concepts presented auditorily

Verbal Expressive Disability

The student

- Mispronounces common words
- Uses incorrect word endings and plurals
- Omits correct verbal endings
- Makes grammatical or syntactical errors that do not reflect those of his or her parents
- Has difficulty blending sounds

Auditory Memory Disability

The student

- Does not know address or phone number
- Fails to remember instructions
- Has difficulty memorizing nursery rhymes or poems
- Has difficulty knowing the alphabet

Assessment of Auditory Perception

There are many tests used in school systems to assess auditory perceptual skills. This section examines the most commonly used auditory perceptual measures and identifies the strengths and weaknesses of each test.

Goldman-Fristoe-Woodcock Test of Auditory Discrimination (G-F-WTAD)

Authors: Ronald Goldman, Macalyne Fristoe, and Richard W. Woodcock

Publisher: American Guidance Service

Description of Test: The *Goldman-Fristoe-Woodcock Test of Auditory Discrimination* is specifically designed to assess young children. Geared to children's vocabulary levels and limited attention spans, the test moves rapidly as responses are made by pointing to appealing pictures of familiar objects. Writing and speaking are not required. In this two-part test the examiner presents a test plate containing four drawings to the subject. The subject responds to a stimulus word (presented via audiocassette to ensure standardized presentation) by pointing to one of the drawings on the plate.

Administration Time: 20 to 30 minutes

Age/Grade Levels: Ages 4 to 70

Subtest Information: The test has three parts:

- *Training Procedure*—During this time, the examinee is familiarized with the pictures and the names that are used on the two subtests.
- *Quiet Subtest*—In this subtest, the examinee is presented with individual words in the absence of any noise. This subtest provides a measure of auditory discrimination under ideal conditions.
- *Noise Subtest*—In this subtest, the examinee is presented with individual words in the presence of distracting background noise on the tape. This subtest provides a measure of auditory discrimination under conditions similar to those encountered in everyday life.

STRENGTHS OF THE G-F-WTAD

More reliability and validity data are given for this test than for most other discrimination tests.

The test is applicable to a wide age range.

The test is easy to administer.

The test manual provides clear instruction.

Lindamood Auditory Conceptualization Test-3 (LAC-3)

Authors: Charles Lindamood and Patricia Lindamood

Publisher: PRO-ED

Description of Test: The LAC-3 is an individually administered, norm-referenced assessment that measures an individual's ability to perceive and conceptualize speech sounds using a visual medium. Because of the importance of these auditory skills to reading, the results are helpful for speech–language pathologists, special educators, and reading specialists. The LAC-3 also measures the cognitive ability to distinguish and manipulate sounds, which success in reading and spelling requires.

Administration Time: 20 to 30 minutes

Age/Grade Levels: 5-0 to 18-11 years

Subtest Information: There are no formal subtests but the test is divided into four parts:

- *Precheck*—This five-item subtest is designed to examine a child's knowledge of various concepts, for example, same/different, first/last.
- *Category I, Part A*—This subtest consists of 10 items in which the student is asked to identify certain isolated sounds and determine whether they are the same or different.
- *Category I, Part B*—This subtest requires the student to identify isolated sounds, sameness or difference, and also their order.
- *Category II*—This subtest consists of a list of 12 items in which the student must change sound patterns when sounds are added, omitted, substituted, shifted, or repeated.

STRENGTHS OF THE LAC-3

More complexity—The number of items in Category II has been increased from 12 to 18. The syllables have been extended from four phonemes to five. This category is now titled Tracking Phonemes (Monosyllables).

Multisyllabic processing—Three new categories of items have been added which extend the test into the multisyllable level of processing. These subtests are titled Counting Syllables (Multisyllables), Tracking Syllables (Multisyllables), and Tracking Syllables and Phonemes (Multisyllables).

More item analysis—All items on the test were evaluated using both conventional item analysis and the new differential item functioning analysis.

More reliability—Reliability coefficients are provided for subgroups of the normative sample (e.g., African Americans, Hispanic Americans, gender groups) as well as for the entire normative sample.

More validity studies—Many new validity studies have been conducted. Special attention has been devoted to showing that the test is valid for a wide variety of subgroups, as well as for the general population.

Test of Auditory Perceptual Skills–Revised (TAPS-R)

Author: Morrison F. Gardner

Publisher: PRO-ED

Description of Test: This test, a highly respected, well-normed, and well-standardized measurement of a client's ability to perceive auditory matter, has been revised. The TAPSR provides valuable information used in the diagnosing of individuals who have auditory difficulties, imperceptions of auditory modality, or language problems that could be the basis for learning problems.

Administration Time: Approximately 10 to 15 minutes

Age/Grade Levels: Ages 4 to 13 years

Subtest Information: The test is divided into six subtests:

- *Auditory Number Memory, Digits Forward*—This subtest measures a student's rote memory of nonsensical auditory matter.

- *Auditory Number Memory, Digits Reversed*—This subtest requires the child's ability to hear the sounds of digits forward and to repeat them in reverse.

- *Auditory Sentence Memory*—This subtest measures a child's ability to remember for immediate recall not only rote auditory matter but also auditory matter in sequence, thus measuring two processes.

- *Auditory Word Memory*—This subtest measures a child's ability to understand and interpret what he or she perceives by ear.

- *Auditory Word Discrimination*—This subtest measures a child's ability to discriminate paired one- and two-syllable words with phonemically similar consonants, cognates, or vowel differences.

- *Auditory Processing (Thinking and Reasoning)*—This subtest measures a student's ability to use common sense and ingenuity in solving common thought problems and avoids as much as possible what a child has learned from informal education and from the home.

STRENGTHS OF THE TAPS-R

This test is useful in the diagnosing of students who have auditory difficulties.

The test is useful in diagnosing language problems that could be the basis for learning problems.

Scoring takes approximately 5 to 10 minutes.

Wepman Test of Auditory Discrimination, 2nd Edition (ADT-2)

Authors: Joseph M. Wepman and William M. Reynolds

Publisher: Western Psychological Services

Description of Test: The ADT-2 is a quick way to individually screen children for auditory discrimination—and to identify those who may have difficulty learning the phonics necessary for reading. Using a very simple procedure, the ADT assesses a child's ability to recognize the fine differences between phonemes used in English speech. The examiner reads aloud 40 pairs of words, and the child indicates, verbally or gesturally, whether the words in each pair are the same or different.

Administration Time: 10 minutes

Age/Grade Levels: Ages 4 to 8

Subtest Information: There are no subtests on this instrument. The mode of presentation is the same for all editions of the test. The test consists of 40 word pairs of similar sounding words or contrasts of similar words. The child has to say if the word pairs read aloud are the same or different.

STRENGTHS OF THE ADT-2

The test has a simple administration procedure.
The test is useful for preschool and kindergarten screening.
The test–retest reliability is high.
The test is easy to score and interpret.

COMPREHENSIVE MEASURES OF PERCEPTUAL ABILITIES

Besides the assessment measures already discussed under visual and auditory perception, there are many comprehensive measures of perceptual ability. These tests are sometimes referred to as multiprocess tests (tests that contain a variety of subtests used to measure many perceptual areas). The following is a review of some available comprehensive perceptual tests.

Bruininks-Oseretsky Test of Motor Proficiency

Author: Robert Bruininks

Publisher: American Guidance Service

Description of Test: The *Bruininks-Oseretsky Test of Motor Proficiency* is an individually administered measure of gross and fine motor skills. It is a 46-item physical performance and paper-and-pencil assessment measure containing eight subtests. The examiner observes and records the student's performance on certain tasks, and the student is given a booklet in which he completes cutting and paper-and-pencil tasks.

Administration Time: The complete battery takes 45 to 60 minutes; the short form takes 15 to 20 minutes.

Age/Grade Levels: Ages 4-6 to 14-5 years

Subtest Information: The test consists of eight subtests in three areas:

- *Gross-Motor Development:* Running speed and agility, balance, bilateral coordination, strength (arm, shoulder, abdominal, and leg)
- *Gross- and Fine-Motor Development:* Upper-limb coordination
- *Fine-Motor Development:* Response speed, Visual–motor control, Upper-limb and speed dexterity

STRENGTHS OF THE BRUININKS–OSERETSKY

The test is relatively inexpensive.

The short form is very useful for testing large numbers of students because of its ease of administration and short test time.

The manual is clearly written.

The test is an enjoyable one for children.

The Bruininks-Oseretsky test thoroughly assesses the motor proficiency of able-bodied students, as well as students with serious motor dysfunctions and

Detroit Tests
of Learning Aptitude
· Fourth Edition

DTLA–4

RESPONSE
FORM

Name of Examinee _____

Date _____

Copyright © 1998, 1991, 1985 by PRO-ED, Inc.
1 2 3 4 5 02 01 00 99 98

Additional copies of this form (#8566) may be purchased from
PRO-ED, 8700 Shoal Creek Blvd., Austin, TX 78757-6897.
512/451-3246, Fax 512/451-8542

FIGURE 12.3 Detroit Tests of Learning Aptitude–Fourth Edition, Cover Sheet

developmental handicaps. The test can also be useful in developing and evaluating motor training programs.

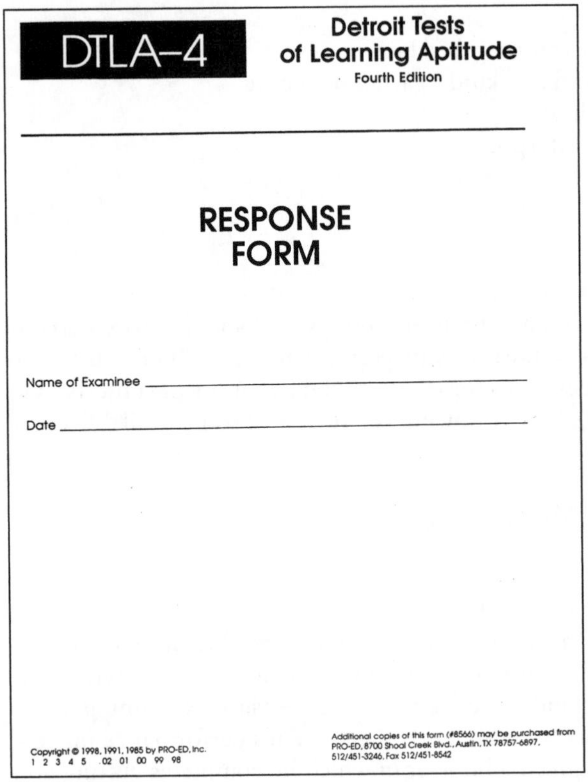

Detroit Tests of Learning Aptitudes–Fourth Edition (DTLA-4)

Author: Donald D. Hammill (1998)

Publisher: PRO-ED

Description of Test: The DTLA-4 is a multiple-item, oral-response, and paper-and-pencil battery of 11 subtests. The test provides the examiner with a profile of the student's perceptual abilities and deficiencies.

Administration Time: 50 to 120 minutes

Age/Grade Levels: Ages 6-0 to 17-11

Subtest Information: The latest edition of this test contains 11 subtests that are grouped into three domains (see Figure 12.3 for the DTLA-4 Cover Sheet). Within each domain there are two subareas called composites. Listed below are the subtests included in each domain:

Linguistic Domain

1. *Verbal Composite*—This composite tests the student's knowledge of words and their use. The subtests making up this composite are

Basic Information   *Story Construction*
Picture Fragments   *Word Opposites (see Figure 12.4)*
Reversed Letters   *Word Sequences*
Sentence Imitation

2. *Nonverbal Composite*—This composite does not involve reading, writing, or speech. The subtests making up this composite are

Design Reproduction   *Story Sequences*
Design Sequences   *Symbolic Relations*

Attentional Domain

1. *Attention-Enhanced Composite*—This composite emphasizes concentration, attending, and short-term memory. The tests that make up this composite are

Design Reproduction   *Sentence Imitation*
Design Sequences   *Story Sequences*
Reversed Letters   *Word Sequences*

2. *Attention-Reduced Composite*—This composite emphasizes long-term memory. The subtests that make up this composite are

   Basic Information *Symbolic Relations*
   Picture Fragments *Word Opposites*
   Story Construction

Motoric Domain

1. *Motor-Enhanced Composite*—This subtest emphasizes complex manual dexterity. The subtests that make up this composite are

   Design Reproduction *Reversed Letters*
   Design Sequences *Story Sequences*

2. *Motor-Reduced Composite*—This subtest requires very little motor involvement. The subtests that make up this composite are

   Basic Information *Story Construction*
   Picture Fragments *Word Opposites*
   Sentence Imitation *Word Sequences*

Subtest I. Word Opposites

Entry Point: 6–9 years = Item 1; 10–14 years = Item 25; 15–17 years = Item 35
Basal: 5 consecutive correct items
Ceiling: 5 consecutive incorrect items

Instructions:
Say, "I am going to say a word, and I want you to tell me one word that means just the opposite. For example, if I say *day*, you would say . . . (pause) *night*. *Night* is correct because *night* is the opposite of *day*. Let's try another one. What is the opposite of *up* . . . (pause) down." Once the examinee understands the task, say, "Listen carefully to what I say, and tell me the one word that is the opposite of the word I say." For all items, say, "What is the opposite of . . . ," pausing a few seconds if necessary for each answer. Items may be repeated on request. Scoreable responses are listed below.

Items:		Stimulus	Response	Items:		Stimulus	Response
______	1.	**Hot**	cold, frigid, freezing, chilling, chilly, gelid, algid	______	26.	**Entrance**	exit, egress, departure, withdrawal
______	2.	**Brother**	sister	______	27.	**Friend**	enemy, adversary, calumniator, slanderer, vilifier, foe, foeman, defamer, detractor
______	3.	**Off**	on	______	28.	**Laugh**	cry, weep
______	4.	**Asleep**	awake	______	29.	**Begin**	end, stop, finish, terminate
______	5.	**Empty**	full, filled, replete	______	30.	**False**	true
______	6.	**Young**	old	______	31.	**Narrow**	wide, expanded, ample, broad, extended, swollen, broad-minded, catholic
______	7.	**Shut**	open	______	32.	**Lengthen**	shorten, cut, curtail, abbreviate
______	8.	**Lost**	found	______	33.	**Dangerous**	safe, harmless, innocuous
______	9.	**Heavy**	light, trivial, inconsequential	______	34.	**Maximum**	minimum
______	10.	**Crooked**	straight, upright, unbent, law-abiding, honest, respectable, right-living, moral	______	35.	**Stale**	fresh, new, sharp
______	11.	**Early**	late	______	36.	**Victory**	defeat, rout, disaster, failure
______	12.	**Near**	far, distant, remote	______	37.	**Create**	destroy, abolish
______	13.	**Noisy**	quiet, silent	______	38.	**Public**	private
______	14.	**After**	before	______	39.	**Complex**	simple, easy, plain, clear, direct, evident
______	15.	**Tight**	loose, slack, sober	______	40.	**Unite**	separate, divide, sever
______	16.	**Add**	subtract, diminish, decrease, lessen, reduce, withdraw, deduct, dissever, remove	______	41.	**Falsehood**	truth
______	17.	**North**	south	______	42.	**Inferior**	superior, top-drawer, first-class
______	18.	**Sour**	sweet, saccharine, syrupy, sugary, honey-eyed, nectarous, agreeable, cheerfu, civil, courteous, polite, cordial, obliging, affable	______	43.	**Optimistic**	pessimistic, gloomy, despairing, doubtful, hopeless, cynical, foreboding
______	19.	**Remember**	forget	______	44.	**Ignorant**	enlightened, learned, scholarly, cultured, cultivated, educated, trained, instructed, informed, well-informed, literate, wise, lettered, erudite, well-read
______	20.	**Love**	hate, hatred, disaffection, enmity, execration, antipathy, repugnance, repulsion, malice, implacability, abhorrence, detestation, aversion, abomination	______	45.	**Gradual**	sudden, intermittent, hasty
______	21.	**Daughter**	son	______	46.	**Bless**	curse
______	22.	**Difficult**	easy, facile, simple, complacent, pleasant	______	47.	**Convex**	concave
______	23.	**Same**	different	______	48.	**Epilogue**	prologue
______	24.	**Deep**	shallow, superficial, unintellectual, unintelligent, flighty, frivolous	______	49.	**Former**	latter, after, succeeding, following, ensuing, consequent
______	25.	**Sharp**	dull, blunt, obtuse, pointless	______	50.	**Tentative**	permanent, definite

[ ] **Total raw score**

Anecdotal Remarks: ______________________________

FIGURE 12.4 Detroit Tests of Learning Aptitude–Fourth Edition, Subtest 1

STRENGTHS OF THE DTLA-4

The test offers the examiner some worthwhile scales for examining various abilities in learning disabled or neurologically impaired subjects.

The test provides some potentially valuable information about diverse abilities.

Internal-consistency reliability is good.

The manual is clear and easy to read.

Illinois Test of Psycholinguistic Abilities–3rd edition (ITPS-3)

Authors: D. A. Hammill, N. Mather, and R. Roberts

Publisher: PRO-ED

Description of Test: The ITPA-3 is an effective measure of children's spoken and written language. All of the subtests measure some aspect of language, including oral language, writing, reading, and spelling.

Administration Time: 45 to 60 minutes

Age/Grade Levels: Ages 5-0 to 12-11 years

Subtest Information:

Spoken Language

- *Spoken Analogies:* The examiner says a four-part analogy, of which the last part is missing. The child then tells the examiner the missing part. For example, in response to "Birds fly, fish _____," the child might say, "swim."
- *Spoken Vocabulary:* The examiner says a word that is actually an attribute of some noun. For example, the examiner may say, "I am thinking of something with a roof," to which the child might respond, "house."
- *Morphological Closure:* The examiner says an oral prompt with the last part missing. For example, the examiner says, "big, bigger, ___," and the child completes the phrase by saying the missing part, "biggest."
- *Syntactic Sentences:* The examiner says a sentence that is syntactically correct but semantically nonsensical (e.g., "Red flowers are smart"). The child repeats the sentence.
- *Sound Deletion:* The examiner asks the child to delete words, syllables, and their phonemes from spoken words. For example, the examiner might ask the student to say "weekend" without the "end."
- *Rhyming Sequences:* The examiner says strings of rhyming words that increase in length, and the child repeats them (e.g., "noon," "soon," "moon").

Written Language

- *Sentence Sequencing:* The child reads a series of sentences silently and then orders them into a sequence to form a plausible paragraph. For example, if the following three sentences were rearranged in B, C, A order they would make sense: A. I go to school. B. I get up. C. I get dressed.
- *Written Vocabulary:* After reading an adjective (e.g., "A broken ____"), the child responds by writing a noun that is closely associated with the stimulus word (e.g., "vase" or "mirror").
- *Sight Decoding:* The child pronounces a list of printed words that contain irregular parts (e.g., "would," "laugh," "height," "recipe").
- *Sound Decoding:* The child reads aloud phonically regular names of make-believe animal creatures (e.g., Flant, Yang).
- *Sight Spelling:* The examiner reads aloud irregular words one by one in a list. The child is given a printed list of these words, in which the irregular part of the words and one or more phonemes are missing. The child writes in the omitted part of the words. For example, the examiner says, "said," the child sees s___d, and writes in the missing letters, "ai."
- *Sound Spelling:* The examiner reads aloud phonically regular nonsense words, and the child writes the word or the missing part.

Composite Scores

To enhance the clinical and diagnostic usefulness of the ITPA-3, the subtests can be combined to form 11 composites. These composites are:

GLOBAL COMPOSITES

- *General Language Composite:* Formed by combining the results of all 12 subtests. For most children, this is the best single estimate of linguistic ability because it reflects status on the widest array of spoken and written language abilities.

- *Spoken Language Composite:* Formed by combining the results of the six subtests that measure aspects of oral language. The subtests assess oral language's semantical, grammatical, and phonological aspects.

- *Written Language Composite:* Formed by combining the results of the six subtests that measure different aspects of written language. The subtests assess written language's semantic, graphophonemic, and orthographic aspects. All subtests that involve graphemes (printed letters) to any degree in reading, writing, or spelling are assigned to this composite.

SPECIFIC COMPOSITES

- *Semantics Composite:* Formed using the results of the two subtests that measure the understanding and use of purposeful speech.

- *Grammar Composite:* Formed using the two subtests that measure grammar used in speech (one measures morphology, the other, syntax).

- *Phonology Composite:* The two subtests that make up this composite measure competency with speech sounds, including phonemic awareness. One subtest involves deleting parts of words, and the other involves recalling strings of rhyming words.

- *Comprehension Composite:* The results of the two subtests that measure the ability to comprehend written messages (i.e., to read) and to express thoughts in graphic form (i.e., to write) make up this composite.

- *Spelling Composite:* The results of the two subtests that measure spelling form this composite.

- *SightSymbol Processing Composite:* The two subtests in this composite measure the pronunciation and spelling of irregular words. A part of these words has to be mastered by sight because it does not conform to the most common English spelling rules or patterns (e.g., thumb).

- *SoundSymbol Processing Composite:* The two subtests in this composite measure the pronunciation and spelling of pseudowords (phonetically regular nonwords). These nonwords conform to the standard English phoneme-to-grapheme correspondence rules involved in pronouncing printed words or spelling spoken words.

STRENGTHS OF THE ITPA-3

The ITPA-3 can help you:

Determine children's specific strengths and weaknesses among linguistic abilities

Document children's development in language as a result of intervention programs

Identify children with general linguistic delays in the development of spoken and written language

Contribute to an accurate diagnosis of dyslexia (adequate spoken language with poor word identification and spelling skill), using the oral language/written language discrepancy score

Clarify the aspects of language that are difficult for a particular child (e.g., phonology, syntax, semantics)

Identify specific strengths and weaknesses in language to assist with the development of appropriate instructional goals

Differentiate between children with poor phonological coding (ability to read and spell phonically regular pseudowords) and those with poor orthographic coding (ability to read and spell words with an irregular element). Furthermore, the SightSymbol processing and SoundSymbol processing scores help identify deficits in written symbol processing, which can aid in planning appropriate strategies and accommodations

Slingerland Screening Tests for Identifying Children with Specific Language Disability

Author: Beth H. Slingerland

Publisher: Educators Publishing Service

Description of Test: This is not a test of language but rather a test of various auditory, visual, and motor skills related to specific academic areas. It is a multiple-item verbally presented paper-and-pencil examination containing eight subtests.

Administration Time: 60 to 80 minutes for Forms A, B, and C; 110 to 130 minutes for Form D

Age/Grade Levels: Grades 1 through 6

Subtest Information: Each subtest focuses on curriculum-related skills. They are as follows:

- *Far Point Copying*—This subtest requires the student to copy a printed paragraph from far points to probe visual perception and graphomotor responses. The subtest assesses visual–motor skills related to handwriting.
- *Near Point Copying*—This subtest requires the student to copy a printed paragraph from near points in order to probe visual perception and graphomotor responses. The subtest assesses visual–motor skills related to handwriting.
- *Visual Perception Memory*—This subtest requires the student to recall and match printed words, letters, and numbers presented in brief exposure with a delay before responding. This subtest assesses visual memory skills related to reading and spelling.
- *Visual Discrimination*—This subtest requires the student's immediate matching of printed words and eliminates the memory component of Visual Perception Memory. The subtest assesses basic visual discrimination without memory or written response.

- *Visual Kinesthetic Memory*—This subtest requires the student's delayed copying of words, phrases, letters, designs, and number groups presented with brief exposure. The subtest assesses the combination of visual memory and written response, which is necessary for written spelling.
- *Auditory Kinesthetic Memory*—This subtest requires the student to write groups of letters, numbers, and words to dictation after a brief delay with distraction. This subtest combines auditory perception and memory with written response.
- *Initial and Final Sounds*—This subtest requires the student to write the initial phoneme and later to write the final phoneme of groups of spoken words. This subtest assesses auditory discrimination and sequencing related to basic phonics with a written response.
- *Auditory/Visual Integration*—This subtest requires the student's delayed matching of spoken words, letters, or number groups. This subtest assesses visual discrimination related to word recognition.

There are four different forms of this test (Forms A, B, C, and D). Some of the forms contain subtests other than those already mentioned:

- *Following Directions*—This subtest requires the student to give a written response from a series of directions given by the examiner. This subtest assesses auditory memory and attention with a written response.
- *Echolalia*—This subtest requires the student to listen to a word or phrase given by the examiner and to repeat it four or five times. This is an individual auditory test. This subtest assesses auditory kinesthetic confusion related to pronunciation.
- *Word Finding*—This subtest requires the child to fill in a missing word from a sentence read by the examiner. This is an individual auditory test; it assesses comprehension and the ability to produce a specific word on demand.
- *Storytelling*—This subtest requires the child to retell a story previously read by the examiner. This is an individual auditory test; it assesses auditory memory and verbal expression of content material.

STRENGTHS OF THE SLINGERLAND

This is a very useful test for those who need a test to screen for academic problems.

The test uses skills related to classroom tasks.

This is one of the few group tests designed for disability screening for treatment purposes.

This test has the power to predict reading problems.

CONCLUSION

Administering auditory and visual perception tests is very important in the special education process. Many children have great difficulties perceiving certain stimuli, yet a perception deficit often goes undetected. An evaluation is greatly enhanced when perceptual difficulties can be ruled out as factors contributing to a child's poor performance.

Perceptual tests often take very little time to administer, so there should never be a concern about time factors when determining the battery of tests to use. In the end, using a perceptual measure can only increase the thoroughness and comprehensive nature of your assessment process and final report.

VOCABULARY

Association or Organization: Relating new information to other information and giving meaning to the information received.

Auditory Association: The ability to organize and associate material presented auditorily.

Auditory Discrimination: The ability to differentiate auditorally the sounds in one's environment.

Auditory Long-Term Memory: The ability to retain and recall general and specific long-term auditory information.

Auditory Modality: The delivery of information through sound.

Auditory Motoric Expression: The ability to reproduce motorically prior auditorally presented material or experiences.

Auditory Sequential Memory: The ability to recall in correct sequence and detail prior auditory information.

Auditory Short-Term Memory: The ability to retain and recall general and specific short-term auditory information.

Auditory Vocal Expression: The ability to reproduce vocally prior auditorily presented material or experiences.

Kinesthetic Modality: The delivery of information through movement.

Memory: The storage or retrieval process that facilitates the associational process to give meaning to information or help in relating new concepts to other information that might have already been learned. This process involves short-term, long-term, and sequential memory.

Multisensory Approaches: The input of information through a variety of receptive mechanisms (i.e., seeing, hearing, touching, etc.).

Perception: The initial organization of information.

Tactile Modality: The delivery of information through touching.

Visual Association: The ability to organize and associate visually presented material in a meaningful way.

Visual Coordination: The ability to follow and track objects with coordinated eye movements.

Visual Discrimination: The ability to differentiate visually the forms and symbols in one's environment.

Visual Figure–Ground Discrimination: The ability to differentiate relevant stimuli (the figure) from irrelevant stimuli (the background).

Visual Form Perception (visual constancy):   The ability to discern the size, shape, and position of visual stimuli.

Visual Long-Term Memory: The ability to retain and recall general and specific long-term visual information.

Visual Modality: The delivery of information through sight.

Visual Motoric Expression (visual motor integration):   The ability to reproduce motorically prior visually presented material or experiences.

Visual Sequential Memory: The ability to recall in correct sequence and detail prior visual information.

Visual Short-Term Memory: The ability to retain and recall general and specific short-term visual information.

Visual Spatial Relationships: The ability to perceive the relative positions of objects in space.

Visual Vocal Expression: The ability to reproduce vocally prior visually presented material or experiences.

ASSESSMENT OF SPEECH AND LANGUAGE

KEY TERMS

Aphasia
Apraxia
Articulation
Broca's Aphasia
Central Auditory Processing Disorder
    (CAPD)
Cluttering
Content
Expressive Language Disorders
Fluency Impairment
Form
Global Aphasia
Language Disorder
Language
Morphology

Phonological Process
Phonology
Phonology
Pitch
Loudness
Quality
Receptive Language Disorders
Speech Disorder
Speech
Stuttering
Syntax
Use
Voice
Wernicke's Aphasia

CHAPTER OBJECTIVES

This chapter focuses on the importance of speech and language assessment in the special education process. After reading this chapter, you should understand the following:

- The difference between speech and language
- Language processes
- Educational implications of speech and language disorders
- Types of speech disorders
- Types of language disorders
- Assessment of speech and language
- Assessment measures of oral language

SPEECH AND LANGUAGE

Speech and language are related, but they are not the same thing. **Speech** is the physical process of making the sounds and sound combinations of a language. Language is much more complex than speech; speech production is one of its components. **Language** is essentially the system according to which people agree to talk about or represent environmental events. Once a group of people agree on a system for representing objects, events, and the relationships among objects and events, the system can be used to communicate all their experiences. The language system consists of words and word combinations.

Language is complex and involves multiple domains—nonverbal language, oral language (i.e., listening and speaking), written language (i.e., reading and writing), pragmatic language (e.g., using language for a specific purpose, such as asking for help), phonology, and audiology. How quickly a person can access words or ideas in memory further influences his or her use of language. A child who must struggle to find an appropriate term is at a great disadvantage in a learning and social environment. As he or she grapples to retrieve a word, others have moved on. The student may miss critical pieces of knowledge, connect incorrect bits of information in memory, or have an ineffective means of showing others all that he or she knows. Such problems can result in lowered levels of achievement and in feelings of confusion, helplessness, and frustration.

Whereas the meaning of language is contained in its words and word combinations, it is speech that permits the transmission of meaning. Speech sounds are not meaningful in themselves, of course. They acquire meaning only if the speaker or listener knows his or her relationship to real events. To state it very simply, speech sounds are a medium for carrying messages.

Language is an integral part of our everyday functioning. At a minimum, we use language for problem solving, communicating, and expressing knowledge. Therefore, when problems in language become evident, they can affect individuals in many different ways. In school, children need language in order to function in the classroom. Without language, a child would have serious disadvantages when compared to other students. Students with difficulties in language may not be able to express to teachers, parents, or peers all that they know. Such problems can result in lower levels of self-esteem, low achievement, confusion, helplessness, and frustration.

Because language plays such a critical role in a child's development, most schools have a speech or language pathologist to help students who are having difficulties with these areas. Speech and language pathologists are specially trained professionals who, working with other professionals throughout the school, gather data and assess the language functioning of individual students. Language processes can be broken down into three general categories:

- **Form:** When special educators speak of form, they normally are speaking of three interconnected concepts. These are
  - **Phonology:** The knowledge a student has of sounds in language.
  - **Morphology:** The smallest meaningful unit of language and involves the stringing together of sounds.
  - **Syntax:** The rules used in combining words to make a sentence.

- **Content:** The importance of meaning. It involves knowledge of vocabulary, relationships between words, and time and event relationships.
- **Use:** The pragmatic functions of language in varying contexts. It sees the individual as an active communicator whose words and sentences are intentionally selected in relation to the effect the speaker wishes to have on a listener.

Assessment of Speech and Language

According to IDEA 2004, a speech and language impairment can be defined as a communication disorder such as stuttering, a language impairment, or a voice impairment that adversely affects a child's educational performance. Simply stated, a child with a **speech disorder** may have difficulties with any of the following:

- Producing sounds properly
- Speaking in a normal flow
- Speaking with a normal rhythm
- Using his or her voice in an effective way

Children with **language disorders** may exhibit the following:

- Difficulty in comprehending questions and following commands (receptive language)
- Difficulty in communicating ideas and thoughts (expressive language)

There are numerous tests that one can give to assess speech and language disorders. According to Wallace and colleagues (1992), "some provide a comprehensive view of all language functioning while others measure specific components of linguistic performance (for example, phonology, linguistic structure or semantics)" (p. 252).

When doing an assessment for speech and language, it is imperative for the evaluator to understand that many diagnostic tests can be insensitive to the subtleties of ongoing functional communication (Swanson & Watson, 1989, p. 5). Consequently, in order to do a thorough and complete speech and language evaluation, one should include obtaining a language sample that seeks to show how the individual performs in a real-life communication setting.

Speech and language evaluations are normally done by the speech and language pathologists in the school. However, teachers and parents play an instrumental role in these evaluations. Through interviews and observations, a student's teacher and the child's parents can gather and give valuable input to the overall assessment. As a result, both teachers and parents should become familiar with developmental language milestones. Listed below are some of the important milestones for ages birth to five years:

Birth to 6 months

- First form of communication—crying
- Makes sounds of comfort such as coos and gurgles

- Babbling soon follows as a form of communication
- Attaches no meaning to words heard from others

6 to 12 months

- Voice begins to rise and fall while making sounds
- Begins to understand certain words
- May respond appropriately to the word *no* or own name
- May perform an action when asked
- May repeat words said by others

12 to 18 months

- Has learned to say several words with appropriate meaning
- Is able to tell what he or she wants by pointing
- Responds to simple commands

18 to 24 months

- Great spurt in the acquisition and use of speech at this stage
- Begins to combine words
- Begins to form words into short sentences

2 to 3 years

- Talks
- Will ask questions
- Has vocabulary of about 900 words
- Participates in conversation
- Can identify colors
- Can use plurals
- Can tell simple stories

3 to 4 years

- Begins to speak more rapidly
- Begins to ask questions to obtain information
- Sentences longer and more varied
- Can complete simple analogies

4 to 5 years

- Average vocabulary of over 1,500 words
- Sentences average five words in length
- Able to modify speech
- Able to define words
- Can use conjunctions
- Can sing songs from memory

Educational Implications

Because all communication disorders carry the potential to isolate individuals from their social and educational surroundings, it is essential to find appropriate timely intervention. While many speech and language patterns can be called "baby talk" and are part of a young child's normal development, they can become problems if they are not outgrown as expected. In this way an initial delay in speech and language or an initial speech pattern can become a disorder which can cause difficulties in learning. Because of the way the brain develops, it is easier to learn language and communication skills before the age of 5. When children have muscular disorders, hearing problems, or developmental delays, their acquisition of speech, language, and related skills is often affected.

Speech–language pathologists assist children who have communication disorders in various ways. They provide individual therapy for the child, consult with the child's teacher about the most effective ways to facilitate the child's communication in the class setting, and work closely with the family to develop goals and techniques for effective therapy in class and at home. The speech–language pathologist may assist vocational teachers and counselors in establishing communication goals related to the work experiences of students and suggest strategies that are effective for the important transition from school to employment and adult life.

Technology can help children whose physical conditions make communication difficult. The use of electronic communication systems allow nonspeaking people and people with severe physical disabilities to engage in the give and take of shared thought.

Vocabulary and concept growth continues during the years children are in school. Reading and writing are taught and, as students get older, the understanding and use of language becomes more complex. Communication skills are at the heart of the education experience. Speech and language therapy may continue throughout a student's school years, either in the form of direct therapy or on a consultant basis.

Many speech problems are developmental rather than physiological, and as such they respond to remedial instruction. Language experiences are central to a young child's development. In the past, children with communication disorders were routinely removed from the regular class for individual speech and language therapy. This is still the case in severe instances, but the trend is toward keeping the child in the mainstream as much as possible. In order to accomplish this goal, teamwork among the teacher, speech and language therapist, audiologist, and parents is essential. Speech improvement and correction are blended into the regular classroom curriculum and the child's natural environment.

TYPES OF SPEECH AND LANGUAGE DISORDERS

Common Types of Speech Disorders

Apraxia of Speech.   **Apraxia** is a motor disorder in which voluntary movement is impaired without muscle weakness. Rather, the ability to select and sequence movements is impaired. Apraxia is a problem in assembling the appropriate sequence of movements for speech production or the executing the appropriate serial ordering of sounds for speech.

Oral apraxia affects one's ability to move the muscles of the mouth for non-speech purposes, such as coughing, swallowing, wiggling their tongue or blowing a kiss. Apraxia of speech, also known as verbal apraxia or dyspraxia, is a speech disorder in which a person has trouble saying what he or she wants to say correctly and consistently. It is not due to weakness or paralysis of the speech muscles (the muscles of the face, tongue, and lips).

Articulation Problems.   **Articulation** is the process by which sounds, syllables, and words are formed when the jaw, teeth, tongue, lips, and palate alter the air stream coming through the vocal folds. It is the production of speech sounds. Articulation disorders result from errors in the formation of individual speech sounds. Intelligibility is a measure of how well speech can be understood. Someone with an articulation disorder can be hard to understand because they say sounds incorrectly. Most errors fall into one of three categories: omissions, substitutions, or distortions. An **omission** might be *at* for *hat*, whereas a **substitution** may be *wabbit* for *rabbit* or *thun* for *sun*. When the sound is said inaccurately, but sounds something like the intended sound, it is called a **distortion**. The terms *articulation development* and *phonetic development* both refer to children's gradual acquisition of the ability to produce individual speech sounds.

Phonological Processing Problems.   **Phonology** is the science of speech sounds and sound patterns. The aims of phonology are to demonstrate the patterns of distinctive sound contrasts in a language, and to explain the ways speech sounds are organized and represented in the mind. We have language rules about how sounds can be combined. If children do not use conventional rules for language but develop their own, they may have a phonological disorder.

A **phonological process** is a pattern a child develops in order to simplify articulation. Phonological processing disorders are characterized by failure to use speech sounds that are appropriate for the individual's age and dialect. Phonological disorders involve a difficulty in learning and organizing the sounds needed for clear speech, reading, and spelling. They are disorders that tend to run in families.

Children with a phonological disorder do not necessarily go on to experience literacy problems, but children who still have a phonological disorder in the form of speech errors (especially those at the severe end of the scale) when they start school are very much at risk for difficulties learning to read and spell.

Developmental phonological disorders affect children's ability to develop speech that can be easily understood. Children with phonological disorders have difficulty learning and organizing the sounds needed for clear speech. Two common phonological processes include consonant sequence reduction (*back* instead of *black*, *sock* instead of *socks*) and velar deviation-fronting (*dame* instead of *game*, *take* instead of *cake*). Phonological disorders have been found to run in families. In some cases, these disorders may affect a child's reading and spelling abilities.

Speech Fluency Problems.   A **fluency impairment** is the condition in which speech is broken by abnormal stoppages (no sound), repetition (st-st-stopping), or prolongations (mmmmmmmmaking). There may also be unusual facial and body movement associated with the effort to speak.

Cluttering is what happens when speech becomes literally cluttered with faulty phrasing and unrelated words to the extent that it is unintelligible. Unlike stuttering, which involves hesitation and repetition of key words, cluttering usually includes effortless repetition of syllables and phrases. The affected person is often not aware of any communication difficulties.

Stuttering is a speech disorder in which the normal flow of speech is disrupted by frequent repetitions or prolongations of speech sounds, syllables, or words or by an individual's inability to start a word. The speech disruptions may be accompanied by rapid eye blinks, tremors of the lips and jaw, or other struggle behaviors of the face or upper body that a person who stutters may use in an attempt to speak. Certain situations, such as speaking before a group of people or talking on the telephone, tend to make stuttering more severe, whereas other situations, such as singing or speaking alone, often improve fluency.

Stuttering may also be referred to as stammering, especially in England, and by a broader term, disfluent speech. Stuttering is different from two additional speech fluency disorders, cluttering, characterized by a rapid, irregular speech, and **spasmodic dysphonia,** a voice disorder. It is estimated that in the United States, more than three million people stutter. Stuttering affects individuals of all ages, but occurs most frequently in young children between the ages of 2 and 6 who are developing language. Boys are three times more likely to stutter than girls. Most children, however, outgrow their stuttering, and it is estimated that less than 1 percent of adults stutter.

Many individuals who stutter have become successful in careers that require public speaking. The list of individuals includes Winston Churchill, actress Marilyn Monroe, actors James Earl Jones, Bruce Willis, and Jimmy Stewart, and singers Carly Simon and Mel Tillis, to name only a few.

Scientists suspect a variety of causes. There is reason to believe that many forms of stuttering are genetically determined. The precise mechanisms causing stuttering are not understood.

The most common form of stuttering is thought to be developmental, that is, it is occurring in children who are in the process of developing speech and language. This relaxed type of stuttering is felt to occur when a child's speech and language abilities are unable to meet his or her verbal demands. Stuttering happens when the child searches for the correct word. Developmental stuttering is usually outgrown.

Voice Problems.   **Voice** (or vocalization) is the sound produced by humans and other vertebrates using the lungs and the vocal folds in the larynx, or voice box. Voice is not always produced as speech, however. Infants babble and coo; animals bark, moo, whinny, growl, and meow; and adult humans laugh, sing, and cry. Voice is generated by airflow from the lungs as the vocal folds are brought close together. When air is pushed past the vocal folds with sufficient pressure, the vocal folds vibrate. If the vocal folds in the larynx did not vibrate normally, speech could only be produced as a whisper. Your voice is as unique as your fingerprint. It helps define your personality, mood, and health.

Approximately 7.5 million people in the United States have trouble using their voices. **Voice Disorders** involve problems with pitch, loudness, and quality. **Pitch** is the highness or lowness of a sound based on the frequency of the sound waves. **Loudness** is the perceived volume (or amplitude) of the sound. **Quality** refers to the character or distinctive attributes of a sound. Many people who have normal speaking skills have great difficulty communicating when their vocal apparatus fails. This can occur if the nerves controlling the larynx are impaired because of an accident, a surgical procedure, a viral infection, or cancer.

Voice disorders can be divided into two categories, organic and functional. Organic disorders stem from disease or pathology, whereas functional voice disorders result from abuse or misuse of the voice. Organic disorders require medical intervention, whereas functional voice disorders can often be managed by voice therapy.

Common Types of Language Disorders

Aphasia Syndromes.   **Aphasia** is a language disorder that results from damage to portions of the brain that are responsible for language. For most people, these are parts of the left side (hemisphere) of the brain. Aphasia usually occurs suddenly, often as the result of a stroke or head injury, but it may also develop slowly, as in the case of a brain tumor. The disorder impairs the expression and understanding of language as well as reading and writing.

Aphasia is caused by damage to one or more of the language areas of the brain. Many times, the cause of the brain injury is a stroke. A stroke occurs when, for some reason, blood is unable to reach a part of the brain. Brain cells die when they do not receive their normal supply of blood, which carries oxygen and important nutrients. Other causes of brain injury are severe blows to the head, brain tumors, brain infections, and other conditions of the brain.

Individuals with **Broca's Aphasia** have damage to the frontal lobe of the brain. These individuals frequently speak in short, meaningful phrases that are produced with great effort. Broca's aphasia is thus characterized as a nonfluent aphasia. Affected people often omit small words such as *is*, *and*, and *the*. For example, a person with Broca's aphasia may say, "Walk dog" meaning, "I will take the dog for a walk." The same sentence could also mean "You take the dog for a walk," or "The dog walked out of the yard," depending on the circumstances. Individuals with Broca's aphasia are able to understand the speech of others to varying degrees. Because of this, they are often aware of their difficulties and can become easily frustrated by their speaking problems. Individuals with Broca's aphasia often have right-sided weakness or paralysis of the arm and leg because the frontal lobe is also important for body movement.

In contrast to Broca's aphasia, damage to the temporal lobe may result in a fluent aphasia that is called **Wernicke's Aphasia.** Individuals with Wernicke's aphasia may speak in long sentences that have no meaning, add unnecessary words, and even create new words. For example, someone with Wernicke's aphasia may say, "You know that smoodle pinkered and that I want to get him round and take care of him like you want before," meaning "The dog needs to go out so I will take him for a walk." Individuals with Wernicke's aphasia usually have great difficulty understanding speech and are therefore often unaware of their mistakes. These individuals usually have no body weakness because their brain injury is not near the parts of the brain that control movement.

A third type of aphasia, **Global Aphasia,** results from damage to extensive portions of the language areas of the brain. Individuals with global aphasia have severe communication difficulties and may be extremely limited in their ability to speak or comprehend language.

Aphasia is usually first recognized by the physician who treats the individual for his or her brain injury. Frequently this is a neurologist. The physician typically performs tests that require the individual to follow commands, answer questions, name objects, and converse. If the physician suspects aphasia, the individual is often referred to a speech–language pathologist, who performs a comprehensive examination of the person's ability to understand, speak, read, and write.

Central Auditory Processing Disorders (CAPD). **Central Auditory Processing Disorder (CAPD)** is a term used to describe what happens when your brain recognizes and interprets the sounds around you. Humans hear when energy that we recognize as sound travels through the ear and is changed into electrical information that can be interpreted by the brain. The "disorder" part of auditory processing disorder means that something is adversely affecting the processing or interpretation of the information.

Children with CAPD often do not recognize subtle differences between sounds in words, even though the sounds themselves are loud and clear. For example, the request "Tell me how a chair and a couch are alike" may sound to a child with CAPD like "Tell me how a couch and a chair are alike." It can even be understood by the child as "Tell me how a cow and a hair are alike." These kinds of problems are more likely to occur when a person with CAPD is in a noisy environment or when he or she is listening to complex information.

What causes central auditory processing difficulty? We are not sure. Human communication relies on taking in complicated perceptual information from the outside world through the senses, such as hearing, and interpreting that information in a meaningful way. Human communication also requires certain mental abilities, such as attention and memory. Scientists still do not understand exactly how all of these processes work and interact or how they malfunction in cases of communication disorders. Even though a child seems to "hear normally," he or she may have difficulty using those sounds for speech and language.

The cause of CAPD is often unknown. In children, auditory processing difficulty may be associated with conditions such as dyslexia, attention deficit disorder, autism, autism spectrum disorder, specific language impairment, pervasive developmental disorder, or developmental delay. Sometimes this term has been misapplied to children who have no hearing or language disorder but have challenges in learning.

Delayed Language. The most intensive period of speech and language development for humans is during the first three years of life, a period when the brain is developing and maturing. These skills appear to develop best in a world that is rich with sounds, sights, and consistent exposure to the speech and language of others.

There is increasing evidence suggesting that there are critical periods for speech and language development in infants and young children. This means that the developing brain is best able to absorb a language, any language, during this period. The ability to learn a language will be more difficult, and perhaps less efficient or effective, if these critical periods are allowed to pass without early exposure to a language. The beginning signs of communication occur during the first few days of life when an infant learns that a cry will bring food, comfort, and companionship. The newborn also begins to recognize important sounds in his or her environment. The sound of a parent or voice can be one important sound. As they grow, infants begin to sort out the speech sounds (phonemes) or building blocks that compose the words of their language. Research has shown that by six months of age, most children recognize the basic sounds of their native language.

As the speech mechanism (jaw, lips, and tongue) and voice mature, an infant is able to make controlled sound. This begins in the first few months of life with cooing, a quiet, pleasant, repetitive vocalization. By six months of age, an infant usually babbles or produces repetitive syllables such as "ba, ba, ba" or "da, da, da." Babbling soon turns into a type of nonsense speech (jargon) that often has the tone and cadence of human speech but does not contain real words. By the end of their first year, most children have mastered the ability to say a few simple words. Children are most likely unaware of the meaning of their first words, but soon learn the power of those words as others respond to them.

By eighteen months of age, most children can say eight to ten words. By age two, most are putting words together in crude sentences such as "More milk." During this period, children rapidly learn that words symbolize or represent objects, actions, and thoughts. At this age they also engage in representational or pretend play. At ages three, four, and five, a child's vocabulary rapidly increases, and he or she begins to master the rules of language. Children vary in their development of speech and language. There is, however, a natural progression or timetable for mastery of these skills for each language. The milestones are identifiable skills that can serve as a guide to normal development. Typically, simple skills need to be reached before the more complex skills can be learned. There is a general age and time when most children pass through these periods. These milestones help doctors and other health professionals determine when a child may need extra help to learn to speak or to use language.

Expressive Language Disorders.   A person with an **expressive language disorder** (as opposed to a mixed receptive/expressive language disorder) understands language better than he or she is able to communicate. In speech–language therapy terms, the person's receptive language (understanding of language) is better than his or her expressive language (use of language). This type of language disorder is often a component in developmental language delay (see section on this disorder). Expressive language disorders can also be acquired (occurring as a result of brain damage/injury), as in aphasia (see section on aphasia). The developmental type is more common in children, whereas the acquired type is more common in the elderly. An expressive language disorder could occur in a child of normal intelligence, or it could be a component of a condition affecting mental functioning more broadly (i.e. mental retardation, autism).

Children with expressive language delays often do not talk much or often, although they generally understand language addressed to them. For example, a 2-year-old may be able to follow two step commands, but not name body parts. A 4-year-old may understand stories read aloud, but may not be able to describe the story even in a simple narrative. Imaginative play and social uses of language (i.e. manners, conversation) may also be impaired by expressive language limitations, causing difficulty in playing with peers. These are children who may have a lot to say, but are unable to retrieve the words they need. Some children may have no problem in simple expression, but have difficulties retrieving and organizing words and sentences when expressing more complicated thoughts and ideas. This may occur when they are trying to describe, define, or explain information or retell an event or activity.

Receptive Language Disorders.   **Receptive Language Disorders** involve difficulties in the ability to attend to, process, comprehend, retain, or integrate spoken language.

ASSESSMENT MEASURES OF SPEECH AND LANGUAGE

There are many tests that assess the strengths and weaknesses of a child's speech and language development. This section focuses on the most commonly used assessment measures for speech and language in school systems.

Peabody Picture Vocabulary Test–3 (PPVT-III)

Authors: Lloyd M. Dunn and Leota M. Dunn, with Kathleen T. Williams

Publisher: American Guidance Service

Description of Test: The test is offered in two parallel forms—IIIA and IIIB—for reliable testing and retesting. Items consist of pictures arranged in a multiple-choice format. To administer an item, the evaluator shows a plate in the test easel and says a corresponding stimulus word. The child or adult responds by pointing to one of the pictures to measure receptive vocabulary.

Administration Time: 10 to 12 minutes

Age/Grade Levels: Ages 2 to 90+

Subtest Information: This test is not divided into subtests.

STRENGTHS OF THE PPVT-3

The test has a wide range of uses.

The test has a quick administration time.

The test has clear black-and-white line drawings.

The test does not require reading or writing by the examinee.

The test has expanded adult norms through the age of 90.

The manual is clear and easy to read.

Test of Auditory Comprehension of Language–III (TACL-3)

Author: Elizabeth Carrow Woolfolk

Publisher: PRO-ED

Description of Test: The test is designed to measure a child's auditory comprehension of language, determine the developmental level, and provide diagnostic information regarding those areas of language comprehension that present difficulty to the child. This is a multiple-item response test assessing auditory understanding of word classes and relations, grammatical morphemes, and elaborated sentence constructions.

Administration Time: 15 to 25 minutes

Age/Grade Levels: Ages 3 to 9

Subtest Information: There are three subtests:

- *Vocabulary*—This subtest contains items composed of nouns, verbs, modifiers, and word relations. It measures mastery of vocabulary and concepts needed by children in preschool, kindergarten, and the elementary grades.
- *Grammatical Morphemes*—This subtest contains items composed of short simple sentences that measure grammatical morphemes, including prepositions, pronouns, noun inflections, verb inflections, noun-verb agreement, and derivational suffixes.
- *Elaborated Phrases and Sentences*—This subtest contains items composed of complex sentences that vary on a number of dimensions. It tests a student's competence with sentences with interrogatives; active and passive voice; direct and indirect objects; and coordination, subordination, and embedding of contextual elements.

STRENGTHS OF THE TACL-3

All-new normative data representing the current population have been obtained.

Characteristics of the normative sample relative to socioeconomic factors, ethnicity, gender, disability, and other critical variables are the same as those estimated for the year 2000 by the U.S. Bureau of the Census in the Statistical Abstract of the United States (1998).

The normative information is stratified by age relative to gender, race, ethnicity, and disability.

Studies to identify gender, racial, disability, or ethnic bias were conducted, and appropriate modifications were made.

Reliability coefficients are computed for subgroups of the normative sample (e.g., individuals with speech disabilities, African Americans, European Americans, Hispanic Americans, females) as well as for the entire normative group.

New validity studies were conducted, showing that the test is valid for a wide variety of subgroups as well as for the general population.

Goldman-Fristoe Test of Articulation– 2nd Edition (GFTA-2)

Authors: Ronald Goldman and Macalyne Fristoe

Publisher: American Guidance Service

Description of Test: The test provides information about a child's articulation ability by sampling both spontaneous and imitative sound production. Examinees respond to picture plates and verbal cues from the examiner with single-word answers that demonstrate common speech sounds. Additional sections provide further measures of speech production.

Administration Time: 5 to 15 minutes for Sounds-in-Words Section, varied for other two sections.

Age/Grade Levels: Ages 2 to 21 years

Subtest Information: The test is comprised of three subtests:

- *Sounds in Words*—This subtest is a picture naming task in which the child is shown pictures of familiar objects and asked to name or answer questions about them.
- *Sounds in Sentences*—This subtest assesses spontaneous sound production used in connected speech.
- *Stimulability Subtest*—This subtest assesses the child's ability to correctly produce a previously misarticulated sound when asked to watch and listen to the examiner's production of the sound.

STRENGTHS OF THE GFTA-2

New items have been added to sample more speech sounds—39 consonant sounds and clusters can now be tested with the GFTA-2. Some objectionable or culturally inappropriate items (e.g., gun, Christmas tree) have been removed.

All artwork has been redrawn and reviewed for cultural bias and fairness.

The age range for the GFTA-2 has been expanded to include ages 2 through 21. Age-based standard scores include separate normative information for females and males.

Normative tables are based on a national sample of 2,350 examinees stratified to match the most recent U.S. Census data on gender, race/ethnicity, region, and SES as determined by mother's education level.

Boehm Test of Basic Concepts–3rd Edition (BTBC-3)

Author: Ann E. Boehm

Publisher: PRO-ED

Description of Test: This new edition of an old favorite helps measure 50 basic concepts most frequently occurring in current kindergarten, first, and second grade curricula.

Administration Time: 30 to 40 minutes

Age/Grade Levels: Grades K to 2

Subtest Information: There are no subtests. The Boehm-3 is group-administered, and designed to effectively identify concepts in areas children need to master to be successful in school:

- Size (i.e., medium-sized)
- Direction (away)
- Quantity (as many)
- Time (first)
- Classification (all)
- General (other)

STRENGTHS OF THE BTBC-R

The administration of this test is straightforward and well explained in the manual.

People being examined seem to enjoy the test.

This test is designed to assess attainment of certain concepts that are used extensively in primary-grade curriculum materials.

The test's standardization sample is impressive in terms of the number of subjects used in the norming population.

The BTBC-R is a very good screening device to assess if further testing may be warranted.

Comprehensive Receptive and Expressive Vocabulary Test–2nd Edition (CREVT-2)

Authors: Gerald Wallace and Donald D. Hammill

Publisher: PRO-ED

Description of Test: *The Comprehensive Receptive and Expressive Vocabulary Test–2nd Edition* (CREVT-2) is an innovative, efficient measure of both receptive and expressive oral vocabulary. This test is a two-subtest measure based on current theories of vocabulary development. Two equivalent forms are available and full-color photos are used on the Receptive Vocabulary subtest. The kit includes examiner's manual, photo album picture book, and record forms (see Figure 13.1).

Administration Time: 20 to 30 minutes

Age/Grade Levels: Ages 4-0 to 89-11 years

Subtest Information: There are two subtests in this measure:

- *Receptive Vocabulary*—The format for the 61-item Receptive Vocabulary Subtest is a variation of the familiar "point-to-the-picture-of-the-word-I-say" technique, featuring the unique use of thematic full-color photographs. The subtest is made up of 10 plates, each of which comprises six pictures. All of the pictures on a plate relate to a particular theme (animals, transportation, occupations, clothing, food, personal grooming, tools, household appliances, recreation, and clerical materials). The themes represent concepts with which most people are familiar. Five to eight words are associated with each plate and the words are spread evenly from young children through adults. The examiner begins with Item 1 on the first plate and asks the person being tested a series of words, one at a time. After each word, the examinee selects from six photographs the one that best goes with the stimulus word. When the person misses two words in a row, the examiner introduces the next plate. The pictures used to give the Receptive Vocabulary Subtest are spiral-bound in a Photo Album Picture Book featuring laminated covers for ease of use and durability. Each plate is printed in full-color on heavy, varnish-sealed cover stock designed for frequent use.

- *Expressive Vocabulary*—The Expressive Vocabulary Subtest uses the "define-the-word-I-say" format—the most popular and precise way to measure expressive vocabulary. This format encourages and requires the individual to converse in detail about a particular stimulus word, making it ideal to measure expressive ability. The 25 items on this subtest pertain to the same 10 common themes used in the Receptive Vocabulary Subtest (i.e., animals, transportation, occupations, etc.) allowing for easy transition from subtest to subtest. The applications of basals and ceilings allow this test to be given quickly and make it appropriate for a wide age range.

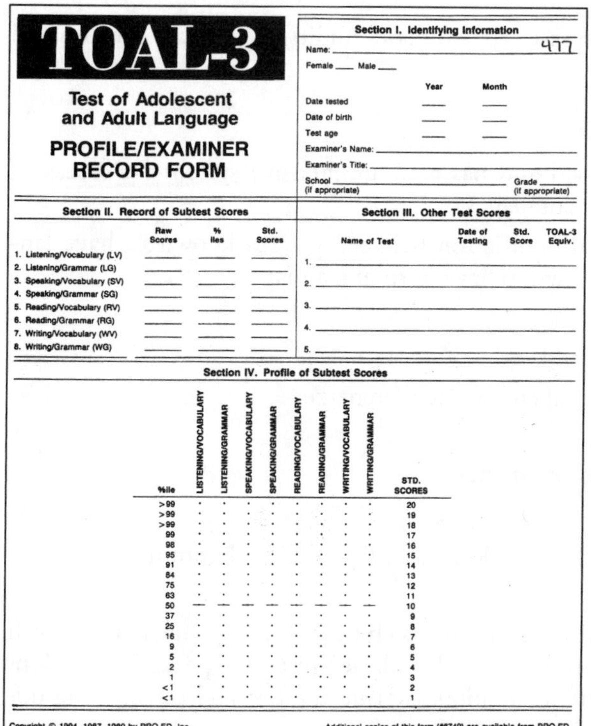

TOAL-3

Test of Adolescent and Adult Language

PROFILE/EXAMINER RECORD FORM

Section I. Identifying Information

Name: 477

Female ___ Male ___

	Year	Month
Date tested	___	___
Date of birth	___	___
Test age	___	___

Examiner's Name: ___

Examiner's Title: ___

School (if appropriate) ___ Grade (if appropriate) ___

Section II. Record of Subtest Scores

	Raw Scores	%iles	Std. Scores
1. Listening/Vocabulary (LV)			
2. Listening/Grammar (LG)			
3. Speaking/Vocabulary (SV)			
4. Speaking/Grammar (SG)			
5. Reading/Vocabulary (RV)			
6. Reading/Grammar (RG)			
7. Writing/Vocabulary (WV)			
8. Writing/Grammar (WG)			

Section III. Other Test Scores

Name of Test	Date of Testing	Std. Score	TOAL-3 Equiv.
1.			
2.			
3.			
4.			
5.			

Section IV. Profile of Subtest Scores

%ile	LISTENING/VOCABULARY	LISTENING/GRAMMAR	SPEAKING/VOCABULARY	SPEAKING/GRAMMAR	READING/VOCABULARY	READING/GRAMMAR	WRITING/VOCABULARY	WRITING/GRAMMAR	STD. SCORES
>99	·	·	·	·	·	·	·	·	20
>99	·	·	·	·	·	·	·	·	19
>99	·	·	·	·	·	·	·	·	18
99	·	·	·	·	·	·	·	·	17
98	·	·	·	·	·	·	·	·	16
95	·	·	·	·	·	·	·	·	15
91	·	·	·	·	·	·	·	·	14
84	·	·	·	·	·	·	·	·	13
75	·	·	·	·	·	·	·	·	12
63	·	·	·	·	·	·	·	·	11
50	—	—	—	—	—	—	—	—	10
37	·	·	·	·	·	·	·	·	9
25	·	·	·	·	·	·	·	·	8
16	·	·	·	·	·	·	·	·	7
9	·	·	·	·	·	·	·	·	6
5	·	·	·	·	·	·	·	·	5
2	·	·	·	·	·	·	·	·	4
1	·	·	·	·	·	·	·	·	3
<1	·	·	·	·	·	·	·	·	2
<1	·	·	·	·	·	·	·	·	1

Additional copies of this form (#6749) are available from PRO-ED, 8700 Shoal Creek Blvd., Austin, TX 78757, 512/451-3246.

FIGURE 13.1 Test of Adolescent and Adult Language–Third Edition, Profile/Examiner Record Form

STRENGTHS OF THE CREVT-2

Identifies students who are significantly below their peers in oral vocabulary proficiency

Notes discrepancies between receptive and expressive oral vocabulary

Documents progress in oral vocabulary development as a consequence of intervention programs

Measures oral vocabulary in research studies

Test of Adolescent and Adult Language–Third Edition (TOAL-3)

Authors: Virginia Brown, Donald Hammill, Stephen Larson, and J. Lee Wiederholt

Publisher: PRO-ED

Description of Test: The *Test of Adolescent and Adult Language–3rd Edition* (TOAL-3) is a current revision of the popular Test of Adolescent Language originally published in 1981 and revised in 1987. A major improvement in the test is the extension of the norms to include 18- through 24-year-old persons enrolled in postsecondary education programs. This improvement required that the name of the test be changed to indicate the presence of the older population in the normative sample.

Administration Time: 60 to 180 minutes

Age/Grade Levels: Ages 12-0 to 24-11 years

Subtest Information: The test consists of the following composites:

- *Listening*—It assesses the student's ability to understand the spoken language of other people.
- *Speaking*—It assesses the student's ability to express one's ideas orally.
- *Reading*—It assesses the ability to comprehend written messages.
- *Writing*—It assesses the student's ability to express thoughts in graphic form.
- *Spoken Language*—It assesses the student's ability to listen and speak.
- *Written Language*—It assesses the student's ability to read and write.
- *Vocabulary*—It assesses the student's ability to understand and use words in communication.
- *Grammar*—It assesses the student's ability to understand and generate syntactic structures.
- *Perceptive Language*—It assesses the student's ability to comprehend both written and spoken language.
- *Expressive Language*—It assesses the student's ability to produce written and spoken language.

STRENGTHS OF THE TOAL-3

The test is carefully developed and has a comprehensive system for assessing selected adolescent and adult languages.

Scores allow for the clear differentiation between groups known to have language problems and those known to have normal language.

The reliability is high.

Items do not appear to be biased.

The TOAL-3 assesses both oral and written language.

Test of Early Language Development– 3rd Edition (TELD-3)

Authors: Wayne P. Iliesko, D. Kim Reid, and Donald D. Hammill

Publisher: PRO-ED

Description of Test: The TELD-3 screens children for language deficiency. It is designed for normal children but can be administered to special populations after making proper adjustments in administering the test and establishing different norms (see Figure 13.2).

Administration Time: 20 minutes

Age/Grade Levels: Ages 2-0 to 7-11

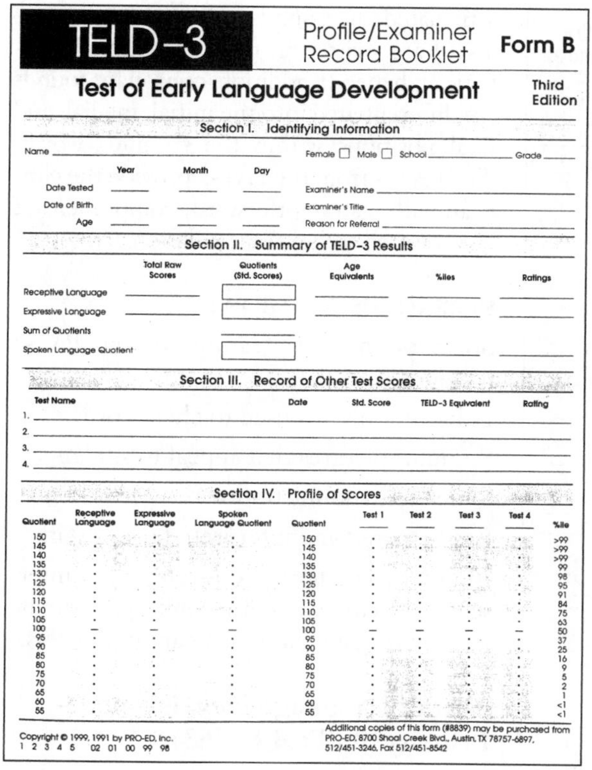
TELD-3 Profile/Examiner Record Booklet Form B

Test of Early Language Development Third Edition

Section I. Identifying Information

Name ______ Female ☐ Male ☐ School ______ Grade ______

	Year	Month	Day
Date Tested			
Date of Birth			
Age			

Examiner's Name ______
Examiner's Title ______
Reason for Referral ______

Section II. Summary of TELD-3 Results

	Total Raw Scores	Quotients (Std. Scores)	Age Equivalents	%iles	Ratings
Receptive Language					
Expressive Language					
Sum of Quotients					
Spoken Language Quotient					

Section III. Record of Other Test Scores

Test Name	Date	Std. Score	TELD-3 Equivalent	Rating
1.				
2.				
3.				
4.				

Section IV. Profile of Scores

Quotient	Receptive Language	Expressive Language	Spoken Language Quotient	Quotient	Test 1	Test 2	Test 3	Test 4	%ile
150				150					>99
145				145					>99
140				140					>99
135				135					99
130				130					98
125				125					95
120				120					91
115				115					84
110				110					75
105				105					63
100				100					50
95				95					37
90				90					25
85				85					16
80				80					9
75				75					5
70				70					2
65				65					1
60				60					<1
55				55					<1

Copyright © 1999, 1991 by PRO-ED, Inc.
1 2 3 4 5 02 01 00 99 98

Additional copies of this form (#8839) may be purchased from PRO-ED, 8700 Shoal Creek Blvd., Austin, TX 78757-6897, 512/451-3246, Fax 512/451-8542

FIGURE 13.2 Test of Early Language Development–Third Edition, Form B

Subtest Information: The TELD3 has two subtests: Receptive Language and Expressive Language.

STRENGTHS OF THE TELD-3

The test is well grounded in theory and measures form and content of language development.

Syntax, morphology, and semantics are measured in receptive as well as expressive modes.

Content validity of the test has been adequately established.

The manual is well written.

Useful examples for establishing basals and ceilings are provided in the manual.

Photo Articulation Test–Third Edition (PAT-3)

Authors: Barbara Lipke, Stanley Dickey, John Selmar, and Anton Soder

Publisher: PRO-ED

Description of Test: The *Photo Articulation Test–3rd Edition* (PAT-3) is a completely revised edition of the popular Photo Articulation Test. It meets the nationally recognized need for a standardized way to document the presence of articulation errors. The PAT-3 enables the clinician to rapidly and accurately assess and interpret articulation errors.

Administration Time: 20 minutes

Age/Grade Levels: Ages 3-6 through 9 years

Subtest Information: The test consists of 72 color photographs (nine photos on each of eight sheets). The first 69 photos test consonants and all but one vowel and one diphthong. The remaining three pictures test connected speech and the remaining vowel and diphthong. A deck of the same 72 color photographs, each on a separate card, is provided for further diagnosis and may be used in speech–language remediation.

To administer the PAT-3, the examiner simply points to each consecutively numbered photograph and asks the child, "What is this?" The child's response is scored on the Summary/Response Form to indicate the presence or absence of errors. The elicited sounds are arranged by age of acquisition. The Summary/Response Form groups the sounds by the ages at which 90% of the sample correctly

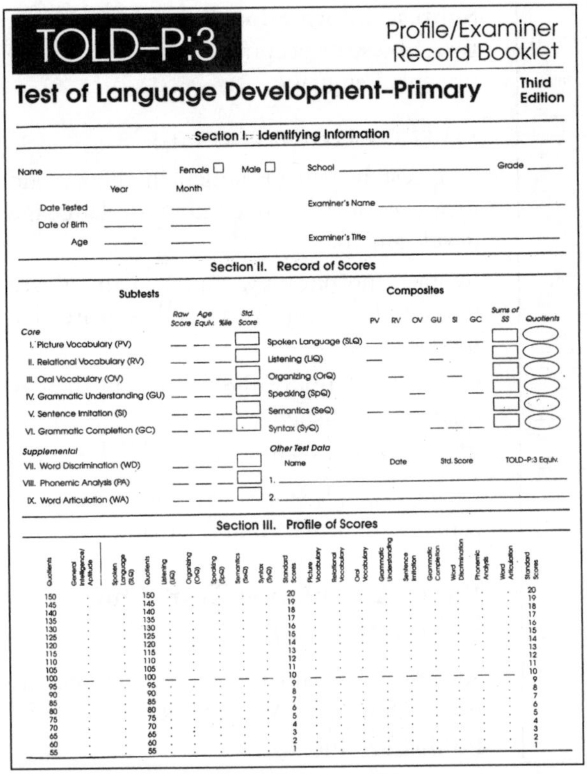
TOLD–P:3 Profile/Examiner Record Booklet

Test of Language Development–Primary Third Edition

Section I. Identifying Information

Name ______ Female ☐ Male ☐ School ______ Grade ______

Year Month

Date Tested ______ ______ Examiner's Name ______

Date of Birth ______ ______

Age ______ ______ Examiner's Title ______

Section II. Record of Scores

Subtests: Raw Score, Age Equiv., %ile, Std. Score

Core

I. Picture Vocabulary (PV)

II. Relational Vocabulary (RV)

III. Oral Vocabulary (OV)

IV. Grammatic Understanding (GU)

V. Sentence Imitation (SI)

VI. Grammatic Completion (GC)

Supplemental

VII. Word Discrimination (WD)

VIII. Phonemic Analysis (PA)

IX. Word Articulation (WA)

Composites: PV RV OV GU SI GC, Sums of SS, Quotients

Spoken Language (SLQ)

Listening (LiQ)

Organizing (OrQ)

Speaking (SpQ)

Semantics (SeQ)

Syntax (SyQ)

Other Test Data: Name, Date, Std. Score, TOLD–P:3 Equiv.

1.

2.

Section III. Profile of Scores

FIGURE 13.3 **Test of Language Development—Primary–Third Edition, Profile/Examiner Record Booklet**

articulated the sounds. All sounds that are tested are written in the international phonetic alphabet. In addition, consonant sounds are differentiated into the initial, medial, and final positions within the stimulus words. The results from the PAT-3 provide the clinician with a straightforward, comprehensive view of each student's articulation errors.

STRENGTHS OF THE PAT-3

Some of the new features of the PAT-3 include:

Full-color photos used to elicit words

Stimulus pictures that appeal to students

Quick test administration

Easily scored and interpreted test results.

Internal consistency, test–retest, and interscorer reliability coefficients approximate .80 at most ages, and many are in the .90s.

Test of Language Development–Primary: 3 (TOLD-P:3)

Authors: Phyllis L. Newcomer and Donald D. Hammill

Publisher: PRO-ED

Description of Test: The test is used to identify children and determine children's strengths and weaknesses in language skills. The TOLD-P:3 uses a two-dimensional linguistic model involving linguistic systems (listening and speaking) and linguistic features (phonology, syntax, and semantics). The subtests of the TOLD-P:3 sample each component of the model (see Figure 13.3).

Administration Time: 60 minutes

Age/Grade Levels: Ages 4-0 to 8-11 years

Subtest Information: The test consists of the following subtests:

SUBTEST	SPECIFIC ABILITY	LANGUAGE AREA MEASURED
Picture Vocabulary	Understanding words	Semantics
Oral Vocabulary	Defining words	Semantics
Grammatic Understanding	Understanding sentence structures	Syntax
Sentence Imitation	Generating proper sentences	Syntax

SUBTEST	SPECIFIC ABILITY	LANGUAGE AREA MEASURED
Grammatic Completion	Morphological usage	Syntax
Relational Vocabulary	Understanding similarities	Semantics
Word Discrimination	Noticing sound differences	Phonology
Word Articulation	Saying words correctly	Phonology
Phonemic Analysis	Segmenting words into smaller units	Phonology

STRENGTHS OF THE TOLD-P:3

The TOLD-P:3 is well designed in terms of utilizing established psychometric criteria for reliability and criterion-related validity.

The test is a useful measure for investigating the oral language skills of young children.

The test is very useful in identifying areas in which the child is proficient and areas that require further evaluation.

Many different language areas can be assessed.

Children may find the test to be fun because the colored pictures are pleasant to observe.

CONCLUSION

There are many areas of assessment that may be done when testing is mandated. The areas discussed in this chapter are very important to understand, even if they are ones that you as a special educator may not have to actually administer in your career. You should now understand that a thorough comprehension of speech and language is critical to developing appropriate hypotheses and theories about whether a specific disability exists in a child. The fact that a professional in the special education process may not be a speech and language clinician does not preclude him or her from knowing the various tests and assessment procedures that are being utilized. When all team members have at least a general understanding of what the other team members are doing, it makes the entire multidisciplinary evaluation stronger.

VOCABULARY

Aphasia: A language disorder that results from damage to portions of the brain that are responsible for language.

Apraxia: A motor disorder in which voluntary movement is impaired without muscle weakness.

Articulation: The process by which sounds, syllables, and words are formed when the jaw, teeth, tongue, lips, and palate alter the air stream coming through the vocal folds. It is the production of speech sounds.

Broca's Aphasia: Damage to the frontal lobe of the brain. These individuals frequently speak in short, meaningful phrases that are produced with great effort. Broca's aphasia is thus characterized as a nonfluent aphasia.

Central Auditory Processing Disorder (CAPD):   A term used to describe what happens when your brain recognizes and interprets the sounds around you. Humans hear when energy that we recognize as sound travels through the ear and is changed into electrical information that can be interpreted by the brain. The disorder part of auditory processing disorder means that something is adversely affecting the processing or interpretation of the information.

Cluttering: What happens when speech becomes literally cluttered with faulty phrasing and unrelated words to the extent that it is unintelligible. Unlike stuttering, which involves hesitation and repetition over key words, cluttering usually includes effortless repetition of syllables and phrases. The affected person is often not aware of any communication difficulties.

Content: The importance of meaning. It involves knowledge of vocabulary, relationships between words, and time and event relationships.

Expressive Language Disorders: A person with an **expressive language disorder** (as opposed to a mixed receptive/expressive language disorder) understands language better than he/she is able to communicate. In speech–language therapy terms, the person's receptive language (understanding of language) is better than his/her expressive language (use of language).

Fluency Impairment: A condition in which speech is broken by abnormal stoppages (no sound), repetition (st-st-stopping), or prolongations (mmm-mmmmmaking). There may also be unusual facial and body movement associated with the effort to speak.

Form: The interconnected concepts of phonology, morphology, and syntax.

Global Aphasia: Global Aphasia results from damage to extensive portions of the language areas of the brain. Individuals with global aphasia have severe communication difficulties and may be extremely limited in their ability to speak or comprehend language.

Language Disorder: Difficulties in language that adversely affects a child's educational performance.

Language: The system according to which a people agree to talk about or represent environmental events.

Morphology: The smallest meaningful unit of language and involves the stringing together of sounds.

Phonological Process: A pattern a child develops in order to simplify articulation. Phonological processing disorders are characterized by failure to use speech sounds that are appropriate for the individual's age and dialect.

Phonology: The science of speech sounds and sound patterns.

Phonology: The knowledge a student has of sounds in language.

Pitch: The highness or lowness of a sound based on the frequency of the sound waves.

Loudness: The perceived volume (or amplitude) of the sound.

Quality: The character or distinctive attributes of a sound.

Receptive Language Disorders: Involve difficulties in the ability to attend to, process, comprehend, retain, or integrate spoken language.

Speech Disorder: Difficulties in speech which adversely affects a child's educational performance.

Speech: The physical process of making the sounds and sound combinations of a language.

Stuttering: A speech disorder in which the normal flow of speech is disrupted by frequent repetitions or prolongations of speech sounds, syllables, or words or by an individual's inability to start a word.

Syntax: The rules used in combining words to make a sentence.

Use: The pragmatic functions of language in varying contexts. It sees the individual as an active communicator whose words and sentences are intentionally selected in relation to the effect the speaker wishes to have on a listener.

Voice (or vocalization): The sound produced by humans and other vertebrates using the lungs and the vocal folds in the larynx, or voice box.

Wernicke's Aphasia: In contrast to Broca's aphasia, damage to the temporal lobe may result in a fluent aphasia that is called Wernicke's aphasia.

CHAPTER FOURTEEN

EARLY CHILDHOOD ASSESSMENT

KEY TERMS

Adaptive

Assessment for Diagnosing and
　Determination of Eligibility

Assistive Technology

At Risk

Authenticity

Casefinding/Child Find

Collaboration

Congruence

Convergence

Developmental

Developmental Tests

Early Childhood Intervention

Equity

Evaluations

Facility or Center-Based Visits

Family

Family Support Groups

Group Development Intervention

Home and Community Based Visits

Home visits

IDEA—Public Law 101-476

IDEA 1997—Public Law 105-17

IDEA 2004—Public Law 108-446

Individualized

Individualized Family Service Plan (IFSP)

Outcomes

Parent-child groups

Part C

Part H

Plan

Program Evaluation

Program Planning

Public Law 94-142

Public Law 99-457

Qualified Personnel

Screening

Sensitivity

Service

CHAPTER OBJECTIVES

This chapter focuses on the importance of early intervention assessment and education in the birth to 5-year-old population. After reading this chapter, you should understand the following:

- The importance of early childhood assessment
- Legal foundations for assessment procedures
- The challenge of early childhood assessment
- Working with the family in early childhood assessment
- Early childhood assessment

EARLY CHILDHOOD ASSESSMENT

Early childhood intervention (often referred to as early intervention) is rapidly becoming an area of study for many special educators. Both undergraduate and graduate schools are beginning to stress the importance of early intervention assessment and education in the birth to 5-year-old population. Many states are becoming increasingly aware of the importance of early intervention for children. The idea of helping children before they get to elementary school with whatever concerns they may be facing has educational, social, and political implications. Whatever the reasons for the initiation of early intervention in a given state, it has become apparent that it is a very important part of the special education process.

It is important to keep in mind that the parents of very young children who are suspected of having a disability will be anxious and in search of answers from the educational professionals. When potential problems occur at such an early age, parents need answers that will inform them as to the diagnosis of the problem, the prognosis or what the child will be like in later years, and remediation and intervention strategies that will help their child. Therefore, special educators need to be familiar with early childhood evaluation instruments that will begin the process of assessment by diagnosing the child's areas of strength and weakness. From this information, a team of professionals can then prepare intervention recommendations for the parent.

The goal of assessment in early childhood is the same as it is for an individual of any age—that is, to derive information to facilitate decision making with respect to that individual. Such decisions revolve around the potential existence, implications, and treatment needs of a problem(s) for the child and family.

One of the problems with early childhood assessment is that many special educators have limited, if any, training with the birth to five-year-old population. Consequently, although there are a number of tests to measure intellectual development, speech and language delays, and behavioral norms, few educators are well versed in the use of these assessment instruments.

The assessment process in early childhood is an attempt to determine the strengths and weaknesses of a child so that a specific program of intervention can be planned and implemented. An important characteristic of a good assessment program is an ecological approach to the evaluation. By this, we mean that the assessment data accurately describe as many aspects of the child's functioning as possible (physical, social, and intellectual) in as many settings as possible (home, school, community) so that we have the necessary information to plan an intervention program that will affect as much of the child's life as possible.

To meet these objectives, an assessment program must be broad enough to include a fair sampling of the child's abilities, yet specific enough to provide useful information. It must include several instruments administered by specialists in various areas of development (e.g., language, motor development, cognition), as well as observational data concerning the child's daily environment.

Bagnato, Neisworth, and Munson (1993) list six standards of assessment materials for use with young children:

- **Authenticity:** Does the assessment focus on actual child behavior in real settings?
- **Convergence:** Does the assessment rely on more than one source of information?
- **Collaboration:** Does the assessment involve cooperation and sharing, especially with parents?
- **Equity:** Does the assessment accommodate special sensory, motor, cultural, or other needs rather than penalize children who have such needs?
- **Sensitivity:** Does the assessment include sufficient items for planning lessons and detecting changes?
- **Congruence:** Was the assessment developed and field tested with children similar to those being assessed?

LEGAL FOUNDATIONS FOR ASSESSMENT PROCEDURES

The field of Early Childhood Special Education is relatively new. Laws that govern the assessment of young children with special needs have recently been passed. *Public Law 94-142, The Education for All Handicapped Children's Act*, mandated services for all school-age children with disabilities and facilitated the provision of services for preschool children with disabilities in some states (see Chapter 2). P.L. 94-142 and its regulations provided guidelines for the assessment of children receiving special education services from state departments of education (McLean et al., 1996).

In 1986, **Public Law 99-457** was passed, amending P.L. 94-142 and requiring the states to provide a free and appropriate public education to children with disabilities ages three through five years. The regulations that governed school-age children were then made applicable to the assessment of preschool children. In addition, a new part (Part H) was added to the law, establishing incentives for serving infants and toddlers with special needs.

In 1990, P.L. 99-457 was retitled the *Individuals with Disabilities Education Act (IDEA)—P.L. 101-476*. The IDEA amendment to P.L. 99-457 requires a timely, comprehensive, multidisciplinary evaluation, including assessment activities related to the child and the child's play. For infants and toddlers (birth to two years of age), a new program (Part H was changed to *Part C* in the Amendments to IDEA '97) was established to help states develop and implement programs for early intervention services. Every U.S. state currently provides services for infants and toddlers with disabilities under IDEA 2004 (P.L. 108-446).

IDEA 2004 (sec. 636(a)(1)(2)) states that

(a) the state shall provide at a minimum for each infant or toddler with a disability, and the infant's or toddler's family, to receive:
  (1) a multidisciplinary assessment of the unique strengths and needs of the infant or toddler and the identification of services appropriate to meet such needs;
  (2) a family-directed assessment of the resources, priorities, and concerns of the family and the identification of the supports and services necessary to enhance the family's capacity to meet the developmental needs of the infant or toddler. (p. 62)

THE CHALLENGE OF EARLY
CHILDHOOD ASSESSMENT

Environmental and cultural influences must be considered when testing young children. Special educators can expect much more variability in test performance due to environmental influences on infants and preschool children than on older school-age children. Measures of the home environment can be very helpful in understanding a child's **developmental** functioning. Such factors as the quality of the mother's or father's verbalization, the toys or variety of activities available in the environment, the restrictiveness of discipline, and the freedom from danger can influence the child's early developmental course. It was very appropriate that P.L. 99-457 included a focus on not only the child with disabilities but also the family of the child.

Cultural influences also must be considered, as they may affect parenting style and the child's responsivity to the examiner and the testing process. For instance, a young Native American child may make less eye contact, act more shy, and be less verbal with the examiner than a Caucasian child, but these differences may represent cultural influences rather than developmental delay. Reviewing the cross-cultural literature regarding the developmental performance of infants who are African American, Asian American, Hispanic, and other cultural groups would be helpful to the prospective examiner.

To effectively meet the challenges posed, the assessment process in early childhood should try to achieve eight fundamental goals (Bailey & Wolery, 1992):

- Determine the eligibility for services and the appropriateness of alternative environments
- Identify developmentally appropriate and functional intervention goals
- Identify the unique styles, strengths, and coping strategies of each child
- Identify parents' goals for their children and their needs for themselves
- Build and reinforce parents' sense of competence and worth
- Develop a shared and integrated perspective on child and family needs and resources
- Create a shared commitment to intervention goals
- Evaluate the effectiveness of services for children and families

The assessment and evaluation process for early intervention normally consists of the following five stages:

- **Casefinding/child find:** To alert parents, professionals, and the general public to children who may have special needs and to elicit their help in recruiting candidates for screening.
- **Screening:** To identify children who are not within normal ranges of development and need further evaluation and who may be candidates for early intervention programs.
- **Assessment for diagnosis and determination of eligibility:** To conduct an in-depth evaluation to verify if a problem exists, determine the nature and severity of the problem, and prescribe the treatment or type of intervention services needed.

- **Program planning:** This refers to procedures used by the assessment team to develop the Individualized Family Service Plan (IFSP, discussed below) and to revise these plans as necessary. The outcome of assessment for program planning is the identification of special services needed by the child and the family, the service delivery format that will be used (including location of services), and the delineation of intervention objectives as specified in the IFSP.
- **Program evaluation:** To evaluate the quality of the overall intervention program and to document its impact on the children or parents it serves. Information collected on an ongoing basis allows the team to determine to what extent progress is being made toward goals and objectives and, as a result, to identify changes that should be made in intervention strategies or objectives. When such data are collected across all of the children in a given program, it may be possible to measure overall program impact.

According to Hanson and Lynch (1995), the following questions can be used to review and evaluate procedures used to assess young children and identify family concerns, priorities, and resources:

- Are diagnostic or eligibility assessment procedures clearly identified?
- Are child assessment and family procedures linked to programming?
- Are the staff members who are conducting child assessments trained in measurement, the particular strategies being used, and assessment of young children and infants?
- Are the assessment instruments that are being used valid and reliable?
- Is the assessment being conducted by an interdisciplinary team that includes the parents or primary caregivers as equal partners?
- Is adequate time allocated for the team to plan assessments jointly with the family?
- Are assessments conducted in a setting that is familiar to the child, with the parents or primary caregivers present and assisting?
- Are assessment data collected in a variety of ways (observation, interview, etc.)?
- Are assessments of the child's strengths and needs and the family's concerns, priorities, and resources culturally and linguistically appropriate?
- Is there a standard procedure for writing reports and sharing the findings with all the members, including the parents?
- Are written and verbal reports free of judgment, stereotyping, and negative labeling?
- Is ample time allocated for discussing and sharing findings and making programming decisions?
- Is follow-up done soon after placement to determine the appropriateness of the program, the child's performance, and the family's and staff's satisfaction with the program?
- Is the identification of family concerns, priorities, and resources nonintrusive, nonjudgmental, and conducted with sensitivity?
- Does the information collected about the family's concerns, priorities, and resources assist in finding resources or developing programs? (p. 179)

THE INDIVIDUALIZED FAMILY
SERVICE PLAN (IFSP)

After a child has been evaluated, it is mandated under federal law that an **Individualized Family Service Plan (IFSP)** be written. This plan sets forth critical information pertaining to both the child and the family's services. IFSP stands for

- **Individualized:** The plan will be specially designed for the child and the family.
- **Family:** The plan will focus on the family and the **outcomes** family members hope for the child and the family through early intervention.
- **Service:** The plan will include all the details about the services provided for both the child and the family.
- **Plan:** The plan is a written plan for services.

The IFSP is based on the premise that a child's home environment strongly influences that child's overall experiences and successes; therefore, it includes goals and objectives for the family as a unit, as well as goals and objectives for the individual child (Bigge & Stump, 1999, p. 15).

Under IDEA 2004, sec. 636(d), the components of an IFSP must include the following:

1. A statement of the infant's or toddler's present levels of physical development, cognitive development, communication development, social or emotional development, and adaptive development, based on objective criteria
2. A statement of the family's resources, priorities, and concerns relating to enhancing the development of the family's infant or toddler with a disability
3. A statement of the measurable results or outcomes expected to be achieved for the infant or toddler and the family, including preliteracy and language skills, as developmentally appropriate for the child, and the criteria, procedures, and time lines used to determine the degree to which progress toward achieving the results or outcomes is being made and whether modifications or revisions of the results or outcomes or services are necessary
4. A statement of specific early intervention services based on peer-reviewed research, to the extent practicable, necessary to meet the unique needs of the infant or toddler and the family, including the frequency, intensity, and method of delivering services
5. A statement of the natural environments in which early intervention services will appropriately be provided, including a justification of the extent, if any, to which the services will not be provided in the natural environment
6. The projected dates for initiation of services and the anticipated length, duration, and frequency of the services
7. The identification of the service coordinator from the profession most immediately relevant to the infant or toddler's family's needs (or who is otherwise qualified to carry out all applicable responsibilities under this part) who will be responsible for the implementation of the plan and coordination with other agencies and persons, including transition services
8. The steps to be taken to support the transition of the toddler with a disability to preschool or other appropriate services

The IFSP must be reviewed at 6-month intervals or more frequently as needed. Every 12 months, the child must be reevaluated. After assessment is completed, a program must be established for each child.

Under Part C of IDEA, the following services can be given to infants and toddlers in the IFSP:

- Family training, counseling, and home visits
- Special instruction
- Speech and language instruction
- Occupational and physical therapy
- Psychological testing and counseling
- Service coordination
- Medical services necessary for diagnostic and evaluation purposes
- Social work services
- Assistive technology
- Early identification, screening, and assessment services
- Health services, when necessary
- Transportation and related costs as necessary

Only **qualified personnel**—individuals who are licensed, certified, or registered in their discipline and approved by their state—can deliver early intervention services. All early intervention services can be given using any of the following service models (NYS Department of Health, 2000):

1. **Home and community-based visits:** In this model, services are given to a child and parent or other family member or caregiver at home or in the community.
2. **Facility or center-based visits:** In this model, services are given to a child and parent or other family member or caregiver where the service provider works (such as an office, hospital, clinic, etc.).
3. **Parent–child groups:** In this model, parents and children get services together in a group led by a service provider. A parent-child group can happen anywhere in the community.
4. **Family support groups:** In this model, parents, grandparents, or other relatives of the child get together in a group led by a service provider for help and support and to share concerns and information.
5. **Group development intervention:** In this model, children receive services in a group setting led by a service provider or providers without parents or caregivers. A group means two or more children who are eligible for early intervention services. The group can include children without disabilities and can happen anywhere in the community.

WORKING WITH THE FAMILY IN EARLY CHILDHOOD ASSESSMENT

Many times, when assessing children who may need early intervention, the special educator will have to interview the parents/caregivers. This is very often done during a **home visit** right in the home of these individuals. Often, this is a new experience for many special educators. With the more recent emphasis on ecological assessment, interviews have begun to examine the relationship of children to their environment. How parents are treated in initial contacts with professionals who will be working with their child shapes their current and future attitudes and behaviors. Thus, planning and conducting the interview thoughtfully and sensitively are important investments. Interviews should allow time for rapport building or "warm-up" for both the interviewer and the interviewee. The purpose of the interview and an overview of the kinds of questions provided should be reviewed (see Chapter 8). Listed here are some practical suggestions for special educators when conducting parent interviews in early intervention (cited in Hanson and Lynch's *Survival Guide for Interviewers*, 1995):

- Write down the address, directions, and a phone number where you can reach or leave a message for the family that you are interviewing. It is easy to get lost when you are busy or nervous.
- There are different cultural rules related to being in someone's house. Do not be surprised if the father or elder does all of the talking in some situations or if a male interventionist cannot visit the home unless the husband is present.
- If you are conducting the interview through an interpreter, allow time to discuss the interview questions with the interpreter first. Give the family and the interpreter time to get acquainted and comfortable with one another, and be sure that you address your questions and comments to the family, not the interpreter.
- Dress professionally yet in keeping with the norms of the family and community.
- If you are taking toys or materials to the home, take something that can remain (picture books, crayons, animal crackers, etc.), remembering that there may be several brothers and sisters who will be very interested in what you are doing and what you have brought.
- Do not be afraid to admit if you are nervous. Parents always recognize bluffing.
- It is not appropriate to tell your own stories or say you know just how the family feels, but it is appropriate to laugh and cry with someone who is sharing joy or pain.
- Do not feel that you have to answer all of the family's concerns or questions. For some you may be able to find answers; for others you may be able to help them find answers; and for some there never will be an answer.
- If you do not feel safe in a neighborhood, take someone with you to the interview or arrange to conduct it outside the home.
- Remember the Golden Rule as you embark on any interview: Interview others as you would like to be interviewed. (p. 161)

EARLY CHILDHOOD ASSESSMENT MEASURES

Bayley Scales of Infant Development–2nd Edition (BAYLEY-II)

Author: Nancy Bayley

Publisher: Harcourt Assessment, Inc.

Description of Test: This individually administered test has three subscales: the Mental Scale, the Motor Scale, and the Behavior Rating Scale. The items in the Mental and Motor scales are mixed together; thus, examiners are required to identify which items go on each scale and tally them separately. The Behavior Rating Scale is completed after the Mental and Motor scales have been administered. This second edition has more than 100 new items created to apply to the expanded age range. The test includes the examiner's manual, stimulus booklet, Mental Scale record forms, Motor Scale record forms (with tracing design sheet), Behavior Rating Scale record forms, visual stimulus cards, map, and all necessary manipulatives.

Administration Time: Under 15 months, 25 to 30 minutes; over 15 months, up to 60 minutes

Age/Grade Levels: Ages 1 through 42 months

Subtest Information: The test is comprised of three subtests:

The *Mental Developmental Index (MDI)* assesses a variety of abilities, including:

- Sensory/perceptual acuity, discriminations, and responses
- Acquisition of object constancy
- Memory
- Vocalization
- Verbal communication
- Mathematical Concept Formation

The *Psychomotor Developmental Index (PDI)* assesses a variety of abilities, including

- Degree of body control
- Large muscle coordination
- Finer manipulatory skills of the hands and fingers
- Dynamic movement
- Postural imitation

The *Behavior Developmental Index (BDI)* is separate scale made up of its own items. It assesses qualitative aspects of the child's test-taking behavior and allows an examiner to rate:

- Arousal
- Attention
- Orientation
- Engagement
- Emotional regulation
- Motor quality

STRENGTHS OF THE BSID-II

The scale's norms are representative in terms of race, ethnicity, geographic region, parental education, and sex.

The BSID-II is a well-standardized and very comprehensive test of infant development.

The BSID-II is a very popular test used by early intervention clinicians.

Data are provided in the manual for the following groups: children who were born prematurely, have the HIV antibody, were prenatally drug exposed, were asphyxiated at birth, are developmentally delayed or have frequent otitis media, are autistic, or have Down syndrome. There is evidence of strong construct validity.

The test is a good screening instrument for children with disabilities.

Preschool Language Scale–3 (PLS-3)

Authors: Irla Lee Zimmerman, Violette G. Steiner, and Roberta L. Evatt

Publisher: Harcourt Assessment, Inc.

Description of Test: This test is designed in a format of three sections: Auditory Comprehension, Verbal Ability, and Articulation. The test consists of pictures and items that each child must point to or explain. The level depends on the child's developmental level at the time of testing. This test may be used as a criterion-referenced test for older children functioning within the range of behaviors assessed by PLS-3 and, with suggested modifications, for children with physical or hearing impairments. The test includes examiner's manual, picture book, and record forms.

Administration Time: 30 minutes

Age/Grade Levels: Birth to 6-11

Subtest Information: The test includes two separate scales:

- *Auditory Comprehension Scale*—The scale requires nonverbal responses such as pointing to a picture that the examiner has named.
- *Expressive Communication Scale*—In this section, items are presented that require the child to name or explain the items. The difficulty varies depending on the child's developmental level during the time of testing.

The items on the test assess the following areas in both the receptive and expressive modes:

Vocabulary	*Morphology*
Concepts of quality	*Syntax*
Concepts of quantity	*Integrative thinking skills*
Space and time	

STRENGTHS OF THE PLS-3

This test may be useful to a preschool teacher who wishes to identify a pattern of strengths and weaknesses in a child's conceptual and auditory abilities.

The test offers a comprehensive assessment of receptive and expressive language in young children.

The test meets general federal and state guidelines—including IDEA legislation—for evaluating preschoolers for special services.

The test is a good screening measure for qualification in early intervention programs such as Head Start, Even Start, or Title I programs.

Metropolitan Readiness Test–6th Edition (MRT-6)

Authors: J. R. Nurss (1995)

Publisher: Harcourt Assessment, Inc.

Description of Test: The MRT-6 assesses literacy development in children from preschool to the first grade. It is the oldest and most widely used readiness test (Taylor, 1997).

Administration Time: 85 to 100 minutes in 4 sessions

Age/Grade Levels: Pre K and Kindergarten

Subtest Information: The MRT-6 assesses five different areas:

- Visual discrimination
- Beginning consonants
- Sound-letter correspondence
- Story comprehension
- Quantitative concepts and reasoning

STRENGTHS OF THE MRT-6

The MRT-6 is a comprehensive and diagnostic tool.

It includes a conference report that explains the purpose and the results of the MRT-6 in a convenient format for teachers to use when conferring with parents (Venn, 2000).

The MRT-6 has a colorful easel format that children appear to enjoy.

The MRT-6 provides excellent standardization.

Boehm Test of Basic Concepts–Revised (BTBC-R)

Author: Ann E. Boehm

Publisher: Harcourt Assessment, Inc.

Description of Test: The test consists of 50 concept items placed in two test booklets, Booklet 1 and Booklet 2, to facilitate administration in two sessions to children in Grades K, 1, 2, and 3. The test has two alternate forms, C and D. The test questions are read by the examiner, and the students are required to mark the correct response directly in the individual test booklet. The test materials include individual student test booklets and the examiner's manual.

Administration Time: Up to 40 minutes for Form C or D, and 15 to 20 minutes for the Applications form

Age/Grade Levels: Grades K through 3

Subtest Information: The test has no subtests.

STRENGTHS OF THE BTBC-R

A section in the manual devoted to score interpretation and to the use of the results is very practical.

Most young children find this test interesting.

The test has two equivalent forms that allow for the determination of progress with pre- and posttesting.

Bracken Basic Concept Scale (BBCS)

Author: Bruce A. Bracken

Publisher: Harcourt Assessment, Inc.

Description of Test: This test measures 11 diagnostic subtests areas. Items are multiple choice, and the child is shown four monochrome pictures and asked to identify the picture that depicts a particular concept. The test includes an examiner's manual, diagnostic stimulus manual, diagnostic record forms, one Screening Test Form A, and one Screening Test Form B.

Administration Time: 20 to 40 minutes

Age/Grade Levels: Age 2-6 to 7-11

Subtest Information: The following lists the subtests and corresponding concepts:

- *Color/Letter Identification*—Children are tested on their knowledge of colors and letters.
- *Numbers/Counting*—Children are required to tell how many items and recognize numbers.
- *Comparisons*—Children are required to compare things.
- *Shapes*—Children are tested regarding their ability to recognize different shapes.
- *Direction/Position*—Children are tested on their ability to distinguish between different directions and positions.
- *Social/Emotional*—This subtest determines children's social and emotional development.
- *Size*—This subtest determines children's ability to differentiate between sizes.
- *Texture/Material*—Children are given objects of different texture and must identify them.
- *Quantity*—Children are tested on their ability to distinguish amounts.
- *Time/Sequence*—Children are given numbers and asked to tell the missing number or the number that comes next.

STRENGTHS OF THE BBCS

One of the major strengths of the BBCS is the detailed and well-organized examiner's manual.

The test administration procedures for the BBCS are fairly well planned and coordinated.

The test is a very comprehensive test of basic concept identification for young children.

The test can be used for norm-referenced, criterion-referenced, or curriculum-based purposes.

A criterion-referenced record form is available in Spanish.

The Preschool Evaluation Scales (PES)

Author: Stephen B. McCarney

Publisher: Hawthorne Educational Services

Description of Test: This test is designed as a rating scale completed by the child's parents or child-care provider. It consists of a technical manual, rating forms, and a computerized scoring system.

Administration Time: 20 to 25 minutes

Age/Grade Levels: Birth to 72 months

Subtest Information: The subscale areas assessed by this instrument follow:

Large muscle skill   *Expressive language*
Small muscle skill   *Social/emotional behavior*
Cognitive thinking   *Self-help skills*

STRENGTHS OF THE PES

This test is a good screening device for developmental delays for preschool-age children.

The test has strong validity.

New norms are being developed for a home version.

Kindergarten Readiness Test (KRT)

Authors: Sue L. Larson and Gary Vitali

Publisher: Slosson Educational Publications

Description of Test: The test assesses five general areas of readiness: awareness of one's environment, reasoning, numerical awareness, fine-motor coordination, and auditory attention span. See Figures 14.1 and 14.2 for the KRT Cover Sheet and Letter.

Administration Time: 15 to 20 minutes

Age/Grade Levels: Ages 4 to 6

Subtest Information: The test has no subtests.

STRENGTHS OF THE KRT

The test can be readily administered by specialists, teachers, or paraprofessionals.

The test assesses various key areas shown to be critical for school readiness and consolidates information on one form.

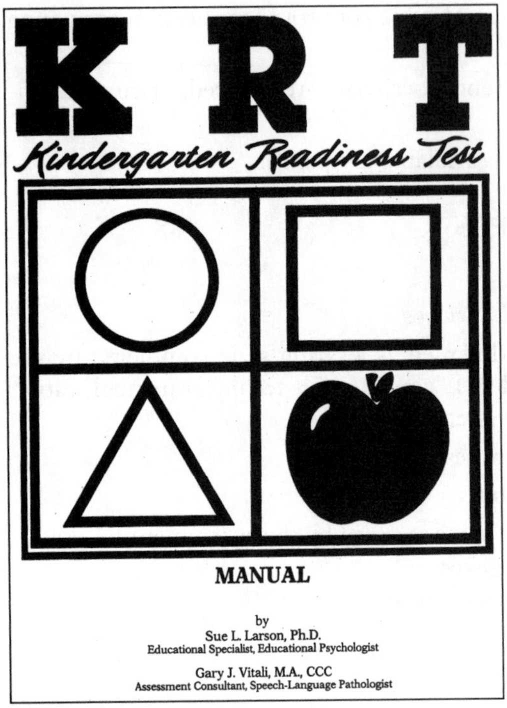

FIGURE 14.1 Kindergarten Readiness Test Cover Sheet

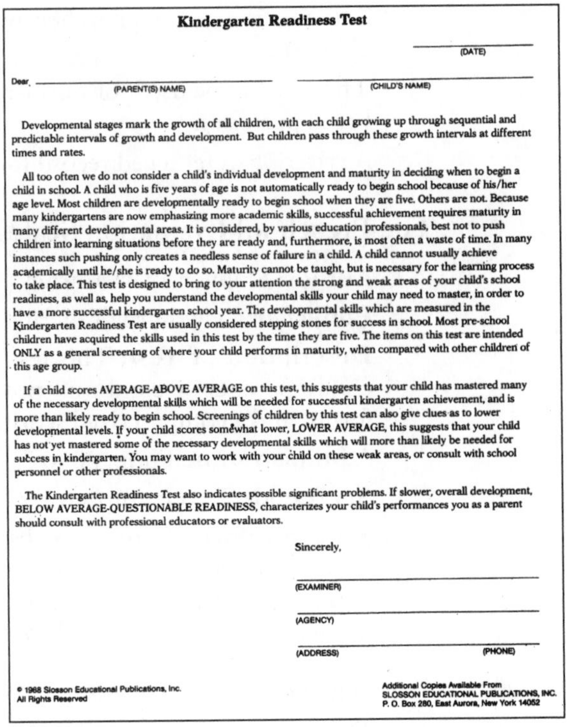

Kindergarten Readiness Test

(DATE)

Dear, (PARENT(S) NAME) (CHILD'S NAME)

Developmental stages mark the growth of all children, with each child growing up through sequential and predictable intervals of growth and development. But children pass through these growth intervals at different times and rates.

All too often we do not consider a child's individual development and maturity in deciding when to begin a child in school. A child who is five years of age is not automatically ready to begin school because of his/her age level. Most children are developmentally ready to begin school when they are five. Others are not. Because many kindergartens are now emphasizing more academic skills, successful achievement requires maturity in many different developmental areas. It is considered, by various education professionals, best not to push children into learning situations before they are ready and, furthermore, is most often a waste of time. In many instances such pushing only creates a needless sense of failure in a child. A child cannot usually achieve academically until he/she is ready to do so. Maturity cannot be taught, but is necessary for the learning process to take place. This test is designed to bring to your attention the strong and weak areas of your child's school readiness, as well as, help you understand the developmental skills your child may need to master, in order to have a more successful kindergarten school year. The developmental skills which are measured in the Kindergarten Readiness Test are usually considered stepping stones for success in school. Most pre-school children have acquired the skills used in this test by the time they are five. The items on this test are intended ONLY as a general screening of where your child performs in maturity, when compared with other children of this age group.

If a child scores AVERAGE-ABOVE AVERAGE on this test, this suggests that your child has mastered many of the necessary developmental skills which will be needed for successful kindergarten achievement, and is more than likely ready to begin school. Screenings of children by this test can also give clues as to lower developmental levels. If your child scores somewhat lower, LOWER AVERAGE, this suggests that your child has not yet mastered some of the necessary developmental skills which will more than likely be needed for success in kindergarten. You may want to work with your child on these weak areas, or consult with school personnel or other professionals.

The Kindergarten Readiness Test also indicates possible significant problems. If slower, overall development, BELOW AVERAGE-QUESTIONABLE READINESS, characterizes your child's performances you as a parent should consult with professional educators or evaluators.

Sincerely,

(EXAMINER)

(AGENCY)

(ADDRESS) (PHONE)

Additional Copies Available From
SLOSSON EDUCATIONAL PUBLICATIONS, INC.
P. O. Box 280, East Aurora, New York 14052

FIGURE 14.2 Kindergarten Readiness Test Letter

The test is easy to administer.

The test is appropriate for school, preschool, and clinical settings.

DeGangi-Berk Test of Sensory Integration (TSI)

Authors: Georgia A. DeGangi and Ronald A. Berk

Publisher: Western Psychological Services

Description of Test: The 36 test items require the child to perform specific tasks or respond to various stimuli. It consists of design sheets, protocol booklets, and a manual. Other test materials (e.g., stopwatch, scooter board, hula hoop) must be supplied by the examiner.

Administration Time: 30 minutes

Age/Grade Levels: Ages 3 to 5 years

Subtest Information: The test measures the child's ability on three clinically significant subdomains:

1. Postural Control
2. Bilateral Motor Integration
3. Reflex Integration

These vestibular-based functions are essential to the development of motor skills, visual–spatial and language abilities, hand dominance, and motor planning.

STRENGTHS OF THE TSI

The test effectively differentiates normal from developmentally delayed children.

When used as the basis for screening decisions, the test's total scores demonstrate a high accuracy rate.

The TSI effectively differentiates normal and developmentally delayed children. When used as the basis for screening decisions, total scores demonstrate an 81% accuracy rate, with a false normal error rate of only 9%.

The Battelle Developmental Inventory (BDI)

Authors: J. Newborg, J. R. Stock, and J. Wnek

Publisher: The Riverside Publishing Company

Description of Test: The BDI is a multiple-item test assessing key developmental skills. Information is obtained through structured interactions with the child in a controlled setting, observation of the child, and interviews with the child's parents, teachers, and caregivers. The test consists of five test-item books, an examiner's manual, scoring booklets, and a VHS overview videotape.

Administration Time: 10 minutes to 2 hours depending on the child's age and cognitive ability

Age/Grade Levels: Birth to 8 years

Subtest Information: The test consists of five subtests:

- *Personal-Social Domain*—This subtest measures coping skills, self-concept, expressions of feelings, and adult interaction.
- *Adaptive Domain*—This subtest measures attention, eating skills, dressing skills, personal responsibility, and toileting.
- *Motor Domain*—This subtest measures muscle control, body coordination, locomotion, fine muscle skills, and perceptual-motor skills.
- *Communication Domain*—This subtest measures receptive and expressive communication.
- *Cognitive Domain*—This subtest measures memory, reasoning skills, perceptual discrimination, academic skills, and conceptual development.

STRENGTHS OF THE BDI

The BDI is a multifactor assessment measure.

The BDI can be administered in the home setting, which may be important when dealing with very young children.

The test is very comprehensive.

Standardization procedures appear to be adequate.

Columbia Mental Maturity Scale (CMMS)

Authors: Bessie B. Burgemeister, Lucille Hollander Blurn, and Irving Lorge

Publisher: Harcourt Assessment, Inc.

Description of Test: The CMMS is an individual-type scale that requires perceptual discrimination involving color, shape, size, use, number, kind, missing parts, and symbolic material. Items are printed on ninety-five 6-inch by 19-inch cards arranged in a series of eight overlapping levels. The subject responds by selecting the picture in each series that is different from, or unrelated to, the others.

Administration Time: 15 to 30 minutes

Age/Grade Levels: Ages 3.5 to 10 years

Subtest Information: There are no formal subtests on this scale; rather, it is a 92-item test of general reasoning abilities.

STRENGTHS OF THE CMMS

Most children enjoy taking this test.

The test can be administered in a relatively short period of time.

A trained examiner can get quality judgments of the child and his or her method of attacking problems.

McCarthy Scales of Children's Abilities (MSCA)

Author: Dorothea McCarthy

Publisher: Harcourt Assessment, Inc.

Description of Test: The test consists of 18 separate tests grouped into 6 scales: Verbal, Perceptual–Performance, Quantitative, Composite (General Cognitive), Memory, and Motor.

Administration Time: 45 to 60 minutes

Age/Grade Levels: Ages 2-4 to 8-7

Subtest Information: The test consists of six scales comprising a variety of 18 subtests. Some subtests fall into more than one scale. Listed below is each scale and the corresponding subtests measuring that skill:

1. *Verbal Scale*—This scale consists of five subtests:
   - *Pictorial Memory*—The child is required to recall names of objects pictured on cards.
   - *Word Knowledge*—In Part 1, the child is required to point to pictures of common objects named by the examiner. In Part 2, the child is required to give oral definitions of words.
   - *Verbal Memory*—In Part 1, the child is required to repeat word series and sentences. In Part 2, the child is required to retell a story read by the examiner.
   - *Verbal Fluency*—The child is required to name as many articles as possible in a given category within 20 seconds.

- *Opposite Analogies*—The child is required to complete sentences by providing opposites.

2. *Perceptual Performance Scale*—This scale consists of seven subtests:
   - *Block Building*—The child is required to copy block structures built by the examiner.
   - *Puzzle Solving*—The child is required to assemble picture puzzles of common animals or foods.
   - *Tapping Sequence*—The child is required to imitate sequences of notes on a xylophone, as demonstrated by the examiner.
   - *Right–Left Orientation*—The child is required to demonstrate knowledge of right and left.
   - *Draw-a-Design*—The child is required to draw geometrical designs as presented in a model.
   - *Draw-a-Child*—The child is required to draw a picture of a child of the same sex.
   - *Conceptual Grouping*—The child is required to classify blocks on the basis of size, color, and shape.

3. *Quantitative Scale*—This scale consists of three subtests:
   - *Number Questions*—The child is required to answer orally presented questions involving number information or basic arithmetical computation.
   - *Numerical Memory*—In Part 1, the child is required to repeat a series of digits exactly as presented by the examiner. In Part 2, the child is required to repeat a digit series in exact reverse order.
   - *Counting and Sorting*—The child is required to count blocks and sort them into equal groups.

4. *Motor Scale*—This scale consists of three subtests:
   - *Leg Coordination*—The child is required to perform motor tasks that involve lower extremities such as walking backward or standing on one foot.
   - *Arm Coordination*—In Part 1, the child is required to bounce a ball. In Part 2, the child is required to catch a beanbag, and in Part 3, the child is required to throw a beanbag at a target.
   - *Imitative Action*—The child is required to copy simple movements such as folding hands or looking through a tube.

5. *General Cognitive*—This scale consists of 17 subtests from many of the measures shown previously. Please refer to the four prior scales for a complete explanation of the subtests.

Pictorial Memory	*Draw-a-Design*
Word Knowledge	*Draw-a-Child*
Verbal Memory	*Conceptual Grouping*
Verbal Fluency	*Number Questions*
Opposite Analogies	*Numerical Memory*
Block Building	*Counting and Sorting*
Puzzle Solving	*Draw-a-Child*
Tapping Sequence	*Draw-a-Design*
Right–Left Orientation	

6. *Memory*—This scale consists of four subtests. Please refer to the first four scales for a complete explanation of these subtests.

Pictorial Memory   *Verbal Memory*
Tapping Sequence   *Numerical Memory*

STRENGTHS OF THE MSCA

The test's technical manual contains elaborate information about the standardization process, norm tables, and guidelines for administration and interpretation.

The test creates a framework within which the child being tested can function comfortably.

The test is like a game, with no threatening material.

Reliability and validity are good determinants of achievement for children in school.

The manual is well written and easy to read.

CONCLUSION

The early years of a child's life are extremely important. During the infant and toddler years, children grow quickly and have much to learn. However, some children and families face special challenges and need extra help. Early help does make a difference. Young children present many challenges to the special educator, who is charged with evaluating their intellectual, language, motor, and adaptive functioning. Normal developmental transitions of infancy and early childhood influence motivation, interest, and cooperation with the testing process. The special educator experienced in testing school-age children may expect a young child to exhibit appropriate "testing behavior"—sitting quietly at a desk, attending to a task at hand, and being motivated to complete the tasks presented. Such characteristic testing behavior is not often present in this age group or, if present, is limited to a few brief moments. The special educator examining young children must be aware of the developmental influences affecting the young child and must be flexible enough to adapt the testing procedures accordingly.

VOCABULARY

Adaptive: Self-help skills the child uses for daily living.

Assessment for Diagnosis and Determination of Eligibility: Part of the assessment and evaluation process for early intervention that conducts an in-depth evaluation to verify if a problem exists, to determine the nature and severity of the problem, and to prescribe the treatment or type of intervention services needed.

Assistive Technology: Equipment or services that are used to improve or maintain the abilities of a child to participate in daily activities.

At Risk: A term used for children who may, in the future, have problems with their development that may affect learning or development.

Authenticity: Does the assessment focus on actual child behavior in real settings?

Casefinding/Child Find: Part of the assessment and evaluation process for early intervention that alerts parents, professionals, and the general public to children who may have special needs and to elicit their help in recruiting candidates for screening.

Collaboration: Does the assessment involve cooperation and sharing, especially with parents?

Congruence: Was the assessment developed and field-tested with children similar to those being assessed?

Convergence: Does the assessment rely on more than one source of information?

Developmental: Having to do with the steps or stages in the growth of a child.

Developmental Tests: Tests that measure a child's development compared to the development of other children at that age.

Early Childhood Intervention (often referred to as early intervention): the early intervention through assessment and education in the birth to 5 year-old population.

Eligibility Requirements: The requirements a child must meet to be able to receive early intervention services.

Equity: Does the assessment accommodate special sensory, motor, cultural, or other needs rather than penalize children who have such needs?

Evaluation: A process used to determine if a child meets the eligibility standards for early intervention.

Facility or Center-Based Visits: In this early intervention services model, services are given to a child and parent or other family member or caregiver where the service provider works (office, hospital, clinic, etc.).

Family Support Groups: In this early intervention services model, parents, grandparents, or other relatives of the child get together in a group led by a service provider for help and support and to share concerns and information.

Family: The Individualized Family Service Plan (IFSP) will focus on the family and the outcomes they hope for the child and the family through early intervention.

Group Development Intervention: In this early intervention services model, children receive services in a group setting led by a service provider or providers without parents or caregivers.

Home Visits: Visits in the parents' home by a professional for the purpose of planning and providing early intervention services.

Home and Community-Based Visits: In this early intervention services model, services are given to a child, parent, or other family member or caregiver at home or in the community.

IDEA '97: An amendment to IDEA 1990—this act made substantial changes to IDEA 1990 for schools and parents to follow in planning and providing special education and related services for children with special needs.

Individualized: The Individualized Family Service Plan (IFSP) will be specially designed for the child and the family.

Individualized Family Service Plan (IFSP): After a child has been evaluated, it is mandated under Public Law 99-457 that an IFSP be written. This plan sets forth critical information pertaining to both the child and the family's services.

Individuals with Disabilities Education Act (IDEA)-Public Law 101-476: This IDEA amendment to P.L. 99-457 required a timely, comprehensive, multidisciplinary evaluation, including assessment activities related to the child and the child's play.

Outcomes: Statements of changes that parents want to see in their child or family. These statements are part of the IFSP.

Parent-Child Groups: In this early intervention services model, parents and children get services together in a group led by a service provider. A parent-child group can happen anywhere in the community.

Plan: The Individualized Family Service Plan (IFSP) is a written plan for services.

Program Evaluation: Part of the assessment and evaluation process for early intervention that evaluates the quality of the overall intervention program and to document its impact on the children or parents it serves.

Program Planning: Part of the assessment and evaluation process for early intervention that refers to those procedures used by the assessment team to develop the IFSP (Individual Family Service Plan) and to revise these plans as necessary.

Public Law 101-476, Part C of Individuals with Disabilities Education Act (IDEA): For infants and toddlers (birth to 2 years of age), a new program established to help states develop and implement programs for early intervention services.

Public Law 108-446: Requires that every state in America provide services for infants and toddlers with disabilities.

Public Law 94-142, The Education for All Handicapped Children Act: Mandated services for all school-age children with disabilities and facilitated the provision of services for preschool children with disabilities in some states.

Public Law 99-457, Part H: Established incentives for serving infants and toddlers with special needs.

Public Law 99-457: Amended P.L. 94-142 requiring states to provide a free and appropriate public education to children with disabilities age 3 through age 5. The regulations that governed school-age children were then made applicable to the assessment of preschool children.

Qualified Personnel: Those individuals who are approved to provide early intervention services within the limits of their licensure, certification, or registration.

Screening: Part of the assessment and evaluation process for early intervention that identifies children who are not within normal ranges of development, need further evaluation, and who may be candidates for early intervention programs.

Sensitivity: Does the assessment include sufficient items for planning lessons and detecting changes?

Service: The Individualized Family Service Plan (IFSP) will include all the details about the services provided for both the child and the family.

. . . . .

CHAPTER FIFTEEN

OTHER AREAS OF ASSESSMENT

KEY TERMS

Audiometric Evaluation Measures
Behavioral Play Audiometry
Bilingual Assessment
Central Auditory Disorders
Conductive Hearing Loss
Deafness
Dominant Language
Evoked Response Audiometry
Functional Hearing Loss
Hearing Impairment

Impedance Audiometry
Mixed Hearing Loss
Occupational Therapy
Otosclerosis
Physical Therapy
Pure Tone Audiometric Screening
Pure Tone Threshold Audiometry
Sensorineural Hearing Loss
Sound Field Audiometry
Speech Audiometry

CHAPTER OBJECTIVES

The focus of this chapter will be to discuss three other areas of assessment: the assessment of hearing, the roles and responsibilities of the physical and occupational therapists, and bilingual assessment. After reading this chapter, you should understand the following:

- Assessment of hearing
- Assessment measures of hearing
- Occupational and physical therapy measures
- Bilingual assessment

ASSESSMENT OF HEARING

When people think of someone who is hearing impaired, they often think that the person is "deaf." However, this is not true. Under IDEA 2004, **deafness** is "A hearing impairment that is so severe that the child is impaired in processing linguistic information through hearing, with or without amplification, that adversely affects a child's educational performance." Yet, under IDEA 2004, a **hearing impairment** is "An impairment in hearing, whether permanent or fluctuating, that adversely affects a child's educational performance but which is not included under the definition of deafness in this section."

In examining these two definitions, it is evident that being deaf means that hearing is disabled to an extent that precludes understanding speech through the ear alone, with or without a hearing aid. Being hearing impaired or hard of hearing makes hearing difficult, but does not preclude the understanding of speech through the ear alone, with or without a hearing aid.

Causes of Hearing Impairments

Hearing difficulties need to be identified as early as possible in order to plan an appropriate educational program. Some hearing problems occur from birth, whereas others occur at later stages in a child's development. There are several causes of hearing impairments.

Conductive hearing loss: This results from problems with the structures in the outer or middle ear, generally attributed to a blockage in the mechanical conduction of sound. In order to overcome this blockage, the sounds must be amplified. These conditions are usually temporary. The leading causes of this type of hearing loss are:

Otitis media (middle ear infection)

Excessive ear wax

Otosclerosis—formation of a spongy-bony growth around the stapes, which impedes its movement

Sensorineural hearing loss: This results from damage to the cochlea or the auditory nerve. This damage is caused by illness and disease and is not medically or surgically treatable. Causes of this hearing loss include:

- Viral diseases (e.g., rubella—German measles, meningitis)
- Rh incompatibility
- Ototoxic medications (medicines that destroy or damage hair cells in the cochlea, e.g., streptomycin) taken by pregnant mothers or very young children
- Hereditary factors
- Exposure to noise
- Aging

Mixed hearing loss: This is a hearing loss caused by both sensorineural and conductive problems.

Functional hearing loss: This results from those problems that are not organic in origin. Examples include:

Psychosomatic causes

- Hysterical conversion
- Malingering
- Emotional or psychological problems

Central auditory disorders: These disorders result in no measurable peripheral hearing loss. Children with this disorder have trouble learning and are often considered learning disabled. Causes include

- Auditory comprehension problems
- Auditory discrimination problems
- Auditory learning difficulties
- Language development delays

Whatever the cause, a parent or teacher may be the first individual to observe the symptoms of a hearing loss, such as

- Significant problems in expressive language
- Significant problems in receptive language
- Difficulties with speech development
- Problems in socialization
- Difficulty with alertness or speaking in class

Degrees of Hearing Impairment

Once the audiologist completes his or her assessment, a determination is made of the level of hearing loss. The following chart offers a comparison of the different levels of hearing loss.

DEGREE OF HEARING LOSS	DECIBEL LOSS	RESULTING IMPAIRMENT
Slight	27–40 dB	Difficulty hearing faint noises or distant conversation. The individual with a slight hearing loss will usually not have difficulties in the regular school setting.
Mild	41–55 dB	This individual may miss as much as 50% of classroom conversations. The individual may also exhibit limited vocabulary and speech difficulties.
Moderate	56–70 dB	The individual will be able to hear only loud conversation, may exhibit defective speech, vocabulary, and language difficulties.
Severe	71–90 dB	Hearing may be limited to a radius of one foot. May be able to discriminate certain environmental sounds, shows defective speech and language ability, and has severe difficulty understanding consonant sounds.
Profound	91 dB or greater	The individual can sense but is unable to understand sounds and tones. Vision becomes the primary sense of communication, and speech and language are likely to deteriorate.

The diagnosis of a hearing loss is the initial step in the treatment and education of the child. Special education teachers need specialized assessment measures to conduct educational screenings and evaluations. These tests for the hearing-impaired child are crucial in the educational planning process.

ASSESSMENT MEASURES OF HEARING

When such symptoms are observed, the first step is usually a referral to an audiologist for a screening. Several assessment measures are utilized in the possible identification of a hearing loss, including the following:

Audiometric evaluation measures: These assessment measures are used by qualified audiologists who measure the level of hearing loss through the use of several techniques. These may include:

- **Pure tone audiometric screening**—Pure tone screening is often referred to as sweep testing, and is usually the child's first encounter with hearing testing. This type of testing, which is common in schools, presents the child with pure tones over a variety of frequency ranges. The child is then asked to respond if he or she hears a tone, usually by some gesture. If a child is unable to hear sounds at two or more frequencies, the child is usually referred for further evaluation.
- **Speech audiometry**—This type of evaluation is used to determine a child's present ability to hear and understand speech through the presentation of words in a variety of loudness levels.
- **Pure tone threshold audiometry**—In this procedure, the child is asked to make a gesture or push a button each time he or she hears a tone. The child is presented with a variety of frequencies through earphones. This type of ear conduction test reveals the presence of hearing loss.

Special audiometric tests: These include:

- **Sound field audiometry**—This measure is used with very young children who cannot respond to manual responses or are unable or unwilling to wear headphones. The child is evaluated by observing the intensity levels at which he or she responds to different levels of sounds broadcast through speakers.
- **Evoked response audiometry**—This measure uses an electroencephalograph, and a computer measures changes in brain wave activity to a variety of sound levels. This measure can be used with infants who are suspected of being deaf.
- **Impedance audiometry**—There are two major impedance audiometry tests: **Tympanometry** measures the functioning level of the eardrum, and **stapedial reflex testing** measures the reflex response of the stapedial muscle to pure tone signals. Because these tests do not require a response on the part of the child, they can be used with very young children.
- **Behavioral play audiometry**—This technique involves placing the child in a series of activities that reward him or her for responding appropriately to tone or speech.

Listed next are some of the tests used most often to assess students for a possible hearing problem when being evaluated for special education services.

Auditory Perception Test for the Hearing Impaired (APT/HI)

Authors: Susan G. Allen and Thomas S. Serwatka

Publisher: M. D. Angus and Associated, LTD

Description of Test: The test is designed to assess the building-block processes used to decode speech. It allows for specific analysis of the individual's ability to decode phonemes in isolation and in the context of words and sentences. It consists of a manual, plates, and record forms.

Administration Time: 30 minutes

Age/Grade Levels: Ages 5 and over

Subtest Information: The test has no subtests.

Scoring Information: The test results are given in a performance profile that enables comparison of an individual's pre- and posttreatment performance to determine the efficacy of treatment and the need for further therapy.

STRENGTHS OF THE APT/HI

Although designed specifically for the hearing impaired, the test can also be used with children who have other auditory processing deficits.

The test analyzes auditory decoding skills at the most basic level.

Carolina Picture Vocabulary Test for Deaf and Hearing Impaired (CPVT)

Authors: Thomas L. Layton and David W. Holmes

Publisher: PRO-ED

Description of Test: The test is designed to measure the receptive sign vocabulary in individuals for whom manual signing is the primary mode of communication. The CPVT consists of a manual, record forms, and a picture book.

Administration Time: 10 to 30 minutes

Age/Grade Levels: Ages 4 to 11-5

Subtest Information: The test contains no subtests.

STRENGTHS OF THE CPVT

The population (N = 767) used in the standardization research was based on a nationwide sample of children who use manual signs as their primary means of communication. Stratification of the sample was based on geographic region, educational facility, parental occupation, gender, race, age, grade, etiology, age of onset of hearing impairment, number of years of signing, IQ, and threshold of hearing loss in the better ear.

Hiskey-Nebraska Test of Learning Aptitude

Author: Marshall S. Hiskey

Publisher: PRO-ED (Note that PRO-ED is only publishing the record form until the test is revised.)

Description of Test: The test is designed as a nonverbal measure of mental ability that has been found helpful in the intellectual assessment of a variety of language-handicapped children and youth. The test is a performance scale that can be administered entirely via pantomimed instructions and requires no verbal response from the subject. The scale consists of a series of performance tasks that are organized in ascending order of difficulty within subscales.

Administration Time: Approximately 60 minutes

Age/Grade Levels: Ages 2 to 18

Subtest Information: The test is comprised of the following subtests:

- *Memory for Colored Objects*—The child is required to perform memory tasks using colored objects.
- *Bead Stringing*—The child is required to put beads on a string.
- *Pictorial Associations*—The child has to decide what various pictures look like.
- *Block Building*—The child is required to build things with blocks.
- *Memory for Digits*—The child is given groups of numbers and asked to repeat them.
- *Completion of Drawings*—The child is required to finish a picture that is not completed.
- *Pictorial Identification*—The child has to say what the picture is that is being shown.
- *Visual Attention Span*—The child must focus on an object for a set period of time.
- *Puzzle Blocks*—The child is required to arrange the blocks into a picture that is shown.
- *Pictorial Analogies*—The child is required to compare two pictures and pick a picture that goes with the third picture.

STRENGTHS OF THE HISKEY-NEBRASKA

The test is easy to administer.

The test results are reported as a learning quotient rather than pure IQ, which may be easier for parents to understand.

It is the only test of learning standardized on individuals who are deaf

Leiter International Performance Scale–Revised (LEITER–R)

Authors: Russel Graydon Leiter and Grace Arthur

Publisher: C. H. Stoelting

Description of Test: The test is designed as a totally nonverbal intelligence and cognitive abilities test; because the Leiter-R is completely nonverbal, it does not require the child to read or write any materials or need any spoken words from the examiner or the child. It is presented in a game-like administration by having the child match the full-color response cards with corresponding illustrations on the easel display.

Administration Time: 30 to 60 minutes

Age/Grade Levels: Ages 2 to 17

Subtest Information: The Leiter-R includes 20 subtests listed below, which are combined to create numerous composites that measure both general intelligence and discrete ability areas. The test consists of two batteries measuring a variety of skills:

1. **Visualization and Reasoning Battery**
   Reasoning skills measured in this battery include

Classification	*Repeated Patterns*
Sequential Order	*Design Analogies*

   Visualization skills measured in this battery include

Matching	*Picture Context*
Figure Ground	*Paper Folding*
Form Completion	*Figure Rotation*

2. **Attention and Memory Battery**
   Memory skills measured in this battery include

Memory Span (Forward)	*Associative Memory*
Memory Span (Reversed)	*Associative Delayed Memory*
Spatial Memory	*Immediate Recognition*
Visual Coding	*Delayed Recognition*

   Attention skills measured in this battery include

Attention Sustained	*Attention Divided*

STRENGTHS OF THE LEITER-R

Because of its nonverbal approach, the scale is a useful instrument and has made possible the testing of many children who could not be properly evaluated by the Stanford-Binet or WISC.

The test has a high correlation (.84) with the WISC-III Full Scale IQ.

The extensive age range measured by the test, ages 2 to 17, allows for the use of one test throughout a child's school career, which enhances comparisons of performance over time.

Because the test is nonverbal, there is no dominant language bias as found on other IQ tests.

Rhode Island Test of Language Structure (RITLS)

Authors: Elizabeth Engen and Trygg Engen
Publisher: PRO-ED

Description of Test: The *Rhode Island Test of Language Structure* (RITLS) provides a measure of English language development and assessment data. It is designed primarily for use with children who are hearing impaired but also is useful in other areas where language development is of concern, including mental retardation, learning disability, and bilingual programs. The RITLS focuses on syntax, unlike other tests that test morphology.

Administration Time: 25 to 35 minutes

Age/Grade Levels: Hearing-impaired children ages 3 to 20, hearing children ages 3 to 6

Subtest Information: This test measures syntax-response errors for 20 sentence types, both simple and complex. The sentence elements tests are

- Relative and Adverbial Clauses
- Subject and Other Complements
- Reversible and Nonreversible Passives
- Datives
- Deletions
- Negations
- Conjunctives
- Embedded Imperatives

STRENGTHS OF THE RITLS

The test includes hearing-impaired individuals as part of the standardized group that adds to the effectiveness of generalizability.

The test is useful in areas in which level of language development is of concern, for example, mental retardation, learning disability, and bilingual programs.

The RITLS is easy to administer, score, and interpret.

A variety of syntactic structures are included in the test.

Test of Early Reading Ability–2: Deaf or Hard of Hearing (TERAD/HH-2)

Authors: D. Kim Reid, Wayne P. Jiresko, Donald D. Hammill, and Susan Wiltshire

Publisher: PRO-ED

Description of Test: The test is designed to measure the ability of children with moderate to profound hearing loss to attribute meaning to printed symbols, their knowledge of the alphabet and its functions, and their knowledge of the conventions of print. It isolates key components of early print experiences and assesses children's relative competence in deriving meaning from these print symbols. The test includes a sheet that allows the examiner to picture the student's "instructional target zone." By examining the student's item performance in the three components of early reading, the examiner can identify the types of concepts that might be profitably taught.

Administration Time: 15 to 30 minutes

Age/Grade Level: Ages 8 years and younger

Subtest Information: Three aspects of early reading behavior are specifically addressed:

- *Constructing meaning from print*—Here, the construction of meaning encompasses a child's ability to read frequently encountered signs, logos, and words; relate words to one another; and understand the contextual nature of written discourse.
- *Knowledge of the alphabet*—This aspect is defined as letter and word decoding (either orally or through sign).
- *Understanding print conventions*—This aspect evaluates the child's awareness of text orientation and organization (e.g., book handling, the spatial orientation of print on a page, and ability to uncover textual or print errors).

STRENGTHS OF THE TERAD/HH-2

The authors provide a comprehensive and informative manual.

The student record form is complete and easy to follow.

This is the only individually administered test of reading designed for children with moderate to profound sensory hearing loss (i.e., ranging from 41 to beyond 91 decibels, corrected).

TERAD/HH is also the only individually administered reading test designed for children younger than age 8 who are deaf or hard of hearing.

It has equivalent forms and taps the child's ability to construct meaning, knowledge of the alphabet and its functions, and awareness of print conventions.

PHYSICAL AND OCCUPATIONAL THERAPY ASSESSMENT

Physical and occupational therapies are important components of the special education process. Many school districts now have physical and occupational therapists as part of their staff. These therapists may help students individually, in small groups, or as consultants. These two services are related therapies but specific in their function. **Physical therapy** concentrates on lower-body and gross-motor difficulties. **Occupational therapy** focuses mainly on fine-motor and upper-body functions. The services are provided for students with disabilities who exhibit a range of difficulties such as learning disabilities (e.g., fine- and gross-motor problems or perceptual problems), developmental delays (e.g., mental retardation, vision or hearing impairment), respiratory problems (e.g., cystic fibrosis or asthma), neuromuscular problems (e.g., muscular dystrophy, cerebral palsy), muscle skeletal problems (e.g., arthritis, orthopedic problems, postural deviations), or traumatic accidents (e.g., amputations, brain injuries, burns). In addition to providing therapy for such students, physical and occupational therapists provide many other services including evaluations, screenings, consultations, education, and training.

Evaluations

Physical and occupational therapy evaluations may be referred to the Multidisciplinary Team (MDT) or Eligibility Committee by any number of school or medical professionals. Parents may also ask for a referral for physical and occupational therapy services for their child. In any case, written parental consent is required for an evaluation.

As with other evaluations, those of physical and occupational therapists need to be individualized, well documented, and specific. The physical and occupational therapists play a significant role in regard to the service provided to the student; the more thorough their documentation, the more appropriate the services will be. The evaluation will serve as a blueprint for the development of an IEP, should one be necessary. The evaluation will identify the child's current level of performance and his or her deficient areas of development in the physical realm. It will also suggest what he or she needs in order to achieve the next higher level of function. Parents need to be aware that the evaluation process is subjective, and varies from district to district. In some districts, if a child can walk into a classroom, he or she would not be provided with physical therapy. In some districts, if a child can hold a pencil, he or she would not be provided with occupational therapy, whereas in other districts such services are provided for only marginal problems.

Assessment Areas

In general, both physical therapy and occupational therapy assess the following:

- Range of motion
- Sensory integration
- Activities for daily living
- Physical and mental development
- Muscular control
- Need for and uses of adaptive equipment

Certain assessments are unique to physical therapy:

- Posture
- Gait
- Endurance
- Personal independence
- Joint abnormalities
- Wheelchair management
- Transportation needs
- Architectural barriers
- Prosthetic and orthotic equipment checks

Other assessments are unique to occupational therapy:

- Neuromuscular functioning
- Sensory processing

- Manual dexterity
- Leisure time abilities
- Prevocational skills
- Oral motor and feeding problems

The Therapist's Many Roles

Occupational and physical therapists should meet with all of the professionals involved with a particular child as well as with the child's parents to fully explain the nature of the disability, to train them to work with the child in the areas of dysfunction, and to provide assistive devices or environmental aids that will help the child function in the least restrictive environment. The therapists should also model remedial techniques that can be duplicated by the parents and by other teaching professionals. Parents should be reminded that many of the school activities suggested by occupational and physical therapists can be duplicated in the home. Many of the exercises are really activities for daily living such as hopping, jumping, buttoning, and the like.

Occupational and physical therapists serve important roles as consultants. Some examples of their services are:

- Referring families to appropriate sources for assistance
- Helping families order adaptive or prosthetic equipment
- Coordinating with physical education programs
- Instructing families regarding methods used in physical therapy
- Formulating long-range developmental plans for children's education
- Training school professionals with special equipment
- Helping families and children learn how to deal with architectural barriers

Occupational and physical therapists should act as liaisons between the Eligibility Committee, the teaching staff, medical professionals, outside agencies, and parents. Many pupils in need of occupational and physical therapy have severe medical conditions. These conditions often require supervision of a family doctor. The therapist should help with the coordination between the school physician and the family doctor. The therapists play an important role in severe cases.

The following is a list of problems requiring occupational therapy:

- Perceptual problems (eye-hand coordination)
- Sensory problems (sensitive to sound, sensitive to visual changes, sensitive to odors, overly sensitive to touch)
- Gross-motor difficulties (trouble with balance, coordination, moving)
- Fine-motor problems (difficulty with coordination, handwriting, using scissors)
- Hardship with daily living activities (cannot dress, feed, or care for self)
- Organizational problems (difficulties with memory, time, spatial concepts)
- Attention span difficulties (difficulties focusing on task, short attention span)
- Interpersonal problems (difficulty with environmental and school-related social situations)

The following is a list of the kinds of evaluations an occupational therapist can conduct:

- Vision
- Abnormal movement patterns
- Range of motion
- Skeletal and joint conditions
- Behavior
- Skin and soft tissue
- Fine motor
- Perceptual
- Gross motor
- Balance and equilibrium
- Activities for daily living
- Equipment analysis

There are many different assessment measures used by occupational and physical therapists. Listed below are some of the most frequently used tests by these professionals.

First Step: Screening Test for Evaluating Preschoolers (FIRSTep)

Author: Lucy Jane Miller

Publisher: Harcourt Assessment, Inc.

Description of Test: This test is designed to identify children who exhibit moderate preacademic problems. The FIRSTep is a short but comprehensive preschool assessment instrument that evaluates children for mild to moderate developmental delays. The test includes an examiner's manual, item score sheets, and all materials needed for administration.

Administration Time: 15 minutes

Age/Grade Levels: Ages 2-9 to 6-2 years

Subtest Information: The test consists of five performance areas:

- *Foundations Index*—It assesses abilities involving basic motor tasks and the awareness of sensations, both of which are fundamental for the development of complex skills.
- *Coordination Index*—It assesses complex gross, fine, and oral motor abilities.
- *Verbal Index*—It assesses memory, sequencing, comprehension, association, and expression in a verbal context.
- *Nonverbal Index*—It assesses memory, sequencing, visualization, and the performance of mental manipulations not requiring spoken language.
- *Complex Tasks Index*—It measures sensory motor abilities in conjunction with cognitive abilities.

STRENGTHS OF THE FIRSTep

The FIRSTep presents detailed information in the manual for the administration of each of the five indexes.

It is a short, carefully developed, and well-standardized test.

The test can be scored quickly.

FirstSTEp is sensitive enough to detect even mild developmental delays. Identify children who need in-depth diagnostic testing.

Address IDEA domains: Cognition, Communication, and Motor.

Reports classify results as Within Acceptable Limits, Caution, or At-Risk.

Quick Neurological Screening Test–II (QNST-II)

Authors: Margaret Motti, Harold M. Steling, Norma V. Spalding, and C. Slade Crawfold

Publisher: Academic Therapy Publications and Western Psychological Services

Description of Test: The test is designed to assess neurological integration as it relates to learning. It is used for the early screening of learning disabilities. The QNST-II is a screening test that assesses 15 areas of neurological integration. It requires the examinee to perform a series of motor tasks adapted from neurological pediatric examinations and from neuropsychological and developmental scales. Each of the 15 areas tested involves a motor task similar to those observed in neurological pediatric examinations. The test includes recording forms, examiner's manual, reproduction sheets, remedial guidelines, and an administration and scoring flip card.

Administration Time: Untimed—takes approximately 20 minutes

Age/Grade Levels: Ages 5 to 18

Subtest Information: The areas of neurological integration measured by the QNST-II include

- Motor development
- Fine/gross-motor control
- Motor planning and sequencing and rhythm
- Visual/spatial perception
- Spatial organization
- Balance/vestibular function
- Attentional disorders

STRENGTHS OF THE QNST-II

The test is useful as a supplement for the pediatric neurological examination.

The test is exceptionally good in identifying subjects with abnormal neurological patterns.

The popular QNST has been updated to include the latest research findings concerning the soft neurological signs that may accompany learning disabilities.

The QNST-II manual explores the importance of such soft neurological signs in educational settings as well as the medical implications.

Special education personnel will appreciate knowing whether behaviors seen in the classroom have physiological (organic) or emotional origins.

The detailed scoring information will also allow other rehabilitation professionals invaluable assistance with planning appropriate remediation.

Sensory Integration and Praxis Tests (SIPT)

Author: Jean Ayres

Publisher: Western Psychological Services

Description of Test: The test is designed to measure the sensory integration processes that underlie learning and behavior. By showing how children organize and respond to sensory input, the SIPT helps pinpoint specific organic problems associated with learning disabilities, emotional disorders, and minimal brain dysfunction. The test measures visual, tactile, and kinesthetic perception as well as motor performance.

Administration Time: The entire battery can be administered in two hours. And any of the individual tests can be administered separately in about 10 minutes.

Age/Grade Levels: Ages 4 to 9 years

Subtest Information: The SIPT measures visual, tactile, and kinesthetic perception as well as motor performance. It is composed of 17 brief tests:

Bilateral Motor Coordination	*Motor Accuracy*
Constructional Praxis	*Oral Praxis*
Design Copying	*Postrotary Nystagmus*
Figure Ground Perception	*Postural Praxis*
Finger Identification	*Praxis on Verbal Command*
Graphesthesia	*Sequencing Praxis*
Kinesthesia	*Space Visualization*
Localization of Tactile Stimuli	*Standing and Walking Balance*
Manual Form Perception	

Scoring Information: All SIPT tests are computer scored, using WPS Test Report. Any combination of the 17 tests can be scored—the entire battery need not be administered.

STRENGTHS OF THE SIPT

This test is a helpful clinical tool.

Any of the individual tests can be administered separately, and therefore, one does not need to administer the entire battery.

The computerized scoring provides a detailed report explaining the SIPT results.

Norms are provided for each test based on a national sample of more than 2,000 children between the ages of 4 years and 8 years, 11 months.

MULTICULTURAL ASSESSMENT

It is a well-known fact that the demographics of American schools are changing. Many students come from ethnic, racial, or linguistic backgrounds that are different from the dominant culture, and this number is steadily increasing (National Center for Education Statistics, 1992). Much concern has been expressed in recent years about the over-representation of minority students in special education programs, particularly in programs for students with mild disabilities, and a great deal of research has been conducted to identify the reasons why. Many factors appear to contribute, including considerable bias against children from different cultural and linguistic backgrounds, particularly those who are poor (Harry, 1992). The style and emphasis of the school may also be very different from those found in the cultures of students who are racially or linguistically diverse. Because culture and language affect learning and behavior (Franklin, 1992), the school system may misinterpret what students know, how they behave, or how they learn. Students may appear less competent than they are, leading educators to refer them for assessment inappropriately. Once referred, inappropriate methods may then be used to assess the students, leading to inappropriate conclusions and placement into special education.

There is also a great deal of research and numerous court decisions (see Chapter 2, for example, *Larry P. v. Riles*, 1979; *Guadalupe Organization Inc. v. Tempe Elementary School District*, 1972) to support the fact that standardized tests (particularly intelligence and achievement tests) are often culturally and linguistically biased against students from backgrounds different from the majority culture. On many tests, being able to answer questions correctly too often depends on having specific culturally based information or knowledge. If students have not been exposed to that information through their cultures, or have not had the experiences that lead to gaining specific knowledge, then they will not be able to answer certain questions at all or will answer them in ways that are considered "incorrect" within the majority culture. This can lead to inappropriate conclusions about students' abilities to function within the school setting.

Under IDEA 2004, all children have the right to tests that are free of cultural bias. Furthermore, all tests must be conducted in the child's native language, and reports must be written in the parent's language. Given these mandates under the federal law, it is evident that educators must be very aware of a child's native language. Consequently, it is critical that assessments done on children who are bilingual be done in a manner that is in compliance with all federal laws. Educators need to be aware of variables associated with the assessment of bilingual children, because the number of bilingual children with suspected disabilities is increasing.

The majority of tests used for assessment in special education are based on standards of the English-speaking culture. Given this fact, the use of these instruments on students who are bilingual may not be appropriate under the federal law. Consequently, special educators must devise a way to assess children whose primary language may not be English. This is commonly referred to as dynamic assessment (see Chapter 3), whereby information is obtained through interviews, observations, and other methods, not simply based on objective criteria based on national norms.

"Professionals must attend carefully to the overall picture of a child's background and performance," (Harry, 1992), and "assessment cannot be complete without an understanding of whether prior instruction has been adequate and appropriate" (p. 87). To this end, Ortiz (1986) recommends that such students first undergo the prereferral process mentioned earlier. Schools are moving toward requiring a prereferral process before any individualized evaluation is done (see Chapter 7). The purpose of the prereferral process is "to determine if appropriate and sufficient approaches have been attempted" (Wallace et al., 1992, p. 467). This allows the school to adjust instruction or make other classroom modifications and see if these changes address the problem being noted.

According to Waterman (1994), from her article "Assessing Children for the Presence of a Disability" (published by the National Information Center for Children and Youth with Disabilities), the prereferral process includes:

- Direct observation of the student in the regular classroom
- Analyzing how the student behaves and interacts verbally in different settings
- Reviewing the methods of instruction that are used in the regular classroom

It is also important to interview people who are familiar with the student, for these individuals can provide a wealth of information about the child's interests, adaptive behavior, how he or she processes information and approaches learning, language ability, and (in the case of students who are not native speakers of English) language dominance. Interviewers should be aware, however, that the differing culture or language of those being interviewed can seriously affect the nature and interpretation of information gathered. Some understanding of how individuals within that culture view disability, the educational system, and authority figures will be helpful in designing, conducting, and interpreting a culturally sensitive interview. It may be particularly useful to gather information from the home environment that will help the assessment team develop an understanding of the student within his or her own culture. To facilitate this, parents need to communicate openly with the school and share their insight into their child's behaviors, attitudes, successes, needs, and, when appropriate, information about the minority culture. Before conducting any formal testing of a student who is a nonnative speaker of English, it is vital to determine the student's preferred language and to conduct a comprehensive language assessment in both English and the native language.

Dominant Language

Examiners need to be aware that it is highly inappropriate to evaluate students in English when that is not their **dominant language** (unless the purpose of testing is to assess the student's English-language proficiency). Translating tests from English is not an acceptable practice either. IDEA 2004 (sec. 614[b][3][ii]) states that tests and other evaluation materials must be provided and administered in the language and form most likely to yield accurate information on what the child knows and can do academically, developmentally, and functionally, unless it is not feasible to so provide or administer. If possible, the evaluator in any testing situation or interview should be familiar to the child and speak the child's language. When tests or evaluation materials are not available in the student's native language, examiners may find it necessary to use English-language instruments. Because this is a practice fraught with the possibility of misinterpretation, examiners need to be cautious in how they administer the test and interpret results.

Alterations may need to be made to the standardized procedures used to administer tests for bilingual students. These can include paraphrasing instructions, providing a demonstration of how test tasks are to be performed, reading test items to the student rather than having him or her read them, allowing the student to respond verbally rather than in writing, or allowing the student to use a dictionary (Wallace et al., 1992). However, if any such alterations are made, it is important to recognize that standardization has been broken, limiting the usefulness and applicability of test norms. Results should be cautiously interpreted, and all alterations made to the testing procedures should be fully detailed in the report describing the student's test performance. As mentioned earlier, it is also essential that other assessment approaches be an integral part of collecting information about the student.

Ascher (1990) addresses options commonly used in testing limited English speakers: nonverbal tests, translated tests, interpreters, and tests that are norm-referenced in the primary language. The following is a brief description of each of these options:

- Nonverbal tests are the most common procedure used with bilingual students. Unfortunately, nonverbal measures of intelligence predict less reliably than verbal measures and, despite appearances, may even be hypersensitive to language background.
- Translated tests are always different tests, unknown and unfair. Although it is not difficult to translate a test, it is extremely difficult, if not impossible, to translate psychometric properties from one language to another. A word in English is simply not the same word in terms of difficulty in Spanish, Hmong, Russian, or Chinese.
- Both trained and untrained interpreters are widely used in assessment. However, this practice remains risky. The research on interpreters is negligible. Although a number of commercial models exist for training and using interpreters, there is no empirical validation of their suggested procedures.
- Many testing specialists have become sensitive to the problems of testing bilingual individuals. However, because standardized tests in any language remain biased in favor of persons for whom that language is native, low test scores received by bilingual students often are interpreted as evidence of deficits or even disorders. This creates difficulties with every kind of assessment, from tests for English-language proficiency—used most often to place students in bilingual classes—to intelligence tests, the prime source of information for special education placement.

Referral of Culturally and Linguistically Diverse Students

The materials and procedures required for a referral of culturally and linguistically diverse children to the Eligibility Committee (see Chapter 18) may involve more than the normal packet of materials. The evaluation team needs to

- Identify the reason for the referral and include any test results in both languages as appropriate.

- Include any records or reports on which the referral is based.
- Attach a home language survey indicating the home language(s).
- Specify the level of language proficiency.
- Describe the extent to which the LEP (limited English proficiency) student has received native language instruction and/or ESL (English as a second language) services prior to the referral.
- Describe experiential and/or enrichment services for students from diverse cultural and experiential backgrounds.
- Describe the school's efforts to involve parents prior to referral.
- Describe the amount of time and extent of services in an academic program for students who have had little or no formal schooling.
- Identify length of residency of the referred student in the United States and prior school experience in the native country and in an English-language school system.
- Describe all attempts to remediate the pupil's performance prior to referral, including any supplemental aids or support services provided for this purpose.

In conclusion, it is necessary for those entering into or currently involved in the field of special education to be aware of the growing number of students designated as limited English proficient. Federal law mandates that minority students have rights for protection when being assessed. Consequently, knowledge of various tests, their limitations, and controversies surrounding the biases of bilingual assessment is imperative.

VOCABULARY

Audiometric Evaluation Measures: These assessment measures are used by qualified audiologists who measure the level of hearing loss through the use of several techniques.

Behavioral Play Audiometry: This technique involves placing the child in a series of activities that reward him or her for responding appropriately to tone or speech.

Bilingual Assessment: An assessment whereby testing may be done in two or more languages based on the child's dominant language.

Central Auditory Disorders: These disorders result in no measurable peripheral hearing loss. Children with this disorder have trouble learning and are often considered learning disabled.

Conductive Hearing Loss: This results from problems with the structures in the outer or middle ear, generally attributed to a blockage in the mechanical conduction of sound.

Deafness: According to IDEA, "A hearing impairment that is so severe that the child is impaired in processing linguistic information through hear-

ing, with or without amplification, that adversely affects a child's educational performance."

Dominant Language: The primary language spoken by an individual.

Evoked Response Audiometry: This measure uses an electroencephalograph, and a computer measures changes in brain wave activity to a variety of sound levels. This measure can be used with infants who are suspected of being deaf.

Functional Hearing Loss: Results from those problems that are not organic in origin.

Hearing Impairment: According to IDEA, "An impairment in hearing, whether permanent or fluctuating, that adversely affects a child's educational performance but which is not included under the definition of deafness in this section."

Impedance Audiometry: There are two major impedance audiometry tests: **Tympanometry** measures the functioning level of the eardrum, and **stapedial reflex testing** measures the reflex response of the stapedial muscle to pure tone signals. Because these tests do not require a response on the part of the child, they can be used with very young children.

Mixed Hearing Loss: A hearing loss caused by both sensorineural and conductive problems.

Occupational Therapy and Physical Therapy: Occupational therapy focuses mainly on fine-motor and upper-body functions, whereas physical therapy concentrates on lower-body and gross-motor difficulties. The services are provided for students with disabilities who exhibit a range of difficulties such as learning disabilities (e.g., fine- and gross-motor problems or perceptual problems), developmental delays (e.g., mental retardation, vision or hearing impairment), respiratory problems (e.g., cystic fibrosis or asthma), neuromuscular problems (e.g., muscular dystrophy, cerebral palsy), muscle skeletal problems (e.g., arthritis, orthopedic problems, postural deviations), or traumatic accidents (e.g., amputations, brain injuries, burns). In addition to providing therapy for such students, physical and occupational therapists provide many other services including evaluations, screenings, consultations, education, and training.

Otosclerosis: Formation of a spongy-bony growth around the stapes, which impedes its movement.

Pure Tone Audiometric Screening: Pure tone screening is often referred to as sweep testing and is usually the child's first encounter with hearing testing. This type of testing, which is common in schools, presents the child with pure tones over a variety of frequency ranges. The child is then asked to respond if he or she hears a tone, usually by some gesture. If a child is unable to hear sounds at two or more frequencies, the child is usually referred for further evaluation.

Pure Tone Threshold Audiometry: In this procedure, the child is asked to make a gesture or push a button each time he or she hears a tone. The child is presented with a variety of frequencies through earphones. This type of air conduction test reveals the presence of hearing loss.

Sensorineural Hearing Loss: Results from damage to the cochlea or the auditory nerve. This damage is caused by illness and disease and is not medically or surgically treatable.

Sound Field Audiometry: This measure is used with very young children who cannot respond to manual responses or are unable or unwilling to wear headphones. The child is evaluated by observing the intensity levels at which he or she responds to different levels of sounds broadcast through speakers.

Speech Audiometry: This type of evaluation is used to determine a child's present ability to hear and understand speech through the presentation of words in a variety of loudness levels.

DETERMINING WHETHER A DISABILITY EXISTS

CHAPTER OBJECTIVES

In this chapter you learn about diagnosing a suspected disability. After reading this chapter, you should be able to understand the following:

- Higher and lower incidence disabilities
- The process involved in diagnosing a suspected disability from the assessment materials gathered
- The definitions, the incidence, the characteristics, an example assessment battery of, and the method to diagnose a learning disability
- The definitions, the incidence, the characteristics, an example assessment battery of, and the method to diagnose a developmental disability/mental retardation
- The definitions, the incidence, the characteristics, an example assessment battery of, and the method to diagnose an emotional disturbance

DIAGNOSING A DISABILITY

One of the most crucial parts of the assessment process is the ability to take all the information, test results, observations, and so forth and put them all together into a practical, informative, diagnostic, and professional manner. This process can be very difficult for evaluators because it requires the integration of many variables to determine the proper diagnosis and possible classification category. In reality, certain classifications under IDEA 2004 will be diagnosed by the local school-based team, some will be diagnosed by medical professionals, and others will be diagnosed by a combination of agencies. For example, the categories most likely to appear in the public school for initial diagnosis, if not previously identified by parents and medical professionals prior to school enrollment, are referred to as **higher incidence disabilities** and include

- Learning disabilities
- Emotional disturbance
- Mental retardation—higher-level functioning other than Down syndrome
- Speech and language impairments
- Other health impairment—AD/HD-Prediagnosis

These diagnostic categories may first show up when the child enters formal schooling and is presented with educational and social demands that may prove to be too difficult. In these cases, the Child Study Team (CST) will be directly involved in the identification, evaluation, diagnosis, and recommendation of classification, program, and services. It is not likely, in most of these cases, that outside agencies or medical personnel would need to be involved in this process unless the team needed further substantiation of the diagnosis (e.g., an audiological exam to rule out hearing impaired in the case of a child with a suspected language disorder).

The classification categories most likely diagnosed by medical professionals or early medical screening prior to formal schooling are referred to as **lower incidence disabilities.** These include:

- Autism
- Orthopedic impairments
- Visual impairments
- Hearing impairments
- Other health impaired
- Traumatic brain injury
- Deaf-blindness
- Deafness
- Mental retardation—lower levels of functioning

These categories would most likely be diagnosed by doctors, early screening programs, or outside agencies involved in the early education (birth to age five) of the child. The child with these conditions would most likely come to the school at age five with a classification from the district's Eligibility Committee on preschool special education. These conditions, if present prior to formal schooling, would not require the diagnosis by the CST. However, there may be times when some of these conditions might occur after entrance into school at age five, for example, traumatic brain injury, deafness, and the like. These would all be diagnosed by medical professionals, not the CST. However, the role of school professionals would involve following the child's progress, determining educational levels, providing the triennial review, and so forth. (For definitions of all of the classifications under IDEA 2004, see Chapter 1.)

The classification categories most likely diagnosed by a combination of professionals and agencies during school could be:

- Visual impairments
- Hearing impairments
- Other health impairment—Attention Deficit Disorder (ADD) or Attention Deficit Hyperactive Disorder (ADHD)

In regard to the above, there may be times when the school becomes the first level of awareness of a suspected medical problem. In these cases, the school would initially be involved in recommending outside evaluations for diagnosis and recommendations. To diagnose a suspected disability properly, you need to understand the necessary information gathered from the assessment process. This material will be quite comprehensive. Now the key question becomes "What do I do with all this information?" Next we describe examples of this process to determine a suspected learning disability, a suspected developmental disability, and a suspected emotional disturbance.

LEARNING DISABILITIES

Definition

Under IDEA 2004, a learning disability (LD) is defined as

> a disorder in 1 or more of the basic psychological processes involved in understanding or in using language, spoken or written, which may manifest itself in the imperfect ability to listen, think, speak, read, write, spell, or to do mathematical calculations. Such term includes such conditions as perceptual disabilities, brain injury, minimal brain dysfunction, dyslexia, and developmental aphasia. Such term does not include children who have a learning problem that is primarily the result of visual, hearing, or motor disabilities, of mental retardation, of emotional disturbance, or of environmental, cultural, or economic disadvantage. When determining whether a child has a specific learning disability, a local education agency shall not be required to take into consideration whether a child has a severe discrepency between achievement and intellectual ability.
>
> In determining whether a child has a specific learning disability, a local education agency may use a process that determines if the child responds to scientific, research-based intervention as part of the evaluation procedures.

Having a single term to describe this category of children with disabilities reduces some of the confusion, but there are many conflicting theories about the causes of learning disabilities. The classification **learning disabilities** is all-embracing; it describes a syndrome (a group of symptoms), not a specific child with specific problems. Therefore the criteria used in the diagnosis of a learning disability may vary.

Incidence

Many different estimates of the number of children with learning disabilities have appeared in the literature (ranging from 1% to 30% of the general population). The U.S. Department of Education (2002) reported that more than 5% of all school-age children received special education services for learning disabilities and that almost 3.0 million children with learning disabilities were served. Differences in estimates perhaps reflect variations in the definition.

Diagnosing a Learning Disability

The diagnosis of a learning disability can be difficult, especially in the very early grades. However, if one follows some practical guidelines, the diagnosis can be more easily substantiated. In order to diagnose a child with a suspected learning disability, the following procedures and criteria should be considered:

Clinical Interview.   The clinical interview involves a series of interviews with the child to assess where the ultimate problems may lie. When interviewing the child with a suspected learning disability, you may want to look and listen for confusion over questions, poor use of vocabulary, problems expressing ideas and thoughts, awkward gait, poor memory, short attention span, lack of focus, poor fine-motor skills, and a history of academic difficulties.

Ecological Assessment.   Ecological assessment involves observing the child in a variety of settings such as the classroom, playground, and other structured and nonstructured settings to determine where the student manifests the greatest difficulties. In the case of a child with a suspected learning disability, you may observe social withdrawal, alienation from peers, inability to focus in unstructured settings, and "class clown" type behaviors as a means of being removed from academically stressful settings.

Parent Interview.   A parent interview requires a personal meeting with the parents to determine essential background history that may be essential for appropriate diagnosis. In the case of a child with a suspected learning disability, you may want to listen during this type of interview for such things as has difficulty dressing him or herself, avoids homework, is disorganized, has a short attention span, forgets easily, forgets to bring home books, gets stomachaches in the morning before school, gets frequent headaches, has few friends, is unwilling to try new things, and gives up easily.

Teacher Interview.   Teacher interviews may require several meetings with the classroom teacher to ascertain the child's basic intellectual, social, and academic performance. In the case of a child with a potential learning disability, the interviewer should be aware of certain LD symptom clusters that may appear in the classroom. Some examples may include poor memory, gross-motor coordination difficulties, lack of focus, short attention span, procrastination, failure to hand in written work or homework, lack of confidence, self-derogatory statements such as "I'm so stupid," consistently low academic performance in certain subjects over time, social difficulties, lack of motivation for schoolwork, poor handwriting, and poor fine-motor skills.

Review of Cumulative Reports and Records.   Review report cards, attendance records, standardized tests, and so forth to determine possible patterns of behavior. In the case of the child with a potential learning disability, a **review of cumulative records** may reveal consistently low group achievement scores in certain subjects over a period of years, past teacher comments showing a pattern to what the child's present teacher reports, a historical pattern of academic difficulties, frequent absences (which may occur when the child feels frustrated and overwhelmed by the work), and a discrepancy between ability and class performance as indicated by report card patterns.

Intelligence Testing.   In the case of a child with a suspected learning disability, the psychologist will administer an individual intelligence test to look for an average to above-average potential intellectual level. This does not mean that the child's IQ need be in the average range, but analysis of the profile indicates that greater potential be shown through a significant uneven pattern between different scores within the same test. For example, two children can score an 85 (Low Average) on the WISC-IV (see Chapter 10 for a detailed explanation of all subtests indicated below), but the score profiles may be very different

Billy, a student with a Full Scale IQ of 85, has subtest scores that are consistent with little scatter (e.g., his subtest scores have little variability, ranging from 8 to 11). Based on IQ, Billy may not exhibit a learning disability. His subtest scores appear relatively flat when plotted on a graph, as opposed to "up and down" and inconsistent.

However, in the case of a child with a learning disability, there will often be great variability and scatter both within and between subtests. For example, Sally, whose IQ subtest range from 7 (Low Average) to 15 (Superior) is showing tremendous differences in scores. Clearly, her scores are inconsistent and look like a roller coaster when plotted. This may be an indicator of a possible learning disability.

Important Point: Many children are commonly misdiagnosed as having a learning disability when, in actuality, they may be slow learners, children with emotional issues, or underachievers not performing for reasons other than a learning disability.

Achievement Testing.   Children with learning disabilities usually exhibit a severe discrepancy between potential ability (as measured on an individual IQ test) and academic achievement. This is a debatable criterion because it is possible that a child functioning on grade level, according to standardized achievement tests, may actually have a severe discrepancy if one takes into account ability levels. For instance:

> **Susan—Grade 5—IQ 125:** With this IQ score, one would expect Susan's potential achievement levels to be above grade level, perhaps by one to two years. Therefore, scores within the seventh-grade range (80th to 90th percentiles) would be more in line with her ability levels, which, based on her IQ score, are at

around the 95th Percentile. If Susan were to score on the second-grade level in achievement areas (around the 10th percentile), then this would represent an 85th-percentile difference between ability and achievement potential, a definite criterion for a possible learning disability.

Jimmy—Grade 5—IQ 100: With this IQ score (50th Percentile), one should expect Jimmy to be functioning right on grade level according to his ability potential. This means that because he is in the fifth grade, scores in that area would be right where we expect. If one uses percentile comparisons, then **achievement testing** scores around the 50th Percentile would indicate no significant discrepancy between ability and achievement.

Shamica—Grade 5—IQ 130: With this IQ score, one would expect Shamica's potential achievement levels to be above grade level, perhaps by one to two years. Therefore, scores within the seventh-grade range (80th to 90th Percentiles) would be more in line with her ability levels, which, based on her IQ score, are at the 98th Percentile. If Shamica were to score on the fifth-grade level in achievement areas (around the 50th Percentile), then this would represent a 40% difference between ability and achievement potential, a definite criterion for a possible learning disability. However, this type of pattern of a learning disability may not be identified in the early grades because the child is "keeping up with the class." In this case it is more likely that the discrepancy between ability and performance may begin to show in later grades as the work becomes more difficult.

The Wechsler Individual Achievement Test-2 and the Peabody Individual Achievement Test-R are examples of tests that are used to measure this variable (refer to Chapter 10 for further examples).

Perceptual Testing.   One of the underlying assumptions with a true learning disability is that it is the result of a subtle neurological impairment. This impairment, if present, affects the child's ability to process information in a timely manner, thereby interfering with performance. **Perceptual testing** needs to be administered to determine if, and where, such processing difficulties occur.

These deficits may affect memory, perception, expression, organization, or reception of information. Further, they may also affect the child's ability to process information if it is received through certain weak channels, such as auditory or visual. These factors, when present, might explain the lack of performance in certain academic areas. The Detroit Tests of Learning Aptitudes-4, Slingerland Screening Test, Bender Visual Motor Gestalt Test, and the Wepman Test of Auditory Discrimination-2 are examples of tests usually administered by either the special education teacher or the psychologist (see Chapter 2 for further information and examples).

Curriculum-Based Assessment.   In the case of a child with a suspected learning disability, the teacher may use **curriculum-based assessment** to find that the child is unable to decode or comprehend information from class texts as fast as other children in the classroom. This may result from poor memory, slow processing, or inadequate reading skills.

Portfolio Assessment.   In the case of a child with a suspected learning disability, the teacher may use **portfolio assessment** to find that the child is missing homework, shows incomplete work, and has consistent problems through error analysis in one or more areas, such as writing skills and spelling, avoidance to show or collect work, crumpled work from embarrassment, and failure to complete group assignments.

Exclusion Factors.   To properly diagnose a true learning disability, several other possible problems or causes have to be excluded or ruled out. Among these **exclusion factors** are

> *Retardation:* This can usually be ruled out if the child's IQ is 70 or higher on the Wechsler Scales.
>
> *Primary emotional issues:* Sometimes serious emotional issues with their increased levels of tension can mirror learning disability symptoms. However, these are learning problems, not learning disabilities, if the primary causes are determined to be emotionally based. In this case, the patterns of academic difficulties may be inconsistent, indicating the effects of ongoing anxiety and stress.
>
> *Problems in acuity:* Any mechanical difficulties with the eye and ear must be ruled out, and should be done first, prior to any evaluation. These can be screened in school and, if need be, substantiated by a doctor's examination. If acuity is causing the distorted perception, then the child cannot be considered truly LD. A child with a learning disability has intact acuity, and the perceptual distortion occurs in the internal psychological processes involved in the learning process.
>
> *Poor teaching:* Poor teaching or inadequate schooling may cause learning problems that are severe in nature and misinterpreted as a learning disability.
>
> *Cultural deprivation:* A student from a foreign country may experience learning problems as a result of the cultural confusion. However, if this is found to be the cause, then this is not a true learning disability. If this student were to be tested and taught in his or her native language, he or she may exhibit no learning problems. However, be careful here to rule out whether cultural confusion is the only factor, because some foreign students would also have learning disabilities in their native lands.
>
> *Motivational factors:* If a child does not possess a serious emotional disturbance, but rather is simply unmotivated for school, this is not a true learning disability. However, be careful, because a lack of motivation may be a symptomatic behavior of a true learning disability.
>
> *Historical Patterns:* A learning disability does not normally just appear out of nowhere for the first time in the later grades unless it has gone undiagnosed due to inadequate screening. If the child has performed up to ability without any **historical pattern** of achievement deficit areas, and then has problems in learning or performance, check out other possibilities as the cause.

Psychological Tests/Scales: Many children with learning disabilities have some form of anxiety or low self-esteem because of their difficulties in the classroom. During assessment, the psychologist will use a variety of psychological testing measures, such as the Thematic Apperception Tests, Children's Apperception Test, or Sentence Completion Test (see Chapter 11), because they measure the individual's inner turmoil, conflicts, or fears, which may be contributing to educational interference. These tests will reveal many underlying themes that can show a pattern of emotional conflict, anxiety, and/or tension. By using psychological tests, the psychologist can determine if a child shows signs of emotional issues such as depression, anxiety, school phobia, and other types of disorders that are being caused by the effects of a learning disability.

Behavioral Manifestations: Students who have learning disabilities may exhibit a wide range of **behavioral manifestations** including inattention, uneven and unpredictable test performance, perceptual impairments, motor disorders, and behaviors such as impulsiveness, low tolerance for frustration, and problems in handling day-to-day social interactions and situations.

Other Diagnostic Symptoms: **Other diagnostic symptoms** may be the first indication of a possible learning disability and, if exhibited, should be investigated as soon as possible. These may include, but are not limited, to:

- Delays, disorders, or discrepancies in listening and speaking
- Difficulties with reading, writing, and spelling
- Difficulty in performing arithmetic functions or in comprehending basic concepts
- Difficulty in organizing and integrating thoughts
- Difficulty in organizing all facets of learning
- Short attention span
- Poor letter or word memory
- Inability to distinguish between letters and sounds
- May be erratic and fluctuate from day to day
- Poor gross- or fine-motor development
- Difficulty telling time
- Difficulty with spatial relationships
- Difficulty developing left or right dominance
- Difficulty making friends
- Adjusts poorly to change or responds inappropriately

MILD MENTAL RETARDATION/ DEVELOPMENTAL DISABILITY

Definition

People with **mental retardation** are those who develop at a below-average rate and experience difficulty in learning and social adjustment. The regulations under the

Individuals with Disabilities Education Improvement Act of 2004 provide the following technical definition for mental retardation:

> Mental retardation means significantly sub-average general intellectual functioning existing concurrently with deficits in adaptive behavior and manifested during the developmental period, that adversely affects a child's educational performance.

General intellectual functioning is typically measured by an intelligence test. Persons with mental retardation usually score 70 or below on such tests. *Adaptive behavior* refers to a person's adjustment to everyday life. Difficulties may occur in learning, communication, and social, academic, vocational, and independent living skills.

Mental retardation is not a disease, nor should it be confused with mental illness. Children with mental retardation become adults; they do not remain "eternal children." They do learn, but slowly, and with difficulty.

Many children with mental retardation have chromosome abnormalities. Other biological factors include (but are not limited to) asphyxia (lack of oxygen); blood incompatibilities between the mother and fetus; and maternal infections, such as rubella or herpes. Certain drugs also have been linked to problems in fetal development.

Incidence

Some studies suggest that approximately 1% of the general population has mental retardation (when both intelligence and adaptive behavior measures are used). According to data reported to the U.S. Department of Education by the states, in the 2002 school year, approximately 600,000 students ages 6 to 21 were classified as having mental retardation and were provided services by the public schools. This figure represents approximately 1.7% of the total school enrollment for that year. It does not include students reported as having multiple handicaps or those in noncategorical special education preschool programs who may also have mental retardation.

Diagnosing Mild Retardation/Developmental Disabilities

In order to diagnose a child with a suspected developmental disability, the following procedures and criteria are considered:

Clinical Interview. A clinical interview involves a series of interviews with the child to assess where the ultimate problems may lie. When interviewing the child with a suspected developmental disability, you may want to look and listen for confusion over questions, immature speech patterns, inappropriate behaviors, poor use of vocabulary, problems expressing ideas and thoughts, awkward gait, poor memory, short attention span, lack of focus, poor fine-motor skills, and a history of academic difficulties.

Ecological Assessment. An ecological assessment requires observing the child in a variety of settings such as the classroom, playground, and other structured and non-structured settings to determine where the student manifests the greatest difficulties.

In the case of a child with a suspected developmental disability, you may observe social withdrawal, alienation, immaturity, and inability to focus in structured or unstructured settings.

Parent Interview.   The parent interview technique involves a personal meeting with the parents to determine essential background history that may be essential for appropriate diagnosis. In the case of a child with a suspected developmental disability, you may want to listen during this type of interview for such things as difficulty dressing him or herself; awkward gait; poor social skills; immaturity; difficulty following directions; delays in walking, talking, toileting, and other developmental milestones.

Teacher Interview.   Teacher interviews may require several meetings with the classroom teacher to ascertain the child's basic intellectual, social, and academic performance. In the case of a child with a potential developmental disability, the interviewer should be aware of certain symptom clusters that may appear in the classroom. Some examples may include having serious problems with abstract concepts; frequently confuses directions; seems lost, overwhelmed, confused; has failing test grades; is anxious and worried, with excessive fears and phobias; is socially immature with social and physical skills far below the rest of the class; is easily frustrated even when confronted with a simple task; is resistant to change; has short attention span; and has difficulty generalizing learned concepts to new situations.

Review of Cumulative Reports and Records.   Review report cards, attendance records, standardized tests, and so forth to determine possible patterns of behavior. In the case of the child with a potential developmental disability, the records may reveal subaverage group achievement scores in all or most subjects over a period of years, past teacher comments showing a pattern to what the child's present teacher reports, a historical pattern of serious academic difficulties, frequent absences (which may occur when the child feels frustrated and overwhelmed by the work), and no discrepancy between ability and class performance as indicated by present and past report card patterns.

Intelligence Testing.   A student may be diagnosed as having a developmental disability if he or she exhibits certain learning, social, and behavior patterns to a marked extent and over a prolonged period of time. Such patterns may include a consistently subaverage intellectual level: According to the AAMR (1992), the IQ score normally needs to fall below 70 (assuming an IQ test with a mean of 100 and a standard deviation of 15, i.e., WISC-III). However, some children with serious emotional disabilities may fall below 70 due to lack of motivation, high levels of tension and anxiety, or other factors that may hinder the exhibited IQ score.

Achievement Testing.   Children with developmental disabilities will have achievement levels similar to those reflected in their IQ. For example, a child with a 65 IQ (2nd Percentile) should also show consistent achievement levels well below the norm over time. For this determination, tests of academic achievement such as the KTEA or

WIAT-2 must be administered and indicate scores significantly lower than expected for the child's age.

Impaired Adaptive Functioning.   Impaired adaptative functioning (see Chapter 11) normally shows up in the child's inability to function at his or her expected age in such areas as social skills, communication, and daily living skills. For this determination, a test of adaptive ability such as the ABS (Adaptive Behavior Scales) must be administered and indicate scores significantly lower than expected for his or her age.

Curriculum-Based Assessment.   In the case of a child with a suspected developmental disability, the teacher may find that the child's ability to decode or comprehend information from class texts is far below that of the other children in the classroom.

Portfolio Assessment.   In the case of a child with a suspected developmental disability, the teacher may find that the child is missing homework, shows incomplete work, exhibits serious problems through error analysis in most areas, avoids showing or collecting work, crumples work from embarrassment, and fails to complete group assignments.

Exclusion Factors.   In order to diagnose a developmental disability properly, several other possible problems or causes have to be excluded or ruled out. Among these are

- *Primary emotional issues:* Sometimes, very serious emotional issues caused by traumatic experiences can lead to performance within the level of functional retardation. Here the child's trauma has reduced functional ability to the point where scores seem to reflect subaverage intellectual and academic ability.
- *Problems in acuity:* Any mechanical difficulties with the eye and ear must be ruled out, and should be done first, prior to any evaluation. These can be screened in school and, if need be, substantiated by a doctor's examination.
- *Poor teaching:* Poor teaching, inadequate schooling, or early sensory deprivation may cause learning problems that are severe in nature and misinterpreted as developmental disabilities.
- *Cultural deprivation:* A student from a foreign country may experience severe learning problems as a result of the cultural confusion. However, if this is found to be the cause, then this is not a developmental disability. If this student were to be tested and taught in his or her native language, he or she may exhibit no learning problems. However, be careful here to rule out whether cultural confusion is the only factor, because some foreign students would also have developmental disabilities in their native lands.
- *Consistently Slow Rate of Learning.* Children with developmental disabilities usually will exhibit levels of development similar to that of a younger child. Normally, in the regular classroom, they tend to take longer to do assignments and have difficulties keeping up with their peers. This information can be obtained through parent and teacher interviews.

■ *Historical Patterns.* Normally a child with developmental disabilities will exhibit developmental delays in his or her medical history. For example, parents may report slower than normal development of language, walking, and talking.

EMOTIONAL DISTURBANCE

The final diagnosis of an **emotional disturbance** is a very serious matter and should be done only on the recommendation of a psychologist, psychiatrist, or approved mental health clinic. Although a special educator will be involved in certain aspects of the assessment, such as achievement or perceptual evaluation, he or she will not make the eventual diagnosis. However, awareness of what is involved in the diagnosis of an emotional disturbance is important for anyone involved in the process.

Definition

Many terms are used to describe emotional, behavioral, or mental disorders. Currently, students with such disorders are categorized as having a serious emotional disturbance, which is defined under the Individuals with Disabilities Education Improvement Act of 2004 as follows:

> a condition exhibiting one or more of the following characteristics over a long period of time and to a marked degree that adversely affects educational performance—
>
> (A) An inability to learn that cannot be explained by intellectual, sensory or health factors;
> (B) An inability to build or maintain satisfactory interpersonal relationships with peers and teachers;
> (C) Inappropriate types of behavior or feelings under normal circumstances;
> (D) A general pervasive mood of unhappiness or depression; or
> (E) A tendency to develop physical symptoms or fears associated with personal or school problems.

As defined by the IDEA, serious emotional disturbance includes schizophrenia but does not apply to children who are socially maladjusted, unless it is determined that they have a serious emotional disturbance (C.F.R., Title 34, Sec 300.7[b][9]). It is important to know that the federal government is currently reviewing the way in which serious emotional disturbance is defined, and that the definition may be revised.

Incidence

Estimates of the prevalence of emotional disorders in children vary because there has been no standard and reliable definition nor screening instrument for its determination. Data reported by numerous studies indicate that approximately 6% to 10% of all school-age children exhibit serious and persistent emotional/behavioral difficulties. Yet, according to its *Nineteenth Annual Report to Congress*, the U.S. Department of Education (2002) found that only about 1% of schoolchildren in the United States are identified as seriously emotionally disturbed.

Diagnosing an Emotional Disturbance

The exact causes of emotional disturbance have not been adequately determined. Although various factors such as heredity, brain disorder, diet, stress, and family functioning have been suggested as possibilities, research has not shown any of these factors to be the direct cause of behavior problems. However, some of the methods used in the diagnosis of emotional disturbance may include the following.

Clinical Interview.   The school psychologist employs the clinical interview by conducting a series of interviews with the child to assess where areas of tension may exist. When interviewing the child with a suspected emotional disability, the psychologist may look and listen for a variety of issues including, but not limited to:

- An inability or unwillingness to develop or maintain satisfactory interpersonal relationships: These problem behaviors may impact on the relationships with peers, teachers, parents, or other adults
- Extreme overreactions to minimally stressful situations over a prolonged period of time
- A general pervasive mood of sadness or depression
- Anxiety
- Low self-esteem
- Being overly dependent
- Tendency to be depressed about life
- Threats of suicide
- Use of offensive language

Ecological Assessment.   As with other disability diagnoses, ecological assessment involves observing the child in a variety of settings such as the classroom, playground, and other structured and nonstructured settings to determine where the student manifests the greatest difficulties. In the case of a child with a suspected emotional disability, the psychologist will be looking for behaviors such as:

- Appears lazy, preoccupied, and uninterested
- Attempts self-injury
- Attempts to injure others
- Has attentional problems
- Displays cruel, malicious, or assaultive thoughts or behavior
- Shows defiance
- Has difficulty making friends
- Does not appear to enjoy being in school
- Does not follow class rules
- Fights with authority figures
- Fights with peers
- Acts impulsively
- Is unable to carry on normal routines

- Displays inappropriate behaviors
- Displays learning problems whereby the student is performing academically below grade level
- Acts out
- Shows aggressive tendencies
- Displays antisocial behavior: lies, steals, or vandalizes
- Uses threats to try and get his way
- Exhibits violent behaviors

Parent Interview.   The parent interview involves a personal meeting with the parents to determine essential background history that may be essential for appropriate diagnosis. In the case of a child with a suspected emotional disability, the psychologist will listen for behaviors including, but not limited to:

- Social isolation or withdrawal
- Excessive latenesses
- Excessive absences
- Negativism
- Open defiance to parental authority or rules
- Poor social relationships
- Feelings of hopelessness
- Verbal aggression
- Confrontational behavior with parents
- Rigid behavior patterns
- Excessive fears and phobias, being anxious and worried
- Easily frustrated even when confronted with a simple task
- Resistance to change

Teacher Interview.   Because the behavior of children with emotional disabilities can vary from withdrawal, in the case of depression, to aggressive tendencies, in the case of a conduct disorder, teachers can provide many symptoms indicative of children with possible emotional disabilities. Behaviors that might show up in the classroom include:

- Attendance problems and tardiness
- Challenges to authority
- Inappropriate verbalizations and outburst
- Incomplete classwork
- Difficulty remaining seated
- Problems with social relationships
- Problems following directions and paying attention
- Aggressive behavior patterns

Review of Cumulative Reports and Records.   Review report cards, attendance records, standardized tests, and so forth to determine possible patterns of behavior. In the case of the child with a potential emotional disability, the records may reveal inconsistent group achievement scores within the same subjects over a period of years due to inconsistent motivation, low energy, oppositional factors, or high levels of tension that may impair the student's ability to focus on a consistent basis. Past teacher comments showing a historical pattern of academic difficulties, frequent absences or latenesses (which may occur when the child feels frustrated and overwhelmed by the work or resulting from a dysfunctional home environment), and a discrepancy between ability and class performance as indicated by report card patterns may be exhibited. For instance, these report card patterns may show high first-quarter grade performance, which deteriorates over the course of the school year. This may be due to the lack of available energy caused by high levels of tension and anxiety.

Intelligence Testing.   In the case of a child with a suspected emotional disturbance, the profile exhibited on an IQ test (e.g., WISC-IV) can vary. For example, the profile on the IQ test may reveal a very inconsistent pattern and/or great deal of variability or scatter within the scaled scores. This type of pattern may be caused by interference of emotional turmoil or tension, or a lack of motivation in the student's ability to think clearly or consistently. As a result, greater focus may be present on some tasks than others, resulting in the roller coaster effect of high and low scores. Also, it is common that Arithmetic and Digit Span scores are lower due to the amount of concentration and focus required, which is normally limited in children with emotional disabilities.

In some cases, an emotional disturbance can depress IQ scores on tasks requiring verbal responses and those tasks similar to school-related activities. Low Verbal scores may be masking depression, while Performance scores may reflect true potential.

Achievement Testing.   Children with emotional disabilities may or may not show discrepancies in achievement testing, depending on the level of focus and motivation at the time of testing. Children who are depressed, for instance, may be apathetic, noncompliant, or unenthusiastic; give up easily; or be unwilling to venture guesses—all resulting in low scores that may not truly reflect ability levels. Other children with emotional disabilities may see this as a short burst of energy to see what they are capable of doing. However, despite high scores, the student usually will be unable to generalize these high scores into consistent classroom performance.

Perceptual Testing.   If perceptual testing is given, one should assume that if the etiology is emotional in nature, then the child's learning process should be intact. Unlike a child with a learning disability, whereby subtle neurological impairments affect perception and reduce scores, students with emotional issues usually will have intact learning processes unless their low scores reflect opposition, lack of motivation, or depression.

Portfolio Assessment.   In the case of a child with a suspected emotional disability, the teacher may find that the child is missing homework, shows incomplete work, exhibits work with inconsistent problems, avoids showing or collecting work, crumples work from embarrassment or frustration, and fails to complete group assignments.

Historical Patterns.   In order to diagnose a problem as an emotional disability, it must exist over a period of time and, to a marked degree, adversely affect educational performance.

Psychological Tests/Scales.   The psychologist will use a variety of psychological measures. Some of these are called projective tests, such as the Sentence Completion Test and Thematic Apperception Tests, because they measure the individual's inner turmoil, conflicts, fears, and so forth, which may be contributing to educational interference. These tests will reveal many underlying themes that can show a pattern of emotional conflict, anxiety, and/or tension. By using psychological tests, the psychologist can determine if a child shows signs of emotional issues such as depression, anxiety, school phobia, and other types of disorders.

CONCLUSION

The diagnosis of any suspected disability is without any doubt the most important part of the assessment process. Having all the data and relevant information available and not knowing what to do with it is a disservice to both the parent and the child with a suspected disability. Therefore, it is your professional responsibility to stay abreast of any changes in the federal laws, state laws, and local policies involving the assessment of children with suspected disabilities.

CHAPTER SEVENTEEN

WRITING A COMPREHENSIVE REPORT IN SPECIAL EDUCATION

CHAPTER OBJECTIVES

Writing a report is not a simple task. It takes knowledge and skill because it is being written for parents, teachers, and administrators. After reading this chapter, you should be able to understand why reports need to be written, general guidelines when writing a report, and all sections of a comprehensive report. These sections include

- Identifying data
- Reason for referral
- Background history
- Observations
- Tests administered
- Test results
- Test by test analysis
- Content area by content area analysis
- Conclusions
- Recommendations

REPORT WRITING

Many different professionals may provide input in the assessment of a child with a suspected disability. When this occurs, a comprehensive report based on the findings must be written. The purpose of this report is to communicate results in such a way that the reader will understand the rationale behind the recommendations, and will be able to use the recommendations as practical guidelines for intervention. This report may be presented to the parent, sent to an outside doctor or agency, or presented to the Eligibility Committee. In any case, the report needs to be professional, comprehensive, and practical.

Writing a good report is a real skill. The fact is, all the wonderful data collection becomes useless if it cannot be interpreted and explained in a clear and concise manner. For example, being too general or explaining results poorly creates many problems and confusion for readers. Also, citing numerous general recommendations will not be practical for the school, teacher, or parents. Writing a report that contains jargon that no one other than you understands is also useless. Completing an extremely lengthy report in an attempt to be too comprehensive will result only in losing your reader. As you review each section in this chapter, you may wish to refer to the example reports we have provided.

PRACTICAL GUIDELINES FOR REPORT WRITING

When writing a report, the key is to be as comprehensive as possible while being clear and concise. To do this effectively, it is important to understand some very practical guidelines. Listed below are some practical guidelines to follow when writing an educational report.

Write the report in the third person. Never write "I think" or "If it were up to me." This is not a term paper but, rather, a legal document. As such, the professional approach is to remain in the third person. Use phrases such as:

- According to the examiner
- It was felt that
- There seems to be
- It is the professional opinion of this evaluator that

Single space your report to condense the length. A report of three to five pages is not overwhelming. There are several ideas suggested throughout this chapter that can break up the report so that the format is very easy on the reader.

In general, try to separate your recommendation section into three parts. This approach will make it easy for a reader to follow the recommendations, and allow those interested parties to see their responsibilities. The three parts should be addressed to:

- The school
- The teacher
- The parents

Try to write the report in the past tense as often as possible. Because the data were already collected, and you have done the assessment, the use of the past tense is most appropriate. For example:

- On the Reading subtest, Jared *scored* in the 95th percentile.
- During testing, Tamika *exhibited* shyness.
- Throughout the interview, David *showed* no signs of hyperactivity.
- Sonya *appeared* to lack confidence when doing tasks that *required* hand-eye coordination.

Underline, bold, or italicize paragraph headings so that they stand out and are easy to locate. When you create a new section in your report, format it so that the reader knows that this starts a different area of the report. Separate sections (e.g., Reason for Referral and Background History) with extra "white space."

Write reports using complete sentences. A report should never read like a telegram. Be sure all sentences make sense. Always check spelling and grammar to make sure there are no errors. Nothing is more unprofessional than a report that looks sloppy and has many mistakes.

CRITERIA FOR WRITING A COMPREHENSIVE REPORT

Now that you have some practical guidelines to follow, take a comprehensive look at each specific section. Reports can be written in many ways, and report format is decided by the personal choice of the examiner, the supervisor, or the district. However, it is important not to overlook certain information. What follows is one suggested outline and sections that would meet all the criteria for a professional and comprehensive report.

Section I: Identifying Data

The first section is called **Identifying Data** and contains all the necessary basic information about the child. This section is important to the reader, especially if further contact is required. It allows the reader to have all the basic information in one place. The parts of this section include:

Name:	Parents' Names:
Address:	Teacher:
Phone:	Referred By:
Date of Birth:	Date/s of Testing:
Grade:	Date of Report:
School:	Examiner:
Chronological Age at Time of Testing (CA):	

For example, in a model report, the first section might be completed as follows:

Name: Sally Jones	**Parents' Names:** Paul and Mary Jones
Address: 123 ABC Dr.	**Teacher:** Mrs. Johnson
Anytown, New York 12345	
Phone: (555) 123-1234	**Referred By:** Mother
Date of Birth: 8-17-92	**Date/s of Testing:** 9-17-05, 9-18-05
Grade: 7	**Date of Report:** 9-25-05
School: Anytown Middle School	**Examiner:** Ms. Sandra Smith, M.S.

Chronological Age at Time of Testing (CA): 13-1

Although most of this information is usually found in the school records, having it all in one place saves time. Make sure that the date/s of testing and the date of the report are always included for comparisons. Some evaluations are finished several months before the report is typed, and the scores can be misleading if the reader assumes that they represent the child's present levels on the date of the report when they may really be reflective of ability levels in prior months. It is always more acceptable when the two dates are within one month of each other. Also keep in mind that the **chronological age,** CA, is at the time of initial testing and is presented in years and months, for example, 12-6 (see Chapter 6).

Section II: Reason for Referral

The second section is called **Reason for Referral,** and explains to the reader the specific reasons why this evaluation is taking place. It should not be longer than two to three sentences, but should be comprehensive enough to clarify the purpose. The following are some examples of this section:

Reason for Referral

- *Jarmel was referred by his teacher for an evaluation as a result of inconsistent academic performance and poor social skills.*
- *Mary was referred by her parents for an evaluation in order to determine if a learning disability was interfering with her ability to learn.*
- *Benjamin is being tested as part of the triennial evaluation.*
- *Matthew is being screened for a suspected disability.*
- *Peter was referred by the child study team in order to determine his present intellectual, academic, and perceptual levels.*

This section should not contain a great deal of parent or teacher information. There may be a tendency here to bring in other information to substantiate the reason for the evaluation. Avoid this, and keep it short and to the point. Substantiation for this referral is part of another section that offers a more detailed explanation of the child.

Section III: Background History

The next section is called **Background History,** and contains a very thorough description of the child's family history, developmental history, academic history, and social history (refer to the parent intake form in Chapter 7).

This general section is very comprehensive and establishes a foundation for what will follow. If you suspect a disability that may have historical features, then you need to present the development of this disability and its interfering factors in depth. The reader should come away from the section seeing the substantiation for a suspected disability. Certain areas should always be covered in the Background History section. These include:

A. Family History.   A family history provides the reader with a general understanding of the family structure, siblings, parental perceptions, and so on. Examples of sentences that would appear in this section include the following:

- *Jacob lives at home with his mother and a younger brother, Jon. His parents are divorced and Jacob has no contact with his father.*
- *Rosa lives at home with her father, mother, and two older sisters.*
- *Julie is an only child who was adopted at the age of six months by her parents, Ted and Jane. She knows that she is adopted and has never had any contact with her biological parents.*

B. Developmental History.   The purpose of a **developmental history** is to give the reader any relevant background history pertaining to developmental milestones. This section need not read like a hospital report but should contain the basic developmental history. Examples of sentences that would appear in this section include the following:

- *All of Julio's developmental milestones were reached in the normal limits.*
- *Yolanda started to talk only at 2 years of age and received early intervention to help her with language ability.*
- *Mike had many ear infections during the first year of life and needed tubes put in when he was 13 months of age.*
- *Emily started to walk later than the norms, as she started at 21 months of age.*

C. Academic History.   An **academic history** section provides the reader with relevant academic performance during the child's school years. If you suspect a learning disability, then the academic section must be extensive. Trace the child's educational performance as far back as possible and establish the consistency of the pattern to the reader. Include all pertinent academic information such as past teacher comments, grades, attendance, group scores, and the like; and lead the reader grade by grade in establishing a pattern of concern or a pattern that may rule out a specific type of suspected disability. Example sentences used in this section might read as follows:

- *Jessica has always done poorly in math and has never received a grade of higher than C in this subject throughout her educational career.*

- *Laura's first-grade teacher reported that she had great difficulty in the area of spelling.*
- *Justin's Reading scores on the ABC National Standardized Test were well below the norm (8th Percentile) when he took it two years ago in the fourth grade.*

D. Social History. A **social history** provides the reader with an understanding of the child in his social world. Group participation, organizations, hobbies, interests, interaction with peers, social style, and so forth should all be discussed. Examples of sentences that would appear in this section include the following:

- *According to Tomas, he enjoys playing baseball and hanging out with his friends at the mall.*
- *Karen reported that she has no friends and does not participate in any extracurricular activities.*
- *Ted is the eleventh-grade class president of his school and plays on the junior varsity basketball and varsity baseball teams.*

When the Background History section is complete, it should provide the reader with a clear understanding of the child and his or her world at the present time.

Section IV: Behavioral Observations

The fourth section is called **Behavioral Observations** and includes a description of the child's behavior during the testing sessions. This can be a very important section because it may reinforce what is seen in the class or be very different, in which case the structure of the testing environment should be explored for clues to learning style. Here, for the first time, you are providing the reader with your professional and first-hand observation of this child in a controlled setting. This type of structure provides a great deal of valuable information that may be later transferred to recommendations about the way in which the child learns best. Examples of sentences that would appear in this section include the following:

- *Jamal approached the testing situation in a reluctant and hesitant manner.*
- *During testing, it was evident that Hannah was frustrated with many of the reading tasks.*
- *Throughout the assessment, Keith appeared anxious and nervous, as he was biting his nails and always asking whether his answers were correct.*

Section V: Tests and Procedures Administered

The next section is called **Tests and Procedures Administered.** This includes a simple list of the individual tests included in the test battery and any procedures used to enhance the report, such as classroom observation, review of records, and parent intake. Do not utilize abbreviations when referring to test names. You may want to add them after the name of each specific test, for example, Wide Range Achievement Test–3rd Edition (WRAT-3). No further explanation is required here other than a list. This section will vary depending upon the professional doing the evaluation. For example, the educational evaluator's list of tests and procedures administered may look like this:

- *Wechsler Individual Achievement Test–2nd Edition (WIAT-2)*
- *Detroit Tests of Learning Aptitudes–4th Edition (DTLA-4)*
- *Gray Oral Reading Test–4th Edition (GORT-4)*
- *Classroom observation*
- *Interview with child*
- *Parent interview*
- *Teacher conferences*
- *Review of cumulative records*

Section VI. Test Results

The sixth section, **Test Results,** is a crucial one because it analyzes the results of each test and looks at the child's individual performance on each measure. There are several approaches to this section, but the two most widely used approaches are the test-by-test analysis and the content area by content area analysis. The approach chosen is the personal choice and preference of the examiner.

A **test-by-test approach** separately analyzes the child's performance on each test. It analyzes the results of the different subtests and provides indications of strengths and weaknesses, manner of approach, and indications of whether the scores on the specific test should be considered valid. In this section, the first paragraph of each test analyzed usually contains all the basic score information provided by that specific test: grade levels, age levels, percentiles, stanines, and ranges. It should not contain raw scores or other statistical information that has no meaning to the reader. The next several paragraphs under each test normally describe the subtest performance, patterns, strengths and weaknesses, and child's style in handling the task. Information on whether the scores should be considered a valid indicator is provided. For example, if a child refuses to do more than two problems and receives a low score, it is important to inform the reader that that score may be misleading and may not reflect the child's true ability due to giving up or an unwillingness to venture a guess.

A **content area by content area approach** takes all the reading, math, spelling, writing, visual, auditory, and motor tests from each evaluation measure and analyzes the results separately by content area. The examiner analyzes each content area in hopes of establishing patterns of strengths and weaknesses. For example, deficient scores on all tests of reading comprehension may establish a pattern of disability, especially if they are discrepant from the child's ability levels. However, extremely high scores on some tests of comprehension and low scores on others need to be explained to the reader.

Here are the key steps that you want to follow in the **Test Results** section. We will go through this step by step. *Italicized* writing indicates the information you might type in a particular step.

1. Step 1 for Writing Test Results: Write out the name of the test.
   Wechsler Individualized Achievement Test, 2nd Edition

2. Step 2 for Writing Test Results: Create a table (Standard Score, Classification, and Percentile).

Name of Subtest	Standard Score	Classification	Percentile Rank
Word Reading	85	Low Average	16
Numerical Operations	135	Very Superior	99
Spelling	110	High Average	75
Reading Comprehension	70	Well Below Average	2

3. Step 3 for Writing Test Results: Write a brief 1- or 2-sentence statement about what each subtest measures. (This is obtained through the Examiner's Manual.)

   The Word Reading subtest of the WIAT-II presents a series of pictures and printed words for assessing decoding and word-reading ability. Only the accuracy of the pronunciation is scored; not comprehension.

   The Numerical Operations subtest of the WIAT-II consists of a series of problems with pencil and paper for assessing the ability to reason mathematically.

   The Spelling subtest of the WIAT-II requires the student to spell a target word based on its meaning in a sentence.

   The Reading Comprehension subtest of the WIAT-II presents stories for the student to read. The student is then asked a question about the story orally, to which she must orally respond with an answer.

4. Step 4 for Writing Test Results: Report the student's standard score, classification, and percentile for each subtest. You are reiterating what is stated on the table. In these examples, you see the brief description from the examiner's manual (from Step 3), followed by a restatement of the student's performance (in italics).

   The *Word Reading* subtest of the WIAT-II presents a series of pictures and printed words for assessing decoding and word-reading ability. Only the accuracy of the pronunciation is scored; not comprehension. *On this subtest, Sally's performance was in the Low Average range, earning a standard score of 85. As indicated by her percentile rank of 16, Sally performed as well or better than 16 percent of all students when compared to the norms for her age.*

   The Numerical Operations subtest of the WIAT-II consists of a series of problems with pencil and paper for assessing the ability to reason mathematically. *On this subtest, Sally's performance was in the Very Superior range, earning a standard score of 135. As indicated by her percentile rank of 99, she performed as well or better than 99 percent of all students when compared to the norms for her age.*

   The Spelling subtest of the WIAT-II requires the student to spell a target word based on its meaning in a sentence. *On this subtest, Sally's performance was in the High Average range, earning a standard score of 110. As indicated by her percentile rank of 75, Sally performed as well or better than 75 percent of all students when compared to the norms for her age.*

The Reading Comprehension subtest of the WIAT-II presents stories for the student to read. The student is then asked a question about the story orally, to which she must orally respond with an answer. *On this subtest, Sally's performance was in the Well Below Average range, earning a standard score of 70. As indicated by her percentile rank of 2, Sally performed as well or better than 2 percent of all students when compared to the norms for her age.*

5. Step 5 for Writing Test Results: Finally, make a statement regarding something to note about the student's performance on each subtest. In the following examples, the descriptions written for steps 3 and 4 are followed by the new information, in italics.

The *Word Reading* subtest of the WIAT-II presents a series of pictures and printed words for assessing decoding and word-reading ability. Only the accuracy of the pronunciation is scored; not comprehension. On this subtest, Sally's performance was in the Low Average range, earning a standard score of 85. As indicated by her percentile rank of 16, Sally performed as well or better than 16 percent of all students when compared to the norms for her age. *An analysis of Sally's errors indicated that she often added and omitted syllables when reading words. Her reading speed was slow, and she self-corrected herself on five different words.*

The Numerical Operations subtest of the WIAT-II consists of a series of problems with pencil and paper for assessing the ability to reason mathematically. On this subtest, Sally's performance was in the Very Superior range, earning a standard score of 135. As indicated by her percentile rank of 99, she performed as well or better than 99 percent of all students when compared to the norms for her age. *Sally's performance shows a strong ability with mathematical problems. On the only two division errors that she made, her errors were due to simple miscalculations that had more to do with carelessness and rushing rather than anything else. Her scores represent a normative strength for her.*

The Spelling subtest of the WIAT-II requires the student to spell a target word based on its meaning in a sentence. On this subtest, Sally's performance was in the High Average range, earning a standard score of 110. As indicated by her percentile rank of 75, Sally performed as well or better than 75 percent of all students when compared to the norms for her age. *Analysis of Sally's errors reveals that she most often either added a single letter or omitted a single letter when misspelling words. The majority of errors were made toward the end of the subtest as the items increased in level of difficulty.*

The Reading Comprehension subtest of the WIAT-II presents stories for the student to read. The student is then asked a question about the story orally, to which she must orally respond with an answer. On this subtest, Sally's performance was in the Well Below Average range, earning a standard score of 70. As indicated by her percentile rank of 2, Sally performed as well or better than 2 percent of all students when compared to the norms for her age. *Sally made numerous errors on items that involved the skill of drawing conclusions and making inferences. She had difficulty recognizing stated detail, predicting events and outcomes, and identi-*

fying the main ideas of passages. As compared to Sally's achievement on other subtests on the WIAT-II, her standard score of 70 on the Reading Comprehension subtest represents a relative weakness for her.

Model Test Results Section.   This section presents a sample test results section for one student, Sally Jones.

Test Results:

Name of Subtest	Standard Score	Classification	Percentile Rank
Word Reading	85	Low Average	16
Numerical Operations	135	Very Superior	99
Spelling	110	High Average	75
Reading Comprehension	70	Well Below Average	2

The Word Reading subtest of the WIAT-II presents a series of pictures and printed words for assessing decoding and word-reading ability. Only the accuracy of the pronunciation is scored; not comprehension. On this subtest, Sally's performance was in the Low Average range, earning a standard score of 85. As indicated by her percentile rank of 16, Sally performed as well or better than 16 percent of all students when compared to the norms for her age. An analysis of Sally's errors indicated that she often added and omitted syllables when reading words. Her reading speed was slow, and she self-corrected herself on five different words.

The Numerical Operations subtest of the WIAT-II consists of a series of problems with pencil and paper for assessing the ability to reason mathematically. On this subtest, Sally's performance was in the Very Superior range, earning a standard score of 135. As indicated by her percentile rank of 99, Sally performed as well or better than 99 percent of all students when compared to the norms for her age. Sally's shows a strong ability with mathematical problems. On the only two division errors that she made, her errors were due to simple miscalculations that had more to do with carelessness and rushing rather than anything else. Her scores represent a normative strength for her.

The Spelling subtest of the WIAT-II requires the student to spell a target word based on its meaning in a sentence. On this subtest, Sally's performance was in the High Average range, earning a standard score of 110. As indicated by her percentile rank of 75, Sally performed as well or better than 75 percent of all students when compared to the norms for her age. Analysis of Sally's errors reveals that she most often either added a single letter or omitted a single letter when misspelling words. The majority of errors were made toward the end of the subtest as the items increased in level of difficulty.

The Reading Comprehension subtest of the WIAT-II presents stories for the student to read. The student is then asked a question about the story orally, to which she must orally respond with an answer. On this subtest, Sally's performance was in the Well Below Average range, earning a standard score of 70. As indicated by her percentile rank of 2, Sally performed as well or better than 2 percent of all students when compared to the norms for her age. Sally made numerous errors on items that involved the skill of drawing conclusions and making inferences. She had difficulty recognizing stated detail, predicting events and outcomes, and identifying the main ideas of passages. As compared to Sally's achievement on other subtests on the WIAT-II, her standard score of 70 on the Reading Comprehension subtest represents a relative weakness for her.

Section VII: Conclusions

The **Conclusions** section is probably the essence of the report. Here the examiner explains in very simple terms to the reader the trends in the child's testing results that may indicate academic strengths and weaknesses, modality strengths and weaknesses, process strengths and weaknesses, and overall diagnosis and level of severity of the problems areas indicated. It is not a restatement of the test results section but a summary of overall performance.

1. **State the name of the student, age, grade, and the reason for referral.**
   Sally Jones is a thirteen-year-old seventh grade girl who was administered the WIAT-II for the purposes of assessing her academic achievement.

2. **In the next sentence, discuss strengths.**
   Sally Jones is a thirteen-year-old seventh grade-girl who was administered the WIAT-II for the purposes of assessing her academic achievement. *The areas of spelling and mathematics (numerical operations) appear to be Sally's greatest strengths.*

3. **The next few sentences discuss weaknesses.**
   Sally Jones is a thirteen-year-old seventh grade girl who was administered the WIAT-II for the purposes of assessing her academic achievement. The areas of spelling and mathematics (numerical operations) appear to be Sally's greatest strengths. *Sally appears to have difficulties in both reading and reading comprehension. She made numerous errors on items that involved the skill of drawing conclusions and making inferences. She had difficulty recognizing stated detail, predicting events and outcomes, and identifying the main ideas of passages. Furthermore, Sally often added and omitted syllables when reading words. Her reading speed was slow and she self-corrected herself on five different words.*

4. **Add a sentence or two about behavior.**
   Sally Jones is a thirteen-year-old seventh grade girl who was administered the WIAT-II for the purposes of assessing her academic achievement. The areas of spelling and mathematics (numerical operations) appear to be Sally's greatest strengths. Sally appears to have difficulties in both reading and reading comprehension. She made numerous errors on items that involved the skill of drawing conclusions and making inferences. She had difficulty recognizing stated detail, predicting events and outcomes, and identifying the main ideas of passages. Furthermore, Sally often added and omitted syllables when reading words. Her reading speed was slow and she self-corrected herself on five different words. *Sally appears to be lacking academic self-confidence. She is frustrated by school.*

Section VIII: Recommendations

The last section of the report is probably the most valuable section for the reader—**Recommendations.** It should contain practical recommendations that will bring some hope and direction for the identified problem areas. Keep in mind that the recommendations should be practical enough and explained in such a way that the reader will have no problem following through. For example, a recommendation to a parent of "Try to spend more time with Jarmel" is useless. It provides the reader with no direction or specifics. Instead, a recommendation such as "Read at home with Jarmel in unison. By this, we mean that both you and Jarmel have the same book and read aloud together so that he receives constant auditory feedback." This more detailed recommendation provides the reader with specific direction.

Try to separate the recommendations into the following three sections:

1. Recommendations to the school: This section might contain suggestions such as further testing from other professionals on staff, vision or hearing tests by the school nurse, recommendation for a review by the Eligibility Committee, remedial reading assistance, or an ESL evaluation.

2. Recommendations to the teacher: This section should contain useful information for the teacher including an indication of the conditions under which the child learns best. The teacher is probably mainly interested in "What do I do to help the child learn?" Keep in mind that even before you begin the evaluation process, you should ask the teacher what he or she has already tried in an attempt to alleviate the problems. This should be done so that your recommendations do not include suggestions already attempted by the teacher. Doing this will avoid having your recommendations being viewed as "nothing I haven't already tried before."

3. Recommendations to the parent: This part should be very practical, direct, and diplomatic. The suggestions should also be inclusive enough to answer the questions "why" and "how" so that parents do not have to interpret them.

Finally, each subsection should contain recommendations in priority order. Try to number each recommendation separately for purposes of clarity. For examples of recommendations to the school, parents, and teachers, see the following model report.

MODEL REPORT

Personal and Confidential
Psychological Assessment for Sally Jones

Identifying Data

Name: Sally Jones

Parents: Mr. and Mrs. Paul and Mary Jones

Address: 123 ABC Dr., Anytown, NY 12345

School: Anytown Middle School

Birthdate: 8-17-92

Age: 13-10

Phone: (555) 123-1234

Grade: 7

Assessment Date: June 4, 11, and 12, 2005

Psychologist: Sandra Smith, M.S., Educational Examiner

Reason for Referral

Sally was referred for testing by her parents, Mr. and Mrs. Paul and Mary Jones, due to serious concerns about her academic performance in the grade.

Background Information

Sally Jones is currently enrolled in the 7th grade at Anytown Middle School and is in all regular education classes. She is the youngest child of Mr. and Mrs. Paul Jones. Mr. and Mrs. Jones are very active in Sally's education. They are very dedicated and concerned parents and will do anything for their daughter. They keep in constant contact with the school to check on Sally's progress.

Sally's father, Paul, is an electrical engineer and her mother, Mary, works part-time as a dental assistant. They live at home with their two other children, Bob, age 17 and Katie, age 15.

Sally is currently on the borderline of failing all her classes. She admits that she needs to try harder and does not complete her assignments. However, she also reports that many times she has trouble remembering what to do or what needs to be done.

At present, Sally appears to enjoy hanging out with friends, watching television (her favorite shows are *Survivor* and the TGIF shows on Friday night on WABC) and going online. According to Sally, her strongest subjects in school are Science and Math. Her greatest difficulties are in English (Reading) and Social Studies (understanding what she reads). She reported that she has a lot of trouble with spelling. Sally knows that she has to try harder in school. She feels as though she is a failure in so many areas.

Sally seems to make friends quite easily but has a tendency to be dramatic. She often thrives on crises and make big issues out of situations which can be solved with a more solution-oriented approach.

Behavioral Observations

Sally approached the testing situation in a very cooperative and friendly manner. She was quite polite and kind, and rapport with the examiner was easily established. She was evidently very nervous throughout testing because she felt as though this was a stupid test and that her being left back was riding on these tests. Although the examiner assured her that this was not the case, she was easily frustrated and visibly upset whenever she knew that she got an answer wrong.

During testing, Sally's attention and effort were very good. However, there were points where repetition and emphasis were needed. When new tasks or new instructions were presented, there was no difficulty adjusting or responding appropriately. However, it is very important to note that Sally had great difficulty with multidirectional tasks. She had problems organizing many tasks into separate components. She also reported that in school, she does have trouble doing this, often causing her to forget to do assignments, projects, or prepare for quizzes or exams.

Given the above-stated information, it is believed that the present scores should be viewed as adequately representing Sally's ability and level of achievement. However, all of Sally's scores may be higher than presented due to her anxiety levels and concerns about doing well.

Test and Procedures Administered

Wechsler Individualized Achievement Test–2nd ed. (WIAT-2)
Review of Cumulative Records and Previous Assessments
Clinical Interview
Behavioral Observations

Test Results:

WIAT-II

Name of Subtest	Standard Score	Classification	Percentile Rank
Word Reading	85	Low Average	16
Numerical Operations	135	Very Superior	99
Spelling	110	High Average	75
Reading Comprehension	70	Well Below Average	2

The Word Reading subtest of the WIAT-II presents a series of pictures and printed words for assessing decoding and word-reading ability. Only the accuracy of the pronunciation is scored; not comprehension. On this subtest, Sally's performance was in the Low Average range, earning a standard score of 85. As indicated by her percentile rank of 16, Sally performed as well or better than 16 percent of all students when compared to the norms for her age. An analysis of Sally's errors indicated that she often added and omitted syllables when reading words. Her reading speed was slow, and she self-corrected herself on five different words.

The Numerical Operations subtest of the WIAT-II consists of a series of problems with pencil and paper for assessing the ability to reason mathematically. On this subtest, Sally's performance was in the Very Superior range, earning a standard score of 135. As indicated by her percentile rank of 99, Sally performed as well or better than 99 percent of all students when compared to the norms for her age. Sally shows a strong ability with mathematical problems. On the only two division errors that she made, her errors were due to simple miscalculations that had more to do with carelessness and rushing rather than anything else. Her scores represent a normative strength for her.

The Spelling subtest of the WIAT-II requires the student to spell a target word based on its meaning in a sentence. On this subtest, Sally performance was in the High Average range, earning a standard score of 110. As indicated by her percentile rank of 75, Sally performed as well or better than 75 percent of all students when compared to the norms for her age. Analysis of Sally's errors reveals that she most often either added a single letter or omitted a single letter when misspelling words. The majority of errors were made toward the end of the subtest as the items increased in level of difficulty.

The Reading Comprehension subtest of the WIAT-II presents stories for the student to read. The student is then asked a question about the story orally, to which she must orally respond with an answer. On this subtest, Sally's performance was in the Well Below Average range, earning a standard score of 70. As indicated by her percentile rank of 2, Sally performed as well or better than 2 percent of all students when compared to the norms for her age. Sally made numerous errors on items that involved the skill of drawing conclusions and making inferences. She had difficulty recognizing stated detail, predicting events and outcomes, and identifying the main ideas of passages. As compared to Sally's achievement on other subtests on the WIAT-II, her standard score of 70 on the Reading Comprehension subtest represents a relative weakness for her.

Conclusions

Sally Jones is a 13-year-old seventh-grade girl who was administered the WIAT-II for the purposes of assessing her academic achievement. The areas of spelling and mathematics (numerical operations) appear to be her greatest strengths. Sally appears to have difficulties in both reading and reading comprehension. She made numerous errors on items that involved the skill of drawing conclusions and making inferences. She had difficulty recognizing stated detail, predicting events and outcomes, and identifying the main ideas of passages. Furthermore, Sally often added and omitted syllables when reading words. Sally appears to be lacking academic self-confidence. She is frustrated by school.

Recommendations to the Teachers and School

1. Help Sally with her organizational skills by speaking to her teachers about her difficulties in organization.
2. Make sure all of Sally's teachers understand her disability. All teachers should be aware of where Sally's limitations lie and do whatever is necessary to help her.
3. Do not count spelling errors when grading Sally on a project. Instead, allow her to fix her mistakes at home so that she can resubmit her work without penalty.
4. To further develop feelings of success, always design spelling problems in ascending order of difficulty.
5. Ask Sally if she understands what she has read. The fact that she has read a passage or story does not mean that she comprehends her reading.
6. Be aware that Sally has problems processing information. Therefore, allow her time to respond that is sufficient for her.
7. Maintain constant contact with Sally's parents to update them on her progress.
8. Provide Sally with a high degree of structure, and clearly explain your expectations to her.

Recommendations to Sally's Parents

1. Be patient and understand that Sally will need more time than other students her age when it comes to reading, writing, and spelling.
2. Work with Sally at home, helping her on various educational concepts that she has difficulty understanding.
3. Provide much positive reinforcement, verbal praise, and words of encouragement.

4. Help Sally deal with her frustration levels by letting her know that you will help her in any way that you can.
5. Provide Sally with any computer programs or outside materials which could benefit her learning style.
6. Think about talking to other parents whose children have a learning disability. There are many organizations available; contact the school for more information.

Sandra Smith, M.S.
Educational Evaluator

CONCLUSION

When all is said and done, the comprehensive report is perhaps the most important part of the special education process. All of the data collection, hard work, statistical analyses, and relevant information now need to be expressed to all those involved. When a report is well written, it explains everything that was found along with appropriate recommendations. As special educators, writing is a critical part of your job. Being able to express yourself clearly helps all those with whom you work. In the end, the comprehensive report should be clear, cogent, and concise. When written professionally, the reader should walk away with a complete and thorough understanding of the testing done, what was found, and the recommendations for the future.

VOCABULARY

Academic History: This section provides the reader with relevant academic performance during the child's school years.

Background History: The section of the comprehensive report that contains a very thorough description of the child's family history, developmental history, academic history, and social history.

Behavioral Observations: The fourth section of the comprehensive report, that includes a description of the child's behavior during the testing sessions. This can be a very important section because it may reinforce what is seen in the class or be very different, in which case the structure of the testing environment should be explored for clues to learning style.

Chronological Age: The age of the child at the time of testing.

Conclusions: In this section of the comprehensive report, the examiner indicates in very simple terms to the reader the trends in the child's testing results that may indicate academic strengths and weaknesses, modality strengths and weaknesses,

process strengths and weaknesses, and overall diagnosis and level of severity of the problem areas indicated.

Content Area by Content Area Approach: In the test results section, results from all the reading, math, spelling, writing, visual, auditory, and motor tests from each evaluation measure are analyzed separately by content area. The examiner hopes to establish patterns of strengths and weaknesses.

Developmental History: The purpose of this information is to give the reader any relevant background history pertaining to developmental milestones. This section need not read like a hospital report but should contain the basic developmental history.

Family History: This information provides the reader with a general understanding of the family structure, siblings, parental perceptions, and so on.

Identifying Data: The first section of a comprehensive report, which contains all the necessary basic information about the child. This section is important to the reader especially, if further contact is required. It allows the reader to have all the basic information in one place.

Reason for Referral: The second section of the comprehensive report that explains to the reader the specific reasons for this evaluation. It should not be more than two to three sentences, but should be comprehensive enough to clarify the purpose.

Recommendations: The last section of the comprehensive report and probably the most valuable section for the reader. It should contain practical recommendations that will bring some hope and direction for the identified problem areas.

Social History: This section should provide the reader with an understanding of the child in his social world. Group participation, organizations, hobbies, interests, interaction with peers, social style, and so forth should all be discussed.

Test by Test Approach: In the test results section, it analyzes the child's performance on each test separately. It analyzes the results of the different subtests and provides indications of strengths and weaknesses, manner of approach, and indications of whether the scores on the specific test should be considered valid.

Test Results: The section of the comprehensive report that analyzes the results of each test and looks at the child's individual performance on each measure.

Tests and Procedures Administered: The section of the comprehensive report that includes a simple list of the individual tests included in the test battery and any procedures used to enhance the report, such as classroom observation, review of records, parent intake.

■ ■ ■ ■ ■

CHAPTER EIGHTEEN

ELIGIBILITY PROCEDURES FOR SPECIAL EDUCATION SERVICES

KEY TERMS

Adaptive Physical Education
Annual Review
Case Manager
Change in Placement
Cooperative Educational Services
Declassification
Due Process Rights
Eligibility Committee
Eligibility Committee Packet
Evaluation Summary Sheet
Extended School Year
Full-time Special Class in a Regular School
Home/Hospital Settings
Homebound Instruction
Hospital or Institution

Impartial Hearing Officer
Inclusion Classroom
Independent Evaluation
Itinerant Services
Least Restrictive Education (LRE)
Local School District
Neighboring School District
Private Approved Schools
Regular Class Placement
Residential School
Resource Room Program
Special Class
Special Day School
State Operated Schools
Triennial Review

CHAPTER OBJECTIVES

This chapter focuses on the preparation for the presentation of the case to the Eligibility Committee, classification, and placement. After reading this chapter, you should be able to understand the following:

- Overview of the Eligibility Committee (EC)
- Members of the Eligibility Committee
- Responsibilities of the Eligibility Committee
- IDEA 2004 and Eligibility Committee meetings
- Development of the information packet for presentation to the Eligibility Committee
- Presentation at the EC by the special education teacher as educational evaluator
- Recommendations for classification

- Specific placement considerations according to IDEA 2004
- Developing the Individualized Education Plan (IEP)
- Appealing the decision of the Eligibility Committee
- Special meetings of the Eligibility Committee
- Presentation at the EC by the special education teacher as classroom teacher
- The annual review
- Suggestions for the special educator's participation in the annual review
- The triennial review
- Declassification of a child in special education

THE ELIGIBILITY COMMITTEE (IEP TEAM)

Once the evaluation process is completed by the MDT, the **Eligibility Committee** will arrange to meet to discuss the results of the evaluations and the school's recommendations. Normally, the individuals who have completed each evaluation discuss the results of the evaluations with the parents prior to the Eligibility Committee meeting. However, this is an informal process, and recommendations for classification and placement usually are not discussed because that is the responsibility of the Eligibility Committee. Formally, parents will receive a notice indicating the time and date of an Eligibility meeting.

According to IDEA 2004, every public school district is required to have an Eligibility Committee, which, as previously mentioned, may be referred to as the IEP Committee, Committee on Special Education, and so forth. If the population of special education students reaches a certain level, then more than one Eligibility Committee may be formed. Eligibility Committees are responsible for the identification of children with disabilities within the district and recommending appropriate education at public expense for students identified as having disabilities.

Members of the Eligibility Committee (EC)

This EC is usually made up of members mandated by IDEA 2004 and assigned members whom the board of education deems necessary. Most states require that certain professionals and individuals be core members. Consistent with IDEA 2004 Regulations, these members must include:

1. The parents of a child with a disability.
2. Not less than 1 regular education teacher of such child (if the child is or may be participating in the regular education environment).
3. Not less than 1 special education teacher of the child or, where appropriate, not less than 1 special education provider of such child.
4. A representative of the school district who is qualified to provide or supervise the provision of special education and is knowledgeable about the general curricu-

lum and the availability of resources in the district. This individual can also be the special education teacher, the special education provider, or the school psychologist, provided he or she meets the other qualifications.

5. An individual who can interpret the instructional implications of evaluation results. This individual can also be the regular education teacher, the special education teacher, the special education provider, the school psychologist, a direct representative, or a person having knowledge or special expertise regarding the student if that person is determined by the district to have knowledge and expertise to fulfill this role.

6. The child, where appropriate.

7. A school physician, if requested in writing by the student's parent or the district at least 72 hours prior to the meeting.

8. An additional parent member who is a parent of a student with a disability residing in the district or a neighboring district. However, the participation of this member is not required if the student's parents request that this additional parent member not participate in the meeting.

9. At the discretion of the parent or the district, other individuals who have knowledge and special expertise regarding the student, including related services personnel, as appropriate.

Responsibilities of the Eligibility Committee

The Eligibility Committee is charged with many important responsibilities both before and after a child is classified in special education. Some of the responsibilities of EC are:

During the Initial Eligibility Meeting

1. Following appropriate procedures and taking appropriate action for a child referred as having a suspected disability

2. Determining the suitable classification for a child with a suspected disability (see Chapter 1 for a detailed explanation of the possible choices for a suspected disability)

3. Reviewing and evaluating all relevant information that may appear for each student with a disability

4. Determining the least restrictive educational (LRE) setting for any child having been classified as having a disability

5. Finalizing the child's IEP

After the Child Is Classified

1. Reviewing, at least annually, the status of the child. This is known as an annual review.

2. Evaluating the adequacy of programs, services, and facilities for the child.

3. Maintaining ongoing communication in writing to parents in regard to planning, modifying, changing, reviewing, placing, or evaluating the program, classification, or educational plan of the child.

4. Advising the board of education as to the status and recommendations of the child.

5. Making sure that every three years the child is retested with a full educational and psychological battery. This is known as a triennial review.

Most Eligibility Committees try to remain as informal as possible to reduce the anxiety of the situation. This is a crucial issue, because a parent may enter a room with numerous professionals and feel overwhelmed or intimidated. The parent member usually serves as a liaison and advocate for the parent(s), establishing contact prior to the meeting to reduce anxiety and alleviate any concerns that the parent(s) may have. School personnel should also be in contact with the parent(s) prior to the meeting to go over the process, their rights, and what may take place at the meeting. At no time should anyone in contact with the parent(s) prior to the meeting give them false hope, make promises, or second guess the Eligibility Committee. What needs to be communicated are procedural issues and options, and the awareness that it is the Eligibility Committee that will make the recommendation, not one individual. Further, the parent(s) must be made aware of their rights, and you should make sure they understand their right to due process if they do not agree with the Eligibility Committee's recommendations. Making sure parents understand their rights before the meeting may reduce the possibility of conflict.

IDEA 2004 AND ELIGIBILITY COMMITTEE MEETINGS

1. IDEA 2004 makes it clear that parents have a right to participate in Eligibility Committee meetings with respect to the identification, evaluation, educational placement, and the provision of FAPE (Free and Appropriate Public Education) for their child.

2. IDEA 2004 regulations provide that a meeting does not include informal or unscheduled conversations involving school district personnel and conversations on issues such as teaching methodology, lesson plans, or coordination of service provision if those issues are not addressed in the child's IEP.

3. IDEA 2004 regulations also provide that if neither parent can participate in a meeting in which a decision is to be made relating to the educational placement of their child, the school district must either use other methods to ensure their participation, including individual conference calls or videoconferencing. The Eligibility Committee may make a placement decision without parental participation in the decision, but in such an instance the school district must have a record of its attempt to ensure parental involvement, including

- *Detailed records of telephone calls made or attempted and the results of those calls*
- *Copies of correspondence sent to the parents and any responses received*
- *Detailed records of visits made to the parents' home or place of employment and the results of those visits.*

4. IDEA 2004 regulations further require that school districts inform parents of the purpose of an Eligibility meeting and those who will be in attendance in addition to the time and location of the meeting.

5. IDEA 2004 regulations indicates that it may be appropriate for a school district to ask the parents to inform it of any individuals the parents will be bringing to an Eligibility meeting and encourage parents to do so.

DEVELOPING THE INFORMATION PACKET
FOR THE ELIGIBILITY COMMITTEE

Once the MDT has considered all the information and completed the evaluations, intakes, assessments, and so on, team members need to prepare the necessary information packet that will be presented to the district's Eligibility Committee for the review of the case for possible classification and special education programs and services. This information will be viewed by all the members of the EC along with the parents and other individuals so designated, such as an advocate or lawyer. This **Eligibility Committee packet** is a crucial part of the special education process because most of the Committee members will not be familiar with the child. The information gathered and forwarded will be used to determine the child's educational future. Therefore, it is imperative that the MDT present the most thorough and practical information to the Committee.

To facilitate the process of preparing the required documentation for presentation, the team usually designates a **case manager,** the specific individual whose responsibility it will be to gather, organize, and forward the packet to the Eligibility Committee. The case manager can be anyone, but in many cases it will be either the special education teacher or the psychologist. All districts will have their own specific forms and guidelines for presentation to the committee. However, in most of these cases the information presented, regardless of the forms, will be somewhat the same.

This section of the chapter presents an example of what the case manager may need to forward to the Eligibility Committee. It is a typical list of materials included in the eligibility packet that might be required by the committee for a review of a student for classification. These materials may vary from district to district and from state to state.

Required Forms

1. Initial referral to the MDT from school staff: The Child Study Team fills out this form when the team suspects that the child being reviewed may have an educational disability. This type of referral occurs when a child is being assessed for special education by the MDT for the very first time and usually involves children previously in the mainstream who have had no prior services. (See Chapter 7 for further explanation and example of this form.)

2. Initial referral to MDT from parent/guardian: This form is filled out if the parent makes the initial referral for assessment to the MDT for a suspected disability, which is part of the parent's **due process rights.** (See Chapter 8 for further explanation and an example of this form.)

3. Assessment plan and parent consent: This plan and form must be signed and dated by a parent prior to evaluation and is part of the parent's due process rights. (See Chapter 7 for further explanation.)

4. Social history form: This form is the result of a recent parent intake and provides the most recent pertinent background information on the child. (See Chapter 8 for further explanation and an example of this form.)

5. Medical report form: This is usually filled out by the teacher or school nurse and includes the latest medical information on the child within the last year that may be related to the child's learning problems.

6. Classroom observation form: This form is the result of an on-site visit observation by some member of the Child Study Team.

Evaluations (Initial Referral)

1. Psychological: A full psychological evaluation including all identifying data, reason for referral, background and developmental history, prior testing results, observations, tests administered, test results (including a breakdown of scaled scores), conclusions, and recommendations is required. This evaluation must be conducted within one year of the Eligibility Committee meeting. It may also be helpful to include any prior evaluations done over the years.

2. Educational: An educational evaluation including identifying data, reason for referral, academic history, prior testing results, observations, tests administered, test results, conclusions, and recommendations is required. This report should identify achievement strengths and weaknesses.

3. Speech/language: A speech/language evaluation including identifying data, reason for referral, observations, tests administered, test results, conclusions, and recommendations should be included if applicable. A description of the severity of the language deficit should also be included and, if possible, the prognosis.

4. Vocational (secondary level only): A copy of the child's Differential Aptitude Test results or other measures of vocational aptitude should be included, if applicable.

5. Other (e.g., occupational therapist, physical therapist, ESL, reading): From time to time, parents or the school will have a variety of reports from outside agencies, such as medical, neurological, psychiatric, occupational therapy screening, physical therapy screening, psychological, audiological, visual training, and so forth. These reports should be included only when they are relevant to the possible disability. If outside reports are to be used in lieu of the district's own evaluations, they should be fairly recent, within the past six months to one year.

Guidance and School Materials (Initial Referral)

1. Child's schedule: This would be a copy of the student's daily school schedule.

2. Transcript of past grades: All the child's report card grades should be attached as far back as possible, or a report indicating the patterns of grades throughout the child's school career should be included.

3. Latest report card: The most up-to-date report card should be included.

4. Teacher's reports: Teacher reports in behavioral terms should be included from all the child's teachers.

5. Standardized achievement test scores: Many schools require standardized achievement testing in certain grades. Any and all scores should be provided to reinforce historical patterns or levels of ability.

6. Discipline information: Any referrals to the principal, dean, and so on should be included as well as descriptions of incidents and disposition.

7. CST related documents (i.e., minutes): This provides the Eligibility Committee with pertinent information regarding prior intervention strategies and procedures followed prior to the referral.

8. Attendance records: Attendance patterns and records should be provided, especially if this is a recurring issue and a serious symptom.

Other Materials

Some schools also may include the following materials in a draft form. This draft becomes a working model at the Eligibility Committee meeting between the Committee and the parent, and the final version is mailed to the parent after the meeting. These may include:

1. SPAMS (Social, Physical, Academic, Management needs): In some states and school districts, a working draft copy of the child's needs should be included in the eligibility packet. These needs will provide the Committee with an idea of the environmental, educational, social, and physical requirements under which the child may learn best.

2. Draft IEP including goals and objectives: In some states and school districts, a working draft copy of the IEP is prepared prior to the Eligibility meeting. This is a basic working draft of the IEP, not the final draft, because no IEP can be finalized without parental involvement (for a more extensive explanation, see Chapter 9).

3. Testing modifications worksheet: This worksheet outlines the suggested test and classroom modifications being suggested and the supporting data for such recommendations. As discussed in Chapter 9, testing modifications are a component of the child's IEP. The modifications must be consistent with the criteria established. The worksheet may be completed by a member of the MDT or school staff to be processed as a draft recommendation for discussion at the Eligibility Committee meeting.

Depending on the state, there are usually four circumstances in which students with disabilities may be eligible to receive test modifications:

- Students with disabilities whose individualized education program includes test modifications
- Students who are declassified by the Eligibility Committee
- Students with disabilities whose Section 504 Accommodation Plan includes test modifications
- Students who acquire disabilities shortly before test administration

In making its decision regarding the need for test modifications, the EC reviews all available information regarding the student's individual needs. Such information might include recent evaluations, previous school records and IEPs, classroom observations, and the student's experience on previous tests. Information and suggestions from the student's teachers, related service providers, and parents should also be sought. Testing modifications are to be limited to specific needs of the student.

If such a determination is made by the EC and documented in the recommendation for declassification, the test modification(s) must continue to be consistently provided to the student for the balance of his or her public school education. The continuation of test modifications upon declassification, however, is not automatic. During subsequent school years, if it is felt that such modification(s) is no longer appropriate, the school staff is to meet with the student's parent to review and document the discontinuation or revision of the test modification(s).

The school principal may modify testing procedures for regular education students who experience temporary (e.g., broken arm) or long-term (e.g., paraplegic) disabilities shortly before the administration of state exams. In such cases when sufficient time is not available for the development of an IEP or 504 plan, principals may authorize testing modifications. Also, if the student is expected to continue to need test modifications, the principal should make the appropriate referral for the development of an IEP or 504 plan.

4. Extended school year worksheet: This worksheet provides the Eligibility Committee with the information and criteria necessary to make a recommendation for extended school services in July and August. At annual review meetings, parents of students with disabilities may ask for special education services during the summer (**extended school year**).

5. Extended school year criteria: Depending on the state, the law may indicate the extended school year service be considered by the Eligibility Committee when a student experiences substantial regression. Substantial regression means a student's inability to maintain developmental levels due to a loss of skill or knowledge during the months of July and August of such severity as to require an inordinate period of review at the beginning of the school year to reestablish and maintain IEP goals and objectives mastered at the end of the previous school year. For example, a teacher would project November 1 of the upcoming school year as the target date for the student to reacquire skills demonstrated at the end of the previous school year (a typical period of review or reteaching is up to 40 school days). Classroom teachers and/or service providers are expected to provide documentation (qualitative and/or quantitative) as to the evidence of regression discussion at the Eligibility Committee meeting.

An analysis of students' substantial regression, if any, may be monitored during school vacation periods (winter, spring, summer). Note the above definition includes not only regression but also an inordinate period of time to reestablish and maintain IEP goals/objectives. Extended school year services are not provided in order for students to improve their skills. Such instruction is a parent responsibility.

Extended year services may differ from services provided during the school year. The Eligibility Committee will determine the type, amount, and duration of services to be provided. Extended school year services may be provided at a different location than provided during the school year.

6. Adaptive physical education worksheet: If a child's disability prevents him or her from participating in a regular mainstreamed physical education program, then the district must provide adaptive alternatives that capitalize on the student's abilities. This worksheet outlines the criteria exhibited by the child for possible **adaptive physical education.** The behaviors, supporting reports, and data are included for the EC in order to make a recommendation. The physical education teacher in consultation with other EC staff members usually completes this. This worksheet then becomes a draft recommendation for discussion at the EC.

7. Other: This includes any other information not noted in the above categories.

In conclusion, the above forms and information will represent a picture of the child with a disability including strengths, weaknesses, recommendations, and any other information that will assist the EC in making the most educationally sound decision.

PRESENTATION TO THE EC BY THE SPECIAL EDUCATION TEACHER AS EDUCATIONAL EVALUATOR

After meeting with the parents to discuss the results, the individuals who evaluated the student must now focus on the presentation of test results at the Eligibility meeting. If your role on the MDT has resulted from your evaluation of the child, then you need to keep the following in mind:

1. Prior to the meeting, many school districts will ask that you meet with the parents and go over your results.

2. Make sure that you have your report complete and typed at least one week to ten days prior to the eligibility meeting. In some districts, the Eligibility Committee requires that the entire packet be forwarded a week in advance.

3. Prior to the meeting, outline the important points of the report that you wish to make. Do not go through the report at the Eligibility meeting looking for the issues that you feel need to be discussed. Preparation will make you look more professional.

4. Make sure you report strengths as well as weaknesses.

5. Even though everyone should have copies of your report in front of them, the length of the report may make it impossible for them to filter out the crucial sections in the time allotted for the meeting. Therefore, you may want to develop a one-page **evaluation summary sheet** that clearly outlines what you will be presenting. This would be handed out as you begin your presentation.

6. Remember that this is not a parent conference to review the entire report. You may have done that earlier and, if so, keep it brief and highlight the important issues. Several individuals may need to report results or speak, and the Committee may have several meetings that day.

7. If you feel that the nature of the case may require more time than that normally set aside by the EC for a review, then call the chairperson and make a request for a longer meeting time. It is very uncomfortable when crucial meetings have to be ended because of time constraints.

8. Prepare to answer questions about your findings or some aspect of the report by either a parent, committee member, lawyer (sometimes brought by the parent), and others. Even though this may not happen, you should be ready to answer without being defensive or anxious. Carefully looking over your report and being prepared is the best advice.

CLASSIFICATION RECOMMENDATIONS OF THE EC

In developing recommendations, all the members of the EC present will discuss the evaluations presented and any other pertinent information on the child. The first issue decided will be whether the child has an educational disability that adversely affects his or her educational performance. The EC will review the EC packet prepared by the school and ask any sitting member pertinent questions necessary to clarify the information. If in fact it is found that this is the case, the child will be classified according to the categories outlined in IDEA 2004. There are a number of classifications from which the committee draws, such as learning disabled or emotionally disturbed (see Chapter 1 for a complete description of these classifications).

The concept of **least restrictive education (LRE)** applies to the placement of students with disabilities in the most advantageous educational placement suitable for their needs. Contrary to the belief of many teachers and parents, LRE does not mean every student with a disability should be placed in a regular classroom.

LRE PLACEMENT CONSIDERATIONS ACCORDING TO IDEA 2004

A placement is the location where the special educational program will be provided. According to IDEA 2004, the requirements involving least restrictive environment are

1. In selecting the LRE for a student with a disability, school districts must consider any potential harmful effect on the child or on the quality of services that he or she needs.

2. School districts may not remove a student with a disability from education in age-appropriate regular classrooms solely because of needed modifications in the general curriculum.
3. LRE requirements apply to both nonacademic and extracurricular activities, including meals and recess periods, athletics, transportation, health services, recreational activities, special interest groups or school sponsored clubs, referral to agencies that provide assistance to individuals with disabilities and employment of students, including both employment by the public agency and assistance in making outside employment available.

IDEA 2004 regulations also indicate that

a. The determination of an appropriate placement for a child whose behavior is interfering with the education of others requires careful consideration of whether the child can appropriately function in the regular classroom if provided appropriate behavioral supports, strategies and interventions.
b. If a student's behavior in the regular classroom, even with the provision of appropriate behavioral supports, strategies and interventions, would significantly impair the learning of others, that placement would not meet her needs and would not be appropriate for that child.

The placement of students with disabilities is the responsibility of the Eligibility Committee with the input of staff and parents and final consent by the parents. This Committee must analyze all the available information and determine the best "starting placement" for the child that will ensure success and provide the child with the highest level of stimulation and experience for his or her specific disability and profile of strengths and weaknesses.

In order to accomplish this task, the Eligibility Committee has a variety of placements from which to choose, which range in levels of restriction, including class size, student-teacher ratio, length of program, and degree of mainstreaming. In the normal course of events, it is hoped that children should be placed in a more restrictive environment only if it is to their educational advantage. However, they should be moved to a less restrictive setting as soon as they are capable of being educated in that environment. The placements below follow a path from least restrictive to most restrictive.

Regular Class Placement.   **Regular class placement** is the least restrictive placement for all children. This placement alone, without some type of special education supportive services, is not suitable for a child with a disability and is usually considered unsuitable by the Eligibility Committee.

Inclusion Classroom.   **Inclusion classroom** placement involves the maintenance of the child in a regular mainstreamed classroom assisted by the presence of a second teacher who is certified in special education.

Regular Class Placement with Consulting Teacher Assistance.   A consultant teacher model is used when supportive special education services are required, but the Eligibility Committee feels that the child will be better served while remaining in the classroom rather than being pulled out for services. Because the child remains within the class, even though he or she is receiving services, this placement is considered the next LRE setting.

Regular Class Placement with Some Supportive Services.   Regular class placement with supportive services may be used for students with mild disabilities who require supportive services but can remain in the regular class for the majority of the day. The services that may be applied to this level include adaptive physical education, speech and language therapy, in-school individual or group counseling, physical therapy, and occupational therapy.

Regular Class Placement with Itinerant Specialist Assistance.   **Itinerant services** are services subcontracted by the district and provided by outside agencies. These services are usually provided for students when the disability is such that the district wishes to maintain the child in the district, but there are not a sufficient number of students with that disability to warrant hiring a teacher. An example of this may be a hard-of-hearing child who can maintain a regular class placement as long as supportive itinerant services by a teacher specializing in hearing impairments are provided.

Regular Class Placement with Resource Room Assistance.   A **resource room program** is usually provided for students who need supportive services but can successfully remain within the regular classroom for the majority of the day. This type of program is a "pullout" program, and the services are usually provided in a separate room. The student–teacher ratio with this type of service is usually 5:1, and the amount of time spent within the resource room cannot exceed 50% of the child's day.

Special Class Placement with Part Time in Regular Class.   Part-time placement is for students who need a more restrictive setting for learning, behavioral, or intellectual reasons; cannot be successful in a full-time regular class or with a pullout supportive service; but can be successfully mainstreamed (part-time participation in a regular classroom setting) for a part of the school day. The special education teacher determines the nature of the mainstream experience.

Full-Time Special Class in a Regular School.   A **full-time special class in a regular school** placement is viewed as the LRE setting for students whose disability does not permit successful participation in any type of regular class setting, even for part of the day. The students in a **special class** usually require a very structured, closely monitored program on a daily basis but not so restrictive as to warrant an out-of-district placement. These students can handle the rules and structure of a regular school building but not the freedom or style of a less restrictive setting within the school.

Special Day School Outside the School District.   A **special day school** is a type of restrictive educational setting that is a desirable placement for students whose disability is so severe that they may require a more therapeutic environment and closer monitoring by specially trained special education teachers or staff members. The child is transported by district expense to the placement, and many state policies try to limit travel time on the bus to no more than one hour.

These types of programs may have student–teacher–aide ratios of 6:1:1, 6:1:2, 9:1:1, 9:1:2, 12:1:1, or 15:1:1, depending upon the severity of the child's disability. The more severe the disability, the lower the number of student–teacher ratio. These programs can run 10 or 12 months, again depending upon the severity of the disability and the individual needs of the child.

Residential School.   **Residential school** placements are considered the next most restrictive placement. Not only does the student with a disability receive his education within this setting but also usually resides there for the school term. The nature and length of home visits depend on several factors that are usually determined by the residential school staff after evaluation and observation. For some students, home visits may not take place at all, whereas others may go home every weekend.

Some students are placed in residential placements by the court. In this case, the child's local school district is only responsible to provide the costs of the educational portion, including related services if needed.

Homebound Instruction.   **Homebound instruction** provides a very restrictive setting that is usually for students who are in the process of transition between programs and have yet to be placed. It should never be used as a long-term placement because of the social restriction and limitations. This option is also used when a child is restricted to his or her house because of an illness, injury, and so on, and this option remains the only realistic educational service until the child recovers. Homebound instruction requires an adult at home when the teacher arrives or can be held at a community center, library, or some other site deemed appropriate by the Eligibility Committee.

Hospital or Institution.   **The most restrictive setting used is a hospital or institution.** Although this is the most restrictive setting, it may be the LRE setting for certain students, such as situations of attempted suicide by an adolescent, pervasive clinical depression, or severe or profound retardation.

In conclusion, the least restrictive educational setting is not something that is etched in concrete. It is normally reviewed every year at the annual review, and changes are made in either direction should the situation warrant it.

Once the EC determines the most suitable LRE, committee members will need to determine the facility or program that best fits their decision. The following examples are types of placements that the Eligibility Committee may consider for the LRE and are listed in order of educational restriction.

Local School District.   The child's home school of the **local school district,** depending on the severity of the disability, will generally provide the types of services he or she requires. This is preferential for the many reasons previously discussed. Maintaining the child in his or her home school should be the parents' and the district's goal. This, of course, is not always possible. If not, the next step is another school in the district.

Neighboring School District.   Due to the nature of special education programs, all special education services are not offered within every district. The child's local school may arrange for participation in necessary programs and services in **neighboring school districts** if they cannot be provided within the child's home district.

Cooperative Educational Services.   **Cooperative educational service** agencies are usually set up by your state to assist local districts with the student population or specific services one or more districts could not provide themselves.

Home/Hospital Settings.   There may be times when a child needs temporary instruction at **home** or in a **hospital setting** due to severe illness or special circumstances indicated on the IEP. The key term here is *temporary*. The instruction should approximate what is offered in school within reasonable limits. Home and hospital instruction is highly restrictive; the continuing need for such services should be assessed frequently, and this service should be seen as temporary. State laws may vary on the minimum amount of educational time allotted to children involved in these services. A general guide should be two hours per day of individual instruction for a secondary student and one hour per day for an elementary-grade student.

Private Approved Schools.   School districts may place students in private schools, special act schools (schools set up by the state to provide services for a child with a disability), or residential placements approved by the State Education Department. These **private approved schools** may be located in or out of state. Students placed in such facilities have such diverse needs that the home school district may not be able to service them due to the severity of their medical, physical, mental, or emotional needs.

State Operated Schools for the Deaf, Blind, and Severely Emotionally Disturbed. These **state operated schools** are examples of educational programs that are available for students with educational needs who require a school with a special focus.

It is the responsibility of the Eligibility Committee to provide programs based on the least restrictive environment concept. Remember, it is important to provide programs that are in close proximity to the child's home (some states limit this to one hour on the bus). The child should have involvement with his or her peers without disabilities. Finally, the program must be based on the student's needs.

When considering any of the above placements, everyone works toward providing the best possible placement for the child in the least restrictive environment. However, the school district, on the other hand, needs to provide only an appropriate placement, not the best placement, in a program that is appropriate to the child's needs, as close to home as possible.

DEVELOPING THE IEP

During the meeting, the EC, along with the parent(s), should finalize the various components of the child's individualized education plan (IEP). This final draft document will then be mailed home along with the minutes of the meeting, the parents' rights, and other necessary forms for their approval. (See Chapter 19 for an extensive discussion of IEP development.)

Appealing the Decision of the Eligibility Committee

The process of identifying and finding an appropriate educational placement for a child with a disability should be a joint process between the district and the family.

Assuming that the parents agree with the Eligibility Committee's decisions, the parents will sign off on the IEP, and the child's program will begin as of the start date mandated in the IEP. When both the parents and the Eligibility Committee work in the best interests of the child, the process can be very positive and rewarding. However, there can be times when the family and the district disagree. When this occurs, the parents or the school has the right to due process. This procedure protects the rights of both the school and the family and allows for another avenue for resolution. An **impartial hearing officer** may be requested to intervene when there is a difference of opinion. This is an independent individual assigned by the district's board of education or commissioner of education to hear an appeal and render a decision. Impartial hearing officers can in no way be connected to the school district, may have to be certified (depending upon state regulations), are trained, and usually must update their skills. Although due process rights of parents to continue this appeal to the State Department of Education exist, if they disagree with the impartial hearing officer's decision, it is hoped that through a thorough understanding of the needs of the parent and the child, conflict resolution, and a positive working relationship, a solution that is acceptable to both sides can be established at the local level.

Special Meetings of the Eligibility Committee

Sometimes, the parents or Eligibility Committee will call a special meeting. This type of review can occur for several reasons and is always held for a child who has been previously classified. Among the reasons for such a meeting are:

- Change in a child's IEP
- Change in a child's program
- Declassification request
- Addition or deletion of a modification
- Parental request for an Eligibility Committee meeting
- Disciplinary concerns
- New student to district previously identified as disabled
- Referral from the building administrator

PRESENTATION TO THE EC: THE SPECIAL EDUCATION TEACHER AS CLASSROOM TEACHER

There may be times when you will be called upon to attend an Eligibility Committee meeting that has been called for one of the reasons listed above. If you are the child's classroom or special education teacher, then you should consider the following:

1. The first thing you need to do when you receive a request for your participation at a meeting is to find out the reason for the meeting. The material required may vary, but your preparation prior to the meeting is crucial. If the parents called the meeting, you may want to have them in for a conference to discuss their concerns.

2. Once you know why the meeting will be held, organize yourself so that you will have information in front of you in the following areas:

- The child's present academic levels in reading, math, spelling, and writing. These may be available as a result of recent individual or group achievement tests, informal evaluations that you may have administered, observation (although try to be more objective), class tests, and so on. Determine grade levels if possible and where the child falls in comparison to others in the class.
- The child's present pattern of classroom behavior. Write this up in behavioral terms (factual, observable, and descriptive notes of behavior that do not include analysis or judgment).
- The child's present levels of social interaction and social skills.
- The child's interest areas and areas of strength.
- The child's present schedule.
- Samples of the child's work.
- Outline of parent conferences, phone conversations, or meetings and the purpose and outcome of each. These notes should be kept on an ongoing basis.
- Your opinion as to whether the child is benefiting from his or her present placement.
- Any physical limitations noted and their implication on the learning process.
- Your opinion of the child's self-esteem.
- Any pertinent comments made by the child that may have a bearing on his or her present situation.

3. You should be well prepared to answer any questions with the above information at hand. When it is your turn to present, do so in an organized manner. You may want to provide the participants with an outline of what you will be covering.

4. Try not to be defensive, even if the reason for the meeting is the parents' concern over the child's placement in your class, the work load, or some such matter. Try to listen carefully as to what the parents are saying or really asking for. It may not be as big of a problem as you may think, and therefore, try to be solution oriented, even if the parents may be blame oriented.

THE ANNUAL REVIEW

Each year the Eligibility Committee is required to review the existing program of a child with a disability. **Annual review** meetings are required for all students receiving special instruction or related services. The required Eligibility Committee participants of an annual review meeting may include the Eligibility Committee chairperson, psychologist, special education teacher, general education teacher (if student is in general education or will receive general education services), parent of child, parent member, and student (if over 16 years of age). During this process, the Eligibility Committee will make recommendations upon review of records that will continue, change, revise, or end the child's special education program. Based on these findings, the Eligibility Committee will make adjustments to the IEP and recommendations to the board of education.

The annual review occurs within a year of initial placement and yearly thereafter. The date of the annual review should be part of the child's IEP. A parent, the child's teacher, or a school administrator may request an Eligibility Committee review at any time to determine if a **change in placement** is needed. If this occurs, the next review must be conducted within one year.

The parents are notified of the date, time, location, and individuals expected to attend their child's meeting. They will also be given a statement about their right to bring other people to the meeting. As earlier stated, parents have the same rights as at the initial Eligibility Committee meeting. They will also be notified that if they cannot attend the meeting, they will have the opportunity to participate in other ways such as through telephone calls or written reports of the annual review meeting. If necessary, they will be able to have an interpreter provided at no cost. The parents' notice of their child's annual review will include their right to have information about the planned review. They may at any time inspect their child's school files, records, and reports and make copies at a reasonable cost. If medication or a physical condition is part of the child's disability, the parent may request that a physician attend the meeting. The parent may request an **independent evaluation,** an impartial hearing, or appeal the decision from the impartial hearing to the State Review Office of the State Education Department.

In some cases, the parent may be entitled to receive free or low-cost legal services and a listing of where those services can be obtained. They also are entitled to **pendency,** having the child stay in the current educational placement during formal due process proceedings, unless both parties agree otherwise.

After the annual review, the parents will receive another notice regarding the recommendation that has been made to the board of education. A copy of their child's IEP will be sent to them indicating that their child has been recommended to continue to receive special education. The notice will also explain all factors used to make the recommendation. Again, the notice will describe the parents' due process rights.

Suggestions for the Special Educator's Participation in the Annual Review

When you attend an annual review meeting as a special educator, there are some key points that you should follow. These include:

- Suggest ways to meet the child's proposed goals and objectives as specified in the IEP.
- Discuss changes or additions for the child's upcoming program and services. Talk about what worked and what needs adjustment from your point of view.
- Present the areas in which the child showed success and significant progress.
- Discuss high school diploma and credential options, if applicable.
- Discuss need for a referral to an adult service provider—that is, state vocational rehabilitation coordinator—for services the child may need as an adult, if applicable.
- Review problems that the child has experienced or encountered throughout the year with the Eligibility Committee and parent.

- When the child is 13, you should begin to consider plans for occupational education and transition services and become very familiar with the transitional process and all the factors involved.

THE TRIENNIAL REVIEW

A child in special education will have a **triennial review** (evaluation) that occurs every three years to provide current assessment information to help determine his or her continued placement in special education. At this triennial evaluation, updated information is provided through reexamining many of the areas previously tested in the initial evaluation. The results of this evaluation, which is usually conducted by school officials, must be discussed at an Eligibility Committee meeting.

DECLASSIFYING A CHILD IN SPECIAL EDUCATION

It is the responsibility of the Eligibility Committee to declassify students previously classified with a disability who no longer meet the requirements for special education. The rationale for **declassification** is as follows:

- The child demonstrates effective compensatory skills.
- The student no longer exhibits difficulty in classroom (no classroom impact on performance) despite a process deficit and discrepancy.
- The student no longer exhibits difficulty in the classroom (performance) or a discrepancy between ability and achievement (no classroom impact) despite a process deficit.
- The student no longer exhibits difficulty in the classroom (performance) or a process deficit (no classroom impact) despite a discrepancy between ability and achievement.

Depending on the state regulations, the child who is declassified may be entitled to transition services that offer up to one year of support following the declassification. However, testing modifications can continue after the student is declassified when the student graduates from high school or receives an IEP Diploma (a diploma offered to children with disabilities who meet the criteria of their IEP but do not meet district or state standards for graduation).

CONCLUSION

The Eligibility Committee packet is a crucial piece of the special education process because it represents the culmination of gathering information, evaluations, observations, intakes, professional opinions, and recommendations necessary for the proper educational direction of a child with a suspected disability. This information will be viewed by all the members of the Eligibility Committee along with the parents and other individuals so designated, such as an advocate or lawyer. This packet is also crucial because most of the Eligibility Committee members will not be familiar with the child, and they will use the information gathered and forwarded to determine the child's educational future. Therefore, it is imperative that the MDT present the most thorough and practical information to the Eligibility Committee.

If a child is classified with a disability, several other procedures will occur in the special education process. Some of these may occur during the year, at the end of the year, or every three years. These procedures are also part of due process rights for students with disabilities and their parents. The Eligibility Committee handles many types of issues, but the three more common ones are special meetings, annual reviews, and triennial reviews. All of these meetings are for the sole purpose of protecting the rights of both the children and the parents. In the end, the Eligibility Committee plays a very significant role within the school district. An effective Eligibility Committee, working as an interdisciplinary team, can make a tremendous difference in the lives of children with disabilities. It is truly the link between the child and his or her educational future.

VOCABULARY

Adaptive Physical Education: Services provided to a child with a disability who is unable to perform the required tasks of a regular mainstreamed physical education class.

Annual Review: Reviewing, at least annually, the status of a child in special education.

Case Manager: The individual designated to collect, organize, and forward the eligibility committee packet to the administrator of the eligibility committee.

Change in Placement: Any change of educational setting from or to a public school, local special school, or state approved school.

Cooperative Educational Services: Cooperative service agencies are usually set up by your state to assist local districts with the student population or specific services one or more districts could not provide themselves.

Declassification: The process of taking a child who is currently in special education and removing his or her classification so that he or she is no longer a part of the special education program.

Due Process Rights: The rights of a child and parent in the special education process.

Eligibility Committee: The team that oversees the identification, monitoring, review, and status of all children with disabilities residing within the school district.

Eligibility Committee Packet: An organized, thorough packet of required forms and information necessary for a presentation to the Eligibility Committee of a child with a suspected disability.

Evaluation Summary Sheet: A summary of all scores and tests administered that becomes part of the Eligibility Committee packet.

Extended School Year: The determination by the Eligibility Committee of continued services through the summer to avoid regression of learning on the part of a child with a disability.

Full-Time Special Class in a Regular School: This placement is viewed as the LRE setting for students whose disability does not permit successful participation in any type of regular class setting, even for part of the day. These are students who usually require a very structured, closely monitored program on a daily basis but not so restrictive as to warrant an out-of-district placement.

Home/Hospital Settings: There may be times when a child needs temporary instruction at home or in a hospital setting due to severe illness or special circumstances indicated on the IEP. Home and hospital instruction is highly restrictive; the continuing need for such services should be assessed frequently, and this service should be seen as temporary.

Homebound Instruction: This very restrictive setting is usually provided for students who are in the process of transition between programs and have yet to be placed.

Hospital or Institution: The most restrictive setting used is a hospital or institutional setting. Although this is the most restrictive setting, it may be the LRE setting for certain students, such as situations of attempted suicide by an adolescent, pervasive clinical depression, or severe or profound retardation.

Impartial Hearing Officer: An independent individual assigned by the district's board of education or commissioner of education to hear an appeal and render a decision. These individuals can in no way be connected to the school district, may have to be certified (depending upon state regulations), are trained, and usually must update their skills.

Inclusion Classroom: This placement involves the maintenance of the child in a regular mainstreamed classroom assisted by the presence of a second teacher who is certified in special education.

Independent Evaluation: A full and comprehensive individual evaluation conducted by an outside professional or agency not involved in the education of the child.

Itinerant Services: Services subcontracted by the district and provided by outside agencies.

Least Restrictive Education (LRE): Applies to the placement of students with disabilities in the most advantageous educational placement suitable for their needs.

Local School District: The child's home school, depending on the severity of the disability, will generally provide the types of services he or she requires.

Neighboring School District: Due to the nature of special education programs, not all special education services are offered within every district. The child's local school may arrange for participation in necessary programs and services in surrounding districts if they cannot be provided within the child's home district.

Private Approved Schools: School districts may place students in private schools, special act schools (schools set up by the state to provide services for child with a disability), or residential placements approved by the State Education Department. These schools may be located in or out of state. Students placed in such facilities have such diverse needs that the home school district may not be able to service them due to the severity of their mental, physical, mental, or emotional needs.

Regular Class Placement: This placement is the least restrictive placement for all children without a disability. This placement alone, without some type of special education supportive services, is not suitable for a child with a disability and is usually considered unsuitable by the Eligibility Committee.

Residential School: Residential placements are where students receive their education within this setting and reside there for the school term. The nature and length of home visits depend on several factors that are usually determined by the residential school staff after evaluation and observation. For some students home visits may not take place at all, whereas others may go home every weekend.

Resource Room Program: A part-time supplementary instruction on an individual or small group basis outside the regular classroom for child with a disability.

Special Day School: This type of restrictive educational setting is a desirable placement for students whose disability is so severe that they may require a more totally therapeutic environment and closer monitoring by specially trained special education teachers or staff members.

State Operated Schools: These schools are examples of educational programs that are available for students with educational needs who require a school with a special focus.

Triennial Review: Under federal law, the mandated assessment battery that must be given to a child in special education every three years.

CHAPTER NINETEEN

DEVELOPMENT OF THE IEP

KEY TERMS

Academic/Educational Achievement and
    Learning Characteristics
Address of Student
Annual Goals
Assistive Technology Devices
Benchmarks
Classification
Committee on Special Education
Community Experiences
County of Residence
Credits Earned to Date
Current Grade
Date for Reevaluation
Date of Birth
Date of Eligibility
Date of Initiation of Services
Date of the Eligibility Committee/CPSE
    Meeting
Dominant Language of Parent/Guardian
Dominant Language of Student
Expected Date of High School Completion
Extended School Year Program

Gender
Individualized Education Program (IEP)
Individuals with Disabilities Education
    Improvement Act (IDEA 2004)
Instruction
Management Needs
Medical Alerts/Prescriptive Devices
Parent/Guardian Name
Participating Agency
Physical Development
Postschool Adult Living Objectives
Projected Date of Review
Race/Ethnicity Group
Related Services
Short-Term Objectives
Social Development
Street, City, Zip
Student Identification Number (ID)
Student Name
Supplementary Aids
Telephone
VESID

CHAPTER OBJECTIVES

This chapter focuses on the individualized education plan (IEP). After reading this chapter,
you should be able to understand the following:

- The purpose of an IEP
- The components of an IEP
- How to read a sample IEP
- How to interpret all parts of an IEP

IEP DEVELOPMENT

All students in special education are expected to leave school prepared to:

- Live independently
- Enjoy self-determination
- Make choices
- Contribute to society
- Pursue meaningful careers
- Enjoy integration in the economic, political, social, cultural, and educational mainstream of American society

As discussed in Chapter 18, the school district's committee on eligibility for special education services (Eligibility Committee) is charged with ensuring that each student with a disability is educated to the maximum extent appropriate in classes and programs with their peers who do not have disabilities. For school-age students with disabilities, this committee must consider the supports, services, and program modifications necessary for a student to participate in general education classes and extracurricular and nonacademic activities. In order to better ensure that this occurs, the **Individuals with Disabilities Education Improvement Act (IDEA 2004)** requires that all students in special education have an **individualized education program (IEP).**

The IEP is the blueprint for attaining improved educational results for students with disabilities. It is used to strengthen the connection between special education programs and services and the general education curriculum. The IEP serves two major purposes:

- It is a written plan for a student in special education: Simply stated, the IEP explains the specific educational objectives and placement for a particular student.
- It is a management tool for the entire assessment process: The IEP becomes the critical link between the student in special education and the special teaching that the student requires (Lerner, 1997).

Components to Be Included in the IEP

According to IDEA 2004 , the components of an IEP must include:

I) a statement of the child's present levels of academic achievement and functional performance, including—(aa) how the child's disability affects the child's involvement and progress in the general education curriculum; (bb) for preschool children, as appropriate, how the disability affects the child's participation in appropriate activities; and (cc) for children with disabilities who take alternate assessments aligned to alternate achievement standards, a description of benchmarks or short-term objectives;

II) a statement of measurable annual goals, including academic and functional goals, designed to—(aa) meet the child's needs that result from the child's disability to enable the child to be involved in and make progress in the general education curriculum; and (bb) meet each of the child's other educational needs that result from the child's disability;

III) a description of how the child's progress toward meeting the annual goals will be measured and when periodic reports on the progress the child is making toward meeting the annual goals will be provided;

IV) a statement of the special education and related services and supplementary aids and services, based on peer-reviewed research to the extent practicable, to be provided to the child, or on behalf of the child, and a statement of the program modifications or supports for school personnel that will be provided for the child—(aa) to advance appropriately toward attaining the annual goals; (bb) to be involved in and make progress in the general education curriculum in accordance with subclause (I) and to participate in extracurricular and other nonacademic activities; and (cc) to be educated and participate with other children with disabilities and nondisabled children in the activities described in this subparagraph;

V) an explanation of the extent, if any, to which the child will not participate with nondisabled children in the regular class and in the activities described in subclause (IV)(cc);

VI) (aa) a statement of any individual appropriate accommodations that are necessary to measure the academic achievement and functional performance of the child on State and districtwide assessments; and (bb) if the IEP Team determines that the child shall take an alternate assessment on a particular State or districtwide assessment of student achievement, a statement of why—(AA) the child cannot participate in the regular assessment; and (BB) the particular alternate assessment selected is appropriate for the child;

VII) the projected date for the beginning of the services and modifications described in subclause (IV), and the anticipated frequency, location, and duration of those services and modifications; and

VIII) beginning not later than the first IEP to be in effect when the child is 16, and updated annually thereafter—(aa) appropriate measurable postsecondary goals based upon age appropriate transition assessments related to training, education, employment, and, where appropriate, independent living skills; (bb) the transition services needed to assist the child in reaching those goals; and (cc) beginning not later than 1 year before the child reaches the age of majority under State law, a statement that the child has been informed of the child's rights under this title, if any, that will transfer to the child on reaching the age of majority.

IEP Requirements under IDEA

The initial draft of the IEP should be developed at the eligibility meeting by the committee members, the parent(s), and, when appropriate, the student (see Chapter 17 for a review of this material). Each student's IEP is a vital document, because it spells out the special education and related services that he or she will receive. A team that includes parents and school professionals and, when appropriate, the student develops the IEP. IDEA 2004 maintains the IEP as a document of central importance and, in the hope of improving compliance, moves all provisions related to IEP to one place in the law—Section 614(d).

Since 1990, several key changes have been made as to what information the IEP must contain and the way in which the IEP is developed. The IEP retains many familiar components from previous legislation, such as statements regarding the student's present levels of educational performance, annual goals, special education and related services to be provided, projected dates for the beginning and end of services, and transition services for youth. However, some modifications have been made to these familiar components to place more emphasis within the law on involving students with disabilities in the general curriculum and in the general education classroom, with supplementary aids and services as appropriate.

For example, "present levels of academic achievement and functional performance" must now include a statement of how the child's disability affects his or her involvement and progress in the general curriculum. Similarly, the IEP must contain a statement of special education and related services, as well as the supplementary aids and services, that the child or youth needs in order to "be involved and progress in the general curriculum and to participate in extracurricular and other nonacademic activities; and to be educated and participate with other children with disabilities and nondisabled children."

With these new IEP requirements, there is a clear intent to strengthen the connection between special education and the general education curriculum. As the Committee on Labor and Human Resources' Report (to Accompany S. 717) stated:

The new emphasis on participation in the general education curriculum is intended to produce attention to the accommodations and adjustments necessary for disabled children to access the general education curriculum and the special services which may be necessary for appropriate participation in particular areas of the curriculum (p. 20).

Along the same line, it is the requirement that the IEP include an explanation of the extent to which the student will not be participating with children without disabilities in the general education class and in extracurricular and nonacademic activities. This explanation of the extent to which the child will be educated separately is a new component of the IEP, yet it is clearly in keeping with the changes noted earlier.

Other aspects of the IEP have changed over the past 15 years. For example, each student's IEP must now include a statement of how the administration of state or district-wide assessments will be modified for the student so that he or she can participate. If the IEP team determines that the student cannot participate in such assessments, then the IEP must include a statement of (1) why the assessment is not appropriate for the child and (2) how the child will be assessed. These changes work in tandem with changes elsewhere in IDEA 2004, requiring that students with disabilities be included in state and district-wide assessments of student achievement.

Other IEP requirements are statements regarding

1. Informing the student about the transfer of rights as he or she approaches the age of majority
2. How parents will be regularly informed of their child's progress toward meeting the annual goals in the IEP
3. Where services will be delivered to the student
4. Transition service needs of the student beginning at age 14

IDEA 2004 maintains essentially the same process for developing the IEP—namely, the document is developed by a multidisciplinary team, including the parents. However, the new legislation increases the role of the general educator on the IEP team to include, when appropriate, helping to determine positive behavioral interventions and appropriate supplementary aids and services for the student.

Also added to the IEP process are "special factors" that the IEP team must consider. These factors include:

- Behavior strategies and supports, if the child's behavior impedes his or her learning or that of others
- The child's language needs (as they relate to the IEP) if the child has limited English proficiency
- Providing for instruction in Braille and the use of Braille (unless not appropriate), if a child is blind or visually impaired
- The communication needs of the child, with a list of specific factors to be considered if a child is deaf or hard of hearing
- Whether the child requires assistive devices and services

The language in the new IDEA 2004 emphasizes periodic review of the IEP (at least annually, as previously required) and revision as needed. A new, separate requirement exists: Schools must report to parents on the progress of their child with disabilities at least as frequently as progress of nondisabled children is reported, which seems likely to affect the revision process for IEPs. If it becomes evident that a child is not making "expected progress toward the annual goals and in the general curriculum," the IEP team must meet and revise the IEP.

The new legislation specifically lists a variety of other circumstances under which the IEP team would also need to review and revise the IEP, including the child's anticipated needs, the results of any reevaluation conducted, or information provided by the parents. The requirements for providing transition services for youth with disabilities have been modified in IDEA 2004 (see Chapter 20 for a detailed discussion on transition services).

Understanding the IEP

When writing an IEP, it is very important to remember that it is being written for both administrators and parents. Therefore, be sure that it is:

- Clear and concise
- User-friendly
- A working document
- A reflection of the abilities of the student
- A document that involves the parents and school personnel in the student's education

Now, we take you through a sample IEP. Each section will be a model of what an IEP can look like, and we then explain that section in detail. IEPs differ from state to state and even from district to district. Therefore, the sample IEP used here may be a little different in format than what your school district uses. However, the areas covered will be similar, if not exactly the same. As this is done, it is important to realize a few important points:

- Some sections of the sample IEP apply only to students who are age 14 and older. These sections will be designated as we go along.
- The term *committee* is used to designate the state's committees for special education eligibility (i.e., EC, **Committee on Special Education,** Multidisciplinary Team, Eligibility Team, Multifactor Team). These teams are responsible for children 3 to 21 years of age.
- Some districts separate responsibilities by having separate teams for ages 3 to 5 (i.e., Committee on Preschool Special Education, or CPSE) and 5 to 21 (those listed above).
- Additional space may be added to any section of the sample IEP to meet the needs of the student. Because the number of goals is determined by the needs of the student, space for additional goals may be added.

SAMPLE IEP

Section 1—Background Information

School District/Agency: _____

Name and Address: _____

Individualized Education Program

Date of Eligibility Committee/CPSE Meeting: _____

Purpose of Meeting: _____

Student Name: _____

Date of Birth: _____   **Age:** _____

Street: _____   **County of Residence:** _____

City: _____   **Zip:** _____   **Telephone:** _____

Male _____   **Female** _____   **Student ID#:** _____   **Current Grade:** _____

Dominant Language of Student: _____

Interpreter Needed: Yes _____   No _____

Racial/Ethnic Group of Student:
(optional information)
        American Indian or Alaskan Native _____

        Black (not of Hispanic origin) _____

White (not of Hispanic origin) ——————

Asian or Pacific Islander ————————

Hispanic ———————————————

Date of Initiation of Services: ————   **Projected Date of Review:** ——————

Date of Eligibility: ————   **Date for Reevaluation:** ——————

Medical Alerts: ————————————————————————

Mother's Name/Guardian's Name: ——————————————————

Street: ——————————   **County of Residence:** ——————————

City: ——————————   **Zip:** ————   **Telephone:** ——————

Dominant Language of Mother/Guardian: ————————————————

Interpreter Needed: Yes ————   No ————

Father's Name/Guardian's Name: ——————————————————

Street: ——————————   **County of Residence:** ——————————

City: ——————————   **Zip:** ————   **Telephone:** ——————

Dominant Language of Father/Guardian: ————————————————

Interpreter Needed: Yes ————   No ————

Explanation of Section 1—Background Information

Date of the Eligibility Committee/CPSE Meeting: The date the committee meeting occurred.

Purpose of Meeting: The Eligibility Committee, Subcommittee on Special Education, or Committee on Preschool Education (Eligibility Committee/ Committee on Preschool Special Education) meeting may be conducted to address several purposes. The type of meeting may be an initial review, an annual review, a review of reevaluation results, or a request for review by the student's parent or teacher, and should be noted accordingly.

Student Name: The full name of the student should be noted.

Date of Birth: Student's birth date.

Age: The age of the student on the date of the meeting.

Address of Student: Legal address and phone number of the student.

County of Residence: The county in which the parent(s) and student reside.

Gender: Male or female.

Student Identification Number (ID): The ID number may be the student's social security number or a number assigned by the school.

Current Grade: For school-age students, the current grade is designated as of the date of the committee meeting. Students with disabilities who are participating in instruction based on the general education curriculum should have a grade designation, which generally is the grade in which the student would be enrolled if the student did not have a disability. For all other students, the term *ungraded* should be noted.

Dominant Language of Student: For a student who is deaf or hearing impaired or whose native language is other than English, specify the language or mode of communication used with the student. The committee must arrange for an interpreter if needed for the student to participate meaningfully in developing the IEP.

Race/Ethnic Group of Student: Listing the race/ethnicity of the student is optional.

Date of Initiation of Services: The date when this IEP is to be implemented.

Projected Date of Review: The date when review of this IEP is expected.

Date of Eligibility: The date when the student was first identified as a student with a disability and eligible for special education programs and services.

Date for Reevaluation: The date when the next reevaluation of the student is expected to occur. Reevaluations must occur at least every three years.

Medical Alerts/Prescriptive Devices: Any information that should be readily available to all teachers and other appropriate school personnel, such as medications or specific health-related conditions requiring either constant or intermittent care by a qualified individual (e.g., eyeglasses, hearing aids, and allergic reactions).

Parent(s)/Guardian's Name: The names of the parent(s) or the name of a guardian, if appropriate.

Street, City, and Zip: If the address of a parent(s)/guardian is different from the student's address, both addresses should be indicated, when appropriate.

Telephone: If appropriate, the telephone numbers of parent(s)/guardian should be indicated.

County of Residence: The county(ies) in which the parent(s) resides.

Dominant Language of Parent(s)/Guardian: For parent(s)/guardians who are deaf or hearing impaired or whose native language is other than English, specify the language or mode of communication used by the parent(s). The committee must ensure that the parent(s)/guardian understands the proceedings of the committee meeting and must arrange for an interpreter if needed for the parent(s)/guardian to participate meaningfully in developing the IEP.

Section 2—Present Levels of Performance and Individual Needs

1. Academic/Educational Achievement and Learning Characteristics: Address current levels of knowledge and development in subject and skill areas, including activities of daily living, level of intellectual functioning, adaptive behavior, expected rate of progress in acquiring skills and information, and learning style.

Present Levels: **Academic development**

Desmond is currently functioning below his chronological age in the area of academic ability.

Present Levels: **Cognitive ability**

Desmond is currently functioning at his chronological age in the area of cognitive ability.

Present Levels: **Language ability**

Desmond is currently functioning below his chronological age in the area of language development.

Desmond is currently functioning below his chronological age in the area of receptive development.

Desmond is currently functioning below his chronological age in the area of pragmatic/social speech development.

Abilities: Desmond understands multistep directions.

Needs: None

Present Levels: **Learning style**

Desmond has a multisensory learning style.

Present Levels: **General**

Given Desmond's functional level, his disability affects his involvement and progress in the general education program.

Desmond models math/goal skills only with teacher support.

Desmond is able to perform language arts goals/skills independently with minimal support.

Present Levels: **Rate of Progress**

Desmond's rate of progress is below average.

Desmond reads on or above grade level.

Desmond's computational skills impact the ability to perform general education at his grade level.

Abilities: Desmond is able to read and follow written directions.

Needs: Desmond requires an individualized and/or small group for instruction in math.

Desmond needs to develop self-monitoring skills as a means of avoiding carelessness and of focusing attention to detail (copying homework assignment, completing classwork).

   2. Social Development: Describe the quality of the student's relationships with peers and adults, feelings about self, social adjustment to school and community environments, and behaviors that may impede learning.

Present Levels: **Social Interaction with Peers**

Desmond is presently functioning below his chronological age in the area of social development.

Abilities: Desmond has developed some friendships.

(continued)

Needs: Desmond needs to relate appropriately to peers in the classroom.

Desmond needs to relate appropriately to adults in the classroom.

Desmond needs to relate appropriately to adults outside the classroom.

Desmond needs to learn how to communicate effectively in social situations.

Present Levels: Feelings about Self
Desmond is currently functioning below his chronological age level with regard to feelings about himself.

Abilities: Desmond identifies himself as an individual.

Needs: Desmond needs to develop positive self-concept.

Present Levels: School/Community
Desmond is currently functioning below his chronological age level with regard to school and community.

Abilities: Desmond initiates social interactions with adults.

Needs: Desmond needs to respond to adult intervention.

Desmond needs to respond to adult praise.

Present Levels: Adjustment to School/Community
Desmond does not display appropriate social adjustment to school, family, and/or community environment skills.

Abilities: Desmond can adapt to changes in routine.

Needs: Desmond needs guidance to participate in small groups.

Desmond needs to take initiative in social situations.

3. Physical Development: Describe the student's motor and sensory development, health, vitality, and physical skills or limitations that pertain to the learning process.

Present Levels: Desmond has ADHD medical diagnosis, which impacts learning—see health file.

Abilities: Desmond may participate in all school activities.

Needs: Desmond needs to develop skills required to sit independently.

Desmond needs to improve attending skills when visual distractions are present.

4. Management Needs: Describe the nature of and degree to which environmental modifications and human or material resources are required to address academic, social, and physical needs.

A functional behavioral assessment should be completed for any student who demonstrates behaviors that impede learning. A functional behavioral assessment becomes the basis for positive behavioral interventions, strategies, and supports for the student.

Present Levels: Desmond has moderate management needs to address academic goals.

Desmond has moderate needs to address social goals.

Desmond has no management needs to address physical goals.

Abilities: Desmond is able to perform effectively and complete tasks in the classroom environment with the assistance of additional personnel.

Needs: Desmond needs full-time general education placement with moderate support through special education.

Explanation of Section 2—Present Levels of Performance and Individual Needs

The IEP must describe the student's present levels of educational performance, including the student's abilities and needs. Present levels of performance are based on relevant functional and developmental evaluation information, including information provided by the parent. Many tests and assessment procedures are used to obtain information about a student's present levels of performance.

Present levels of performance must include a statement that explains how the student's disability affects his or her involvement and progress in the general education curriculum. The committee uses this information to determine a student's eligibility for special education, the specific classification, annual goals and objectives, and the specific type and extent of special education programs and services. The committee must assess present levels of performance and individual needs in the following areas:

Academic/Educational Achievement and Learning Characteristics: The levels of knowledge and development in subject and skill areas, including activities of daily living, level of intellectual functioning, adaptive behavior, expected rate of progress in acquiring skills and information, and learning style are addressed. Performance in subject areas should be based on the student's ability in relation to the learning standards and performance indicators established for all students.

Social Development: The degree and quality of the student's relationships with peers and adults, feelings about self, and social adjustment to school and community environments are explained.

Physical Development: The degree or quality of the student's motor and sensory development, health, vitality, and physical skills or limitations that pertain to the learning process, including pertinent information from the student's physical examination are noted.

Management Needs: The nature of and degree to which environmental modifications and human or material resources are required to enable the student to benefit from instruction are discussed.

Section 3—Long-Term Adult Outcome Statement

Long-Term Adult Outcomes: Beginning at age 14, or younger if appropriate, state long-term adult outcomes reflecting student's needs, preferences, and interests in:

Postsecondary Education/Training:
Desmond anticipates receiving the following postsecondary education/training:

Desmond will attend college.

The transition service needs of Desmond to meet long-term adult outcomes are:

Desmond will receive guidance/career counseling.

Desmond will take college entrance courses.

Desmond will take Regents courses.

Employment: *NA*

Community Living: *NA*

Explanation of Section 3—Long-Term Adult Outcome Statement

The IEP must include a long-term adult outcome statement related to the student's individual needs, preferences, and interests for adult employment, postsecondary education, and community living. At age 14, federal law requires that the IEP include a statement of the transition services needs of the student that focuses on the student's courses of study, such as advanced-placement courses or an occupational education program. The IEP must reflect the full array of transition service needs in instruction, related services, community experiences, development of employment, and other **postschool adult living objectives,** including, as appropriate, acquisition of daily living skills and a functional vocational evaluation.

The long-term adult outcome statements establish clear expectations for the school, the student, the student's family, and any agencies participating in planning and implementing the transition programs and services in the IEP. These statements are the basis for planning the student's movement from school to postschool activities and for discussion with appropriate public and private community agencies regarding their contributions to the student's transition process.

Once the statements are established, annual goals and objectives and other activities can be developed to help the student incrementally develop skills, experiences, and contacts with resources, as needed, to work toward these desired adult outcomes. Vocational rehabilitation counselors from the Office of Vocational and Educational Services for Individuals with Disabilities (**VESID**), in consultation with the student, parents, and school personnel, can provide advice on long-term adult outcomes, including appropriate vocational assessments, postsecondary services, and selection of employment goals for students who meet vocational rehabilitation eligibility criteria.

Section 4—Measurable Annual Goals and Short-Term Instructional Objectives

Annual Goal: *Desmond will maintain and improve study skill levels.*

Short-Term Instructional Objective	Evaluation Procedures	Evaluation Schedule
1. *Improve work habits and study skills* 2. *Organize material including classwork, major assignments, and homework*	*Classroom teacher contact*	*Quarterly*

Annual Goal: *Desmond will successfully complete academic course requirements.*

Short-Term Instructional Objective	Evaluation Procedures	Evaluation Schedule
1. *Incorporate writing process strategies*		
2. *Improve math computation*	*Quizzes, tests*	*Quarterly*

Annual Goal: *Desmond will increase attentiveness and concentration skills.*

Short-Term Instructional Objective	Evaluation Procedures	Evaluation Schedule
1. *Develop necessary behaviors, attitudes, and observation, expectations that will lead to self-growth*	*Teacher contact*	*Quarterly*
2. *Learn to express feelings, both positive and negative*		

Explanation of Section 4—Measurable Annual Goals and Short-Term Instructional Objectives

Annual goals are statements, in measurable terms, that describe what the student can reasonably be expected to accomplish within a 12-month period. There must be a direct relationship between the annual goals and the present levels of performance. Annual goals focus on addressing needs resulting from the disability so that the student can appropriately participate in the general curriculum. The committee should consider goals from all areas of the student's individual needs, including those associated with behavior and long-term adult outcomes, where appropriate. The following criteria of annual goals should be considered:

- Should be determined from the abilities and needs of the student as described in the present levels of performance
- Should focus on offsetting or reducing the learning or behavioral problems resulting from the student's disability
- Should focus on meeting the special education needs of the student
- Must be written in measurable terms

Short-Term Objectives or Benchmarks. After the Eligibility Committee has developed measurable annual goals, they must develop **short-term objectives** or **benchmarks** relating to each annual goal. Short-term objectives are measurable, intermediate steps between the present levels of performance and the annual goals. Benchmarks are major milestones between the present levels of performance and the annual goals.

Short-term objectives and benchmarks are based on a logical breakdown of the major components of the annual goals and can serve as milestones to determine the extent to which the student is progressing to meet the annual goals. Short-term objectives provide a mechanism to determine the extent of the student's progress during the year, to ensure the IEP is consistent with the student's instructional needs, and to revise the IEP, if appropriate.

The following criteria for short-term objectives and benchmarks should be considered:

- Must be written in measurable terms
- Must include evaluative criteria specified in such a way that they can be measured
- Must specify evaluation procedures such as systematic observation, teacher-made tests, informal tests or graphs, and work samples
- Must include a schedule to measure progress toward the annual goal

Section 5—Special Education Programs and Related Services/Program Modifications

1. **Special Education Programs/**

Related Services	**Initiation Date**	**Frequency**	**Duration**
In-school counseling	*September 2005*	*1 × a week*	*45 min.*

2. **Extended School Year Programs/Services**   Yes _____   No _____

3. **Supplementary Aids and Modifications or Supports**

	Initiation Date
For the Student	
Modification of curriculum	*September 2005*
Extra time between classes	*September 2005*
Calculator	*September 2005*

4. **Describe any assistive technology devices or services needed:**

   Given Desmond's functional level, he does not need assistive technology services and devices in order to have an equal opportunity to succeed academically.

5. **Describe the program modifications or supports for school personnel that will be provided on behalf of the students to address the annual goals and participation in general education curriculum and activities:**

   School staff will be provided with information on a specific disability and implications for instruction for Desmond.

6. **A. Individual Testing Modification(s):**

   Desmond requires time and a half to complete standardized tests.
   Desmond requires double time to complete classroom tests.
   Desmond requires tests to be administered in a small group in a separate location.
   Desmond will have tests administered in a location with minimal distractions.

   B. State why the student will not participate in a state or district-wide assessment: _____

   C. Explain how the student will be assessed:

   _____

Explanation of Section 5—Special Education Programs and Related Services/Program Modifications

The IEP must indicate the special education programs and related services, supplementary aids and services, assistive technology devices, and program supports or modifications that are to be provided to the student or on behalf of the student.

Special Education Programs.   Special education means specially designed individualized or group instruction or special programs or services to meet the individual needs of students with disabilities. Specially designed instruction ensures access of the student to the general curriculum so the student can meet the educational standards that apply to all students.

The IEP must indicate the type of program or service (e.g., special class, consultant teacher, resource room, related service), the initiation date, frequency (the number of times per week a service will be provided), duration (number of minutes per session), and location (e.g., general education class, separate location) for each special education program and service. The IEP must describe the special class size, if appropriate. If the student needs direct and/or indirect consultant teacher services, the IEP should indicate the general education classes, including occupational education, in which the student will receive such service. The location where special education and related services will be provided to a student may influence decisions about the nature and amount of these services and when they should be provided. For example, the appropriate location for the related service to be provided may be the regular classroom or a separate location.

Related Services.   These are school-based services that the child with a disability will be receiving that provide support for him or her and enhance educational performance. Examples of related services include but are not limited to:

In-school individual counseling: When this service is recommended on an IEP, it usually means that the child would benefit from a more intimate therapeutic situation with emphasis on control, insight, cause and effect awareness, special attention, and developing a trusting relationship with an authority figure. Although some children need only individual counseling, others might move from individual to group to try out the insights and experiences learned from the individual experience.

In-school group counseling: When this service is recommended on an IEP, it means that the child would benefit from a group situation that emphasizes interpersonal relations, social skills, cooperative play and interaction, interdependence, social delay of gratification, peer feedback, and social connections. The group usually meets once or twice a week and many times may be combined with individual in-school counseling.

Resource room: This service is recommended when the Eligibility Committee feels that the child would benefit from extra academic assistance depending on the recommendations of the diagnostic evaluation, IEP recommendation, and teacher observation. This assistance might involve remediation, compensation, or survival skills depending on the age and grade of the child. Most children will be recommended for a minimum of three hours per week (divided as needed) to a maximum of 50% of the child's school day.

Speech/language therapy: This service is recommended when the Eligibility Committee feels that the child's poor performance is directly related to disabilities in language or speech development. The emphasis with this service might include remediation in expressive or receptive language, articulation, voice disorders, fluency disorders, and so on. These services may be administered in small group or individual settings. This recommendation can also be made in conjunction with some other service such as resource room, if indicated.

Physical therapy and occupational therapy: The Eligibility Committee usually makes this recommendation when the child is suffering from some physical or motor impairment. Physical therapists usually provide exercise therapy and special devices to improve the total physical functioning and strength of a student with a disability. Generally, occupational therapists focus more on fine-motor skills such as hand control, using the mouth to chew, and any other factor involved in daily living skills.

Art therapy: This recommendation, although not as common as some other services, is usually recommended when the Eligibility Committee feels that the production of art in its various forms would have beneficial qualities for exceptional students. Major factors involved in this recommendation include the opportunity for the child with a disability to express creativity, to improve fine-motor skills, and to develop appropriate leisure-time activities.

Adaptive physical education: This service is usually recommended when the Eligibility Committee feels that the general physical development of a child with a disability is impaired or delayed. When these programs are instituted, they tend to have a therapeutic orientation. The teachers utilized for this service must have special training in the use of specialized equipment to improve muscle development and coordination.

Music therapy: This recommendation may be made by the Eligibility Committee when it feels that music can be used to prompt the development of various functional behaviors for students with disabilities such as motivation, improvement of speech, language, and communication skills through singing.

Extended School Year Programs and Services. Some students may require special education services during the months of July and August to prevent substantial regression. Substantial regression means a student's inability to maintain developmental levels due to a loss of skill or knowledge during the months of July and August of such severity as to require an inordinate period of review at the beginning of the school year to reestablish and maintain IEP goals and objectives mastered at the end of the previous school year. The Committee should consider **extended school year programs** for those students

- Whose management needs are determined to be highly intensive, who require a high degree of individualized attention and intervention, and who are placed in special classes
- With severe multiple disabilities, whose programs consist primarily of rehabilitation and treatment, and who are placed in special classes
- Who are recommended for home and hospital instruction, whose special education needs are determined to be highly intensive, who require a high degree of individualized attention and intervention, or who have severe multiple disabilities and require primarily rehabilitation and treatment
- Whose needs are so severe that they can be met only in a seven-day residential program
- Receiving other special education services who, because of their disabilities, exhibit the need for special service and/or program provided in a structured learning environment of up to 12 months' duration in order to prevent substantial regression

The Committee must specifically state the initiation date, frequency, duration, and location of services the student is to receive during July and August. In addition, the IEP must indicate the provider of such services.

An IEP developed for an extended school year program may differ from the IEP developed for the school year program. The Eligibility Committee determines the type and amount of services that a student needs for an appropriate extended school year program. The IEP developed for the extended school year program should focus on the areas in which the student is expected to experience substantial regression. The Eligibility Committee must determine the least restrictive environment required for the student to benefit from special education services during July and August. Extended school year programs or services may be provided in a location that differs from the one the student attends during the school year, provided the Eligibility Committee determines that the setting is appropriate for the student to benefit from the special education services and to meet the IEP goals.

Supplementary Aids and Services and Program Modifications or Supports. **Supplementary aids** and services and/or program modifications or supports means aids, services, and other supports that are provided in general education classes or other education-related settings to enable students with disabilities to be educated with students without disabilities to the maximum extent appropriate in the least restrictive environment. Examples of supplementary aids and services include:

- A note taker
- Written materials in Braille format
- Extra time to go between classes
- Modification of curriculum
- Special seating arrangements

Providing modifications to students with suspected disabilities must be substantiated and documented by evidence within the testing results. Although these criteria may vary from district to district, examples that may be used to determine the type of modification recommended are listed below:

Flexible Scheduling.   Flexible scheduling is usually applied to students who may have problems in the rate in which they process information, for example, physical disabilities such as motor or visual impairments. Examples of modifications that fall under this category include:

- Time extensions on tests
- Administration of a test in several sessions during the course of the day
- Administration of a test in several sessions over several days

The documentation required to make this recommendation should include evidence of at least one of the following:

1. Slow processing speed
2. Slow psychomotor speed
3. Severe anxiety

Flexible Setting.   Flexible setting is a modification that allows students with disabilities to take a test in a setting other than a regular classroom. This may become necessary in cases in which a child has health impairments and may be unable to leave home or the hospital, where a child's disability interferes with his or her remaining on task, or a child is easily distracted. In other cases, a student with a disability may require special lighting or acoustics or a specially equipped room. Examples include:

- Individual administration of a test in a separate location
- Small group administration of a test in a separate location
- Provisions for special lighting
- Provisions for special acoustics
- Provision for adaptive or special furniture
- Administration of test in a location with minimal distractions

The documentation required to make this recommendation should include evidence of one of the following:

1. Students with serious attentional difficulties
2. Students who are easily distracted and have difficulty remaining on task due to processing difficulties, anxiety, and so on.

Revised Test Format.   A revised test format is utilized by students whose disability may interfere with their ability to take a test using the standard test format, for example, students with visual or perceptual disabilities who may not be able to read regular-size print. Examples include:

- Use of a large print edition
- Increased spacing between items
- Reduction in the number of items per page
- Use of a Braille edition
- Increase of the size of answer bubbles on test answer forms
- Rearrangement of multiple-choice items with answer bubble right next to each choice

The documentation required to make this recommendation should include evidence of visual-perceptual processing deficits that would cause difficulty transferring answers onto a machine scorable booklet or sheet.

Revised Test Directions.   Revised test directions allow students with certain disabilities a greater chance of understanding directions and thereby successfully completing a test. Examples include:

- Have directions read to child
- Reread the directions for each page of questions
- Simplify the language in the directions
- Provide additional examples

The documentation required to make this recommendation should include evidence of at least one of the following:

1. Students who have documented reading comprehension skills below the 25th Percentile on standardized tests
2. Documented language processing deficits
3. Significant receptive language weaknesses

Use of Aids.   Some students with disabilities—for example, children with hearing impairments—require the use of aids in order to interpret test items. These may include:

- Auditory amplification devices
- Visual magnification devices
- Auditory tape of questions
- Masks or markers to maintain the student's place on a page
- Having questions read to the student
- Having questions signed to the student

The documentation required to make the recommendation for use of a word processor or a scribe (individual who copies notes for the child) should include evidence of one of the following:

1. Documented graphomotor deficits
2. Documented written language deficits significantly below current grade level

The documentation required to make the recommendation of the opportunity to record answers in any manner should include evidence of one of the following:

1. Documented graphomotor deficits
2. Documented written language deficits significantly below current grade level

The documentation required to make the recommendation of not being penalized for spelling errors should show evidence of one of the following:

1. Below 25th percentile on standardized tests
2. A 50% discrepancy between aptitude and spelling achievement score on standardized tests

Revised Format.   Some students with disabilities may be unable to record their responses to test questions on conventional answer forms and as a result may require a change in the test format. These may include:

- Recording answers directly in the test booklet
- Increasing the spacing between questions or problems

- Increasing the size of the answer blocks
- Providing cues (stop sign, arrows) directly on the answer form

The documentation required to make the above recommendations should show evidence of visual–perceptual processing deficits that would cause difficulty transferring answers onto a machine scorable booklet or sheet or with other tasks involving visual discrimination or spatial difficulties.

Testing Modifications.   When making testing modification recommendations for a student, remember the following:

- Testing modifications are to give students the same opportunities as their peers. They are not designed to achieve the identical result or give an unfair advantage to students with disabilities.
- Testing modifications should *not* be excessive. They should alter standard administration to the least extent possible.
- Testing modifications may allow a student access to higher-level classes.
- Higher scores are *not* reasons for giving test modifications.
- Testing modifications are to be specific.
- Students should have to take state exams and the IEP must indicate why a student is exempted from them, if necessary. Only IEP-diploma-bound students may be exempted from certain tests.
- It is the building principal's responsibility to ensure that test modifications are correctly implemented.
- Diagnostic evaluations (newly referred students) do not require test modifications. Administration of test modifications is at the discretion of the examiner.
- If a student refuses to utilize a test modification, it should be documented and if necessary be eliminated from the IEP.
- The principal, as well as all teachers of appropriate students, should receive information on test modifications.
- Students should not be counseled toward more restrictive career objectives because they have disabilities.
- The general education teacher *must* administer test modifications as described in the IEP.

THE ONLY STUDENTS ALLOWED TO HAVE MODIFICATIONS ARE

1. Students with disabilities
2. Declassified students (until graduation or before if no longer appropriate)
3. Students (same as classified) with accommodation plans
4. Students who acquire short-term disabilities shortly before the test

Specialized Equipment or Assistive Technology Devices and/or Services.   The IEP must describe any specialized equipment and adaptive devices needed for the student to benefit from education. IDEA 2004 requires each school district to ensure that assistive technology devices and/or services are made available to a preschool or school-age student with a disability as part of the student's special education, related services, or supplementary aids or services as described in the IEP. **Assistive technology devices** are any item, piece of equipment, or product system—whether acquired commercially off the shelf, modified, or customized—that is used to increase, maintain, or improve the functional capabilities of a child with a disability.

A school district is not responsible to make available, through purchase or rental, devices that a student would require only for nonschool settings or activities. In addition, the district would not, unless specifically stated in the IEP, have to provide items that a student routinely would require for daily life functions regardless of the setting (e.g., wheelchair, hearing aid, or some prosthetic or orthotic devices) that are prescribed by a licensed physician. If a student requires assistive technology to meet the IEP goals and objectives or to participate in the general education curriculum or classes, the committee must consider who will be responsible for day-to-day maintenance as well as developing a contingency plan to provide repairs, replacements, or backup equipment.

Program Modifications or Supports for School Personnel on Behalf of the Student.   The IEP must describe the program modifications or supports for school personnel that will be provided on behalf of the student to address the student's annual goals and participation in general education curriculum and activities. Examples of modifications or supports that may be provided for school personnel are:

- Information on a specific disability and implications for instruction
- Training in use of specific positive behavioral interventions
- Information on the need for special placement of the student within the classroom
- Training in the use of American Sign Language

Individual Testing Modifications Required, Nonparticipation in a State or District-Wide Assessment, and How the Student Will Be Assessed

1. Individual testing modifications: The IEP must indicate the testing modifications. Test modifications must be clearly stated to ensure a consistent understanding by the committee, the principal, the teacher(s), the student, and the parents. Specific test modifications (e.g., use of word processor with a spell-check function) should be indicated, not generic test modification categories (e.g., answers recorded in another manner). It is appropriate to indicate the conditions or nature of tests that will require test modifications (e.g., use of a note taker for tests having answer sheets requiring answers to be blackened); however, qualifying terms such as *as appropriate* or *when necessary* should not be used on the IEP.

2. Statement of nonparticipation in a state or district-wide assessment and how the student will be assessed: The Committee must consider the far-reaching effects of nonparticipation in a particular state or district-wide assessment of student achievement (or part of such an assessment) before determining that a student will not participate in the assessment. If the Committee determines that the student will not participate in a particular state or district-wide assessment, the IEP must contain a statement of why that assessment is not appropriate for the student. In addition, the IEP must indicate how the student will be assessed.

Section 6—Participation in General Education Classes, Nonacademic and Extracurricular Activities

Explain the extent of participation in general education programs and extracurricular and other nonacademic activities including physical education or adaptive (adapted) physical education and occupational education (if appropriate). Explain the extent, if any, to which the student will not participate with students without disabilities in the regular class and in other activities.

Desmond will participate in all general education classes with support personnel.

If the student is exempt from the second language requirement, explain why.

Desmond will be exempt from foreign language requirements due to the following reasons: Desmond exhibits a significant discrepancy between verbal and performance areas on IQ testing, in which the profile suggests significant verbal difficulties, and exempts Desmond from participation in a required second language course.

Explanation of Section 6—Participation in General Education Classes, Nonacademic and Extracurricular Activities

IDEA 2004 presumes that all students with disabilities are to be educated in general education classes. The IEP must explain both how the student will participate in general education classes, programs, and activities and the extent to which, if any, the student will not participate in such classes, programs, and activities with peers without disabilities. For preschool students, the Committee must explain why the student will not participate in age-appropriate activities with peers without disabilities.

The IEP must specifically indicate how the school-age student will participate in general education programs, including:

- Physical education or adaptive (adapted) physical education
- Occupational education, if appropriate
- Second language instruction
- Nonacademic activities
- Extracurricular activities

All students are expected to participate in the second language requirement unless specifically exempted by the Committee. The Committee must explain why the student is exempt from the second language requirement.

Students with severe disabilities can also benefit from participation in general education classes and activities with appropriate supports to them and their teachers.

In determining the placement of a student with severe disabilities, the Committee must determine whether to require the assistance of supplementary aids and services. Only upon determining that such goals and objectives cannot be achieved in a general education classroom, with supports and services, should the student be educated in an alternative placement. Moreover, the Committee should also consider the nonacademic benefits to the student (e.g., language development and role modeling) that will result from interaction with students without disabilities.

Section 7—Participating Agencies for Students Who Require Transition Services

Participating agencies that have agreed to provide transition services/supports (before the student leaves the secondary school program):

Agency Name: _____   **Telephone Number:** _____

Service: _____

Implementation date if different from IEP implementation date: _____

Agency Name: _____   **Telephone Number:** _____

Service: _____

Implementation date if different from IEP implementation date: _____

Agency Name: _____   **Telephone Number:** _____

Service: _____

Implementation date if different from IEP implementation date: _____

Agency Name: _____   **Telephone Number:** _____

Service: _____

Implementation date if different from IEP implementation date: _____

Explanation of Section 7—Participating Agencies for Students Who Require Transition Services

Beginning at age 15 or younger, if appropriate, the IEP must reflect the full array of transition programs and services designed to develop postsecondary education, employment, and community living skills. The Committee is responsible for identifying appropriate and necessary participating agencies that will be a part of the student's transition to postschool opportunities.

A **participating agency** is defined as a state or local agency, other than the school district responsible for a student's education, that may have financial and/or legal responsibility for providing transition services to the student. Prior to the Eligibility Committee meeting to determine needed transition services, Eligibility Committee members should have knowledge of both the eligibility criteria and the services provided by agencies that could be expected to send a representative. This will enable the Eligibility Committee to invite appropriate agencies to participate in discussions regarding the provision of transition services for each student. When an agency agrees to provide a service, the IEP must include that service and the implementation date of the service if it is different from the implementation date of the IEP. The Eligibility Committee must document these contacts on the IEP and the services and supports to be provided to the student as he or she transitions from school. The Eligibility Committee must reconvene as soon as possible to consider other strategies to meet the transition objectives should the participating agency fail to deliver agreed-upon services stated in the IEP.

Section 8—Coordinated Set of Activities Leading to Long-Term Adult Outcomes

If any of the following areas are not addressed, explain why.

1. Instruction:
2. Related Services:
3. Employment/Postsecondary Education:
4. Community Experience:
5. Activities of Daily Living:
6. Functional Vocational Assessment:

Explanation of Section 8—Coordinated Set of Activities Leading to Long-Term Adult Outcomes

For a student age 14 and older, the IEP, as a whole, must demonstrate the use of a coordinated set of activities as the means by which the student can achieve the long-term adult outcomes. Beginning at age 14, the focus of activity is on instruction. At age 15 and older, the coordinated set of activities must address instruction, related services, community experiences, and the development of employment or other postschool adult living objectives. If one of these activities is not included in the IEP in a particular year, then the IEP must explain why that activity is not reflected in any part of the student's program. Activities of daily living and functional vocational evaluation activities should also be included when appropriate to the student's needs. The coordinated set of activities, in conjunction with the special education programs and services, should incrementally provide the student with skills and experiences to prepare him or her to attain the long-term adult outcomes.

The coordinated set of activities are:

1. Instruction: Educational instruction will be provided to the student to achieve the stated outcome(s) (e.g., general and/or special education course instruction, occupational education, and advanced placement courses).

2. Related services: These are specific related services, such as rehabilitation counseling services, which will support the student in attaining the stated outcome(s).

3. Employment and other postschool adult living objectives: These are educational services that will be provided to the student to prepare for employment or other postschool activity. Postschool activities determine what other skills or supports will be necessary for the student to succeed as independently as possible. Examples include participation in a work experience program, information about colleges in which the student has an interest, and travel training.

4. Community experiences: These are community-based experiences that will be offered, or community resources utilized, as part of the student's school program, whether utilized during school hours or after school hours, to achieve the stated outcome(s) (e.g., local employers, public library, local stores).

5. Activities of daily living skills (ADL, if appropriate): These are ADL skills necessary to be worked on to achieve the stated outcome(s) (e.g., dressing, hygiene, self-care skills, self-medication).

6. Functional vocational assessment (if appropriate): If the vocational assessment has not provided enough information to make a vocational program decision, additional assessment activities can be performed to obtain more information about the student's needs, preferences, and interests.

Section 9—Graduation Information for Secondary Students

Credential/Diploma Sought: _____

Expected Date of High School Completion: _____

Credits Earned to Date: _____

Explanation of Section 9—Graduation Information for Secondary Students

Credential/Diploma Sought. Students with disabilities must be afforded the opportunity to earn a local high school diploma, if appropriate. Access must be provided to required courses, electives, and tests. This opportunity must be afforded to students regardless of the placement. Not all students with disabilities will pursue a high school diploma. Some students with disabilities will earn an IEP diploma. IEP diplomas are accepted as a minimum requirement by the Armed Forces to take the Armed Services Vocational Aptitude Battery and by some colleges to take college entrance examinations. However, all of these examinations have set passing scores. Additionally, each college sets its own admission requirements and, therefore, may or may not accept students with disabilities with IEP diplomas.

Expected Date of High School Completion. This is the expected date of high school completion.

Credits Earned to Date. This indicates the number of high school units of credit earned.

Section 10—Summary of Selected Recommendations

Classification of the Disability: _____

Recommended Placement: September to June: _____

Extended School Year (ESL) Services?   Yes ____   No ____

Recommended Placement, July and August: _____

Transportation Needs: _____

Explanation of Section 10—Summary of Selected Recommendations

The summary of selected recommendations is completed after the committee has reviewed the student's present levels of performance and individual needs and has finalized all other components of the IEP.

Classification of the Disability.   In **classification,** the Committee determines a specific disability category based on the definitions of these categories for school-age students or preschool students.

Recommended Placement.   After the completion of all other components of the student's IEP, the committee determines the recommended placement. The placement of a student with a disability in a special class, special school, or other removal from the general educational environment should occur only when the nature of the disability is such that the student cannot be educated, even with the use of supplementary aids and services, in the general education setting.

Extended School Year Program/Services.   The necessity of a July and August program, and where such services will be made available, may be documented in the Summary of Selected Recommendations for convenience in locating this information.

Transportation.   The IEP must document any special transportation to be provided to and from school and/or extracurricular activities. In determining whether to include transportation on a student's IEP, the Committee must consider how the student's disability affects the student's need for transportation, including determining whether the student's disability prevents him or her from using the same transportation provided to those without disabilities or from getting to school in the same manner.

Section 11—Reporting Progress to Parents

State the manner and frequency in which progress will be reported: Parents/guardians or student over 18 will be informed of the student's progress toward meeting the academic goals and objectives with the same frequency as students without disabilities using the following criteria:

- Textbook tests, quizzes, and standardized tests
- Review of report card grades
- Contact with classroom teachers on an ongoing basis

Explanation of Section 11—
Reporting Progress to Parents

The IEP must contain a statement of how parents will be regularly informed of their child's progress, at least as often as parents of children without disabilities are informed of their child's progress. Specifically, the parents must be informed of their child's progress toward the annual goals and the extent to which this progress is sufficient to achieve the child's goals by the end of the year.

CONCLUSION

Unless the student's IEP requires some other arrangement, the student with a disability must be educated in the school he or she would have attended if the student did not have a disability. The determination of the recommended placement is the final step in developing an IEP. The placement decision must address the full range of the student's cognitive, social, physical, linguistic, and communication needs. According to the least restrictive environment (LRE) requirements of federal and state law and regulations, a student may be removed from the general education environment only when the nature or severity of the disability is such that the student's education cannot be satisfactorily achieved even with the use of supplementary supports and services in the general education setting.

VOCABULARY

Academic/Educational Achievement and Learning Characteristics: The current levels of knowledge and development in subject and skill areas, including activities of daily living, level of intellectual functioning, adaptive behavior, expected rate of progress in acquiring skills and information, and learning style.

Address of Student: Legal address and phone number of the student.

Annual Goals: Statements, in measurable terms, that describe what the student can reasonably be expected to accomplish within a 12-month period. There must be a direct relationship between the annual goals and the present levels of performance.

Assistive Technology Devices: Any item, piece of equipment, or product system—whether acquired commercially off the shelf, modified, or customized—that is used to increase, maintain, or improve the functional capabilities of a child with a disability.

Benchmarks: Major milestones between the present levels of performance and the annual goals.

Classification: The committee determination of a specific disability category based on the definitions of these categories for school-age students or preschool students.

Committee on Special Education: The committee charged with ensuring that each student with a disability is educated to the maximum extent appropriate in classes and programs with their peers who do not have disabilities.

Community Experiences: Community-based experiences that will be offered, or community resources utilized as part of the student's school program, whether utilized during school hours or after school hours, to achieve the stated outcome(s).

County of Residence: The county(ies) in which the parent(s) and student reside.

CPSE: Committee on Preschool Special Education.

Credits Earned to Date: The number of high school units of credit earned.

Current Grade: For school-age students, the current grade is designated as of the date of the committee meeting.

Date for Reevaluation: The date when the next reevaluation of the student is expected to occur. Reevaluations must occur at least every three years.

Date of Birth: Student's birth date.

Date of Initiation of Services: The date when this IEP is to be implemented.

Date of Eligibility: The date when the student was first identified as a student with a disability and eligible for special education programs and services.

Date of the Eligibility Committee/CPSE meeting: The date the committee meeting occurred.

Dominant Language of Parent/Guardian: For parents/guardians who are deaf or hearing impaired or whose native language is other than English, the language or mode of communication used by the parents.

Dominant Language of Student: For a student who is deaf or hearing impaired or whose native language is other than English, the language or mode of communication used with the student.

Expected Date of High School Completion: The expected date of high school completion.

Extended School Year Programs and Services: The necessity of a program during July and August.

Gender: Male or female.

Individualized Education Program (IEP): The blueprint for attaining improved educational results for students with disabilities. It is used to strengthen the connection between special education programs and services and the general education curriculum. It is a written plan for a student in special education: Simply stated, the IEP explains the specific educational objectives and placement for a particular student. It is a management tool for the entire assessment teaching process. The IEP becomes the critical link between the student in special education and the special teaching that the student requires.

Individuals with Disabilities Education Improvement Act (IDEA 2004): Federal law that requires that all students in special education have an individualized education program (IEP).

Instruction: Educational instruction that will be provided to the student to achieve the stated outcome(s) (e.g., general and/or special education course instruction, occupational education, and advanced placement courses).

Management Needs: The nature of and degree to which environmental modifications and human or material resources are required to address academic, social, and physical needs.

Medical Alerts/Prescriptive Devices: Any information that should be readily available to all teachers and other appropriate school personnel, such as medications or specific health-related conditions requiring either constant or intermittent care by a qualified individual (e.g., eyeglasses, hearing aids, and allergic reactions).

Parent/Guardian's Name: The names of the parent(s) or the name of a guardian, if appropriate.

Participating Agency: A state or local agency, other than the school district responsible for a student's education, that may have financial and/or legal responsibility for providing transition services to the student.

Physical Development: The student's motor and sensory development, health, vitality, and physical skills or limitations that pertain to the learning process.

Postschool Adult Living Objectives: Educational services that will be provided to the student to prepare for employment or other postschool activity. Postschool activities determine what other skills or supports will be necessary for the student to succeed as independently as possible. Examples include participation in a work experience program, information about colleges in which the student has an interest, and travel training.

Projected Date of Review: The date when review of this IEP is expected.

Race/Ethnic Group: The race/ethnicity of the student is optional.

Related Services: These are specific related services, as defined in Section 200.1 of the Regulations of the Commissioner of Education, such as rehabilitation counseling services, which will support the student in attaining the stated outcome(s).

Short-Term Objectives: Measurable, intermediate steps between the present levels of performance and the annual goals.

Social Development: The quality of the student's relationships with peers and adults, feelings about self, social adjustment to school and community environments, and behaviors that may impede learning.

Street, City, and Zip: If the address of a parent(s)/guardian is different from the student's address, both addresses should be indicated, when appropriate.

Student Identification Number (ID): The ID number may be the student's social security number or a number assigned by the school.

Student Name: The full name of the student should be noted.

Supplementary Aids: Aids, services, and other supports that are provided in general education classes or other education-related settings to enable students with disabilities to be educated with nondisabled students to the maximum extent appropriate in the least restrictive environment.

Telephone: If appropriate, the telephone numbers of parent(s)/guardian should be indicated.

VESID: Vocational and Educational Services for Individuals with Disabilities.

CHAPTER TWENTY

SPECIAL TOPICS IN ASSESSMENT

This chapter will focus on three areas of great importance in the field of special education. These involve the topics of: (1) state and district-wide assessment, (2) transition services in special education, and (3) the Individuals with Disabilities Education Improvement Act. The first part on state and district-wide assessment will be presented in a question and answer format, looking specifically at the most frequently asked questions by parents and teachers on this topic. The second part on transition services will present a general overview of the topic. Finally, the third part will address the reauthorization changes of IDEA '97, focusing on the Individuals with Disabilities Education Improvement Act (IDEA 2004).

QUESTIONS AND ANSWERS ABOUT STATE AND DISTRICT-WIDE ASSESSMENTS

Requirements for including all children in assessments are based on a number of federal laws, including Section 504 of the Rehabilitation Act of 1973 (Section 504), Title II of the Americans with Disabilities Act of 1990 (ADA), Title I of the Elementary and Secondary Education Act (Title I), and the Individuals with Disabilities Education Improvement Act Amendments of 2004 (IDEA 2004). Assessment is often associated with direct individual benefits such as promotion, graduation, and access to educational services. In addition, assessment is an integral aspect of educational accountability systems, which provide valuable information that benefits individual students by measuring individual progress against standards or by evaluating programs.

Title I and IDEA 2004 include a number of specific requirements for including all children in assessments. In adding these requirements, Congress recognized that many students were not experiencing levels of achievement in school that would enable them to successfully pursue postsecondary educational or competitive work opportunities. Students with disabilities, minority children, migrant and homeless children, children with limited English proficiency, and children in poverty were especially at risk. Many of these children's educational programs were marked by low expectations, limited accountability for results, and exposure to a poorer curriculum than that offered to other children.

Originally, Congress's findings for the IDEA '97 amendments noted that "the implementation of this Act has been impeded by low expectations. . . . Over twenty years of research and experience has demonstrated that the education of children with disabilities can be made more effective by having high expectations for such children and ensuring their access in the general curriculum to the maximum extent possible."

According to the report from the Committee on Labor and Human Resources of May 9, 1997, IDEA '97 provided parents and educators with tools to "promote improved educational results for children with disabilities through early intervention, preschool, and educational experiences that prepare them for later educational challenges and employment." The report further notes that:

> The new focus is intended to produce attention to the accommodations and adjustments necessary for disabled children to access the general education curriculum and the special services which may be necessary for appropriate participation.
>
> Children with disabilities must be included in State and district-wide assessments of student progress with individual modifications and accommodations as needed. Thus, the bill requires that the IEP include a statement of any individual modifications in the administration of State and district-wide assessments.

This section is provided in response to frequently asked questions submitted to the Office of Special Education Program by parents, teachers, assessment coordinators, state education agency staff, and other policy makers. In some cases, the responses provided are clarifications of legal issues. In other instances, the responses are intended to stimulate reflection about the implications of policies and practices for students with disabilities. Clearly, high expectations for students entail high expectations for teachers and schools. This document is intended not only to provide guidance in meeting specific legal requirements, but also to help achieve the benefits of these provisions for students with disabilities.

Accountability

Question: Are students with disabilities required to participate in a State's accountability system?

Although IDEA 2004 makes no specific reference as to how states include children with disabilities in the state accountability system, IDEA 2004 requires states to establish performance goals and indicators for children with disabilities—consistent to the maximum extent appropriate with other goals and standards for all children established by the State—and to report on progress toward meeting those goals.

Under Title I of the Elementary and Secondary Education Act, in the 2000–01 school year, each state must have an assessment system that serves as the primary means for determining whether schools and districts receiving Title I funds are making adequate yearly progress toward enabling all students in Title I schools to reach high standards. All students with disabilities in those schools must be included in the State assessment system, and the scores of students with disabilities must be included in the assessment system for purposes of public reporting and school and district accountability. Under Title I, state assessment systems must assign a score, for accountability purposes, to every student who has attended school within a single school district for a full academic year. States must also explain how scores from alternate assessments are integrated into their accountability systems.

Question: How do states and LEAs use their assessment results?

Under IDEA 2004, states must use information about the performance of children with disabilities in state and district-wide assessment programs to revise their State Improvement Plans as needed to improve their performance. Under Title I, states and LEAs also use the results to review the performance of LEAs and schools, respectively, and to identify LEAs and schools in need of improvement. States and LEAs also use results for rewards and sanctions for schools and districts, and for some decisions about student promotion or graduation. Assessment results can also be used in planning teacher training, summer school and after school programs, and in reviewing alignment between assessments and curriculum. These are state and local district decisions. In addition, IEP teams can consider individual assessment results as they develop programs for students with disabilities.

IEP Processes

Question: What is the role of the IEP team in determining whether the child will participate in general or alternate assessments?

The IEP team determines *how* the child participates in state and district-wide assessments of student achievement. The IEP team determines if any individual modifications in administration are needed in order for the student to participate in the assessment. If the IEP team determines that the child will not participate in a particular state or district-wide assessment of student achievement (or part of an assessment), the IEP team states why the assessment is not appropriate for the child and how the child will be assessed. IEP teams should have the level of expertise needed to make these decisions in an effective manner.

Question: May IEP teams exempt children with disabilities from participating in the State or district-wide assessment program?

No. The IEP team determines *How* individual students with disabilities participate in assessment programs, *not whether*. The only students with disabilities who are exempted from participation in general State and district-wide assessment programs are students with disabilities convicted as adults under state law and incarcerated in adult prisons. With this statutory exception, there should be no language in state or district assessment guidelines, rules, or regulations that permits IEP teams to exempt students from state or district-wide assessment programs.

Section 504 prohibits exclusion from participation of, denial of benefits to, or discrimination against, individuals with disabilities on the basis of their disability in federally assisted programs or activities. Title II of the ADA provides that no qualified individual with a disability shall, by reason of such disability, be excluded from participation in or be denied the benefits of the services, programs, or activities of a public entity or be subjected to discrimination by such an entity.

Inclusion in assessments provides valuable information that benefits students either by indicating individual progress against standards or in evaluating educational programs. In some states, participation in assessments is a means to access benefits such as promotion and graduation. Given these benefits, exclusion from assessment programs based on disability would potentially violate Section 504 and Title II of the ADA.

Question: Can the IEP statement of how the child will participate in state and district-wide assessments of student achievement be changed without reconvening the IEP team?

No. If the IEP team wishes to modify a provision of the IEP, it must meet again to make the change.

Parental Permission

Question: Is parental permission required for children with disabilities to participate in state and district-wide assessment programs if parental permission is not required for the participation of nondisabled students?

No. If parental permission is not required for participation in the State and district-wide assessment programs for nondisabled children, it is not required for children with disabilities. However, parents of children with disabilities as members of the IEP team will be involved in IEP team decisions on how an individual child will participate in such assessment programs.

Question: If a state permits parents of nondisabled children to choose not to have their child participate in state or district-wide assessments, do parents of children with disabilities have the same right in regard to assessments and alternate assessments?

Yes. Parents of a child with a disability should have the same right to "opt out" as parents of nondisabled students consistent with any allowable justification criteria established by the SEA or LEA. Denying parents of children with disabilities the same rights afforded parents of nondisabled children would raise concerns about discrimination on the basis of disability. However, parents and students should be informed of the consequences of participation and nonparticipation in state or district-wide assessments. For example, parents should know that state and district-wide assessments can improve accountability and promote services that better meet the needs of the participating students, while nonparticipation may limit opportunities for promotion, graduation, and access to programs. Parents should not be pressured to "opt out" of assessment programs.

Most states already keep track of students who are "opted out" of assessment programs by parents. States and districts should keep track of parent-requested "opt out" exemptions for students with disabilities disaggregated from those for students without disabilities. This should help the state to determine if "opting out" pressure is occurring.

Accommodations and Modifications

Question: Can the SEA or LEA limit the authority of the IEP team to select individual accommodations and modifications in administration needed for a child to participate in the assessment?

IDEA 2004 requires that the IEP team have the responsibility and the authority to determine what, if any, individual modifications in the administration of state or district-wide assessments of student achievement are needed in order for a particular child with a disability to participate in the assessment. If the IEP Team determines that individual modifications in the administration of state or district-wide assessments of student achievement are needed, the Team must include a statement of any such modifications in the IEP. In addition, IDEA 2004 requires that appropriate accommodations and modifications in administration of state or district-wide assessments must be provided if necessary to ensure the participation of children with disabilities in those assessments. As part of each state's general supervision responsibility under IDEA 2004, it must ensure that these requirements are carried out. States that have developed a comprehensive policy governing the use of testing accommodations (including the conditions and instructions for appropriate use of specific accommodations and how scores are to be reported and used) need to ensure that they are consistent with this IDEA requirement.

At the same time, IEP teams need to understand and consider the implications of SEA/LEA policies on the reporting and use of scores in addressing what individual modifications and accommodations are appropriate for an individual child with a disability. SEAs and LEAs should carefully consider the intended and unintended consequences of accommodation policies that may impact student opportunities such as promotion or graduation (e.g., receipt of a regular diploma, a certificate of attendance). Parents and students need to be fully informed of any consequences of such policies.

A major challenge for assessment programs is how to maintain assessment rigor (reliability and validity of assessments), implement and protect the individual rights of students, and simultaneously ensure that schools teach all children what they need to know and to do (knowledge and skills). Much of the current research on accommodations and modifications is inconclusive, so in many cases the impact of specific accommodations is not known. Continued research is underway, and more is needed.

A number of legal principles and concerns apply if a student may be denied benefits such as promotion or graduation because of questionable validation of accommodations. One solution suggested by the National Center on Educational Outcomes (NCEO) at the University of Minnesota is to collect and use additional evidence that allows the student to demonstrate competency in lieu of a single test score. Further information is available from the NCEO (612–626–1530; www.coled.umn.edu/NCEO).

Alternate Assessments

Question: What is an alternate assessment?

Generally, an alternate assessment is understood to mean an assessment designed for those students with disabilities who are unable to participate in general large-scale assessments used by a school district or state, even when accommodations or modifications are provided. The alternate assessment provides a mechanism for students, including those with the most significant disabilities, to participate in and benefit from assessment programs.

Alternate assessments need to be aligned with the general curriculum standards set for all students and should not be assumed appropriate only for those students with significant cognitive impairments. The need for alternate assessments depends on the individual needs of the child, not the category of the child's disability. Although it is expected that the number of students participating in alternate assessments will be relatively small, participation in alternate assessments should not, in and of itself, preclude students from access to the same benefits available to nondisabled students for their participation. Thus, the alternate assessment is sufficiently flexible to meet the needs of difficult-to-assess students with disabilities who may need the alternate assessment to demonstrate competency for benefits such as promotion or a diploma. It may also enable IEP teams, including informed parents, to make choices about appropriate participation that may lead to an IEP diploma or other type of certification.

Question: Do the requirements to establish participation guidelines for alternate assessments and to develop alternate assessments apply to both SEAs and LEAs?

Yes. IDEA 2004 specifically requires inclusion of children with disabilities in both state and district-wide assessment programs and requires both the SEA and the LEA, as appropriate, to develop guidelines for the participation of children with disabilities in alternate assessments for those children who cannot participate in state and district-wide assessments, and develop alternate assessments.

Of course, if an LEA does not conduct district-wide assessments other than those that are part of the state assessment program, then the LEA would follow SEA guidelines and use the SEA alternate assessment(s). The requirements apply to district-wide assessments regardless of whether or not there is a state assessment.

Question: If the SEA has developed guidelines for participation in state alternate assessments, can the LEA use those guidelines to meet its LEA responsibility?

There is nothing that prohibits the LEA from adopting the SEA guidelines if the SEA guidelines are consistent with the assessment program objectives of LEA district-wide assessments. However, if the district-wide assessment is used for significantly different purposes than the state assessment, the LEA should ensure that the participation guidelines developed for the state assessment are consistent with the purposes of the district-wide assessment, or should develop guidelines consistent with the purposes of its district-wide assessment.

Question: Does a state need to have an alternate assessment for each content area assessed in the regular assessment program?

The number of alternate assessments is a state decision. In many state and district-wide assessment programs, the assessment consists of multiple components or batteries. The alternate assessment(s) should at a minimum assess the broad content areas such as communication, mathematics, social studies, science, and so forth assessed in the state or district-wide assessment. The alternate assessment may assess additional content, including functional skills, as determined necessary by the state or local district.

Functional skills can also be aligned to state standards as real-world indicators of progress toward those standards. Title I requires that at a minimum reading/language arts and math are assessed, but Title I also requires that if other subject areas are assessed by the state for Title I purposes, then all students in Title I schools in the grades assessed need to be assessed in those content areas as well. The purpose of an alternate assessment should match at a minimum the purpose of the assessment to which it is intended to serve as an alternate.

Question: Can LEAs use the state alternate assessment to meet its obligation to develop an alternate to its district-wide assessment?

The issue is alignment between the alternate assessment and the large-scale assessment. Districts must adopt local guidelines for participation in alternate assessments and they must have developed and conducted alternate assessments no later than July 1, 2000. Whether an alternate assessment developed by the state for use with a state-wide assessment is also an appropriate alternate assessment to the local district-wide assessment depends on the type of alternate assessment selected, the nature of the district-wide assessment, the content measured, and the purposes for which the results will be used. The purpose of an alternate assessment should match at a minimum the purpose of the assessment to which it is intended to serve as an alternate.

Question: Can LEAs use their own alternate assessment or must they use the state's alternate assessment?

In states with statewide assessment programs, local districts must administer the state alternate assessment. Moreover, local districts must develop and conduct alternate assessments if they have district-wide assessments, or use the state alternate if appropriate.

Out-of-Level Testing

Question: Is out-of-level testing by states acceptable?

"Out-of-level testing" means assessing students in one grade level using versions of tests that were designed for students in other (usually lower) grade levels. Some states allow out-of-level testing in an effort to limit student frustration and provide appropriate assessment levels. Although IDEA does not specifically prohibit its use, out-of-level testing may be problematic for several reasons when used for accountability purposes. IDEA 2004 requires that the performance goals for children with disabilities should be consistent, to the maximum extent appropriate, with other goals and standards for all children established by the state. The purpose is to maintain high expectations and provide coherent information about student attainment of the state's content and student performance standards.

Out-of-level testing may not assess the same content standards at the same levels as are assessed in the "grade-level" assessment. Thus, unless the out-of-level test is designed to yield scores referenced to the appropriate grade-level standards, out-of-level testing may not provide coherent information about student attainment of the state or LEA content and student performance standards. Also, many assessment experts argue that out-of-level testing produces scores that are (even using transformation formulations) insufficiently comparable to allow aggregation, as required by IDEA 2004. If out-of-level tests are used, IEP teams need training and clear information about the statistical appropriateness of administering such tests at each possible level different from the student's grade level.

Out-of-level tests may lower expectations for students, prevent them from demonstrating their full competence, subject them to a lower-level curriculum, and restrict their access to the general curriculum. Important goals of both IDEA 2004 and Title I are to maintain high expectations for all children and to ensure that teachers and schools are able to teach diverse learners. Students with disabilities are entitled to the same rich curriculum as their nondisabled peers.

One source for additional information about out-of-level testing is the National Center on Educational Outcomes (NCEO) at the University of Minnesota (612-626-1530; www.coled.umn.edu/NCEO).

Question: Can an out-of-level test be considered an "alternate" assessment?

Out-of-level tests are considered modified administrations of the state or district-wide assessments rather than alternate assessments, and scores on out-of-level tests should be converted to reflect performance at grade level and reported as performance at the grade level at which the child is placed unless such reporting would be statistically inappropriate.

Reporting

Question: IDEA 2004 refers to children with disabilities being included in general state and district-wide assessment programs, but only requires that state education agencies report to the public on the participation and performance of children with disabilities on assessments. Are local education agencies also required to report to the public in a similar fashion?

The IDEA 2004 requirement is for reporting by the state education agency. Many states have similar requirements for local education agencies to report similarly on local assessment programs. Under IDEA 2004, this is a state decision.

Question: What are the requirements for aggregation and disaggregation of data? Are aggregation and disaggregation required at the state level only? State level and district level only? Or state level, district level, and site level?

Under IDEA 2004, states must report aggregated data that include the performance of children with disabilities together with all other children and disaggregated data on the performance of children with disabilities. There is no requirement for disaggregation by category of disability, only disaggregation of the performance of children with disabilities separate from the performance of nondisabled children. These reports must be made with the same frequency and in the same detail as reports on the assessment of nondisabled children. For example, if school-level results are reported, then school-level results for students with disabilities generally must be disaggregated. It is the SEA's decision how to collect sufficient data from LEAs to meet the Federal SEA reporting requirement consistent with these provisions.

Question: What is meant by "statistically sound" in 34 CRF 300.139?

There are at least two issues for consideration. One has to do with the sample size. In some instances, for example, if a state chooses to disaggregate by disability categories (not a federal requirement) or report on the performance of students with disabilities in small school districts, the relatively small number of students in that category or district might raise questions about statistical soundness if generalizations are to be made about student performance. A second issue centers around the reporting of performance for students who take nonstandard or modified administrations of an assessment. In such cases, there may be questions about the validity of the assessment and its comparability to the standard assessment.

Question: Can a state or local education agency provide individual performance results to its schools, or would this violate the requirement to avoid disclosure of performance results identifiable to individual children?

The reference to disclosure simply refers to the inappropriateness of public reports that deal with samples so small as to publicly disclose the performance of individual students, not to providing results to schools for students served by the school.

Question: To avoid publicly disclosing performance results identifiable to individual students, can a state or local education agency adjust the administrative levels at which it reports these results? For example, can it report the alternate assessment at the district level even though the general assessment is reported at the school level?

Yes, but only if necessary to avoid publicly disclosing results identifiable to individual students.

TRANSITION SERVICES

The past two decades have witnessed significant changes for people with disabilities, in large part due to the disability rights movement that, in many ways, paralleled the civil rights movement. People with disabilities used to be thought of as the invisible minority. They were overlooked and hidden away. They were embarrassments and treated as objects of pity and shame. Now these individuals are taking their place in an inclusive society. Individuals with disabilities are now a presence in all the media, commercial advertising, and many forms of public life. Changes in the laws and progress and technology have helped make these advances possible. Despite these gains, the barriers to acceptance remain society's myths, fears, and stereotypes about those with disabilities. Consequently, the efforts for change need to be viewed as an ongoing process. The implementation of transition services is a significant component of this pathway to acceptance.

As many adults know from their own experience, adolescence is often the most difficult and unsettling period of adjustment in one's development. It is a time filled with physical, emotional, and social upheavals. Until a child leaves secondary school, parents and teachers may experience a sense of protective control over the child's life.

This protective guidance normally involves educational, medical, financial, and social input to assist the child's growth. When the child leaves this setting, there is normally a personal struggle on the part of parents in letting go. There is always a normal amount of apprehension associated with the child's entrance into the adult world. Today, greater responsibility for adjustment falls on educators.

However, for the child with a disability, this developmental period can be fraught with even greater apprehension for a variety of reasons. Depending on the nature and severity of the disability, parents may play more of an ongoing role in their child's life even after he or she leaves secondary education. Historically, parents and their children have spent years actively involved in IEP development and meetings, transitional IEP development, and Eligibility Committee meetings concerning educational and developmental welfare. Depending on the mental competence (the capability to make reasoned decisions) of the child with disabilities, some parents may have to continue to make vital decisions affecting all aspects of their child's life. On the other hand, the parents of such children not affected by diminished mental competence should use all their energies to encourage their child's steps toward independence. Consequently, parents need not shy away thinking that they are being too overprotective if they are involved in their child's life after they leave school.

Because planning for the future of a student with disabilities can arouse fear of the unknown, there may be a tendency for parents to delay addressing these issues and instead focus only on the present. However, working through these fears and thinking about the child's best future interest has a greater chance of ensuring a meaningful outcome. Regardless of the nature and severity of a disability, educators and parents will be exposed to a transitional process during the child's school years that will provide a foundation for the adult world. This transitional process will include many facets of planning for the future and should be fully understood by everyone concerned each step of the way. Planning for the future is an investment in a child's well-being.

The Intent of Transition Services

For many years, educators have been concerned about the lack of success in adult life for students with disabilities. Many did not go for further training, and often did not receive postschool support and services. As these children aged out (at age 21, students were no longer eligible for a free and appropriate education including services and support) of the educational system, the families felt that they were being dropped into a void. Although there were many services out in the community, parents were left to their own devices and would find out about such services and supports by chance, luck, or fate. Parents and students were confronted with a complex array of service options and resources, each with unique roles, services, funding sources, forms, and eligibility requirements. A need for a collaborative, readily accessible system was obvious.

What seemed to be missing was the bridge between a student's school system and services for postsecondary-school life. As a result, the concept of transitional services was developed to bridge this gap and hopefully provide students who have special needs with a more structured path to adulthood.

The Introduction of Transition Services

In 1992, the laws governing the education of children with disabilities took a major step forward with the introduction of transition services. The rules and regulations for the IDEA released in 1992 define transition services as:

> A—a coordinated set of activities for a student, designed within an outcome oriented process that promotes movement from school to postschool activities, including post-secondary education, vocational training, integrated employment (including supported employment), continuing and adult education, adult services, independent living, or community participation.

> B—the coordinated set of activities must be based on the individual student's needs, taking into account the student's preferences and interests; include instruction, community experience, the development of employment and other postschool adult living objectives and if appropriate, acquisition of daily living skills and functional evaluation (IDEA, P.L. 101-476, 34 C.F.R. 300.18).

Simply put, transition is

> *helping students and family think about their life after high school, identify long-range goals, designing the high school experience to ensure that students gain the skills and connections they need to achieve these goals, the provision of funds, and services to local school districts to assist in the transition process.* (Pierangelo & Giulianin, 2004)

In May 1994, President Clinton signed the **School to Work Opportunities Act.** This act contains the blueprint to empower all individuals, including those with disabilities, to acquire the skills and experiences they need to compete. This landmark bill demonstrates that transition is clearly now a national priority, important to ensure our economic viability as well as to offer every young person a chance at a productive life.

Every state receives federal special education moneys through Part B of IDEA 2004 and in turn, most of these funds flow through to local school districts and other state-supported programs providing special education services. As a requirement of receiving these funds, there are state education agencies that monitor the programs for which the funds are made available.

The Individualized Transitional Education Program (ITEP)

The IEP, as it has been defined over the years by legislation and court rulings, is not changed by the presence of the transition services section. The IEP is still a contract between the students, the parents, and the school. It is not a performance contract. The IEP spells out what the school will do (services and activities). If it is written on the IEP, the school is responsible for performing this stated service activity.

The IEP should carry the information about transition services that the school district can only provide, directly or indirectly (by arranging for another agency to provide services coordinated with the school services). As in previous interpretations of the IEP, parents cannot be listed as responsible for achieving an outcome or providing a service. This is the school district's responsibility.

The **Individual Transitional Education Plan** (ITEP) is a part of the overall IEP but represents a very important piece in determining a child's future. The ITEP should include long-term adult outcomes from which annual goals and objectives are defined. The ITEP should address the following:

1. A statement of transition services should be responsive to the child's preferences, interests, and needs. The beginning date for the service should be provided.
2. Annual goals and objectives, such as employment services, living arrangements.
3. Long-term adult outcomes in the IEP should include statements on the child regarding his or her performance in employment, postsecondary education, and community living.
4. A coordinated set of activities must be included on the ITEP. This set must demonstrate the use of various strategies, including community experiences, adult living objectives, and instruction. If one of these activities is not included in the IEP in a particular year, then the IEP must explain why that activity is not reflected in any part of the student's program. Activities of daily living and functional vocational evaluation activities also should be included.
5. A list of participants involved in the planning and development of the individualized transitional educational program.

Examples of Transition Services

Transition services are aimed at providing students and their families with the practical and experiential skills and knowledge that will assist in a successful transition to adult life. Although transition services are provided in each of the following areas, it is important to understand that not every student with disabilities will need to receive all of these services. The available services included in the transition process involve services and experiences for both students and parents, such as:

1. Employment services
2. Living arrangements
3. Leisure/recreational services
4. Transportation services
5. Financial services
6. Postsecondary education services
7. Assistive technology
8. Medical services

As an educator working with students with disabilities, it is crucial for you to become familiar with all the aspects of transition so that you can assist both parents and the student in this process toward adulthood. In order to accomplish this, you will need to become familiar with the different areas associated with transition. A brief explanation of the areas involved in the transition process follows.

Employment Services.   Crossing the threshold from the world of school to the world of work brings a significant change in everyone's life. School is an entitlement, meaning that it is an environment that our system of government supplies for all our citizens. The workplace is the opposite; no one is "entitled" to a job. The workplace is governed by the competitive market, and students with or without disabilities have to be able to function in that setting or they will not survive.

One of the first and most important aspects of transition planning is the preparation for some students for the world of work. This is a very practical issue that can create many concerns. With the proper information and resources, this phase of the transition process can also be rewarding. Parents and teachers must fully understand the options in order to help the child make the best decision for his or her future. The first step in planning for employment may begin with vocational assessments to help determine the best direction based on the child's interests and skill levels.

Vocational Assessments.   One of the techniques used to determine a child's interests, aptitudes, and skills is a vocational assessment. A *vocational assessment* is the responsibility of the district's special education program. It begins by assessing referrals for special education services and continues throughout subsequent annual reviews. The planning of transitional services includes the Eligibility Committee's development of transitional employment goals and objectives based on the child's needs, preferences, and interests. These will be identified through the child-centered vocational assessment process.

A good vocational assessment should include the collection and analysis of information about a child's vocational aptitudes, skills, expressed interests, and occupational exploration history (volunteer experiences, part-time or summer employment, club activities). The collection of this information should also take into account the child's language, culture, and family.

A **Level I vocational assessment** is administered at the beginning of a child's transitional process, usually around age 13 or 14, and is based on the student's abilities, expressed interests, and needs. This Level I assessment may include the review of existing school information and the conduct of informal interviews. Level I takes a look at the student from a vocational perspective. A trained vocational evaluator or knowledgeable special education teacher should be designated to collect the Level I assessment data. The information gathered for analyses should include existing information from:

- Cumulative records
- Student interviews
- Parent/guardian and teacher interviews
- Special education eligibility data
- A review of the child's aptitudes
- Achievements
- Interests
- Behaviors
- Occupational exploration activities

The informal student interview involved in a Level I assessment should consider the student's vocational interest, interpersonal relationship skills, and adaptive behavior.

A **Level II vocational assessment** usually includes the administration of one or more formal vocational evaluations. A Level II assessment follows and is based on the analyses obtained from the Level I assessment. This may be recommended by the eligibility committee at any time to determine the level of a student's vocational skills, aptitudes, and interests but not before the age of 12. The same knowledgeable staff members involved in prior assessments should be used. Collected data should include:

- Writing
- Learning styles
- Interest inventory
- Motor (dexterity, speed, tool use, strength, coordination)
- Spatial discrimination
- Verbal reading
- Perception (visual/auditory/tactile)
- Speaking numerical (measurement, money skills)
- Comprehension (task learning, problem solving)
- Attention (staying on task)

A **Level III vocational assessment** is a comprehensive vocational evaluation that focuses on real or simulated work experiences. This assessment is the basis for vocational counseling. Unlike Level I and Level II assessments, a trained vocational evaluator should administer or supervise this level of assessment. Level III assessment options include:

- **Vocational evaluations:** This includes aptitudes and interests that are compared to job performance to predict vocational success in specific areas. Work samples must be valid and reliable.
- **Situational vocational assessments that occur in real work settings:** This on-the-job assessment considers what has been learned and how.
- **Work study assessments:** These are progress reports from supervisors or mentors that provide information on the student's job performance. A standard observational checklist may be utilized.

If a student plans a postsecondary educational program, he or she may benefit from two types of assessments:

1. General assessments of postsecondary education skills are necessary to determine academic skills, critical thinking skills, requirements for reasonable accommodations, social behaviors, interpersonal skills, self-advocacy and self-determination skills, learning strategies, and time management or organizational skills. This information is usually obtained through consultation with peers, teachers, or a self-evaluation.
2. Assessments specific to field of study or setting are necessary to assess needs in relation to daily living skills that may be experienced in a classroom setting or college campus, such as dormitory living versus commuting, lab work, large lecture versus seminar courses.

Parents should be encouraged to visit campuses that provide supportive services for children with disabilities. Sources of information regarding colleges that provide these services can be obtained in the local libraries, bookstores, or high school guidance offices.

Living Arrangements. There may be times after a student with disabilities leaves secondary education when parents may have to explore housing alternatives other than the family home. There may be a variety of motivations for this decision. These may include:

- The physical, medical, economic, and psychological resources of some families to care for the needs of a family member with disabilities may diminish over time.
- There is the need to foster independence and autonomy.

Parents who are confronted with the need for residential options may face a confusing and sometimes overwhelming fund of information. A large part of this confusion is attributable to the variety of terms used to describe these available programs, such as **group homes** or **community residences.** In trying to unravel the many options, it is important to be as open as possible, because two group homes may be vastly different because they may serve people with different levels of disability.

Three major factors influence what types of service may be available to persons with disabilities:

1. Some residential services are available only to those who are eligible for medical assistance and county mental retardation services.

2. Service options are based on the level of care needed. The family subsidy program aids families in keeping children with disabilities at home rather than placing them in a residential facility. For those who need some supervision and training to live independently but do not need care 24 hours a day, **semi-independent living services** (SILS) may be an option. Community-based wavered services or placement in an intermediate care facility (group home) are options for persons who need 24-hour supervision.

3. The funding level for the programs influences the type of residential services available. Unfortunately, the need for residential facilities far outweighs the availability of these resources. Some of this is due to a lack of funding, but in addition there has been tremendous resistance on the parts of local communities to have such residences in their midst ("not in my backyard"). Historically, there have been costly and lengthy legal fights addressing this issue.

Given this information, educators and parents must begin addressing these issues years before this need may become necessary. Some parents report waiting five to six or more years for a space to open up at a facility. One of the pathways, in addition to putting the student's name on a list, is to assist the parents in getting involved with their child in the activities of a local service provider. This will enable the family to develop an ongoing relationship with that service provider that will be helpful when space in a facility becomes available. When the search for residential options begins, the goal should be to identify as many as possible. Knowing where to look will enable educators and parents to find contacts who can answer questions.

Types of Living Arrangements for Individuals with Disabilities

Residential Services. A **residential program** is a type of housing other than the individual's natural home, usually designed for persons with similar needs in terms of age, independence, and/or abilities. A residential program usually provides:

- A home-like environment with supervision and guidance as needed
- Living experiences appropriate to the functioning level and learning needs of the individual
- A location within the mainstream of community life
- Access to necessary supportive, habilitative programs

The goal of residential programs is to provide access to the highest possible quality of services that a person with certain disabilities needs, while at the same time permitting and encouraging the person to be as independent as possible.

Adult Foster Care. The **adult foster care** homes are provided by families who, for altruistic, religious, or monetary reasons, provide a home care environment for the adult with disabilities. In this residential option, the foster care family receives government reimbursement for this service. Although this living arrangement is meant to be a permanent situation, some factors may prevent this from occurring because no guarantees exist.

Boarding Homes. A **boarding home** is a residential facility that provides minimal structure and training for the adult with disabilities. These homes may provide sleeping and meal arrangements, and deal with a varied clientele with a variety of disabilities.

Family Subsidy Program. The **family subsidy program** provides financial assistance to families to enable them to care for their children with disabilities up to age 22 at home. The Department of Human Services pays eligible families a monthly allowance for certain home care costs such as medical equipment, respite care, transportation, and special diets. Eligibility for the program is based on the needs of the family in their ability to provide the necessary level of care in the home. The program is not based on financial need.

Freestanding Weekend Respite. **Free standing weekend respite** is a community-based program for families in need of respite on a planned or emergency basis. The objective is to afford families a reprieve from the day-to-day caregiving responsibilities. Respite provides room and board, 24-hour supervision, and appropriate recreational activities to individuals with developmental disabilities.

Group Homes. The general characteristics of **group homes** include:

- A home with fewer than 16 people
- A family-like structure
- Similarity to surrounding homes in the community
- Tasks being accomplished by the residents of the home to the extent of their abilities, such as cooking, mowing the lawn, laundry
- The expectation that the individual with a disability will graduate to a more independent situation that will meet his or her needs and preferences

The term **group home** has taken on many different meanings. Group homes have certain general characteristics but these may vary from facility to facility. Specifically, group homes are divided into two specific arrangements: semi-independent living arrangements and supervised living arrangements. These options differ in the following ways:

- Staffing arrangements
- Level of disability
- The need for supervision

Semi-Independent Living Arrangements (SILS).   Semi-independent living arrangements provide intensive support and training to persons with disabilities 18 years of age and over to enable them to learn to live independently in the community or to maintain semi-independence. Persons eligible for SILS do not require daily support services, but are unable to live independently without some training or occasional support. SILS recipients live in their own homes or apartments, in rooming houses, or in foster homes. They often share living arrangements with other persons who have disabilities. The key characteristic is that the staff does not live in the facility. In some cases, they may be on call in cases of emergency.

Home Care Attendants or Personal Assistant Services.   **Home care attendants** are available to assist consumers in housekeeping and personal care needs. These arrangements are utilized by the consumer in order to live more independently.

Supervised Living Arrangements.   Supervised living arrangements provide intensive support and training for persons with severe disabilities. Unlike semi-independent living arrangements, these facilities have full-time residential staff. This type of arrangement is usually provided for individuals who are not able to care for themselves and need full-time supervision.

Due to individual preferences and needs, you may want to check out a variety of different group living arrangements.

Intermediate Care Facility for Those with Mental Retardation (ICF/MR).   ICF/MR facilities are specially licensed residential settings for persons who require 24-hour care and supervision. Group homes may range in size from small six-person homes to larger institutions. Most of them are small residences serving under 16 people. This is a Medicaid residential setting for the more severely impaired individual. The ICF provides a full array of direct-care and clinical services within the program model. Clinical services include psychology, social work, speech therapy, nursing, nutrition, pharmacology, and medical services. ICF admission normally requires participants be Medicaid eligible, have an IQ below 59, and manifest deficits in basic skills such as grooming and hygiene.

Supportive Living Units (SLU).   **Supportive living units** are state-funded small residential sites, typically housing one to three high-functioning individuals. These individuals may or may not be Medicaid eligible, are typically competitively employed, and require 21 hours or less per week of individual protection and oversight by a direct-care person.

Wavered Services.   **Wavered services** apply to persons with mental retardation who are presently in ICF/MRs or who are at risk of being placed in ICF/MRs unless the wavered services can be provided to them in a home or community setting. The possible living arrangements are intended to be much less restrictive and isolated from the mainstream world than the traditional ICF/MR settings. The new home or community-based residence could include a person's own parental home, a foster home, an apartment, or a small group home. It is believed that through providing an array of wavered services to the individual in his or her home or in a community-based setting, placement in the more restrictive ICF/MR setting can be avoided. These services are available to individuals who would otherwise qualify for Medicaid only if they were in an out-of-home setting.

Home Care Attendants.   There may be times when an individual with a disability can function independently with only the care of a home care attendant. **Home care attendants** may be paid for by the individual, if economically capable, or by public funds through Medicaid.

Just as in the school setting in which the policy fosters the least restrictive educational environment, it follows that the same philosophy should be encouraged in seeking out adult living arrangements. This least restrictive independent arrangement may require utilization of many agencies, support personal, family, and so on. However, everything should be done to attain an individual's own personal least restrictive living arrangement.

Further, individuals with disabilities should also be aware that funding may be available to assist in making their residences adaptive to their personal needs, by providing ramps, modifications in doorways, and bathrooms.

Leisure/Recreational Experiences.   *Leisure* is some activity that we do by choice for relaxation rather than for money as part of our job. When a student is involved in the transition from school to adult life, a healthy part of this journey should include leisure activities. Teachers and parents may generally discover the student's leisure interests by having him or her sample a variety of activities and learning which ones are the most interesting and exciting. Parents of very young children in today's society normally expose them to a wide variety of experiences, such as

Dance classes	*Sports activities*
Little League	*Cultural experiences*
Music lessons	*Travel*
Scouting	*Art lessons*

As students without disabilities grow older, this process of sampling leisure interests depends less on the parents and more on their peer group. For young people with disabilities, however, teachers, parents, and other family members may continue to guide or structure leisure experiences. This extended period of guidance and involvement should be considered a realistic part of the transitional process to adulthood. Learning specific leisure skills can be an important component for successful integration into community recreation programs. Research has shown that leisure skill training contributes to a sense of competence, social interaction, and appropriate behavior.

Advantages of Special Leisure Programs. One of the conflicts that teachers and parents have to address is whether the child should participate in activities designed specifically for people with disabilities or enter activities that are geared for a more mainstreamed population. The advantages of a special program designed for children with disabilities are:

- They may allow the only opportunity for some children with severe disabilities to participate (e.g., Special Olympics).
- They allow for a sense of group identity.
- They provide a setting for social interaction.
- They create a more level playing field so that the individual's abilities become the focus rather than the disability.

On the other hand, concentrating on "disabled only" activities may unnecessarily exclude individuals from many leisure opportunities and prevent interaction with the nondisabled community.

Individual Concerns When Faced with Leisure Activities. One of the greatest concerns of individuals with disabilities is the problem they may face assimilating into the social world. Many students receive special services while in school that expose them to other children with disabilities. This social interaction and connection provide a foundation for improving social skills. However, once the school experience ends and the child is confronted with the mainstream world, many of these social opportunities are not available, and social isolation is often the result. Social isolation is probably the most painful aspect that individuals with disabilities face when they enter adulthood. Therefore, parents play a crucial role in assisting their child in providing the exposure to leisure and recreational activities. Parents may often find themselves as the only agent for this particular aspect of life, especially once the child leaves the school setting.

Parents and professionals should be aware of the enormous benefit of recreational activities in the role of social and personal confidence. Having a disability should not preclude a person from activities that enhance enjoyment. It is always important in one's life to maintain a balance between work and play.

Recreation activities have been one of the most visible areas of change for people with disabilities. There is hardly a sport activity that cannot include the participation of people with disabilities. For those that accept the challenge, nothing is off limits. Not everyone needs or wants to be a superstar. But everyone can attain a level of confidence in an activity that interests him or her. Parents and educators need to be supportive and encouraging to help their children develop those interests and skills because for all people, it is through the mastery of tasks that we raise our level of self-esteem.

Transportation Services. **Transportation services** provide us all with access to the wider opportunities of society employment, postsecondary education, job training programs, and recreation, to name a few. Traveling by car, by cab, or by public transportation systems such as bus and subway enables us to go to work and come home, go to school or other training programs, visit friends, take care of daily needs such as grocery shopping, and enjoy recreational activities. Yet, many individuals with disabilities have traditionally been isolated from these societal opportunities, because they lacked a means of transportation. For many, driving a car was not possible, due to a visual, physical, or cognitive disability. Public transportation systems were often inaccessible due to structural barriers. Still other individuals were unable to use the transportation systems that were available, because they lacked the training, or "know-how," to use these systems safely.

Today, the lack of access to transportation that many individuals with disabilities have experienced is changing. The **Americans with Disabilities Act** (ADA) recognizes the critical role that public transportation plays in the lives of many people. The ADA mandates that public transportation systems where available become accessible to people with disabilities. Unfortunately, availability of transportation is not the only impediment to independent travel for people with disabilities. For many individuals, learning how to travel on public transportation requires systematic training. Travel training, then, is often a crucial element in empowering people with disabilities to use the newly accessible transportation systems in our country and is part of the transition process.

Travel Training. *Travel training* is short-term, comprehensive, intensive instruction designed to teach students with disabilities how to travel safely and independently on public transportation. The goal of travel training is to train students to travel independently to a regularly visited destination and back. Specially trained personnel provide the travel training on a one-to-one basis. Students learn travel skills while following a particular route, generally to school or a work site, and are taught the safest, most direct route. The travel trainer is responsible for making sure the student experiences and understands the realities of public transportation and learns the skills required for safe and independent travel.

The term travel training is often used generically to refer to a program that provides instruction in travel skills to individuals with any disability except visual impairment. Individuals who have a visual impairment receive travel training from orientation and mobility specialists usually under the jurisdiction of the State Commission for the Blind. Travel trainers have the task of understanding how different disabilities affect a person's ability to travel independently and devising customized strategies to teach travel skills that address the specific needs of people with those disabilities.

A travel trainer usually begins training a student at the student's residence, which allows the trainer to:

- Observe the student in a familiar environment
- Reassure the family through daily contact
- Assess the student's home environment at regular travel times for potential problems

In a quality travel training program, a travel trainer works with one student at a time. The trainer follows the travel route with the student and instructs the student in dealing with problems such as getting lost or taking a detour around a construction site. The trainer should teach the student to make decisions, deal with the consequences of decisions, and maintain appropriate safety and behavior standards.

Being able to get around on one's own accord is an important component of independence; this is as true for people with disabilities as it is for those without disabilities. Nearly all people who have disabilities can (with training and the use of accessible vehicles) board, travel on, and exit a public transportation vehicle. However, a certified travel training program is often needed to teach people who have a disability to do these procedures safely and independently. Programs that maintain high-quality procedures for travel training are crucial in helping people who have a disability to develop autonomy and practice their right to move freely through a community.

A logical place to implement travel training programs is within the public school system. As the primary providers of education for students with a disability, local school districts have a full range of resources available to develop quality travel training programs. Because students are part of a school system for many consecutive years, educators can plan and deliver a full program of travel instruction. Then, as students become young adults and are close to exiting the school system, explicit travel training can become part of their education and can form the basis of the transition from school transportation to public transportation. While the public school system is the optimal environment in which to begin travel training, individuals with disabilities can also get travel training from independent living centers or similar agencies.

Society, too, benefits when people with disabilities participate actively in everyday life. Travel training programs can enable students with disabilities to become adults who can travel to and from their jobs without support, who are involved citizens of their communities, and who have the opportunity to live independently.

Although many transportation options for the disabled exist in certain areas, there is still work to be done in making all public transportation accessible. The availability of these options needs to be coordinated with the skills required to use such services. These skills begin early in one's life and need to be reinforced continuously if one is to move toward a world of independence.

Financial Services.   Many people with disabilities are eligible for benefits under one or more of several government programs. These programs are designed to protect the person with a disability by making sure that his or her financial resources are sufficient to provide the basic necessities of life—food, clothing, and health care.

To plan for the future of a child with disabilities, individuals must be aware of and use the many programs sponsored by the federal government and operated through a federal state partnership. These are called *entitlement programs*. Some of them are provided for large portions of the population in general and not just for persons with disabilities. Other programs are specifically for people with disabilities. Through a well-planned combination of services determined in the transition process and, where possible, by supplementing these services with private assets, one can establish a relatively secure financial future for the student.

When it comes to parents financing their child's future, there are several paths they can explore depending on:

- The nature and severity of the child's disability
- The personal assets of the family

The following options should be explored, and any one or combination may be sufficient for a particular situation:

- Using the family's own financial assets
- Government assistance through a variety of programs

Because support from personal assets is self-explanatory, we focus on the government programs that can provide financial support for individuals with disabilities.

Social Security Administration. The **Social Security Administration** (SSA) directs two programs that can be of financial benefit to eligible individuals with disabilities throughout the transition process. These programs are:

- Supplemental Security Income (SSI) program
- Social Security Disability Insurance (SSDI) program

Because the Social Security Administration considers many variables before determining if a person is eligible for SSI or SSDI benefits, the discussion here is intended only as an overview to the benefits of these programs. Ultimately, an individual's eligibility can be determined only by contacting the Social Security Administration and filing an application.

Supplemental Security Income (SSI). The **Supplemental Security Income** program is targeted for individuals who are both (1) in financial need and (2) blind or have disabilities. People who get SSI usually receive food stamps and Medicaid, too. The evaluation process to determine eligibility varies depending upon whether the applicant is under or over the age of 18. Recently, there have been many significant changes in how the SSA determines the SSI eligibility of individuals under the age of 18. These changes are expected to make it easier for children and youth with disabilities to qualify for SSI benefits. More information about these changes and the specific evaluation process the SSA now uses for individuals under the age of 18 is available by contacting the Social Security Administration directly. When a child reaches the age of 18, the Social Security Administration no longer considers the income and resources of parents when determining if the youth is eligible for benefits.

Under the SSI program, individuals over the age of 18 are eligible to receive monthly payments if they:

- Have little or no income or resources such as savings accounts
- Are considered medically disabled or blind
- Do not work or earn less than a certain amount, defined by the Social Security Administration as substantial gainful activity (SGA)

Social Security Disability Insurance (SSDI). The **Social Security Disability Insurance** program is a bit different, because it considers the employment status of the applicant's parents. "SSDI benefits are paid to persons who become disabled before the age of 22 if at least one of their parents had worked a certain amount of time under Social Security but is now disabled, retired, and/or deceased" (National Association of State Directors of Special Education, 1990, p. 9). As with SSI, eligibility for SSDI generally makes an individual eligible for food stamps and Medicaid benefits as well.

In the past, the benefits an individual might receive from either or both of these programs would be substantially reduced or even eliminated by income earned at a job. Recent legislation, however, has made major changes in both the SSI and SSDI programs to encourage people receiving these benefits to try to work and become independent. These changes are called work incentives, because they make it possible for individuals with disabilities to work without an immediate loss of benefits.

Whatever financial status a family has at the time a child turns 18, a thorough knowledge of his or her financial entitlements should be fully understood by all.

Food Stamps. The **Food Stamp program** provides financial assistance by enabling recipients to exchange the stamps for food. It is a major supplement for income if an individual with a disability meets the income requirements. This program is federally funded through the Department of Agriculture's Nutrition and Food Service (NFS). It is administered by state and local social service agencies. In most cases, if an individual is eligible for SSI, food stamps will also be available. For more information, contact your local department of social services.

Although we are aware that dealing with this issue may cause frustration, we strongly suggest perseverance. For specific information about the benefits provided through SSI and SSDI, the student or parents should contact your local Social Security Office (listed in the telephone directory under Social Security Administration) and request a copy of the publications addressing SSI and SSDI. Single copies are free. Individuals can also contact the SSA through its toll-free number: 1-800-234-5772 (voice) or 1-800-325-0778 (TDD), available 24 hours a day. Due to the volume of inquiries that SSA receives, it is best to call early in the morning or late in the afternoon. SSA also recommends calling later in the week.

Postsecondary Education Services.   Some students with disabilities may be capable of graduating high school with all the requirements and moving to a postsecondary education experience. A number of years ago, students with disabilities had limited choices when it came to choosing a college or university that could provide accommodations. With the advent of ADA and the disabilities rights movement, accommodations for students with disabilities are relatively commonplace today. As a result, one is able to apply to several different types of postsecondary educational institutions. The first type of school is the college or university that is specifically geared for a certain type of disability.

Colleges and Career Education. Colleges offer an opportunity for individuals with disabilities to continue their education and earn tangible evidence of education such as a certificate or degree. Junior and community colleges offer a variety of courses that, upon successful completion of the prescribed courses, may lead to a Certificate or Associate's degree. Community colleges are publicly funded, have either no or low-cost tuition, and offer a wide range of programs, including vocational and occupational courses. They exist in or near many communities; generally the only admissions requirement is a high school diploma or its equivalent. Junior colleges are usually privately supported, and the majority provide programs in the liberal arts field. Four-year colleges and universities offer programs of study that lead to a Bachelor's degree after successful completion of four years of prescribed course work.

The Law and Its Impact.   In high school, the school district was responsible for providing any or all support services necessary for an individual with disabilities to participate in the educational process. The college or university does not have the same legal obligation. It is required by law to provide any reasonable accommodation that may be necessary for those with disabilities to have equal access to educational opportunities and services available to nondisabled peers if requested.

   Title II of the ADA covers state-funded schools such as universities, community colleges, and vocational schools. Title III covers private colleges and vocational schools. If a school receives federal dollars, regardless of whether it is private or public, it is also covered by the regulation of **Section 504 of the Rehabilitation Act** requiring schools to make their programs accessible to qualified students with disabilities.

   Under the provisions of Section 504, universities and colleges may not:

- Limit the number of students with disabilities
- Make preadmission inquiries as to whether an applicant has a disability
- Exclude a qualified student with a disability from a course of study
- Discriminate in administering scholarships, fellowships, and so forth on the basis of a disability
- Establish rules or policies that may adversely affect students with disabilities

For college students with disabilities, academic adjustments may include adaptations in the way specific courses are conducted, the use of auxiliary equipment and support staff, and modifications in academic requirements. These modifications may include:

- Removing architectural barriers
- Providing services such as readers, qualified interpreters, or note takers for deaf or hard-of-hearing students
- Providing modifications, substitutions, or waivers of courses, major fields of study, or degree requirements on a case-by-case basis
- Allowing extra time to complete exams
- Using alternative forms for students to demonstrate course mastery
- Permitting the use of computer software programs or other assistive technological devices to facilitate test-taking and study skills

Disability-Related Support Services.   Many college campuses have an office of student services or special services for those with disabilities. Others have designated the dean of students or some other administrator to provide this information and to coordinate necessary services and accommodations. At vocational schools or other training programs, the person responsible for disability services can usually provide this information. There are also many publications that can tell more about the policies and programs that individual colleges and universities have established to address the needs of students with disabilities.

Assistive Technology.   Computers were designed to perform at maximum efficiency when used by those without disabilities. But almost all of us employ some type of adaptive technology when using the computer. Adaptive technology ranges from wearing eyeglasses or wrist supports, to simply adjusting the brightness of the screen display or the height and angle of the monitor. Broadly defined, **assistive technology** includes any device or piece of equipment that increases the independence of a person with disabilities. Assistive technology, of course, is not new. For instance, the wheelchair has long been an indispensable assistive device for those with impaired mobility.

The distinction between adaptive technologies employed by the nondisabled and assistive technologies for those with disabilities blurs at times. Some of the assistive technologies designed for the disabled have proven so ergonomically sound that they have been incorporated as standard features. One such example is the placement of the keyboard on/off switch, which was designed so that people with motor impairments would not have to reach to the back of the machine to turn the power on and off.

Assistive technology has enormously increased the ability of those with disabilities to lead independent lives. Computer-based environmental control units allow users to turn on lights and appliances and open doors from a wheelchair. Augmentative communication devices enable those who cannot speak to voice thoughts and needs using touch- or light-activated keyboards coupled to synthetic speech systems. Screen reading programs for the blind, screen magnification systems for those with low vision, and special ability switches that permit the mobility-impaired to use a computer are only a few examples of the technology by which the individuals gain access to the computer screen and keyboard.

Medical Services.   When chronic illness, disability, or severe injury occurs, it is a time of great stress for family and friends. The adjustment for a family with a child with a severe or complex health issue can be very intense and taxing. The special needs for this type of child require a focus on many more issues than may be found under other situations. There is a magnification of concerns surrounding the child's well-being, health, daily life, and constantly changing future expectations. As the health field changes and technology and terminology expand, parents must learn new skills and acquire a wide range of knowledge to ensure that their child's ongoing health needs are properly addressed.

However, with the expansion of technology and improved medical care comes the added burden of growing medical costs. As a result, parents of children with chronic disabilities have the added anxiety of finding the resources necessary for medical attention and recommended equipment.

Although a great deal of financial, social, and medical support is available within one's community, state, or country, it is up to the parents to be able to wade through the vast amount of terminology, forms, agencies, issues, and so on to find the best direction for their particular child. This solution or path to the correct resources will differ from family to family as a result of the:

- Family's personal financial situation
- Type of available health insurance
- Child's specific medical needs

- State in which the family resides
- Family's understanding of its rights and responsibilities

Medicare. Born out of the 1960s, **Medicare** was a result of a response to growing concerns about the high cost of medical care for older Americans. Since that time, however, the program has expanded to include not only older Americans but millions of adults with disabilities. Unlike Medicaid, which is based solely on financial need, the right to Medicare benefits is established primarily by payroll tax contributions. Medicare is a federal health-care-insurance program that provides some medical coverage to people over 65 and also to individuals with disabilities for a limited period of time. Medicare will help meet some bills for long-term care, but will not fund unlimited long-term care. To meet uncovered costs, you may need supplemental or "medigap" insurance policies. *Medigap* insurance is offered by private insurance companies, not the government. It is not the same as Medicare or Medicaid. These policies are designed to pay for some of the costs that Medicare does not cover.

Medicaid. **Medicaid** is a federal-state program that helps pay for health care for nonelderly people who are financially needy or who have a disability. Individual states determine who is eligible for Medicaid and which health services will be covered. Most people do not qualify for Medicaid until the majority of their money has been spent. It is important to realize, however, that some individuals whose incomes are not in the lowest category, but who have substantial medical expenses, do qualify for Medicaid. These individuals—who either have incomes higher than the **Aid for Families with Dependent Children (AFDC)** cutoff or have very high medical bills that drop their incomes below the level established for categorically needy—are termed *medically needy*. Once an individual is covered by Medicaid, he or she is entitled to receive the following minimal services:

- Physician services
- Laboratory and X-ray services
- Outpatient hospital services
- Skilled nursing facilities (SNF) for persons over 21
- Family planning services
- Medical diagnosis and treatment for persons under 21
- Home health services for individuals
- Inpatient hospital service

In many states Medicaid also will pay for some or all of the following:

- Dental care
- Medically necessary drugs
- Eyeglasses
- Prosthetic devices
- Physical, speech, and occupational therapy
- Private duty nursing
- Care from alternative medicine, such as chiropractors, acupuncturists

THE INDIVIDUALS WITH DISABILITIES EDUCATION IMPROVEMENT ACT

The Individuals with Disabilities Education Improvement Act (IDEA 2004), P.L. 108-446, builds on the bipartisan education reforms in the No Child Left Behind Act, which gives important new educational opportunities to students with disabilities. At the foundation of the bill are the findings of President Bush's Commission on Excellence in Special Education, which in 2002 called for special education reform based on paperwork reduction, early intervention, parental choice, and academic results for students. The Individuals with Disabilities Education Improvement Act seeks to improve results for students with disabilities by shifting the focus away from compliance with duplicative, burdensome, and confusing rules, and placing a renewed emphasis on ensuring that children with disabilities are actually learning. The bill reauthorizes the Individuals with Disabilities Education Act (IDEA), the nation's special education law. P.L. 108-446 seeks to improve educational results for students with disabilities by:

- Making special education stronger for students and parents
- Ensuring school safety and reasonable discipline
- Reducing unnecessary lawsuits and litigation
- Supporting teachers and schools
- Reforming special education funding, and building on historic funding increases

Making Special Education Stronger for Students and Parents

Improving Education Results for Children with Disabilities. As noted by the President's Commission on Excellence in Special Education, the IDEA '97 system placed too much emphasis on compliance with complicated rules, and not enough emphasis on academic results for children with special needs. As a result of this misplaced focus, too many children in special education classes had been left behind academically. P.L. 108-446 ensures that states will align their accountability systems for students with disabilities to the No Child Left Behind (NCLB) accountability system, ensure that Individualized Education Programs (IEPs) specifically address academic achievement of students with disabilities; and give local school districts greater flexibility in reviewing the progress of a child by replacing arbitrary and bureaucratic benchmarks and short-term objectives with the strong new NCLB system, which measures students' actual academic progress.

Encouraging Innovative Approaches to Parental Involvement and Parental Choice. Parents should be active participants in their children's education experience. However, under IDEA '97, parents of students with disabilities were often not fully informed or are given limited options of where or how their children can be educated. P.L. 108-446 expands parental rights and options by enabling parents and local school districts to agree to change the IEP without holding a formal IEP meeting, allowing school districts to use state IDEIA funds to support supplemental educational services chosen by parents for students with disabilities in schools identified as needing improvement under NCLB because students with disabilities are not making adequate yearly progress, reforming parent training centers to focus on all children with disabilities and serve all parents of children with disabilities, especially low-income, minority, and limited English proficient parents; and giving parents more choices before their children enter school by allowing children with disabilities to remain in the same program (Part C) from birth until kindergarten.

Addressing the Needs of Home-Schooled Children.   For some parents, educating their children at home is the best option for their children and their families. To ensure that parents have full freedom over the education of their children, IDEA 2004 allows parents of home-schooled children to refuse services for their children when the parents actively reject those services. IDEA 2004 also makes it clear that local schools do not need to conduct an evaluation or create an IEP if parents state that they will refuse both the evaluation and services, helping avoid unnecessary and unwanted involvement that can lead to lawsuits.

Protecting Parents from Being Forced to Medicate Their Children.   IDEA 2004 will protect parents by preventing schools from forcing children to be medicated as a condition of attending school, receiving an evaluation, or receiving services. Although schools will continue to allow teachers and school personnel to share concerns and insights with parents, this will ensure that medical diagnoses are properly handled between the parent, child, and their medical professional.

Ensuring Equitable Participation for Students in Private Schools.   Parents should have the right to choose a private school for their children without losing important special education services. To provide equitable participation of students in private schools, the bill expands child find and consultation responsibilities, including a discussion of direct services and alternative service delivery mechanisms. When local public schools disagree with private school officials, a written explanation will be provided.

Improving Early Intervention Strategies.   Currently, too many children with reading problems are identified as learning disabled and placed in special education classes. This over-identification hinders the academic development of students who are misidentified, and also takes valuable resources away from students who truly have disabilities. Experts agree that strengthening the quality of reading instruction programs will improve special education and address this problem directly. P.L. 108-446 gives flexibility to local school districts to use up to 15 percent of their funds for early intervening services for students before they are identified as needing special education, as recommended by the President's Commission on Excellence in Special Education.

Reducing Over-Identification and Misidentification of Nondisabled Children, Including Minority Youth.   A disproportionate number of minority students are wrongly placed in special education rather than provided intensive educational interventions and positive behavioral interventions. As former Education Secretary Rod Paige has noted, studies show that the proportion of minority students identified in some disability categories is dramatically greater than their share of the overall population. More specifically, African American students are labeled as mentally retarded and emotionally disturbed far out of proportion to their share of the student population. For minority students, misclassification or inappropriate placement in special education programs can have significant adverse consequences, particularly when these students are removed from regular education settings or given limited access to the core curriculum. IDEA 2004 requires districts with significant over-identification of minority students to operate early intervening programs that work to reduce over-identification; eliminate the outdated "IQ-discrepancy" model that relies on a "wait to fail" approach, introduce a "response to intervention" model that identifies specific learning disabilities before the students are failing at grade level, and encourage greater use of programs that rely on positive behavioral interventions and supports.

Strengthening Accountability Measures for States.   To complement the accountability provisions in NCLB, IDEA 2004 asks states to create their own plans on how they will meet the requirements of the law. This will ensure that states struggling to meet their own plans will have access to extra help, such as technical assistance. The improved monitoring and enforcement system sends a strong signal about the importance of providing a high quality education to students with disabilities.

Ensuring School Safety and Reasonable Discipline

Giving Teachers and Schools Greater Discretion to Exercise Reasonable Discipline and Ensure Safety for All Students.   Schools should be safe for all students and teachers, and discipline problems should be addressed with common sense. IDEA 2004 helps school personnel ensure school safety and hold students responsible for their actions while protecting the rights of students with disabilities. Unless a disciplinary infraction is the direct result of a child's disability, the child will be disciplined in the same manner as a nondisabled student. If the disciplinary infraction involves the serious safety issues of drugs, weapons, or serious bodily injury, the student will automatically be out of the classroom for up to 45 days. In cases of suspensions longer than 10 days, the child will continue to receive educational services to make progress on his or her IEP.

Reducing Unnecessary Lawsuits and Litigation

Restoring Trust and Reducing Litigation.   Litigation under IDEA '97 had taken on the role of finding and punishing school districts for technical violations rather than being used to protect the substantive rights of children with disabilities. That type of litigation breeds an attitude of distrust between parents and school personnel, hindering efforts to work cooperatively to find the best education placement and services for students. P.L. 108-446 creates the opportunity for a resolution session within 30 days of a complaint being filed to quickly resolve problems before they escalate, encourages the use of mediation as early as possible, requires complaints to be clear and specific when they are filed, and establishes a statute of limitations of two years from the date of the alleged violation to file a complaint.

Reducing Frivolous Lawsuits and Addressing Attorney's Fees.   Too often, parents are manipulated into court by attorneys with their own interests in mind, rather than the best interests of children and families. To curb this abuse of the system, attorneys will be held liable for the costs of frivolous lawsuits. To address concerns about exorbitant attorney's fees, both parents and school districts will be able to collect the cost of attorney's fees as the prevailing party.

Supporting Teachers and Schools

Reducing the Paperwork Burden on Teachers.   Good special education teachers are leaving the profession in frustration with IDEA '97 system's overwhelming and unnecessary paperwork burden, contributing to what has become a chronic shortage of quality special education teachers. P.L. 108-446 incorporates a 15-state pilot program that will allow school districts to offer parents the *option* of a 3-year IEP and a 15-state pilot program that will allow states to reduce the IEP paperwork burden on teachers and increase instructional time. IDEA 2004 also streamlines and decreases the paperwork burden on states and local school districts through innovative strategies such as the use of teleconferencing and streamlining of duplicative requirements.

Supporting General Education and Special Education Teachers.   A continuing shortage of special education teachers, coupled with a shortage of regular education teachers who are adequately trained to work with students with disabilities, hinders students' educational achievement under the IDEA 2004 system. Both current and prospective teachers should have professional development to address the educational needs of students with disabilities. IDEA 2004 refocuses State Professional Development Grants on professional development for school personnel working with students with disabilities, streamlines Personnel Preparation programs, and encourages training of both special education teachers and regular education teachers to work with students with disabilities.

Defining What It Means to Be a "Highly Qualified" Special Education Teacher. States and schools are asking for clarity on what it means to be a "highly qualified" special education teacher. The No Child Left Behind Act calls for a highly qualified teacher in every public school classroom by the 2005–2006 school year to ensure that all children learn from high quality teachers. To align IDEA 2004 with NCLB, and provide guidance for states and schools on how special education teachers can meet the highly qualified standard, P.L. 108-446 requires *all* special education teachers to be certified in special education. For special education teachers teaching students with the most significant cognitive disabilities—those who take alternate assessments aligned to alternate standards—the teachers will also be required to have an elementary certification, or for those teaching above the elementary grade level, demonstrate the ability to teach at the appropriate instructional level for their students. New special education teachers teaching multiple subjects must meet the NCLB highly qualified standard in at least one core subject area (language arts, math, or science) and will have two years from the date of employment to take advantage of the NCLB High Objective Uniform

State Standard of Evaluation (HOUSSE) to demonstrate competence in other core subject areas. Veteran special education teachers teaching multiple subjects can take advantage of the HOUSSE to demonstrate competence in other core subject areas.

Reforming Special Education Funding, and Building on Historic Funding Increases

Simplifying Special Education Finance and Building on Funding Increases.   The funding streams under IDEA '97 are needlessly complex and should be simplified while establishing a clear path to reach the federal spending goal of 40 percent of the additional cost of educating children with disabilities. P.L. 108-446 simplifies funding streams for IDEA 2004 Part B grants to states and establishes a clear 6-year path to reach the 40 percent goal through the discretionary appropriations process.

Giving Local Communities More Control.   The federal government is not yet meeting its commitment to pay up to 40 percent of special education costs, and states and local communities are making up the difference. Under Republican leadership, the federal share of special education costs has risen dramatically, and the funding increases will continue. As the federal share of special education costs continues to increase, local communities should have more flexibility in how they spend their own resources. To increase options for local communities, P.L. 108-446 allows local schools, as the federal government moves closer to paying 40 percent of special education costs, to redirect a share of their own, local resources for other educational purposes, consistent with activities in the No Child Left Behind Act.

CONCLUSION

It has only been through the personal struggles and efforts of parents, professionals, and individuals with disabilities that laws and attitudes have changed. Initially, the collaborative efforts of parents and professionals best meet the needs of young children with disabilities. However, as these children enter the adult world, they should become partners of this collaborative team in promoting issues that result in their well-being.

REFERENCES AND SUGGESTED READINGS

Algozzine, B., Christensen, S., & Ysseldyke, J. (1982). Probabilities associated with the referral-to-placement process. *Teacher Education and Special Education, 5,* 19–23.

Allen, S. G., & Serwatka, T. S. (1994). *Auditory Perception Test for the Hearing Impaired.* East Aurora, NY: Slosson Educational Publications.

American Association on Mental Retardation (1992). *Mental definition, classification, and systems of support* (9th ed.). Washington, DC: Author.

American Psychological Association (1985). *Standards for educational and psychological testing.* Washington, DC: Author.

American Psychological Association (1990). *Guidelines for providers of psychological services to ethnic, linguistic, and culturally diverse populations.* Washington, DC: Author.

America's Learning Exchange (2000). www.alx.org/aboutalx.asp. Telephone 202-219-8854.

Anastasi, A. (1998). *Psychological testing.* New York: Macmillan.

Anderson, K. (1989). *Screening instrument for targeting educational risk.* Austin, TX: PRO-ED.

Anderson, W., Chitwood, S., & Hayden, D. (1990). *Negotiating special education maze: A guide for parents and teachers* (2nd ed.). Rockville, MD: Woodbine House. (Available from Woodbine House, 6510 Bells Mill Road, Bethesda, MD 20817. Telephone: 1-800-843-7323; [301]-897-3570.)

Archibald, D. A. (1991). Authentic assessment: Principles, practices, and issues. *School Psychology Quarterly, 6,* 279–293.

Artiles, A. J., & Trent, S. C. (1994). Overrepresentation of minority students in special education: A continuing debate. *Journal of Special Education, 27,* 410–437.

Ascher, M. (1990, February). A river-crossing problem in cross-cultural perspectives. *Mathematics Magazine, 63*(1), 26–29.

Ayres, J. (1991). *Sensory Integration and Praxis Test.* Los Angeles, CA: Western Psychological Services.

Baca, L., & Cervantes, H. T. (1984). *The bilingual special education interface.* Columbus, OH: Merrill.

Baca, L., Escamilla, K., & Carjuzaa, J. (1994). Language minority students: Literacy and educational reform. In N. J. Ellsworth, C. N. Hedley, & A. N. Baratta (Eds.), *Literacy: A redefinition* (pp. 61–76). Hillsdale, NJ: Lawrence Erlbaum.

Bagnato, S. J., Neisworth, J. T., & Munson, S. M. (1993). Sensible strategies for assessment in early intervention. In D. M. Bryant & M. A. Grahams (Eds.), *Implementing early intervention: From research to effective practice* (pp. 148–156). New York: Guilford Press.

Bailey, D. B., & Wolery, M. (1992). *Assessing infants and preschoolers with handicaps.* Columbus, OH: Merrill.

Bailey, D. B., Wolery, M., & McLean, M. (1996). *Assessing infants and preschoolers with special need* (2nd ed.). Englewood Cliffs, NJ: Prentice Hall.

Bambara, L., & Knoster, T. (1995). Embedding choice in the context of daily routines: An experimental case study. *Journal of the Association for Persons with Severe Handicaps, 20*(3), 185–195.

Batsche, G. M. (1997). The future of school psychology: Perspectives on effective training. *School Psychology Review, 26*(1), 93–103.

Batzle, J. (1992). *Portfolio assessment and evaluation: Developing and using portfolios in the classroom.* Cypress, CA: Creative Teaching Press.

Bayley, N. (1993). *Bayley Scales of Infant Development—2nd Edition (BSID-II).* San Antonio, TX: The Psychological Corporation.

Beaumont, C., & Langdon, H. W. (1992). Speech-language services for Hispanics with communication disorders: A framework. In H. W. Langdon & L. L. Cheng (Eds.), *Hispanic children and adults with communication disorders* (pp. 1–19). Gaithersburg, MD: Aspen.

Beery, K. E. (1997). *Developmental Test of Visual Motor Integration—4th Edition (VMI-4).* Austin, TX: PRO-ED.

Bellack, L., & Bellak, S. (1974). *Children's Apperception Test.* Larchmont, NY: C.P.S. Incorporated.

Bender, L. (1938). *Bender Visual Motor Gestalt Test (BVMGT).* New York: The American Orthopsychiatric Association.

Berdine, W. H., & Meyer, S. A. (1987). *Assessment in special education.* Boston: Little, Brown (available from HarperCollins).

Berk, R. A., & DeGangi, G. A. (1993). *DeGangi-Berk Test of Sensory Integration.* Los Angeles, CA: Western Psychological Services.

Bernstein, D. K. (1989). Assessing children with limited English proficiency: Current perspectives. *Topics in Language Disorders, 9,* 15–20.

Bigge, J. L. (1990). *Teaching individuals with physical and multiple disabilities* (3rd ed.). Columbus, OH: Merrill.

Bigge, J., & Stump, C. (1999). *Curriculum, assessment, and instruction for students with disabilities.* Belmont, CA: Wadsworth.

Black, J., & Ford, A. (1989). Planning and implementing activity-based lessons. In A. Ford, R. Schnorr, L. Meyer, L. Davern, J. Black, & P. Dempsey (Eds.), *The Syracuse community-reference curriculum guide for students with moderate and severe disabilities* (pp. 295–311). Baltimore: Paul H. Brookes.

Blankenship, C. (1985). Using curriculum-based assessment data to make instructional decisions. *Exceptional Children, 52,* 233–238.

Bloom, L., & Lahey, M. (1978). *Language development and language disorders.* New York: John Wiley.

Boehm, A. E. (1986). *Boehm Test of Basic Concepts—Revised (BTBC-R).* San Antonio, TX: The Psychological Corporation.

Bogdan, R., & Knoll, J. (1988). The sociology of disability. In E. L. Meyen & T. M. Skrtic (Eds.), *Exceptional children and youth* (3rd ed.) (pp. 449–477). Denver, CO: Love.

Bogdan, R., & Kugelmass, J. (1984). Case studies of mainstreaming: A symbolic interactionist approach to special schooling. In L. Barton & S. Tomlinson (Eds.), *Special education and social interests* (pp. 173–191). New York: Nichols.

Bracken, B. A. (1984). *Bracken Basic Concept Scale (BBCS).* San Antonio, TX: The Psychological Corporation.

Braddock, D. (1987, September). National study of public spending for mental retardation and developmental disabilities. *American Journal of Mental Deficiency, 92*(2), 121–133.

Brigance, A. H. (1991). *Brigance Diagnostic Inventory of Basic Skills.* Billerica, MA: Curriculum Associates.

Brown v. Board of Education (1954). 347 U.S. 483.

Brown, L., Serbenov, R. J., & Johnsen, S. K. (1997). *Test of Nonverbal Intelligence—3rd Edition.* Austin, TX: PRO-ED.

Brown, V. L., Cronin, M. E., & McEntire, E. (1994). *Test of Mathematical Abilities—2.* Austin, TX: PRO-ED.

Brown, V., Hammill, D., Larson, S., & Wiederholt, J. L. (1994). *Test of Adolescent and Adult Language—Third Edition (TOAL-3).* Austin, TX: PRO-ED.

Brown, V. L., Hammill, D. D., & Wiederholt, J. L. (1995). *Test of Reading Comprehension—Third Edition.* Austin, TX: PRO-ED.

Bruininks, R. (1985). *Bruininks-Oseretsky Test of Motor Proficiency.* Circle Pines, MN: American Guidance Service.

Buckley, E. (1985). *Diagnostic Word Patterns.* Cambridge, MA: Educators Publishing Service Inc.

Bullis, M., & Gaylord-Ross, R. (1991). *Moving on: Transitions for youth with behavioral disorders.* Reston, VA: Council for Exceptional Children. (Available from the Council for Exceptional Children, 1920 Association Drive, Reston, VA 22091-1589. Telephone: 703-620-3660.)

Burgemeister, B. B., Blurn, L. H., & Lorge, I. (1972). *Columbia Mental Maturity Scale (CMMS).* San Antonio, TX: The Psychological Corporation.

Campione, J. C., & Brown, A. L. (1987). Linking dynamic assessment with school achievement. In C. S. Lidz (Ed.), *Dynamic assessment: An interactional approach to evaluating learning potential* (pp. 82–115). New York: Guilford.

Carl D. Perkins Vocational Education Act. 20 U.S.C. Sections 2331-2342.

Carlson, J. S., & Wiedl, K. H. (1978). Use of testing-the-limits procedures in the assessment of intellectual capabilities of children with learning difficulties. *American Journal of Mental Deficiency, 82,* 559–564.

Carlson, J. S., & Wiedl, K. H. (1979). Toward a differential testing approach: Testing-the-limits employing the Raven Matrices. *Intelligence, 3,* 323–344.

Carrow-Woolfolk, E. (1995). *Written Expression Scale.* Circle Pines, MN: American Guidance Service.

Chalfant, J. C. (1989). Learning disabilities: Policy issues and promising approaches. *American Psychologist, 44*(2), 392–398.

Clark, C. (1994, August). *Exito: A dynamic team assessment approach for culturally diverse students.* Presentation at the BUENO Bilingual Special Education Institute, Boulder, CO.

Code of Federal Regulations (C.F.R.). Title 34; Education; Parts 1 to 499, July 1986. Washington, DC: U.S. Government Printing Office.

Code of Federal Regulations (C.F.R.). Title 34; Parts 300 to 399, July 1, 1993. Washington, DC: U.S. Government Printing Office.

Colarusso, R., & Hammill, D. D. (1996). *Motor-Free Perceptual Test—Revised (MVPT-R).* Novata, CA: Academic Therapy Publications.

Collier, C. (1994). *Multicultural assessment: Implications for regular and special education* (3rd ed.). Boulder, CO: BUENO Center for Multicultural Education.

Conners, K. C. (1997). *Conners' Parent and Teacher Rating Scales.* N. Tonawanda, NY: Multi-Health Systems Incorporated.

Connolly, A., Nachtman, W., & Pritchett, M. (1997). *Key Math Diagnostic Arithmetic Tests—Revised.* Circle Pines, MN: American Guidance Service.

Conoley, J. C., & Kramer, J. J. (Eds.). (1992). *Eleventh mental measurement yearbook.* Lincoln: University of Nebraska Press.

Copenhaver, J. (1995). *Section 504: An educator's primer: What teachers and administrators need to know about implementing accommodations for eligible individuals with disabilities.* Logan, UT: Mountain Plains Regional Resource Center.

Cortâs, C. E. (1986). The education of language minority students: A contextual interaction model. In Bilingual Education Office, California State Department of Education (Comp.), *Beyond language: Social and cultural factors in schooling language minority students* (pp. 3–33). Los Angeles, CA: Evaluation, Dissemination, and Assessment Center.

Covarrubias v. San Diego Unified School District (Southern California) (1971). No. 70-394-T, S.D., Cal. February.

Cox, L. S. (1975). Diagnosing and remediating systematic errors in addition and subtraction computations. *The Arithmetic Teacher, 22,* 151–157.

Cummins, J. (1986). Empowering minority students: A framework for intervention. *Harvard Educational Review, 56*(1), 18–36.

Cummins, J. (1989). A theoretical framework for bilingual special education. *Exceptional Children, 56*(2), 111–119.

Curwin, R., & Mendler, B. (1994). Helping students rediscover hope. *Journal of Emotional and Behavioral Problems, 3*(1), 27–30.

Cutler, B. C. (1993). *You, your child, and "special" education: A guide to making the system work.* Baltimore: Paul H. Brookes.

DeStefano, L., & Wermuth, T. R. (1992). IDEA (P.L. 101-476): Defining a second generation of transition services. In F. R. Rusch, L. DeStefano, J. Chadsey-Rusch, L. A. Phelps, & E. Szymanshi (Eds.), *Transition from school to adult life: Models, linkages, and policy* (pp. 537–549). Sycamore, IL: Sycamore Publishing. (Available from Sycamore Publishing Company, P.O. Box 133, Sycamore, IL 60178. Telephone: [815] 756-5388.)

Developmental Disabilities Assistance and Bill of Rights Act. 42 U.S.C. Section 6012.

Diana v. California State Board of Education (1970). No. C-70 37 RFP, District Court of Northern California, February.

Duffy, J. B., Salvia, J., Tucker, J., & Ysseldyke, J. (1981). Nonbiased assessment: A need for operationalism. *Exceptional Children, 7,* 427–434.

Dunlap, G., et al. (1991). Functional assessment, curricular revision and severe behavior problems. *Journal of Applied Behavioral Analysis, 24*(2), 387–397.

Dunn, L. M., Dunn, L. M., & Williams, K. T. (1997). *Peabody Picture Vocabulary Test—3 (PPVT-III).* Circle Pines, MN: American Guidance Service.

Durrell, D. O., & Catterson, J. H. (1980). *Durrell Analysis of Reading Difficulty.* San Antonio, TX: The Psychological Corporation.

Dykes, M. K. (1980). *Developmental Assessment for the Severely Handicapped—2nd edition.* Austin, TX: PRO-ED.

Elksnin, L., & Elksnin, N. (1990). Using collaborative consultation with parents to promote effective vocational programming. *Career Development for Exceptional Individuals, 13*(2), 135–142.

Elliott, R. (1987). *Litigating intelligence: IQ tests, special education, and social science in the courtroom.* Dover, MA: Auburn House.

Engen, E., & Engen, T. (1983). *Rhode Island Test of Language Structure.* East Aurora, NY: Distributed by Slosson Educational Publications.

Falvey E. (1989). *Community-based curriculum: Instructional strategies for students with severe handicaps* (2nd ed.). Baltimore: Paul H. Brookes.

Federal Regulations for Individuals with Disabilities Education Act (IDEA) Amendments of 1997 for Wed. October 22 (1997). Available from U.S. Government Printing Office, P.O. Box 371954, Pittsburgh, PA 15250-7954.

Figueroa, R., Fradd, S. H., & Correa, V. I. (1989). Bilingual special education and this issue. *Exceptional Children, 56,* 174–178.

Figueroa, R. A. (1993). The reconstruction of bilingual special education. *Focus on Diversity, 3*(3), 2–3.

Figueroa, R. A., & Ruiz, N. T. (1994). The reconstruction of bilingual special education II. *Focus on Diversity, 4*(1), 2–3.

Flaugher, R. (1978). The many definitions of test bias. *American Psychologist, 33,* 671–679.

Franklin, M. E. (1992, October/November). Culturally sensitive instructional practices for African-American learners with disabilities. *Exceptional Children, 59*(2), 115–122.

Frostig, M., Lefever, W., & Whittlessey, J. R. (1993). *Marianne Frostig Developmental Test of Visual Perception (DTVP).* Austin, TX: PRO-ED.

Frostig, M., Maslow, P., LeFev, D. W., & Wittleson, J. R. (1966). *The Marianne Frostig Developmental Test of Visual Perception.* Palo Alto, CA: Consulting Psychology Press.

Fuchs, D., & Fuchs, L. (1989). Effects of examiner familiarity on Black, Caucasian, and Hispanic children: A meta-analysis. *Exceptional Children, 55,* 303–308.

Fuerstein, R. (1979, May). Cognitive modifiability in retarded adolescents: Effects of instrumental enrichment. *American Journal of Mental Deficiency, 83*(6), 539–550.

Gardner, M. F. (1996). *Test of Auditory Perceptual Skills—Revised (TAPS-R)*. Chesterfield, MO: Psychological and Educational Publications.

Gates, A. I., McKillop, A. S., & Horowitz, E. (1981). *Gates-McKillop-Horowitz Reading Diagnostic Tests.* New York: Teachers College Press.

Gearheart, C., & Gearheart, B. (1990). *Introduction to special education assessment. Principles and practices.* Denver, CO: Love.

General Information About Disabilities Which Qualify Children and Youth for Special Education Services Under the IDEA Act (1995). *News Digest.* National Information Center for Children and Youth with Disabilities (NICHCY), P.O. Box 1492, Washington, DC 20013. Telephone: 1-800-695-0285.

Gerard, J., & Weinstock, G. (1981). *Language Proficiency Test.* Novato, CA: Academic Therapy Publications.

Gessel, A. (1983). *Diagnostic Mathematics Inventory/Mathematics System.* Monterey, CA: CTB Macmillan/McGraw Hill.

Gilmore, J. V., & Gilmore, E. C. (1968). *Gilmore Oral Reading Test.* San Antonio, TX: The Psychological Corporation.

Ginsberg, H. P., & Baroody, A. J. (1990). *Test of Early Mathematics Ability—2.* Austin, TX: PRO-ED.

Goldman, R., & Fristoe, M. (1970). *Goldman-Fristoe Test of Articulation.* Circle Pines, MN: American Guidance Service.

Goldman, R., Fristoe, M., & Woodcock, R. (1970). *Goldman-Fristoe-Woodcock Test of Auditory Discrimination.* Circle Pines, MN: American Guidance Service.

Goodenough, F. L., & Harris, D. B. (1963). *Goodenough-Harris Drawing Test.* San Antonio, TX: The Psychological Corporation.

Goodman, Y., & Burke, C. (1972). *Reading miscue inventory manual: Procedure for diagnosis and evaluation.* New York: Macmillan.

Graden, J. L. (1989). Redefining "prereferral" intervention as intervention assistance: Collaboration between general and special education. *Exceptional Children, 56*(3), 227–231.

Graham, M., & Scott, K. (1988). The impact of definitions of high risk on services of infants and toddlers. *Topics in Early Childhood Special Education, 8*(3), 23–28.

Greenbaum, C. (1987). *Spellmaster Assessment and Teaching System.* Austin, TX: PRO-ED.

Grossman, H. J. (Ed.). (1983). *Manual on terminology and classification in mental retardation* (3rd ed. rev.). Washington, DC: American Association on Mental Deficiency (no longer available from the publisher).

Guadalupe Organization Inc. v. Tempe Elementary School District (1972). No. CIV 71-435, Phoenix (D. Arizona, January 24).

Guerin, G. R., & Maier, A. S. (1983). *Informal assessment in education.* Palo Alto, CA: Mayfield.

Hager, R. (1999). *Funding of assistive technology.* Assistive technology funding and systems change project. www.nls.org/spacedat.htm.

Halgren, D. W., & Clarizio, H. F. (1993). Categorical and programming changes in special education services. *Exceptional Children, 59,* 547–555.

Hammill, D. D. (1998). *Detroit Tests of Learning Aptitudes—Fourth Edition (DTLA-4).* Austin, TX: PRO-ED.

Hammill, D. D., Brown, L., & Bryant, B. R. (1992). *A consumer's guide to tests in print.* Austin, TX: PRO-ED.

Hammill, D. D., & Larsen, S. C. (1996). *Test of Written Language—3.* Austin, TX: PRO-ED.

Hammill, D., Pearson, N., & Voress, J. (1993). *Developmental Test of Visual Perception—2.* Austin, TX: PRO-ED.

Hammill, D. D., Pearson, N. A., & Wiederholt, L. (1996). *Comprehensive Test of Nonverbal Intelligence.* Austin, TX: PRO-ED.

Haney, W., & Madaus, G. (1989). Searching for alternatives to standardized tests: Whys, whats, and whitlers. *Phi Delta Kappan, 70*(9), 683–687.

Hanson, M., & Lynch, E. (1995A). *Early intervention: Implementing child and family services for infants and toddlers who are at risk or disabled* (2nd ed.). Austin, TX: PRO-ED.

Hanson, M. J., & Lynch, E. W. (1995B). *Survival Guide for Interviewers.* Austin, TX: PRO-ED.

Harcourt Brace Educational Measurement (1996). *Stanford-Diagnostic Mathematical Test—4th edition.* San Antonio, TX: Harcourt Brace.

Haring, K. A., Lovett, D. L., Haney, K. F., Algozzine, B., Smith, D. D., & Clarke, J. (1992). Labeling preschoolers as learning disabled: A cautionary position. *Topics in Early Childhood Special Education, 12*(2), 151–173.

Harnisch, D. L., & Fisher, A. T. (Eds.). (1989). *Transition literature review: Educational, employment, and independent living outcomes.* Champaign, IL: Secondary Transition Intervention Effectiveness Institute.

Harry, B. (1992). *Cultural diversity, families, and the special education system: Communication and empowerment.* New York: Teachers College Press.

Hart, D. (1994). *Authentic assessment: A handbook for educators.* Menlo Park, CA: Addison-Wesley.

Hartman, R. C. (Ed.). (1991). Transition in the United States: What's happening. *Information from HEATH, 10*(3), 1, 4–6.

Hayden, M. F., & Senese, D. (Eds.). (1994). *Self-advocacy groups: 1994–95 Directory for North America.* This publication lists the addresses and phone numbers of over 700 self-advocacy groups and organizations in the U.S., Canada, and Mexico. Available from Publications Office, Institute on Community Integration, University of Minnesota, 150 Pillsbury Drive SE, Minneapolis, MN 55455. Telephone: (612) 624-4512.

Heiman, G. (1999). *Research methods in psychology* (2nd ed.). Boston: Houghton Mifflin.

Herman, J., Aschbacher, P., & Winters, L. (1992). *A practical guide to alternative assessment.* Alexandria, VA: Association for Supervision and Curriculum Development.

Heward, W. L., & Orlansky, M. D. (1992). *Exceptional children: An introductory survey of special education* (4th ed.). New York: Merrill.

Hiskey, M. S. (1966). *Hiskey-Nebraska Test of Learning Aptitude.* Lincoln, NB: Marshall Hiskey.

Hodgkinson, L. (1985). *All one system: Demographics of education.* Washington, DC: Institute for Educational Leadership.

Hoover, J., & Collier, C. (1994). *Classroom management and curriculum development* (3rd ed.). Boulder, CO: BUENO Center for Multicultural Education.

Hoy, C., & Gregg, N. (1994). *Assessment: The special educator's role.* Pacific Grove, CA: Brookes/Cole.

Hresko, W. P. (1988). *Test of Early Written Language— 2.* Austin, TX: PRO-ED.

Iliesko, W. P., Reid, D. K., & Hammill, D. D. (1997). *Test of Early Language Development—Third Edition (TELD-3).* PRO-ED.

Individuals with Disabilities Education Act (P.L. 101-476) (1990). 20 U.S.C. Chapter 33, Sections 1400-1485.

Individuals with Disabilities Education Act Amendments of 1997, P.L. 105-117, 105th Congress.

Individuals with Disabilities Education Act (IDEA, 20 U.S.C. 1400 et seq, 1997).

Individuals with Disabilities Act (1997). Copies of reauthorized IDEA in its entirety are located on the Internet. Go to the web site of the Department of Education's Office of Special Education and Rehabilitation Services (OSERS): www.ed.gov/offices/OSERS/IDEA. At the site, select "The Law."

Jitendra, A. K., & Kameenui, E. J. (1993, September– October). Dynamic assessment as a compensatory assessment approach: A description and analysis. *Remedial and Special Education, 14*(5), 6–18.

John, J. L. (1985). *Basic reading inventory* (3rd ed.). Boise, Iowa: Kendall-Hunt.

Johnson, B. H., McGonigel, M. J., & Kauffmann, R. K. (1991). *Guidelines and recommended practices for the Individualized Family Service Plan* (2nd ed.). Bethesda, MD: Association for the Care of Children's Health.

Kamphaus, E. W. (1993). *Clinical assessment of children's intelligence.* Boston: Allyn and Bacon.

Kaufman, A. S., & Kaufman, N. L. (1983). *Kaufman Assessment Battery for Children (K-ABC): Mental processing scales.* Circle Pines, MN: American Guidance Service.

Kaufman, A. S., & Kaufman, N. L. (1985). *Kaufman Tests of Educational Achievement.* Circle Pines, MN: American Guidance Service.

Kaufman, A. S., & Kaufman, N. L. (1990). *Kaufman Brief Intelligence Test.* Circle Pines, MN: American Guidance Service.

Kazvo, N., Leland, H., & Lambert, N. (1993). *AAMR Adaptive Behavior Scale-Residential and Community—2.* Austin, TX: PRO-ED.

Keith, T. Z. (1985). Questioning the K-ABC: What does it measure? *School Psychology Review, 14,* 9–20.

Keith, T. Z. (1997). What does the WISC-III measure? A reply to Carroll and Kranzler. *School Psychology Quarterly, 12*(2), 117–118.

Keogh, B., & Margolis, T. (1976). Learn to labor and wait: Attentional problems of children with learning disorders. *Journal of Learning Disabilities, 9,* 276–286.

Kephart, N. (1971). *The Slow Learner in the Classroom.* Columbus, OH: Merrill.

King-Sears, M. E. (1994). *Curriculum based assessment in special education.* San Diego, CA: Singular.

Kirk, S. A., McCarthy, J. J., & Kirk, W. D. (1968). *Illinois Test of Psycholinguistic Abilities (ITPA).* Urbana, IL: University of Illinois Press.

Kozloff, M. (1994). *Improving educational outcomes for children with disabilities: Principles for assessment, program planning, and evaluation.* Baltimore: Paul H. Brookes.

Lambert, W. E. (1977). The effects of bilingualism on the individual: Cognitive and sociocultural consequences. In P. Hornby (Ed.), *Bilingualism: Psychological, social and educational implications.* New York: Academic Press.

Langdon, H. W. (1992). Speech and language assessment of LEP/bilingual Hispanic students. In H. W. Langdon & L. L. Cheng (Eds.), *Hispanic children and adults with communication disorders* (pp. 201–265). Gaithersburg, MD: Aspen.

Larsen, S. C., & Hammill, D. D. (1999). *Test of Written Spelling—4.* Austin, TX: PRO-ED.

Larson, S. L., & Vitali, G. (1988). *Kindergarten Readiness Test (KRT).* Aurora, NY: Slosson Educational Publications.

Layton, T. L., & Holmes, D. W. (1985). *Carolina Picture Vocabulary Test for Deaf and Hearing Impaired.* Austin, TX: PRO-ED.

Leach, L. N., & Harmon, A. (1990). *Annotated bibliography on transition from school to work* (Vol. 5). Champaign, IL: Transition Research Institute.

Leiter, R. G., & Arthur, G. (1997). *Leiter-R International Performance Scale.* Wood Dale, IL: C. H. Stoelting.

Lerner, J. (1997). *Learning disabilities: Theories, diagnosis, and teaching strategies* (7th ed.). Boston: Houghton Mifflin.

Lezak, M. D. (1995). *Neuropsychological assessment* (4th ed.). New York: Oxford University Press.

Lindamood, C., & Lindamood, P. (1985). *Lindamood Auditory Conceptualization Test.* Itasca, IL: The Riverdale Publishing Company.

Lipke, B., Dickey, S., Selmar, J., & Soder, A. (1999). *Photo Articulation Test—Third Edition (PAT-3).* Hydesville, CA: Psychological and Educational Publications.

Luria, A. R. (1980). *The working brain.* New York: Basic Books.

MacGinitie, W., & MacGinitie, R. (1989). *Gates-MacGinitie Silent Reading Tests—Fourth Edition.* Itasca, IL: The Riverside Publishing Company.

Maldonado-Colon, E. (1983). The communication disordered Hispanic child. *Monograph of BUENO Center for Multicultural Education, 1*(4), 59–67.

Markwardt, F. C. (1997). *Peabody Individual Achievement Test—Revised (PIAT-R).* Circle Pines, MN: American Guidance Service.

Mather, W., & Woodcock, R. (1997). *Mather-Woodcock Group Writing Tests.* Chicago: Riverside Publishing.

McCarney, S. B. (1992). *The Preschool Evaluation Scales (PES).* Columbia, MO: Hawthorne Educational Services.

McCarney, S. B. (1989). *Attention Deficit Disorders Evaluation Scale—Revised.* Columbia, MO: Hawthorne Educational Services.

McCarney, S. B. (1995). *The Adaptive Behavior Evaluation Scale—Revised.* Columbia, MO: Hawthorne Educational Services.

McCarthy, D. (1972). *McCarthy Scales of Children's Abilities.* San Antonio, TX: The Psychological Corporation.

McGloughlin, J., & Lewis, R. (1994). *Assessing special students* (4th ed.). Columbus, OH: Merrill.

McLean, M., Bailey, D. B., & Wolery, M. (1996). *Assessing infants and preschoolers with special needs* (2nd ed.). Englewood Cliffs, NJ: Merrill.

McLoughlin, J. A., & Lewis, R. B. (1990). *Assessing special students* (3rd ed.). Columbus, OH: Merrill.

McNair, J., & Rusch, F. R. (1991). Parent involvement in transition programs. *Mental Retardation, 29*(2), 93–101.

Mercer, J. R., & Lewis, J. F. (1978). *System of Multicultural Pluralistic Assessment.* San Antonio, TX: The Psychogical Corporation.

Miller, L. J. (1993). *First Step: Screening Test for Evaluating Preschoolers.* San Antonio, TX: The Psychological Corporation.

Morris, G. (1999). *Psychology: An introduction.* Englewood Cliffs, NJ: Prentice Hall.

Motti, M., Steling, H., Spalding, M. V., & Crawford, C. S. (1998). *Quick Neurological Screening Test.* Novato, CA: Academic Therapy Publications.

Murray, H. A. (1943). *Thematic Apperception Test.* Cambridge, MA: Harvard University Press.

Myers, A., & Hansen, C. (1999). *Experimental psychology* (4th ed.). Belmont, CA: Brooks/Cole.

Naglieri, J. A. (1985). *Matrix Analogies Test—Expanded Form.* San Antonio, TX: The Psychological Corporation.

Naglieri, J. A., McNeish, T. J., & Bardos, A. N. (1991). *Draw-A-Person: Screening Procedure for Emotional Disturbance.* San Antonio, TX: The Psychological Corporation.

National Association of School Psychology (1991). *Position statement on early childhood assessment.* Washington, DC: Author.

National Association of State Directors of Special Education (1992). Alexandria, VA. Telephone: 1-703-519-3800.

National Center for Education Statistics (1992). *American Education at a Glance.* Washington, DC: Author.

National Council of Supervisors of Mathematics (1978). Position Statement on Basic Skills; *Mathematics Teacher, 71,* 147–152.

National Council on Disability (1995). *Improving the implementation of the Individuals with Disabilities Education Act: Making schools work for all of America's children.* Washington, DC: Author.

National Information Center for Children and Youths with Disabilities (NICHCY) (1999). *Questions and answers about IDEA.* www.nichcy.org/pubs/newsdig/nd21txt.htm.

National Information Center for Children and Youths with Disabilities (NICHCY) (1997). *The education of children and youth with special needs: What do the laws say?* http://www.nichcy.org.

The network news (1996, Summer). National Transition Network, Institute on Community Integration, University of Minnesota, Minneapolis, MN, 55455. Telephone: 612-626-8200.

Neill, D. M., & Medina, W. J. (1989). Standardized testing: Harmful to educational health. *Phi Delta Kappan, 70*(9), 688–697.

Newborg, J., Stock, J. R., & Wnek, J. (1984). *The Battelle Developmental Inventory (BDI).* Itasca, IL: The Riverside Publishing Company.

Newcomer, P.L., & Hammill, D. D. (1997). *Test of Language Development—Primary: 3 (TOLD-P:3)*. Austin, TX: PRO-ED.

New York State Department of Health (2000). *Early intervention program: A parent's guide*. Albany, NY: NYS Department of Health.

Nihira, K., Leland, H., & Lambert, N. (1993). *AAMR Adaptive Behavior Scale—Residential and Community—2*. Austin, TX: PRO-ED.

Nisbet, J. (1992). *Natural supports in school, at work, and in the community for people with severe disabilities*. Baltimore: Paul H. Brookes.

Norris, M. K., JuÊrez, M. J., & Perkins, M. N. (1989). Adaptation of a screening test for bilingual and bidialectal populations. *Language, Speech, and Hearing Specialists in Schools, 20*, 381–390.

Nurss, J. R., & McGauvran, M. E. (1986). *Metropolitan Readiness Tests—5th Edition (MRT-5)*. San Antonio, TX: The Psychological Corporation.

Office of Special Education and Rehabilitative Services. Summary of existing legislation affecting persons with disabilities. Washington, DC: Clearinghouse on Disability Information. (An updated edition of this book is available from the Clearinghouse on Disability Information, Office of Special Education and Rehabilitative Services, 330 C Street, SW, Room 3132, Switzer Bldg., Washington, DC 20202-2319.)

Ortiz, A. (1986). *Characteristics of limited English proficient Hispanic students served in programs for the learning disabled*. Bilingual special education newsletter, University at Texas, Austin, Vol. 4.

Ortiz, A. A., & Rivera, C. (1990). *AIM for the BEST: Assessment and intervention model for bilingual exceptional students (Contract No. 300-87-0131)*. Washington, DC: Office of Bilingual Education and Minority Languages Affairs.

Otis, A. S., & Lennon, R. T. (1996). *Otis-Lennon School Ability Test* (7th ed.). San Antonio, TX: The Psychological Corporation.

Overton, T. (1992). *Assessment in special education: An applied approach*. Upper Saddle River, NJ: Merrill.

Overton, T. (1996). *Assessment in special education: An applied approach* (2nd ed.). Upper Saddle River, NJ: Merrill.

Overton, T. (2000). *Assessment in special education: An applied approach* (3rd ed.). Upper Saddle River, NJ: Merrill.

PARC v. Commonwealth of Pennsylvania (1972). 343 F. Supp. 279, E.D. PA.

Pase v. Hannon (1980). No. 74 C 3586 N.D. Ill.

Paulson, E. L., Paulson, P. R., & Meyer, C. A. (1991). What makes a portfolio a portfolio? *Educational Leadership, 48*(5), 60–63.

Pennsylvania Department of Education, Bureau of Special Education (1993, March). *Instructional support*. East Petersburg, PA: Pennsylvania Department of Education.

Pierangelo, R., & Giuliani, G. (1999). *The special educator's guide to 109 diagnostic tests*. West Nyack, NY: Center for Applied Research.

Pierangelo, R., & Giuliani, G. A. (2000). *Special educator's complete guide to 109 diagnostic tests* (4th ed.). West Nyack, NY: Center for Applied Research.

Pierangelo, R., & Giuliani, G. (2004). *Transition services in special education: A practical approach*. Boston: Allyn & Bacon.

Pikulski, J. (1990, March). Informal reading inventories, (Assessment). *Reading Teacher, 43*(7), 314–316.

The pocket guide to federal help: For individuals with disabilities. Clearinghouse on Disability Information Office of Special Education and Rehabilitative Services, U.S. Department of Education, Room 3132, Switzer Building, Washington, DC 20202-2524.

Plake, T., & Impara, B. (2001). *Fourteenth mental measurement yearbook*. Lincoln: University of Nebraska Press.

Politte, A. (1971). *The Politte Sentence Completion Test*. Chesterfield, MO: Psychologists and Educators Incorporated.

Public Law 94-142, Education of the Handicapped Act, 1975.

Public Law 99-372, Handicapped Children's Protection Act of 1986.

Public Law 100-407, Technology-Related Assistance for Individuals with Disabilities Act of 1988.

Public Law 101-127, Children with Disabilities Temporary Care Reauthorization Act of 1989.

Public Law 101-336, Americans with Disabilities Act of 1990.

Public Law 101-476, Individuals with Disabilities Education Act, 1990.

Questions and Answers about IDEA. National Information Center for Children and Youth with Disabilities (NICHCY), News Digest 1991, P.O. Box 1492, Washington, DC 20013. Telephone: 1-800-695-0285.

Rehabilitation Act of 1973, 29 U.S.C. Sections 701–794.

Reid, K. D., Jiresko, W. P., Hammill, D. D., & Wiltshire, S. (1991). *Test of Early Reading Ability—2: Deaf or Hard of Hearing*. Austin, TX: PRO-ED.

Repetto, J., White, W., & Snauwaert, D. (1990). Individual transition plans (ITP): A national perspective. *Career Education for Exceptional Individuals, 13*(2), 109–119.

Reschley, D. (1986). Functional psychoeducational assessment: Trends and issues. *Special services in the schools, 2*, 57–59.

Roddy, M. (1989). *ESL Adult Literacy Scale*. Novato, CA: Academic Therapy Publications.

Rueda, R. (1989). Defining mild disabilities with language-minority students. *Exceptional Children, 56*, 121–128.

Ruiz, N. T. (1989). An optimal learning environment for Rosemary. *Exceptional Children, 56*(2), 130–144.

Runyon, R., & Haber, A. (1991). *Fundamentals of behavioral statistics* (7th ed.). New York: MacGraw-Hill.

Rusch, F. R., Hughes, C., & Kohler, P. D. (1991). *Descriptive analysis of secondary school education and transition services model programs*. Champaign, IL: Secondary Transition Intervention Effectiveness Institute.

Salvia, J., & Hughes, C. (1990). *Curriculum-based assessment: Testing what is taught*. New York: Macmillan.

Salvia, J., & Ysseldyke, J. (1998). *Assessment* (7th ed.). Boston: Houghton Mifflin.

Sattler, J. (1992). *Assessment of children* (3rd ed.). San Diego: Sattler Publishers.

Sewell, T. E. (1987). Dynamic assessment as a nondiscriminatory procedure. In C. S. Lidz (Ed.), *Dynamic assessment: An interactional approach to evaluating learning potential* (pp. 426–443). New York: Guilford.

Shapiro, E. (1989). *Behavioral assessment in school psychology*. Hillsdale, NJ: Lawrence Erlbaum.

Shapiro, E. S. (1989). *Academic skills problems: Direct assessment and intervention*. New York: Guilford.

Skrtic, T. M. (1988). The crisis in special education knowledge. In E. L. Meyen & T. M. Skrtic (Eds.), *Exceptional children and youth* (3rd ed.) (pp. 415–447). Denver, CO: Love.

Sleeter, C. E. (1986). Learning disabilities: The social construction of a special education category. *Exceptional Children, 53*(1), 46–54.

Slingerland, B. H. (1993). *Slingerland Screening Tests for Identifying Children with Specific Language Disability*. Cambridge, MA: Educators Publishing Service.

Slosson, R. L. (1990). *Slosson Oral Reading Test—Revised*. East Aurora, NY: Slosson Educational Publications.

Slosson, R. L. Revised by Nicholson, C. L., & Hibpschman, T. L. (1991). *Slosson Intelligence Test—Revised (SIT-R)*. East Aurora, NY: Slosson Educational Publications.

Smith, D. (1998). *Introduction to special education: Teaching in an age of challenge* (3rd ed.). Boston: Allyn and Bacon.

Smith-Davis, J., & Littlejohn, W. R. (1991). Related services for school-aged children with disabilities. *NICHCY News Digest, 1*(2), 1–24.

Spache, G. D. (1981). *Spache Diagnostic Reading Scales*. Monterey, CA: CTB Macmillan/McGraw-Hill.

Sparrow, S., Balla, D., & Cicchetti, D. (1984). *Vineland Adaptive Behavior Scale*. Circle Pines, MN: American Guidance Service.

Sprinthall, R. (1994). *Basic statistical analysis* (4th ed.). Boston: Allyn and Bacon.

Stainback, W., & Stainback, S. (1984). A rationale for the merger of special and regular education. *Exceptional Children, 51*(2), 102–111.

Stanovich, K. (1982). Individual differences in the cognitive processes of reading. I: Word decoding. *Journal of Learning Disabilities, 15*, 485–493.

Swanson, H. C., & Watson, B. L. (1989). *Educational and psychological assessment of exceptional children* (2nd ed.). Columbus, OH: Merrill.

Sweetland, R. C., & Keyser, D. J. (Eds.). (1991). *Tests: A comprehensive reference for assessments in psychology, education, and business* (3rd ed.). Austin, TX: PRO-ED.

Taylor, R. (1997). *Assessment of exceptional students: Educational and psychological procedures* (5th ed.). Boston: Allyn and Bacon.

Taylor, R. L. (1991). Bias in cognitive assessment: Issues, implications, and future directions. *Diagnostique, 17*(1), 3–5.

Terrell, S. L. (Ed.). (1983, June). Nonbiased assessment of language differences [Special issue]. *Topics in Language Disorders, 3*(3).

Tharp, R. G. (1989). Psychocultural variables and constants: Effects on teaching and learning in schools. *American Psychologist, 44*(2), 349–359.

Tharp, R. G. (1994, June). *Cultural compatibility and the multicultural classroom: Oxymoron or opportunity*. Paper presented at the Training and Development Improvement Quarterly Meeting, Albuquerque, New Mexico.

Thorndike, R. L., Hagen, E. P., & Sattler, J. M. (1986). *The Stanford-Binet Intelligence Scale* (4th ed.). Chicago, IL: The Riverside Publishing Company.

Thorndike, R. M., & Lohman, D. F. (1990). *A century of ability testing*. Chicago, IL: The Riverside Publishing Company.

Trohanis, P. L. (1995). Progress in providing services to young children with special needs and their families: An overview to and update on implementing the Individuals with Disabilities Education Act. *NEC*TAS Notes*, (7), 1–20.

Turnbull, A., Turnbull, H., Shank, M., & Leal, D. (1995). *Exceptional lives: Special education in today's schools*. Englewood Cliffs, NJ: Merrill.

Turnbull, H. R. (1990). *Free and appropriate public education: The law and children with disabilities* (3rd ed.). Denver, CO: Love.

Ulrich, D. (1999). *Test of Gross Motor Development—Second Edition (TGMD-2)*. Austin, TX: PRO-ED.

U.S. Department of Education. (1995). *Seventeenth annual report to Congress on the implementation of the*

Individuals with Disabilities Education Act. Washington, DC: Author.

U.S. Department of Education. (1997). *Nineteenth annual report to Congress on the implementation of the Individuals with Disabilities Education Act.* Washington, DC: Author.

U.S. Department of Education. (2002). *Twenty-fourth annual report to Congress on the implementation of the Individuals with Disabilities Education Act.* Washington, DC: Author.

Vacca, J., Vacca, R., & Grove, M. (1986). *Reading and learning to read.* Boston: Little, Brown.

Valles, E. C. (1998). The disproportionate representation of minority students in special education: Responding to the problem. *Journal of Special Education, 32,* 52–54.

Vellutino, F. R. (1979). *Dyslexia: Theory and research.* Cambridge, MA: MIT Press.

Venn, J. (2000). *Assessing students with special needs* (2nd ed.). Upper Saddle River, NJ: Merrill.

Wagner, M. (1989, March). *The transition experiences of youth with disabilities: A report from the National Longitudinal Transition Study.* Paper presented at the annual meeting of the Council for Exceptional Children, San Francisco, CA.

Wallace, G., & Hammill, D. D. (1994). *Comprehensive Receptive and Expressive Vocabulary Test (CREVT).* Austin, TX: PRO-ED.

Wallace, G., Larsen, S. C., & Elksnin, L. K. (1992). *Educational assessment of learning problems: Testing for teaching* (2nd ed.). Boston: Allyn and Bacon.

Walsh, B., & Betz, N. (1985). *Test and assessment.* Upper Saddle River, NJ: Prentice Hall.

Wandry, D., & Repetto, J. (1993). Transition services in the IEP. *NICHCY Transition Summary,* (1), 1–28.

Ward, M. J. (1992). Introduction to secondary special education and transition issues. In F. R. Rusch, L. DeStefano, J. Chadsey-Rusch, L. A. Phelps, & E. Szymanshi (Eds.), *Transition from school to adult life: Models, linkages, and policy* (pp. 387–389). Sycamore, IL: Sycamore Publishing.

Warden, M. R., & Hutchinson, T. (1992). *Writing Process Test.* Chicago: Riverside Publishing.

Waterman, B. (1994). Assessing children for the presence of a disability. *NICHCY News Digest, 4*(1), 1–15.

Wechsler, D. (1958). *The measurement and appraisal of adult intelligence* (4th ed.). Baltimore: Williams & Wilkins.

Wechsler, D. (1991). *The Wechsler Scales of Intelligence.* San Antonio, TX: The Psychological Corporation.

Wechsler, D. (1999). *Wechsler Individual Achievement Test—2nd edition.* San Antonio, TX: The Psychological Corporation.

Wehman, P. (1992). *Life beyond the classroom: Transition strategies for young people with disabilities.* Baltimore: Paul H. Brookes.

Wepman, J. M., & Reynolds, W. M. (1986). *Wepman Test of Auditory Discrimination, 2nd Edition (ADT-2).* Los Angeles, CA: Western Psychological Services.

Wiederholt, J. L., & Byrant, B. R. (1992). *Gray Oral Reading Test—3.* Austin, TX: PRO-ED.

Wiggins, G. (1989, May). A true test: Toward more authentic and equitable assessment. *Phi Delta Kappan, 70*(9), 703–713.

Wilkinson, S. (1993). *Wide Range Achievement Test—3.* Wilmington, DE: Jastak Associates/Wide Range Inc.

Williams, R., & Zimmerman, D. (1984). On the virtues and vices of standard error of measurement. *Journal of Experimental Education, 52,* 231–233.

Wilson, A. J., & Silverman, H. (1991). Teachers' assumptions and beliefs about the delivery of services to exceptional children. *Teacher Education and Special Education, 14*(3), 198–206.

Wilson, N. O. (1992). *Optimizing special education: How parents can make a difference.* New York: Insight Books.

Wood, F. (1994). Using oral self-reports in the functional assessment of adolescents' behavior disorders. *Preventing School Failure, 38*(4), 16–20.

Wood, J. W., Lazzari, A., Davis, E. H., Sugai, G., & Carter, J. (1990). National status of the prereferral process: An issue for regular education. *Action in Teacher Education, 12*(3), 50–56.

Woodcock, R. (1997). *Woodcock Reading Mastery Tests—Revised.* Circle Pines, MN: American Guidance Service.

Woodcock, R. W., & Johnson, M. B. (1989). *Woodcock-Johnson Achievement Battery.* Itasca, IL: The Riverside Publishing Company.

Woolfolk, E. C. (1999). *Test of Auditory Comprehension of Language—III (TACL-3).* Itasca, IL: The Riverside Publishing Company.

Wyatt v. Stickney (1972). 344 F. Supp. 387 M.D. Ala.

Yell, M. L. (1995). *The law and special education.* Upper Saddle River, NJ: Prentice Hall.

Ysseldyke, J., & Algozzine, B. (1982). *Critical issues in special and remedial education.* Boston: Houghton Mifflin.

Ysseldyke, J., Algozzine, B., Regan, R., & Potter, M. (1980). Technical adequacy of tests used by professionals in simulated decision making. *Psychology in the Schools, 17,* 202–209.

Ysseldyke, J., & Regan, R. (1980). Nondiscriminatory assessment: A formative model. *Exceptional Children, 46,* 465–466.

Zimmerman, I. L., Steiner, V. G., & Evatt, R. L. (1992). *Preschool Language Scale—3 (PLS-3).* San Antonio, TX: The Psychological Corporation.

NAME INDEX

SUBJECT INDEX

TEST NAME INDEX